W9-CXK-568

The Professional Job Hunting System

World's Fastest Way to Get a Better Job

By Robert Jameson

Edited by the Staff of
PerformanceDynamics

©1970, 1972
by
PERFORMANCE DYNAMICS, INC.

2nd Edition Publication Date — September 1, 1972
Standard Book Number 0-912940-01-8
Library of Congress Catalog Number 72-83183

Published by: Performance Dynamics, Inc.
                 Publishing Division
                 17 Grove Avenue
                 Verona, New Jersey 07044

Printed in the United States of America

TABLE OF CONTENTS

THE PROFESSIONAL JOB HUNTING SYSTEM — WORLD'S FASTEST WAY TO GET A BETTER JOB

1.

FOREWORD

SOME PRELIMINARY THOUGHTS ON JOB HUNTING

On job hunting in general: . . . The average person grossly overestimates his knowledge of job hunting, the job market, and his own job hunting skills. The fact is, that in any group of job hunters, there are very few professionals and many rank amateurs.

. . . To the sophisticates, job hunting can be somewhat of a game in which superior job hunting skills will more than compensate for lesser qualifications. Those who arrive at the right time and who appear the best qualified are the ones who get the jobs.

On getting interviews: . . . This is very definitely an art, not a science. However, for the majority, getting interviews can be a numbers game. The more good letters you mail . . . the more interviews you'll get.

. . . One of the keys to your success will be your ability to find the openings. If you rely solely on advertised positions, you may be job hunting a long time; less than 10% of all management jobs are advertised, and when they are advertised they attract hundreds of your competitors.

On job security: . . . This will never be a source of worry — if you really possess the ability to secure another position.

. . . Getting fired from a management position will make you a member of a fairly large fraternity. It's a rare man who completes a career without ever having been fired, dehired, or otherwise invited to resign.

. . . The higher you go in management, the greater the chances that you'll be fired due to a personality conflict.

. . . 80% of the "over 40" executives who lose jobs end up accepting lesser positions — but it's not all that hard to make sure you are in the other 20%.

On resume content: . . . There is no such thing as the perfect resume. Regardless of the pains which you take — there will always be room for improvement.

. . . The more your career is projected as a series of progressive accomplishments, the easier your job search will become.

. . . You write for your audience; 1. for a man who skims because he is also looking at 200 other resumes, and 2. for the man who will eventually hire you and who will read your resume thoroughly. The resume without a quickly visible summary and which looks like all other resumes will never help your chances.

On resume validity: . . . The most successful job hunters never underestimate their achievements. This is certainly not the time to be modest.

On resumes vs. letters: . . . Even the best of resumes will rarely produce interviews at the rate you can generate from well written letters.

On being interviewed: . . . Never beg for a job — you won't get it.

. . . It's hard to overestimate the importance of making a good first impression; the first 5 minutes of the interview are usually more important than all of the other minutes combined.

. . . Not 1 person in 100 can give articulate answers to the stress interview questions listed in this book. When you can . . . you'll begin to coast through interviewing.

On salary negotiation: . . . People expect job hunters to be searching for at least 20% more salary. In fact, it's not all that unusual today for candidates to say they're worth 50% more. Even if they settle for 20% more, at least they help the new employer feel he's getting a bargain.

. . . You should negotiate your salary based upon (1) the results you can produce, and (2) your estimate of what the firm will pay. Individuals who negotiate salary, using their present income as the base for discussions, usually end up disappointed. Who wants to pay $20,000 for something that's presently going for $15,000?

On job hunting strategy: . . . Successful job hunters don't beat competitors as much as they avoid them. If you expect your competition to be more qualified for the job you seek, then you'd better use some different avenues in your search for a new job.

On the effectiveness of a different letter or resume:

. . . An individual did a mailing of 300 resumes and cover letters. He netted 3 interviews and zero job offers. Ninety days later another similar size mailing of new materials produced 24 job interviews and culminated in 4 job offers. After the first mailing, this man felt like a complete failure, rejected by the business society. After the second mailing, he was on top of the world. There can be a very fine line between success and despair.

On job hunting frequency and job hunting competition:

. . . The average American professional changes jobs every five years — and soon it will be every four years.

. . . An average managerial job opening is sought by twenty-five candidates; an advertised opening for an attractive job — by hundreds. This can make things seem pretty difficult, regardless of your skills. However, bear in mind that the employer may still be saying, "There is no one any good in the market". The truth is that of 200 candidates, often none will appear "good", and this is where the skillful job hunter, who presents himself well, can succeed.

On the realtive importance of job hunting skills vs. an individual's background:

. . . Job hunting success depends . . . 50% upon job hunting skills and . . . 50% upon the individual's background and ability. While you can't change your past, you can change how you communicate it and you can always sharpen your job hunting skills.

On the dollar value of the intelligent job change:

. . . A man of 30 who advances from a $12,000 to $16,000 job will generally maintain that salary differential for the remainder of his career. In 30 years this means $120,000 in additional income.

"He is not only idle who does nothing, but he is idle who might be better employed."

— Socrates

2.

INTRODUCTION

This is a book for any individual who may ever seek a job in a professional, managerial or executive capacity. The advice it contains can be of value to both graduating students as well as senior executives seeking positions at the $60,000 level. It is for both potential and active job hunters and should prove effective regardless of the particular factors which have prompted an interest in job hunting. In general, it is directed at what we believe to be a critical void, a knowledge gap, concerning the strategy, techniques, and systematic execution of a professional job hunting effort.

Individuals seek to change jobs because of many reasons. Some seek better pay, while others are motivated by a desire for freedom from frustrating personalitites, inadequate conditions, office politics, or generally insecure feelings. Still others seek a change due to lack of recognition, responsibility, or growth opportunity. Some people, of course, are forced to look for a new job because they have been terminated from their previous position. All these reasons for wanting to change jobs are very similar to those which people gave twenty years ago. However, in the 1970's the frequency of job changing has accelerated dramatically.

There are many forces behind this development. Better education, communication, and transportation have all been stimulants. The continued growth of inflation has also resulted in a much higher percentage of people seeking change because they need a higher income. All of this has resulted in a business environment in which the average person now changes positions every five years. In the near future, this figure will probably go down to every four years. At the present time, there can be little doubt that individualism is dominating what were previously traditional feelings of corporate loyalty. While some people express great concern over this situation, it is our belief that the increased rate of job changing has its advantages for the business society at large. One of the principal benefits is that people transfer the valuable part of their experiences to new industries, and, as a result, there is a more rapid exchange of information and ideas throughout the business community.

We believe that any individual in the business world owes it to himself to always be cognizant of the job market in his field. For greatest personal growth, it is essential for anyone to view his own inventory of talent and knowledge as something to be marketed for the maximum price consistent with his long range plans and other goals. In the future, job hunting will be a rather inevitable event in the lives of most people. The individuals who are familiar with both job hunting and the mechanics of the job market will fare much better when the need to change positions develops.

The Nature of the Job Market and Job Hunting Competition

The competition for jobs is a rather unique competitive situation. It is a form of competition where a job hunter never really knows who his competition is or exactly what they are doing. The inability to clearly view the competitive market place seems to have the effect of making people substantially less keen, intelligent and precise than they would be in any other competitive situation. The result is that the majority approach job hunting with far less drive and creativity, and in general relate to their past instead of concentrating on the future. Few people seem to recognize that jobs are won by those who become candidates, and who appear to be the best qualified, rather than those who may, in fact, be best qualified.

During the year 1973, 1,500,000 people with income in excess of $10,000 will change companies. However, more than seven times this number will prepare and circulate resumes at some time during the year. A recent survey cited that within a single ninety day period, 78% of the people surveyed in middle management had thought about seeking a job change. There can be little doubt that there is presently tremendous competition at all levels for attractive positions, even if it cannot be precisely measured. In this type of a market, most people are not winners, and less than one in ten finds a situation which offers the financial and responsibility levels that he may have originally thought possible.

While the competition is substantial, the critical point for the job hunter to grasp is that it takes place as part of a terribly archaic and inefficient process, which is generally referred to as the "job market". Here we refer to the process by which people and jobs are brought together. We call the system inefficient because at any given moment, firms with attractive positions are unable to fill their openings, while at the same time, unhappily employed but talented individuals are plodding along without any awareness that such openings exist.

During the last few years, the style of job hunting has begun to undergo some very significant changes. As mentioned, more people are attempting to change jobs at a much more frequent rate than ever before. In response to the increased competition, the art of job hunting has been experiencing some refinements which eventually will affect anyone who competes in the job market. There is now a small but growing segment of job hunters who possess real job hunting expertise, and who are applying their knowledge every few years. These individuals have parleyed their job hunting expertise into very high salaries for their age, education and depth of experience.

Other individuals who gain an understanding of the system and who take the time to master the revised art of job hunting, can also be among the ones who get the best positions at the largest salary increases. At the very same moment that they are moving forward, there will be equally qualified individuals who will be in great despair and saying (and believing) that "it is simply impossible to locate a decent job."

What This Book Contains

In this book we have attempted to provide all the strategy and techniques which will enable an individual to conduct a superior job campaign. We have covered all of the so-called professional secrets of job hunting and have focused on those techniques which have actually produced salary increases of 20% to 50% for other individuals.

The basis of these techniques is that they evolve from a view of job hunting as a competitive situation. They are aimed at permitting an individual to take advantage of his competition's weakness. In this case, the weakness is that 95% of all job hunters will be pursuing a new position in a very haphazard, standard and unprofessional manner. With a creative and carefully planned approach, you should be able to project yourself in a manner which will bring you interviews and offers ahead of many other candidates. All of the strategy advice and techniques which we advocate are nothing more than common sense directions. However, they can be deceptively simple and intelligent execution is still required. We have presented them in a manner which is as brief and direct to the point as possible. The entire book has been prepared in a straight-talking, functional, and systematic style which should make it easy for any job hunter to directly copy and apply the information.

We believe that our recommendations offer you the fastest way of being sure of getting a better job. However, it is not intended to be a magic formula type of program. It would be an oversimplification on our part to assume that every individual job hunter can utilize all the approaches that are covered. Every job hunting situation is an individual case and most people will not have to use all the avenues that are reviewed. However, our experience indicates that almost every person will be able to effectively use most of them. In addition, many individuals should find the information useful as a base for developing creative ideas which may be even more effective in terms of their personal needs.

What This Book Does Not Contain

This book does not contain advice about how to succeed in your occupation; which fields you should pursue; what you should do about your present position; what career goals you should have; how much salary you are worth, etc. If you require answers to these types of questions you will have to seek personal counsel.

The Role of Attitude

As we have mentioned, the great majority of people seek interviews in a very haphazard manner. Although they learn as they progress, they end up wasting a tremendous amount of time and frequently get discouraged in the process. The chief barrier to their being effective relates to weakness from both a knowledge and confidence standpoint. Without adequate preparation, the process of securing offers can seem like an impossible task. If you have been job hunting without success, we suggest that you simply scrap everything you have done so far and use this book as a base for launching an entirely new campaign. In this case, you may have to make a super effort to dismiss the psychological discouragement that might have been associated with your previous efforts.

If you are serious in your objective to better yourself, you must be prepared to place your campaign at the top of all priorities. Almost all of your competition will defer their efforts because of social or personal interests. In fact, to take maximum advantage of this book, your job hunting efforts should be approached with the same zeal you would apply to almost any other work which you knew had to be accomplished. Your campaign should be executed in the most intelligent and precise manner possible. You should work at it steadily, both evenings and weekends, until you reach your objectives.

The Authors

Mr. Jameson is Chairman of the Board of Performance Dynamics, Inc., a firm active in publishing, executive search and executive marketing. All of the members of the Performance Dynamics staff who have shared in producing this book were originally employed for many years by major corporations. We had initially started out as students of the managerial job market; an interest which eventually led us into our corporate association. Our work for individuals seeking new positions has included everything from analysis of student's resumes through the handling of complete job hunting campaigns for corporate presidents.

It might interest readers to know that all of the executives associated with Performance Dynamics have successfully practiced the advice we advocate in this book. This is not to imply that we recommend the concept of changing jobs as every person's route to success. Nevertheless, we were all in situations which required the application of these ideas and we did so for notable financial gain.

Over the last twenty years, there have been almost endless articles, books and commentaries about job hunting. In fact, if someone had the time to bring together all the comments that have appeared in print, he could probably cite points of view which differ from all the material we cover. Unfortunately, this field has always seemed to attract the attention of many pseudo-experts, who are probably responsible in part for the generally low level of real job hunting savvy. This book offers readers a body of proven job hunting strategy along with a clear cut plan of action which can be adapted to almost any personal situation. We have seen the materials in this book produce countless job hunting success stories; situations involving young people on the way up as well as unemployed senior executives who had felt their personal situation was hopeless. We sincerely believe that careful adaptation and execution of the techniques set forth will almost certainly guarantee an individual the ability to find a better job.

Rapidly Expanding Corporations

You should also plan to contact expanding firms or companies within the so called growth industries. These are the firms who will have to seek junior and senior executive talent from the outside, even if they generally try to promote from within. There are many of these companies today whose growth creates a need for talent at a much faster rate than they can possibly locate individuals. It is not unusual for them to always have forty to fifty attractive positions available.

If you are not familiar with the faster growing industries and companies, we suggest you check the Business Periodical Index under "Growth Firms". A number of the general business magazines have quarterly listings of both the firms and industries who are enjoying above-average growth. The Business Periodical Index will provide you with the magazine and date in which this information appeared. This will be particularly important if at the time of your job campaign the economy happens to be in a slump and job openings seem scarce. In this case, fast growing small firms that are relatively unknown may prove to be your best prospects.

The Timing of Your Job Campaign

Many individuals have written to our firm about their job hunting success probabilities in various economies. We know of many individuals who delayed job hunting campaigns because they noted that unemployment was very high and therefore assumed that jobs were very few and far between. On the surface this observation may seem to make enough sense. However, during the recent recession, when the highest levels of unemployment were being experienced, the reverse seems to have been partially true. At the same time the media were running lead articles about the unemployed, there was a concurrent shortage of job candidates in many fields. In fact, we know of many executive search firms and personnel agencies who had listings for attractive positions, but who were unable to submit candidates to their clients. Evidently, our national psychology is shaped so much by the media, that the wealth of bad news about unemployment convinced people that they should simply be thankful for having their present position.

Obviously the job market is slower during the summer months and during November and December than it is at other times of the year. During January, many firms begin searching for new employees who have just been authorized under their new budgets for the year. Except for some adjustments for seasonal timing, we would recommend that you launch a job campaign when you feel the need exists, without particular concern about the state of the economy.

4.

CAMPAIGN APPROACHES

&

THE DEVELOPMENT & USE OF PERSONAL CONTACTS

CAMPAIGN APPROACHES

In the following sections we discuss campaign approaches and the professional job hunting techniques which can set people aside from others who use the same channels. For the sake of organization, we have arranged our comments in terms of specific channels which job hunters can use to generate interviews. These include:

* Developing and Using Personal Contacts

* Answering Advertisements
  &
  Placing Situation Wanted Advertisements

* The Direct Letter Approach

* Personnel Agencies
  &
  Executive Search Firms

* Professional Associations
  &
  Unusual Approaches for Generating Interviews

* Commercial Job Hunting Services

3.

PRIOR TO STARTING YOUR CAMPAIGN

&

WHERE TO DIRECT YOUR CAMPAIGN

PRIOR TO STARTING YOUR CAMPAIGN

Our philosophy of job hunting is centered around a well-planned campaign. However, before you actually begin job hunting, you'll have to do a considerable amount of preliminary spadework. By taking care of details initially, you will enable your effort to be executed much more smoothly. You will also free yourself of many things which can otherwise be a continuing source of irritation once you have begun interviewing.

It is impossible for us to list all preliminary requirements until you have actually read this entire book. At the back there is a complete plan-of-action check list. It is divided into two sections: (a) the preliminary items which you must initially resolve, and (b) the actual steps of your campaign. This check list will be quite a help in enabling you to plan your work in an orderly fashion.

A few of the major things which you will have to initially handle include the factors discussed below:

You Must Set Personal Goals

We are always surprised at the number of people who have great difficulty in deciding upon their objectives, and who subsequently have postponed their job campaigns. Obviously, in order to conduct an effective campaign, you will have to define both your position and financial goals. Sometimes people who are in doubt simply choose a given position, title, and salary level in order to get their campaign moving. It is not at all unusual because most individuals refine their objectives in the course of their job search. Other people have found it helpful to sit down and make a listing of all their strengths and weaknesses, and to actually force themselves into yes-no type choices concerning what they really want to achieve in life. When people write things down on paper, including job hunting plans, they sometimes have a way of subjugating themselves to the written words which have become law. Obviously this depends on the individual. However, for some it can be an effective way to harness your thoughts, define some objectives, and get things underway.

You Will Need an Outstanding Resume

You will almost certainly have to develop a basic resume which is a truly superior expression of your own talents and background. It cannot be an ordinary resume. Everything in this book is based on the assumption that you will have accomplished this step. In another section you will find guidance that will enable you to do this with a minimum of inconvenience.

Chances are that you will need an outstanding resume to help you create your own breaks, put yourself in the right place at the right time, and meet the right people. It must be clean, distinctive, and easily read. It must also be a smooth and persuasive advertisement for yourself which is prepared in excellent taste. At the same time, it should be a credit to your own creativity and ability to express yourself. The most effective resumes are ones that sell ability and talent rather than just experience. Creativity which is in good taste is a prerequisite for those who seek something more than modest salary increases.

The reason that the above statement is true is that a terrible sameness exists among most resumes. If you have a resume now you may think it's good but if it isn't really producing for you it can probably be greatly improved. Most resumes are normally poor expressions of an individual person, and usually have a tendency to make him look simply like every other applicant for a given position. This is not to say that we recommend being cute or using tricks, for good taste is paramount. However, the resume which you develop should utilize a creative approach stressing past accomplishments. By doing so, you will have a tremendous competitive advantage throughout your job hunting campaign.

You Will Need a Series of Standard Letters

You will also have to prepare a shortened version of your resume in letter form. You will find many situations that call for a letter rather than a resume. In fact, certain firms and advertisements will request that you write about yourself rather than send a printed summary. This letter is especially important if you are a senior executive or are considering a variety of types of positions. A letter rather than a resume will enable you to slant your background and accomplishments to more specifically meet the requirements likely to exist for each position. The job hunter with expertise will frequently have three or four standard letters prepared before he begins his campaign. All will simply be variations of a basic resume. Different letters will be required for sending to executive search firms and corporations, as well as for answering advertisements. Again, for your guidance, samples are included in a separate section of this book.

Your resume and letters will be only one element in your entire campaign. The simple possession of outstanding materials will never guarantee you interviews for good positions. They will have to be used in connection with a planned placement effort to glean maximum value.

Throughout your campaign one of your continuing objectives will be to create an image of yourself as one among hundreds. To be effective you cannot do just what everyone else does or the way they do it. Your aim is to place yourself far above your competition, regardless of their qualifications.

The very first thing you must do is to read this book a number of times. The next thing is to lay out an ordered schedule for yourself. It will have to be set up in steps and will indicate both what you will do and when you will do it. During the course of your campaign, you will need to refer back to segments of this book. Remember that these techniques are the results of other individuals' trial and error. On the average, they will maximize your exposure to available opportunities and minimize the time which you must waste in experimentation.

WHERE TO DIRECT YOUR CAMPAIGN

Your Primary Targets

Any job campaign should have direction in terms of the key industries and companies on which an individual will focus. As an initial step you should prepare a list of all firms that are prime candidates for your talents (the sources for getting names of companies are listed later in this manual). Obviously you will find opportunities with firms not on your initial list, but those on it will get the attention of your first efforts. There is one major exception to this rule. If you are at a junior level and are not skillful at being interviewed, you should put your best prospects aside until you have gained some interviewing experience.

Ordinarily you should first consider approaching the companies in your industry and the firms serving it both vertically and horizontally. These are the people who would value your experience the most. Another primary target group would be allied industries. For example, if you are working for a camera manufacturer, you obviously should try to reach firms that sell other consumer durable products. Firms in the same general field market their products in similar ways, are generally organized along similar lines, and usually face similar problems. In some cases, dependent upon your specialty, your initial effort should be directed at firms that are the same size as your present employer. For example, if you were in accounting, you might want to seek employment with firms that are likely to utilize similar systems and procedures. If you were in data processing, you might try firms which have or could use the same EDP equipment on which you are experienced.

Unless you want to relocate, you should also restrict your efforts to companies in your immediate geographical area in the initial stages of your campaign. Obviously these will be the firms you can visit without taking excessive personal time for interviews.

Avoid the 'Overly Fraternal' Corporations

Try not to spend time at seeking positions with school-oriented banks, brokerage and law firms, or other corporations. Unfortunately, there still are many firms where your lack of attendance at the "right" school(s) will put you at a marked and continuous disadvantage. You should be able to identify these firms through your personal contacts. (If you do have the right school background, you should of course, take maximum advantage of it.)

Large vs. Small . . . . Strong vs. Weak Companies

There is always a question as to whether people should direct their campaign toward large or small companies, or wealthy or poor companies. The choice between large and small companies is largely a matter of personal preference and individual background. Small firms may pay less to start but frequently have a personality all their own, and can usually offer an individual much more room for accomplishment. They also have to look outside for talent more often. Furthermore, if they are a new venture, or likely to go public, they usually offer young executives a better chance to rapidly accumulate a lot of money. Regarding wealthy versus poor companies, it has been our experience that companies in trouble should not be eliminated from consideration. If you are at a top management level you ought to give this considerable thought. It is risky but in such firms your competition will generally be less, and you will not be just another talent. These types of companies can also be more open to independent action; more flexible in salaries and contracts, and in general, less rigid than very successful large companies. You can identify them simply by scanning the financial magazines and business papers. With these firms we generally recommend that you approach the president on a direct personal letter basis. He can make exceptions to any employment freeze that might exist, even if he was the one who initiated the restriction. Before contacting this type of company, you had better carefully research the firm, and subsequently orient your letter toward what you could do for them.

Rapidly Expanding Corporations

You should also plan to contact expanding firms or companies within the so called growth industries. These are the firms who will have to seek junior and senior executive talent from the outside, even if they generally try to promote from within. There are many of these companies today whose growth creates a need for talent at a much faster rate than they can possibly locate individuals. It is not unusual for them to always have forty to fifty attractive positions available.

If you are not familiar with the faster growing industries and companies, we suggest you check the Business Periodical Index under "Growth Firms". A number of the general business magazines have quarterly listings of both the firms and industries who are enjoying above-average growth. The Business Periodical Index will provide you with the magazine and date in which this information appeared. This will be particularly important if at the time of your job campaign the economy happens to be in a slump and job openings seem scarce. In this case, fast growing small firms that are relatively unknown may prove to be your best prospects.

The Timing of Your Job Campaign

Many individuals have written to our firm about their job hunting success probabilities in various economies. We know of many individuals who delayed job hunting campaigns because they noted that unemployment was very high and therefore assumed that jobs were very few and far between. On the surface this observation may seem to make enough sense. However, during the recent recession, when the highest levels of unemployment were being experienced, the reverse seems to have been partially true. At the same time the media were running lead articles about the unemployed, there was a concurrent shortage of job candidates in many fields. In fact, we know of many executive search firms and personnel agencies who had listings for attractive positions, but who were unable to submit candidates to their clients. Evidently, our national psychology is shaped so much by the media, that the wealth of bad news about unemployment convinced people that they should simply be thankful for having their present position.

Obviously the job market is slower during the summer months and during November and December than it is at other times of the year. During January, many firms begin searching for new employees who have just been authorized under their new budgets for the year. Except for some adjustments for seasonal timing, we would recommend that you launch a job campaign when you feel the need exists, without particular concern about the state of the economy.

4.

CAMPAIGN APPROACHES

&

THE DEVELOPMENT & USE OF PERSONAL CONTACTS

CAMPAIGN APPROACHES

In the following sections we discuss campaign approaches and the professional job hunting techniques which can set people aside from others who use the same channels. For the sake of organization, we have arranged our comments in terms of specific channels which job hunters can use to generate interviews. These include:

* Developing and Using Personal Contacts

* Answering Advertisements
    &
  Placing Situation Wanted Advertisements

* The Direct Letter Approach

* Personnel Agencies
    &
  Executive Search Firms

* Professional Associations
    &
  Unusual Approaches for Generating Interviews

* Commercial Job Hunting Services

In almost every case an individual job hunter will not have to make use of all of these channels. The ones which you select will depend on your own background and goals. However, if you have the time, you should execute the broadest possible campaign. By doing so you will simply improve your chances of rapidly finding a good position at a level consistent with your objectives.

THE DEVELOPMENT AND USE OF PERSONAL CONTACTS

There is not much that can be said about personal contacts that you don't already know. Obviously, the most common and easiest way to seek interviews is via personal contacts. The higher you are, the more important they become. These contacts may include former employers, suppliers, business associates, priests, rabbis, ministers, alumni from your college or fraternity, social and community contacts, creditors, insurance agents, merchants, friends, relatives, former teachers, trade association officers, congressmen, senators, etc.

If you're in the $40,000 to $60,000 category, you're going to have to rely quite heavily on personal contacts. However, the problem in depending on contacts is that you can end up wasting a lot of time on the phone and at lunch, that could have been better spent elsewhere. People have a tendency to provide associates with interviews as a courtesy, even though they know they lack any suitable openings at the moment. We have known many job hunters who thought that their wealth of contacts would make job hunting easy. However, this rarely turns out to be the case.

We think that before you use your personal contacts, it is generally most wise to let your campaign get underway by first trying the approaches set forth in other sections. Our experience has been that for employed individuals, the best policy in initial stages is to keep your job hunting plans to yourself. We are frequently amazed by the large numbers of otherwise expert job hunters who fail to do this. They subsequently create all sorts of problems for themselves and also dilute the potential effectiveness of their really good contacts. After you have organized your effort and gotten your campaign underway, you probably will have refined your position and financial goals. Only at that stage should you make a positive effort to use your personal contacts.

Contact Development — Through Socializing and Achieving Prominence

Anyone who is considering a job search should, of course, make a real effort to meet and cultivate contacts. The time to do this is before you actually have a need to aggressively begin a job campaign. Aside from keeping in touch with your existing personal contacts, you can generally expand your potential leads by doing everything from dining in restaurants patronized by men in your field, through attending seminars, parties, trade association meetings, and supplier get-togethers. At all times you should keep a careful record of individuals you meet, as nothing is more impressive than the correct recall of an individual's name from a single brief meeting.

Achieving even a small degree of prominence can bring you leads and make it much easier to develop and expand personal contacts. If you can write, you would be wise throughout your career to occasionally by-line articles in the trade press. This is always an attention getter which gains many people status and recognition as an authority in their field. The increased visibility can in turn result in easier initiation of new contacts. Taking an active role in community affairs, politics, service clubs, trade associations, etc. will also serve as a means of accomplishing the same end.

Contact Development — Through Seeking Personal Advice

In terms of developing personal contacts from a zero level, there is one technique which we have seen prove successful on many occasions. If you are at a junior level or seeking your first civilian job, we suggest that you encourage suggestions from senior executives concerning your job campaign and career direction. You could consider writing top executives with whom you are not personally acquainted, and seeking their advice. Of course, your letter would have to be well phrased. The idea is to have your respect for their authority and expertise on these matters appeal to them, and hopefully this may result in their taking more than a passing interest in your success. During any initial discussions you should lay the groundwork for additional phone call contact during the course of your campaign. Your objective would be to obtain job opening leads in either the firms of these executives or those of their associates.

Contact Development — Through Pyramiding

Another strategy for expanding contacts is called pyramiding and involves capitalizing on the names of individuals. The idea is simply to use the power of one executive's name to gain an interview in another firm. For example, if you were meeting with the executive of a company and you felt that the interview would not produce anything, you could lead into a discussion concerning another company. You would then ask your interviewer whether or not he felt that it would be a firm for you to explore. He will probably give you a routine:

"Of course, you ought to contact them".

Your next step would be to write the president of the new firm saying that

"Mr. X suggested that I write your company", etc.

Another way of phrasing the same thing would be to say,

"In my recent meeting with Mr. X, he suggested that it might be of value if I arranged to speak with you concerning my career".

If handled properly, this whole strategy can be enormously effective. We have seen individuals conduct entire job campaigns using this technique for getting interviews. In terms of level of application, it will prove most effective for those in junior or middle management. If you are seeking a top level position, the process becomes much more delicate since verbal contact may take place between one company executive and another. In high level situations, personal recommendations count more than anything else, and any thoughts about pyramiding should be carefully reviewed before implementation.

The whole process of developing personal contacts can be time consuming and very difficult. Making your efforts effective will require careful planning and record keeping. Throughout your campaign one of your best sources for information and personal leads will be from other people who are seeking new jobs. For example, if you are in an executive position, you will be able to get a surprising number of useful leads from individuals whose resumes cross your desk. This will require taking advantage of certain situations, but from a competitive standpoint, you owe it to yourself to be as alert as possible. You will also find it useful to check with any friends who have recently accepted new positions. If they happen to be in the same field, they may be able to supply you with a number of fresh leads on positions which still remain open.

5.

ANSWERING ADVERTISEMENTS

&

PLACING SITUATION WANTED ADVERTISEMENTS

MAXIMIZING YOUR RESPONSE WHEN ANSWERING ADVERTISEMENTS

It is generally very difficult to achieve your job hunting goals simply by answering advertisements. For one thing, only a small fraction of available positions are ever advertised. This is particularly true of the higher executive positions. Secondly, your resume is generally forced to compete for attention with hundreds of other resumes. In fact, the response to advertisements for attractive positions is in many cases overwhelming. For example, a display advertisement in the New York Sunday Times may generate anywhere from a low of 30 resumes to a high of 1,000 in response to the advertisement. Nevertheless, with a superior resume or letter, answering ads will bring interviews. In order to maximize your response rate, we suggest that you give careful consideration to the techniques set forth in the following pages.

Where to Locate Position Ads

You should check the following publications for advertisements. The New York Sunday Times, The Wall Street Journal (especially early in the week when most ads appear), your industry and trade magazines, and your functional specialty magazines. If you will consider relocation or are located outside of the metro New York area, you should of course, check the nearest metropolitan newspaper. You might also consider a three-month subscription to the Los Angeles Sunday Times, and the Chicago Sunday Tribune, as well as the New York Sunday Times. These papers carry advertisements (in their financial pages) for positions which are available throughout the country. You may also want to subscribe to regional issues of The Wall Street Journal. This may be worthwhile because many advertisers restrict their advertisements to the area where the opportunity exists. The Standard Periodical Directory will give you the address of any newspaper or magazine.

Selecting the Ads to Answer

When answering advertisements you shouldn't restrict your replies to the ads which sound exactly suited to your talents. The vast majority of advertisements grossly exaggerate the qualities necessary for both consideration and subsequent success in a given position. Answer advertisements despite the fact that the requirements sound too high for you, or request industry experience (or degrees) which you do not possess. When you answer these positions, your appeal may be because of your being available at a lower salary than they would otherwise have to pay. Another reason you should answer this type of ad is that firms rarely find anyone who meets all the criteria as specified. Also, on advertisements for senior positions, you will often find that the individual eventually hired will be looking for new subordinates and outstanding resumes are occasionally kept on hand. This is a good way to be first in the door before a firm begins to advertise opportunities just below the senior level.

If you are just starting your campaign, you should go back and answer all interesting advertisements that have appeared during the past 10 weeks. Many good positions may take three months to fill although they are only advertised once or twice.

Note: If you have developed a new resume be sure to answer ads to which you earlier responded with your former resume. If it was a mediocre resume and you heard nothing, the chances are that it has already been thrown away.

Checking the Classified Ads

If you are considering a position at $30,000 or under, it will generally be worthwhile to check the classified section of large Sunday papers under different key words. For example, if you were a marketing executive you would obviously look under Marketing. However, you should also look under Advertising, Executive, Management, and International. Many advertisers, especially the smaller firms and companies with inexperienced employment managers, are not on target in their advertisements.

Answering Blind Advertisements

Blind advertisements are placed by executive search firms and corporations that are doing their own recruiting. Personnel agencies are generally not permitted to run advertisements without identifying themselves.

These blind advertisements are generally placed for one of three reasons:

(1)   A firm can avoid the burden of a reply to applicants, and further more will not be badgered by unwanted "phone call" and "in person" applicants.

(2)   A blind advertisement permits a firm to maintain secrecy from both competitors and employees.

(3)   Small firms and companies with a bad image can get more applicants for a position if they use advertisements which do not identify themselves.

You should be aware that some firms will run deceptive blind advertisements (i.e. when no available position exists). They may wish to simply gauge the market both in terms of numbers and quality. Sometimes they also scan the market in hopes of finding a specialist with more talent than an employee who will not be terminated unless a replacement is secure. This type of advertisement has frequently trapped a firm's own employees into responding. More than a handful of people have made the mistaken assumption that an advertisement could not have been their company, because they believed that in their firm the advertised position was adequately filled.

While blind advertisements can present problems, they can also give the alert job hunter an advantage he will not have on a company identified advertisement. This is because a blind advertisement by a major corporation will generally attract less than half the applicants they would get by using their name. In addition to having half the competition, the quality of respondents drops sharply. It is our belief that you should give particular consideration to responding to blind advertisements. Some techniques for maintaining secrecy when you do answer them are listed in a later section.

You can gain a further competitive advantage by checking both the classified and display blind advertisements and then attempting to identify the companies who have positions available. Your object is to identify firms which run the blind advertisements and then make a direct approach. For example, a blind advertisement may say that the position is a financial job with a cosmetic firm in Southern Connecticut. You could then send letters to the vice presidents of finance at the handful of cosmetic firms in Southern Connecticut and reduce the risk of being screened out by a company personnel department.

Time Your Answer to Each Advertisement

The timing of your answer to an advertisement is also important. It is generally advisable to delay responding to an advertisement until five to seven days after the ad appears. This is significant for a couple of reasons.

(1)   The response pattern to an advertisement which will draw 250 resumes and which appears on a Sunday, usually runs about as follows (assuming the firm is running an ad for a position in New York under their own name and address):

Sunday	(date ad appears)
Monday	15 resumes received
Tuesday	80 resumes received
Wednesday	75 resumes received
Thursday	40 resumes received
Friday	10 resumes received
—Later	30 resumes received

As you can see, a resume which arrives before the end of the first week runs a greater risk of being lost in the competitive shuffle.

(2) Most companies rarely fill good positions in a hurry. Almost everyone likes to screen a number of candidates, and if you are among the early candidates screened, you're likely to be delayed. If you are interviewed after many others, the hiring executive is in a better position to act quickly. This is because his own ideas about the individual he wants are likely to have been refined. In addition, as time goes on, the hiring individual usually becomes more anxious than ever to fill a given position. There are of course, exceptions to this as every hiring party is an individual. However, since you will have to play percentages, arriving on the late side is generally better than being interviewed early.

Follow-up on Attractive Advertisements

Plan a follow-up campaign on every attractive advertisement you answer. Your follow-up should be timed approximately two weeks after you first respond. This is a key factor because again hardly any of your competition will bother to demonstrate such initiative. The second time you answer an advertisement, send a short letter and one resume, and stress how well you felt you met the requirements in the advertisement.

Using a Letter Rather than a Resume

People who must sift through many resumes tend to screen-out non-qualifiers. Since resumes provide more facts and history, they can unfortunately work against you in this situation. If your resume is not outstanding, or if it is narrow in direction, you will increase your response by only sending a letter. A strong well-written letter can be effectively directed at the specific requirements of any position. However, if you plan to answer many advertisements, our experience indicates that a brief letter and outstanding broad gauge resume will prove almost as useful, and will be much more convenient.

Summary Comments on Answering Advertisements

Applying the advice in this section will in itself improve your interview rate many times over. However, remember that on the average, your response to advertisements will still be low. Not only do hundreds of people answer advertisements, but many times, the jobs are written to sound attractive and actually offer much lower salaries than you would assume. Anything that you can do to make yourself stand out from your competition will further improve your percentage response.

When answering advertisements you will do best if you use a cover letter and two resumes. Your replies should be on a delayed time schedule and you should follow-up on attractive advertisements which result in no response. If you are just beginning your campaign, you should go back and answer all interesting advertisements which appeared in the last 10 weeks. You should be sure to answer blind advertisements as well as attempting to identify the firms and use a direct approach. In selecting ads to answer, be sure to take a broad approach to both classified and display advertisements -- rather than only answering advertisements where you match the stated requirements. If an advertiser requests your salary requirements you should generally meet the request. Failure to do so may eliminate you from consideration or can result in your wasting time on low-paying positions. If you state a salary range (e.g. $25,000 to $30,000 depending on location and benefits), be sure that your range begins with an amount which is a reasonable increase. The first figure is the one which tells any alert executive the price level of your availability.

Just to give you an idea of the actual competition and the type of people that answer advertisements, we have reproduced the statistics below from the replies to a single advertisement which we placed. The advertisement was a blind ad for JUNIOR AND SENIOR MARKETING AND FINANCIAL EXECUTIVES. It was an eighth of one page in size and appeared in the Business and Financial Section of the New York Sunday Times. The ad itself was general, but very attractively worded in terms of growth potential and compensation. There was however, no indication of actual compensation, the nature of the industry or the location of our client.

Number of Total Responses	842	Sent Resumes		807
		Sent Resumes on 8½ x 11 White Paper		782
From New York Area	496	Sent Resumes Without Typed Cover Letter		161
Outside of New York Area	346	Sent Letters Without Resume		35

Age:	Under 25	14	Earnings:	Under $10,000	10
	25 - 29	126		10,000 - 14,999	131
	30 - 34	152		15,000 - 19,999	150
	35 - 39	169		20,000 - 24,999	128
	40 - 44	153		25,000 - 29,999	62
	Over 45	154		Over $30,000	61
	Not Stated	164		Not Stated	300

Degrees:	Bachelors	492	Employed	702
	Masters	223	Unemployed	56
	PHD	18	Could not identify	84
	All Others	109		

PLACING ADVERTISEMENTS FOR YOURSELF UNDER EMPLOYMENT WANTED

Most Executives Fail with Their Own Ads

The results achieved by most executives indicates that this is a rather unsuccessful method for getting interviews. Most people who run advertisements which describe their own talents simply end up wasting their money. Though a great many individuals do place ads, it has been our experience that most lower and middle management people only receive answers from firms who want to scatter their resumes, and letters from career counseling firms, testing services and resume writers. Of course, there are exceptions, however for most people this route usually proves ineffective.

The Cost of Position Wanted Advertisements

Position wanted advertisements can be placed in almost any newspaper, trade magazine, or specialized business publication. The cost of space varies depending on the circulation and type of audience. It can be as low as $10 for a one-inch by one column advertisement.

The media which do the largest volume of business in 'position wanted' advertising are the Sunday editions of major metropolitan newspapers. In the case of most large papers a person can place an advertisement either in the classified section or in the business pages. The classified sections are generally much less expensive than the latter. For example, a one-inch by one column advertisement in the classified section of the New York Sunday Times costs approximately $26.00. A display advertisement of the same size in the business section would cost approximately $61.00. In the case of the Chicago Sunday Tribune or the Los Angeles Sunday Times this cost gap is not quite so large. In these papers the same size display advertisement would cost about $46.00. For the Tribune the cost of the classified space would be about $28.00 while the Los Angeles Times classified runs about $27.00 per column inch. (As a general rule you can figure on getting a maximum of 14 lines per inch and an average of 5 words per line.) A sampling of the approximate rates charged by major newspapers is given below. The rates listed are for one-inch display advertisements in Sunday papers, with the exception of The Wall Street Journal, which is a daily.

Boston Globe	$30.10	Minneapolis Star Tribune	$26.60	Dallas News	$13.30
New York Times	60.90	Des Moines Register	22.40	San Francisco Examiner	
Philadelphia Inquirer	37.80	Omaha World Herald	14.00	Chronical	48.30
Baltimore Sun	21.42	St. Louis Post Dispatch	21.84	Los Angeles Times	50.54
Pittsburgh Press	32.20	Kansas City Star	15.96	Seattle Times	14.98
Buffalo Courier Express	14.00	Denver Post	16.03	Wall Street Journal	
Cleveland Plain Dealer	23.80	Atlanta Constitution Journal	24.22	National Edition	165.20
Cincinnati Enquirer	13.02	New Orleans Times Picayune	20.02	Eastern Edition	63.84
Detroit News	30.52	Memphis Commercial		Midwest Edition	52.22
Indianapolis Star	15.26	Appeal	14.98	Pacific Coast Edition	32.48
Chicago Tribune	49.98	Birmingham News	13.72	Southwestern Edition	19.46

Many of the nation's thousands of trade magazines carry both job ads and position wanted ads. If you need a list of their names and addresses you can generally research them in most libraries. Burrelle's Press Clipping Bureau also publishes an 80 page guide entitled "Consumer and Trade Publications Directory." This lists the 3,500 major magazines according to 125 industry categories. It's updated annually and is available for $3.00 from their offices at 75 E. Northfield Rd., in Livingston, New Jersey (07039).

Display Advertisements vs. Classified

It is our opinion that position wanted advertisements in classified sections offer potential value only for lower level junior executives (below $15,000) and then only if they are in rather specialized occupations (e.g. specific types of engineers, accountants, etc.). Only an unusual requirement for hard-to-find specialized talent will prompt large firms to watch the position wanted advertisements in the classified. Many smaller firms with occasional staffing requirements do check these ads. They do so in the hopes of recruiting someone without going to the expense that would be required if they used a personnel agency or placed their own advertisement.

There have been occasions when we have seen higher level executives be successful with the more expensive display advertisements. Individuals have had good luck with fairly large advertisements (two column by three inches and up); as well as with a series of small teaser advertisements which appeared in the same media at the same time. We also know of men who were successful with display advertisements which did not appear in the employment sections or business pages, but which had a corner placement in a section which was usually well-read.

A Technique which can Save You Trial and Error

If you do feel that you must try one advertisement for yourself in a specific media, we strongly urge that you first do some research. Before spending your money, you might consider scanning the position wanted ads placed by men approximately one month ago. Try to pick out what you feel is the best advertisement that was similar to what you had in mind, and send a blank check made out for a small amount to the individual who ran it. Enclose a stamped and self-addressed return envelope and ask if the ad was successful.

Summary Comments on Employment Wanted Advertising

If you are a high level or generalist executive we believe that you will require quite a bit of luck to make this type of investment worthwhile. If you do want to run an advertisement, try to select some print media which you know will be read by large numbers of individuals that you desire to reach. An example would be an advertisement placed in a special convention issue magazine or newspaper. If you decide on a general publication, give consideration to placing the advertisement in an area other than the normal employment section. Remember however, that your best insurance will be to do some research as suggested in the preceding paragraph.

If you are at a lower level or are a specialist, we suggest that you consider using the classified section. It is less expensive and you could employ the same research technique prior to spending your money. In either case, whether you are at a relatively low or high level, we suggest that you thoroughly explore other approaches before investing in an advertisement for yourself. If you've just lost your job, or have been unemployed for quite some time, go ahead and do the best creative job you can and run either a few different classified ads or a good size display advertisement. You might even consider skipping the usual cover-up approach to your unemployed situation. One of the most successful position wanted ads we've seen began with the caption "Just Fired!"

MAJOR U.S. NEWSPAPERS WHICH CARRY ADVERTISEMENTS FOR JOBS, AND WHICH YOU MIGHT CONSIDER FOR "SITUATION WANTED" ADVERTISING

Note: The circulation listed is the approximate Sunday circulation, unless otherwise specified.

ADDRESS	SUNDAY CIRCULATION
ALABAMA	
Birmingham News Post Herald, 2200 Fourth Ave. N., Birmingham, Ala. 35202	221,000
Mobile Press Register, P.O. Box 2488, Mobile, Ala. 36601	93,000
ARIZONA	
Phoenix Republic Gazette, 120 E. Van Buren, Phoenix, Ariz. 85004	263,000
Tucson Star Citizen, 208 N. Stone Ave., P.O. Box 5866, Tucson, Ariz. 85701	98,000
ARKANSAS	
Little Rock Arkansas Gazette, P.O. Box 1821, Little Rock, Ark. 72203	132,000
CALIFORNIA	
Fresno Bee, Fresno, Calif. 93721	140,000
Long Beach Independent Post Telegram and Orange County News, 604 Pine Ave., Long Beach, Calif. 90801	149,000
Los Angeles Herald Examiner, P.O. Box 2416, Terminal Annex, 1111 South Broadway, Los Angeles, Calif. 90051	519,000
Los Angeles Times, Times-Mirror Square, Los Angeles, Calif. 90053	1,208,000
Oakland Tribune, P.O. Box 509, Oakland, Calif. 94604	234,000
Orange County Register, P.O. Drawer 11626, Santa Ana, Calif. 92711)	
Orange County Bulletin, 232 S. Lemon St., Anaheim, Calif. 92805)	combined 180,000
Orange County Star Progress, La Habra, Calif. 90631)	

ADDRESS	SUNDAY CIRCULATION
CALIFORNIA (Continued)	
Sacramento Bee, P.O. Box 15779, 21st and Q Sts., Sacramento, Calif. 95813	211,000
San Diego Union Tribune, 940 3rd Ave., San Diego, Calif. 92112	269,000
San Francisco Examiner & Chronicle, 925 Mission St., San Francisco, Calif. 94119	641,000
Wall Street Journal (Pacific Coast Edition), San Francisco, Calif. 94111	228,000 (daily)
San Jose Mercury News, 750 Ridder Park Dr., San Jose, Calif. 95131	205,000
Santa Ana, Anaheim, La Habra, Brea Register, Bulletin Star Progress	180,000
Van Nuys Valley News & Green Sheet, 14539 Sylvan, Van Nuys, Calif.	226,000
COLORADO	
Denver Post, P.O. Box 1709, Denver, Colo. 80201	357,000
Rocky Mountain News, 400 W. Colfax Ave., Denver, Colo. 80204	223,000
CONNECTICUT	
Hartford Courant, 285 Broad St., Hartford, Conn. 06101	199,000
Hartford Times, 10 Prospect St., Hartford, Conn. 06101	130,000
New Haven Register Journal-Courier, 367 Orange St., New Haven, Conn. 06503	128,000
DELAWARE	
Wilmington News Journal, 831 Orange St., Wilmington, Del. 19899	136,000 (daily)
DISTRICT OF COLUMBIA	
Washington News, 1013 - 13th St. N.W., Washington, D.C. 20005	210,000 (daily)
Washington Post, 1515 L St. N.W., Washington, D.C. 20005	680,000
Washington Star, 225 Virginia Ave. S.E., Washington, D.C. 20003	333,000
FLORIDA	
Fort Lauderdale News Sun Sentinel, P.O. Box 131, Fort Lauderdale, Fla. 33302	155,000
Jacksonville Times Union Journal, 1 Riverside Ave., Jacksonville, Fla. 32201	176,000
Miami Herald News, 1 Herald Plaza, Miami, Fla. 33101	509,000
Orlando Sentinel Star, P.O. Box 2833, Orlando, Fla. 32802	178,000
St. Petersburg Times Independent, P.O. Box 1121, St. Petersburg, Fla. 33731	206,000
Tampa Tribune Times, P.O. Box 191, Tampa, Fla. 33601	197,000
GEORGIA	
Atlanta Journal Constitution, 10 Forsyth St., Atlanta, Ga. 30303	570,000
HAWAII	
Hawaii Star-Bulletin & Advertiser, P.O. Box 3350, News Bldg., 605 Kapiolani Blvd., Honolulu, Hi. 96801	179,000
ILLINOIS	
Chicago News, 401 N. Wabash Ave., Chicago, Ill. 60611	446,000 (daily)

ADDRESS	SUNDAY CIRCULATION
ILLINOIS (Continued)	
Chicago Sun Times, 401 N. Wabash Ave., Chicago, Ill. 60611	735,000
Chicago Today, 435 N. Michigan Ave., Chicago, Ill. 60611	449,000
Chicago Tribune, 435 N. Michigan Ave., Chicago, Ill. 60611	1,040,000
Wall Street Journal (Midwest Edition), 711 W. Monroe St., Chicago, Ill. 60606	392,000 (daily)
Peoria Journal Star, 1 News Plaza, Peoria, Ill. 61601	115,000
INDIANA	
Evansville Courier & Press, 201 N.W. 2nd St., Evansville, Ind. 47701	114,000
Fort Wayne Journal Gazette, 600 W. Main St., Fort Wayne, Ind. 46802	106,000
Indianapolis Star News, 307 N. Pennsylvania St., Indianapolis, Ind. 46206	371,000
South Bend Tribune, 225 W. Colfax, South Bend, Ind. 46626	125,000
IOWA	
Des Moines Register Tribune, 715 Locust St., Des Moines, Iowa 50304	493,000
KANSAS	
Wichita Eagle Beacon, 825 E. Douglas, Wichita, Kans. 67201	177,000
KENTUCKY	
Louisville Courier-Journal & Times, 525 W. Broadway, Louisville, Ky. 40202	353,000
LOUISIANA	
New Orleans Time Picayune, 3800 Howard Ave., New Orleans, La. 70140	306,000
Shreveport Journal Times, Lake & Market Sts., Shreveport, La. 71101	117,000
MAINE	
Portland Express, 390 Congress St., Portland, Me. 04104	110,000
MARYLAND	
Baltimore News American, Lombard & South Sts., Baltimore, Md. 21202	293,000
Baltimore Sun, Calvert & Centre Sts., Baltimore, Md. 21203	333,000
MASSACHUSETTS	
Boston Globe, 135 Morrissey Blvd., Boston, Mass. 02107	556,000
Boston Herald Traveler, 300 Harrison Ave., Boston, Mass. 02106	262,000
Boston Record-American, 5 Winthrop Sq., Boston, Mass. 02106	419,000
Springfield Union News Republican, P.O. Box 113, Springfield, Mass. 01101	123,000
Worcester Telegram Gazette, 20 Franklin St., Worcester, Mass. 01613	109,000
MICHIGAN	
Detroit Free Press, 321 Lafayette Blvd., Detroit, Mich. 48231	656,000
Detroit News, 615 Lafayette Blvd., Detroit, Mich. 48231	869,000
Flint Journal, 200 E. First St., Flint, Mich. 48502	115,000
Grand Rapids Press, Press Plaza, Vandenberg Center, Grand Rapids, Mich. 49502	132,000

ADDRESS	SUNDAY CIRCULATION
MINNESOTA	
Minneapolis Star Tribune, 427 Portland Ave., Minneapolis, Minn. 55415	634,000
St. Paul Dispatch Pioneer Press, 55 East Fourth St., St. Paul, Minn. 55101	231,000
MISSISSIPPI	
Jackson Clarion-Ledger & News, 311 E. Pearl St., Jackson, Miss. 39205	112,000
MISSOURI	
Kansas City Star Times, 1729 Grand, Kansas City, Mo. 64108	400,000
St. Louis Globe-Democrat, 12th Blvd. & Delmar Sts., St. Louis, Mo. 63101	309,000
St. Louis Post-Dispatch, 1133 Franklin Ave., St. Louis, Mo. 63101	563,000
NEBRASKA	
Omaha World Herald, 14th & Dodge Sts., Omaha, Nebr. 68102	278,000
NEW JERSEY	
Hackensack -Bergen Record, 150 River St., Hackensack, N.J. 07602	178,000
Newark Star Ledger, Court & Plane Sts., Newark, N.J. 07101	579,000
Trenton Times Advertiser, 500 Perry St., Trenton, N.J. 08605	107,000
NEW MEXICO	
Albuquerque Journal Tribune, P.O. Box J-T, Albuquerque, N.M. 87103	96,000
NEW YORK	
Albany Times Union, 645 Albany-Shaker Rd., Albany, N.Y. 12201	143,000
Buffalo Courier Express, 785 Main St., Buffalo, N.Y. 14240	308,000
Buffalo News, 218 Main St., Buffalo, N.Y. 14240	292,000
Long Island Press, 92-20 168th St., Jamaica, N.Y. 11433	388,000
New York News, 220 E. 42nd St., New York, N.Y. 10017	3,014,000
New York Times, 229 W. 43rd St., New York, N.Y. 10036	1,481,000
Wall Street Journal (Eastern Edition), 30 Broad St., New York, N.Y. 10004	519,000 (daily)
Rochester Democrat & Chronicle Times Union, 55 Exchange St., Rochester, N.Y. 14614	223,000
Syracuse Herald-American Herald-Journal Post-Standard, Clinton Sq., Syracuse, N.Y. 13201	241,000
NORTH CAROLINA	
Charlotte Observer News, P.O. Box 2138, 600 S. Tryon St., Charlotte, N.C. 28201	207,000
Greensboro News Record, P.O. Box 20848, Greensboro, N.C. 27420	104,000
Raleigh News & Observer Times, P.O. Box 191, Raleigh, N.C. 27602	151,000
Winston-Salem Journal-Sentinel, Winston-Salem, N.C. 27102	97,000
OHIO	
Akron Beacon Journal, 44 E. Exchange St., Akron, Ohio 44309	208,000
Cincinnati Enquirer, 617 Vine St., Cincinnati, Ohio 45201	300,000
Cincinnati Post & Times Star, 800 Broadway, Cincinnati, Ohio 45202	223,000 (daily)

ADDRESS	SUNDAY CIRCULATION
OHIO (Continued)	
Cleveland Plain Dealer, 1801 Superior Ave. N.E., Cleveland, Ohio 44114	522,000
Cleveland Press, 901 Lakeside, Cleveland, Ohio 44114	377,000 (daily)
Columbus Dispatch, 34 S. Third St., Columbus, Ohio 43216	330,000
Dayton News-Journal Herald, 4th & Ludlow Sts., Dayton, Ohio 45401	223,000
Toledo Blade Times, 541 Superior St., Toledo, Ohio 43604	201,000
Youngstown Vindicator, Vindicator Sq., Youngstown, Ohio 44501	161,000
OKLAHOMA	
Oklahoma City Oklahoman Times, P.O. Box 25125, Oklahoma City, Okla. 73125	278,000
Tulsa World Tribune, 315 S. Boulder, Tulsa, Okla. 74102	812,000
OREGON	
Portland Oregonian-Oregon Journal, Portland, Ore. 97201	407,000
PENNSYLVANIA	
Allentown Call Chronicle, 6th & Linden Sts., Allentown, Pa. 18105	134,000
Harrisburg Patriot News, 812 Market St., Harrisburg, Pa. 17105	169,000
Lancaster New Era Intelligencer Journal News, 8 W. King St., Lancaster, Pa. 17604	119,000
Philadelphia Bulletin, 30th & Market Sts., Philadelphia, Pa. 19101	717,000
Philadelphia Inquirer, Inquirer Bldg., Philadelphia, Pa. 19101	877,000
Philadelphia Daily News, 401 N. Broad St., Philadelphia, Pa. 19101	240,000 (daily)
Pittsburgh Press, P.O. 566, Pittsburgh, Pa. 15230	732,000
Pittsburgh Post Gazette, P.O. 566, Pittsburgh, Pa. 15230	234,000 (daily)
RHODE ISLAND	
Providence Journal Bulletin, 75 Fountain St., Providence, R.I. 02902	209,000
SOUTH CAROLINA	
Charleston Post News & Courier, 134 Columbus St., Charleston, S.C. 29402	87,000
Columbia State Record, Stadium & Key Rds., Columbia, S.C. 29202	122,000
Greenville News Piedmont, P.O. Box 1688, 305 S. Main St., Greenville, S.C. 29602	98,000
TENNESSEE	
Knoxville Journal-News Sentinel, 208 W. Church, Knoxville, Tenn. 37901	159,000
Memphis Commercial Appeal, 495 Union Ave., Memphis, Tenn. 38101	277,000
Nashville Banner Tennessean, 1100 Broadway St., Nashville, Tenn. 37202	233,000
TEXAS	
Corpus Christi Times Caller, P.O. Box 9136, Corpus Christi, Tex. 78408	89,000
Dallas News, Communications Center, Dallas, Tex. 75202	298,000
Dallas Times Herald, Herald Sq., Dallas, Tex. 75202	283,000
Wall Street Journal (Southwest Edition), 1233 Regal Row, Dallas, Tex. 75247	122,000 (daily)
El Paso Herald Post Times, 401 Mills St., El Paso, Tex. 79999	87,000

ADDRESS	SUNDAY CIRCULATION
TEXAS (Continued)	
Fort Worth Star-Telegram, 400 W. 7th St., Fort Worth, Tex. 76101	222,000
Houston Chronicle, 512-20 Travis St., Houston, Tex. 77002	356,000
Houston Post, 4747 Southwest Freeway, Houston, Tex. 77001	327,000
San Antonio Express News, P.O. Box 2171, San Antonio, Tex. 78206	128,000
San Antonio Light, P.O. Box 161, San Antonio, Tex. 78206	162,000
UTAH	
Salt Lake City Desert News Tribune, P.O. Box 838, 143 S. Main St., Salt Lake City, Utah 84110	189,000
VIRGINIA	
Norfolk Virginia Beach Pilot, 150 W. Brambleton Ave., Norfolk, Va. 23501	180,000
Richmond News-Leader Times Dispatch, 333 E. Grace St., Richmond, Va. 23219	198,000
Roanoke Times World-News, P.O. Box 2491, Roanoke, Va. 24010	111,000
WASHINGTON	
Seattle Post-Intelligencer, 6th & Wall Sts., Seattle, Wash. 98121	254,000
Seattle Times, Fairview Ave., North & John Sts., Seattle, Wash. 98111	315,000
Spokane Chronicle Review, 926 Sprague Ave. W., Spokane, Wash. 99210	125,000
Tacoma News Tribune, 711 Street Helens Ave., Tacoma, Wash. 98401	102,000
WEST VIRGINIA	
Charleston Gazette Mail, 1001 Virginia Street E., P.O. Box 2993, Charleston, W. Va. 25330	106,000
WISCONSIN	
Madison Capital Times, 115 S. Carroll St., Madison, Wisc. 53701	112,000
Milwaukee Journal Sentinel, 333 W. State, Milwaukee, Wisc. 53201	540,000
NEGRO NEWSPAPERS	
Afro-American Group, Baltimore, Md.; Washington, D.C.; Richmond, Va.; Newark, N.J.; 628 N. Eutaw St., Baltimore, Md. 21201	99,000 (semi-weekly)
Los Angeles Central Southwest News, 1016 W. Vernon Ave., Los Angeles, Calif. 90037	233,000 (weekly)
San Francisco Bay Area Post Group, P.O. 489, Berkeley, Calif. 94701	121,000 (weekly)

6.

THE DIRECT LETTER APPROACH

The Best Way to Get Interviews

Our experience indicates that the most consistently effective means of generating interviews is through the mailing of personally typed letters to select individuals. Proper execution of a large scale direct letter campaign will almost certainly result in a number of job offers. We believe this to be true whether you are a graduating student or a senior executive. In fact, this method of generating interviews has probably resulted in more people winning positions at great advances in salary than any other approach. The primary advantage of a letter campaign rests with the fact that you have the ability to tailor your background to the person or company you are contacting. Furthermore, you have far less competition than when answering advertisements or going through agencies.

Your Direct Letter Objective

Your objective here is to place a well written personal letter (with or without your resume) in the hands of top executives of companies which may have a need for your services. We have listed examples of effective letters for most occasions in a separate section of this book. Any letters which you send out should be on your own personal stationery. It should be printed in a discreet manner and generally should contain your name, address and phone number. Under no circumstances should you consider using the stationery of your present employer. In terms of content, the letters which will prove most effective will be tailored to the potential needs of the company you are contacting. This "individualization" is far more important than the particular style of letter which you choose to write. In some cases a style which emphasizes your accomplishments will be advisable, while in others a curiosity-arousing style might be in order. On still other occasions a letter which emphasizes what happened as a result of your presence in a given firm, rather than focusing on your accomplishments, may be of maximum effectiveness.

Unless you seek an officer's position, you should direct your letters by name to the vice-president in charge of your specialty. As a second choice, you might consider the president. It should be noted that more than a few chief executives, who owe a major part of their success to their ability to select and use exceptional people, have rapidly hired individuals who use this approach. Obviously your timing must be right, however the potential for rapid achievement of your goals certainly exists with this method of seeking interviews. When you write to "Presidents" we think you should mark your letters private and confidential. Unfortunately, even with this double warning your correspondence may never reach its goal. A standard procedure in most well organized corporations is for the president's secretary to automatically send all resumes to the personnel department. In the case of large firms your letter should go to each division as they will only rarely become aware of your letter to other parts of the corporation.

Sources for Names of Firms and Executives

A partial source for names and addresses for companies and executives in corporations is listed in a separate reference section at the end of this book. The sources given are generally available in the business sections of most large libraries. If you are interested in a specific city or geographical area, you can generally call the business office of your telephone company for free copies of both the white and yellow page phone books.

Contact Recently Promoted Executives

In addition to sending letters to executives in large corporations, you should also contact men who have recently been promoted as evidenced by press releases in the business papers. Many of them may be good prospects for you because they often prefer to hire outsiders (who will be loyal to them) rather than promote from within their firm. The best time to reach them is generally after they have been in their new job for about three months.

Contact Successful Alumni from your University

You may also consider directing some letters to successful executives who have graduated from your college. You probably have an alumni directory which indicates positions and companies, or you can find a source for identifying the successful men who graduated from your school. If possible, you should direct your letter to their home address. In your letter you can refer to your mutual interest in the college attended and solicit assistance. Our experience has been that you will frequently get a quick and sincerely interested response.

Be Careful to Avoid the Obvious Mistakes

Be sure to never commit the obvious mistake of misspelling an executive's name or writing an executive who is no longer with the corporation. Even the best sources for getting an executive's name will rapidly become out-of-date. In the case of local companies in which you are very interested, you should give them a phone call and ask the operator if he is still there and if you have the correct spelling of the person's name.

At the Executive Level . . . . . Try to Avoid Personnel Departments

The importance of personnel executives varies greatly. If you earn more than $20,000, you will generally do better if you do not contact the personnel executive, regardless of what his title may be. In almost all cases, he will not be the person actually doing the hiring and you'll only be placing one more obstacle in your path. If you are seeking a position at less than the above amount, we suggest you send a carbon copy to the top personnel executive. Though he may not be the one who will hire you, his opinion on your qualifications is likely to have influence, and he may know of openings in other departments that might interest you.

Follow-Up Every Letter After Two Weeks

Every letter which you send that is not answered should be followed-up after two to three weeks. Your follow-up letters should restate your interest in a corporation and the contribution you feel you can make. We have even seen people follow-up reject letters and achieve successful results. Many times, people receive letters which thank them for their interest in a corporation and which appear to turn them down. However, large corporations inevitably have turnover and employment opportunities do become available. If you have followed-up your initial contact, you have a reasonable chance of hearing from about 33% of them within a ten week period.

The average person in the job market will only generate interviews from an exceptionally small percent of the direct letters which he mails. There is a great futility in the way people scatter resumes. Obviously, a prime factor in anyone's success rate will be the general demand for his profession at the time of his job search. However, most people add greatly to their own futility because they do not use a good letter; or a good letter with a superior resume; and they do not have a carefully planned follow-up campaign.

The range of responses which you will receive to your mailing will include the following:

1. A phone call or telegram requesting you to call the firm.

2. A letter requesting that you call for an interview.

3. A letter asking you to send more information; to complete an application form; or to forward a detailed resume.

4. A rejection letter from either the person you wrote or someone in the personnel department; normally with a statement that your resume will be kept in their active files.

5. No response at all.

If you are on target with good materials, and are in a profession of average demand you should be able to achieve interviews with 10% of the companies to which you write. On the other hand, if you use a completely random circulation basis, it would not be unusual for you to produce one or two interviews from a mailing of 300 letters. The highest effectiveness rate we have seen was the case of a very marketable thirty-two year old junior executive who was then earning $15,000. He did a mailing of 27 letters, perfectly tailored to each company's needs, and received offers for interviews from 16 of these firms. These interviews eventually resulted in four concrete job offers and the gentleman accepted a position at $22,000.

Summary Comments on the Direct Letter Approach

A direct letter campaign will probably offer you the easiest method of generating interviews. It is by far the best approach if you seek a large increase in salary. In your campaign, you will need a well-written personal letter (with or without your resume attached) and should direct it toward corporate officers by name and title. As a general rule, all of your correspondence to company presidents should be marked private and confidential. If you do not receive an answer you should follow-up on your initial letter after approximately two to three weeks.

There are many general sources which list the names and titles of executives. However, it will also be important for you to use as much ingenuity as possible in selecting the names of executives to write. For example, one of the most effective campaigns we have seen was based entirely on letters to leads secured through newspaper announcements of executive transfers. If you are at a fairly high level you might give consideration to watching the business pages for the names of former employers of executives taking positions with new firms. The chances are that the jobs they formerly occupied are still free. A good letter to the president, or appropriate vice-president, (at the former employer) may open a door to an executive who is anxious to find a replacement. Another overlooked advantage of the direct letter approach is that it is not uncommon for a person's resume to reach the hands of an executive who may be considering replacing a subordinate, but who has been worried about the problems of recruiting someone to take his place. A superior resume along with a good letter can serve to expedite the inevitable.

As you progress in your campaign, you should try to rework your direct letter. Generally, we recommend that people try a few different types of letters and carefully gauge their response to each one.

Examples of well-written letters are included in a later section of this manual. They should provide you with an excellent basis for developing superior materials for yourself. In executing your letter campaign, you should turn out as many letters as possible. Even though it is expensive, you may find it useful to use autotype services and to have your letters advance dated. As an alternative, if you check your local newspaper you are sure to find typists who work at home and charge reasonable fees. A frequent result of a large and well-executed program can be more interviews for positions than people can effectively handle. However, any letter campaign will depend on large numbers of letters being initiated at the same time. If you only circulate fifteen letters a week, it is unlikely that you will have more than one offer mature at any given time. With a limited approach you are also likely to become discouraged by the form letter rejects which you will receive. The best way to approach a letter campaign is to have all of them typed at once and to drop them in the mail at precisely the same time.

LIST OF MAJOR EMPLOYERS

The pages which immediately follow contain the names and addresses of more than 2500 major corporate employers. The firms which are listed cover a variety of industries, and are coded according to a firm's primary activity. The codes, which are listed next to the name of a company, have the following meaning:

AA	Advertising Agency
B	Bank
I	Industrial Firm
LI	Life Insurance Company
M	Merchandiser
MC	Management Consultant
P	Publisher
S	Service Firm
T	Transportation Company
U	Utility

The limitations of any list of this nature are obvious. Our purpose for including it is simply to provide a beginning check list as a measure of convenience for those who will execute a direct letter campaign to major corporations. It should also prove of some help to those people who have an interest in specific geographical areas, or who are located in remote areas.

ALABAMA

ALABAMA GAS CORP. (U): 1918 First Avenue, N. Birmingham, 35203

ALABAMA POWER CO. (U): 600 N. 18th Street, Birmingham, 35205

AMERICAN CAST IRON PIPE CO. (I): Box 2727, Birmingham, 35202

AVONDALE MILLS (I): Avondale Ave., Sylacauga, 35150

BLAIR ALGERNON INC. (S): First National Bank Bldg., P.O. Box 749, Montgomery, 36104

BLOUNT BROS. CORP. (S): 4520 Executive Park Dr., Montgomery, 36111

FIRST NATIONAL BANK (B): 17 N. 20th St., Birmingham, 35203

GULF, MOBILE & OHIO RR (T): 104 St. Francis St., Mobile 36602

GULF STATES PAPER (I): River Rd., Tuscaloosa, 35401

HAYES INTERNATIONAL CORP. (I): Box 2287, Birmingham 35201

LIBERTY NATIONAL LIFE INSURANCE CO. (LI): 301 S. 20th St., Birmingham, 35202

MORRISON, INC. (S): P.O. Box 2608, Mobile, 36601

RUSSELL MILLS INC. (I): Alexander City, 35010

SOUTHERN NATURAL GAS CO. (U): Watts Bldg., Birmingham, 35203

U.S. PIPE & FOUNDRY CO. (I): 3300 First Ave., N. Birmingham, 35202

VULCAN MATERIALS CO. (I): One Office Park, Birmingham, 35223

ARIZONA

ARIZONA COLORADO LAND & CATTLE CO., 5001 E. Washington, Phoenix, 85034

ARIZONA PUBLIC SERVICE CO. (U): P.O. Box 21666, Phoenix, 85036

A. J. BAYLESS MARKETS (M): 111 E. Buckeye Rd., Phoenix, 85004

CUDAHY CO. (I): 100 West Clarendon, Phoenix, 85013

RAMADA INNS, INC. (S): 3838 E. Van Buren St., Phoenix 85008

SOUTHWEST FOREST INDUSTRIES (I): 3443 N. Central Ave., Phoenix, 85012

VALLEY NATIONAL BANK OF ARIZONA (B): 141 N. Central Ave., Phoenix, 85004

DEL E. WEBB CORP. (S): 3800 N. Central Ave., Phoenix 85011

ARKANSAS

ALLIED TELEPHONE CO. (U): Box 2177, Little Rock, Ark. 72203.

ARKANSAS BEST CORP. (S): 1000 S. 21st St., Fort Smith, 72901

ARKANSAS POWER & LIGHT CO. (U): 9th & Louisiana, Little Rock, 72203

CENTRAL TRANSFORMER CORP. (U): 2400 W. 6th St., Pine Bluff, 71601

DILLARD DEPARTMENT STORES (M): 313 Main St., Little Rock 72203

MURPHY OIL CORP. (I): 200 Jefferson Ave., El Dorado 71730

TYSON FOODS, INC., 317 E. Emma Ave., Springdale, 72764

UNITED DOLLAR STORES (M): Highway 54, Dumas 71639

LOS ANGELES, CALIFORNIA

A. J. INDUSTRIES, INC. (I): 10889 Wilshire Blvd. 90024

AKRON (I): 5120 Melrose Ave., 90038

ALISON MORTGAGE INVESTMENT TRUST (B): 1900 Ave. of the Stars, 90067

AMERICAN CEMENT CORP. (I): 2404 Wilshire Blvd. 90057

AMERICAN MEDICAL ENTERPRISES: 660 S. Bonnie Brae St. 90057

ARDEN-MAYFAIR, INC. (M): 2500 S. Garfield Ave. 90022

AUTOMATION INDUSTRIES (S): 1901 Bldg., Century City, 90067

BAKER OIL TOOLS, INC. (I): 7400 E. Slauson Ave. 90022

BEKINS VAN & STORAGE CO. (T): 1335 S. Figueroa St. 90015

BENEFICIAL STANDARD LIFE INS. CO. (LI): 3700 Wilshire Blvd. 90010

BETTER FOODS, INC. (M): 6801 E. Washington Blvd., City of Commerce, 90040

BLUE CHIP STAMP CO. (S): 5801 S. Eastern Ave. 90022

BROADWAY-HALE STORES (M): 600 S. Spring St., 90014

BUFFUMS' (M): 127 Pine Ave., Long Beach, 90802

BULLOCK'S MAGNIN CO. (M): 601 S. Westmoreland Ave., 90005

CALAVO GROWERS OF CALIF. (I): 4833 Everett Ave., 90058

CARNATION CO. (I): 5045 Wilshire Blvd., 90036

CERTIFIED GROWERS OF CALIFORNIA LTD. (M): 2601 S. Eastern Ave., 90040

CHALLENGE CREAM & BUTTER ASSN. (I): 5729 E. Smithway St., City of Commerce, 90040

COMPUTER SCIENCES CORP. (S): 1901 Bldg., Century City, 90067

CONTINENTAL AIR LINES, INC. (T): Los Angeles Intl. Airport, 90009

CYPRUS MINES CORP. (I): 523 W. 6th St., 90014

DART INDUSTRIES (I): 8480 Beverly Blvd., 90054

DUCOMMON INCORPORATED (I): 612 S. Flower St., 90017

ELECTRONIC SPECIALITY CO.: 4585 Electronics Pl., 90039

EQUITY FUNDING CORP. OF AMERICA: 1900 Ave. of the Stars, 90067

ERWIN WASEY, INC. (AA): 5455 Wilshire Blvd., 90036

FINANCIAL FEDERATION, INC. (S): 615 S. Flower St., 90117

FIRESTONE TIRE & RUBBER CO. OF CALIFORNIA (I): Box 2037 Terminal Annex, 90054

FIRST LINCOLN FINANCIAL CORP. (S): 640 W. 6th St., 90017

FLUOR CORP. (I): 2500 So. Atlantic Blvd., 90022

THE GARRETT CORPORATION (I): 9851 Sepulveda Blvd., 90009

GETTY OIL CO. (I): 3810 Wilshire Blvd., 90005

GREAT SOUTHWEST CORP.: 609 S. Grand Ave., 90017

GREAT WESTERN SAVINGS & LOAN ASSN. (B): 4401 Crenshaw Blvd., 90043

HOLMES & NARVER, INC. (S): 828 S. Figueroa St., 90017

INTERNATIONAL RECTIFIER CORP. (I): 9220 Sunset Blvd., 90069

INVESTMENT CO. OF AMERICA (S): 611 W. 6th St., 90017

EARLE M. JORGENSEN CO. (I): 10650 S. Alameda St., 90054

LOS ANGELES TIMES (P): Times Mirror Sq., 90053

McCULLOCH CORP. (I): 6101 W. Century Blvd., 90045

MONOGRAM INDUSTRIES, INC. (I): 10889 Wilshire Blvd., 90024

NATIONAL GENERAL CORP. (S): 1 Carthay Plaza, 90048

NORRIS INDUSTRIES INC. (I): 5215 S. Boyle Ave., 90058

OCCIDENTAL LIFE INSURANCE CO. OF CALIFORNIA (LI): Hill & Olive at 12th St., 90015

OCCIDENTAL PETROLEUM CORP. (I): 10889 Wilshire Blvd., 90024

PACIFIC INDEMNITY CO. (LI): 3200 Wilshire Blvd., 90005

PACIFIC LIGHTING CORP. (U): 810 S. Flower St., 90017

PACIFIC LIGHTING SERVICE AND SUPPLY CO. (U): 720 W. Eighth St., 90017

PACIFIC MUTUAL LIFE INSURANCE CO. (LI): Pacific Mutual Bldg., 90054

THE RALPH M. PARSONS CO. (S): 617 W. Seventh St., 90017

ALBERT PARVIN & CO. (S): 120 N. Robertson Blvd., 90048

PENDLETON TOOL INDUSTRIES, INC. (I): 2209 Santa Fe Ave., 90051

SANTA FE INTERNATIONAL CORP. (I): One Wilshire Bldg., 90017

SECURITY PACIFIC NATIONAL BANK (B): 561 S. Spring St. 90054

SIGNAL COMPANIES INC. (I): 1010 Wilshire Blvd., 90017

SOUTHERN CALIFORNIA EDISON CO. (U): 601-W. 5th St., 90017

SOUTHERN CALIFORNIA GAS CO. (U): 810 S. Flower St., 90017

SUNKIST GROWERS, INC.: 707 W. 5th St., 90017

TI CORP. (I): 433 S. Spring St., 90054

TELEDYNE INC. (I): 1901 Ave. of the Stars, 90067

THRIFTIMART INC. (I): 1837 S. Vermont Ave., 90006

THRIFTY DRUG STORES CO. (M): 5051 Rodeo Rd., 90016

TIMES MIRROR CO. (P): Times Mirror Sq., 90053

TRANSCON LINES (T): 1206 S. Maple Ave., 90015

TRANSAMERICA INSURANCE CO. (LI): 1150 S. Olive St., 90015

UNIONAMERICA, INC., Figueroa at 5th St., 90017

UNION BANK (B): 445 S. Figueroa St., 90054
UNION OIL CO. OF CALIFORNIA (I): 461 S. Boylston, 90017
UNITED CALIFORNIA BANK (B): 600 S. Spring St., 90054
UNITED FINANCIAL CORP. OF CALIFORNIA (S): 9800 S. Sepulveda Blvd., 90045
UNITED STATES BORAX & CHEMICAL CORP. (I): 3075 Wilshire Blvd., 90010
VITRO CORP. OF AMERICA 1901 Building, 90067
WESTERN AIR LINES (T): 6060 Avion Dr., 90009
WESTERN BANCORPORATION (S): 600 S. Spring St., 90054
WHITTAKER CORP. (I): 10880 Wilshire Blvd., 90024

CALIFORNIA (OTHER THAN LOS ANGELES)

AEROJET-GENERAL CORP. (I): 9100 E. Flair Dr., El Monte, 91734
AERONICA, INC. (I): 24751 S. Crenshaw Blvd., Torrance, 90505
AEROSPACE CORP. (MC): 2350 E. El Segundo Blvd., El Segundo, 90245
ALLIED EQUITIES CORP. (I): 555 California St., San Francisco, 94104
AMERICAN AUTOMOBILE INSURANCE COMPANY: 3333 California St., San Francisco, 94119
AMERICAN BUILDING MAINTENANCE INDUSTRIES (S): 335 Fell St., San Francisco, 94102
AMERICAN FOREST PRODUCTS CORP. (I): 2740 Hyde St., San Francisco, 94109
AMERICAN INSURANCE COMPANY: 3333 California St., San Francisco, 94119
AMERICAN PRESIDENT LINES LTD. (T): 601 California St., San Francisco, 94108
AMERICAN SAFETY EQUIPMENT CORP.: 16055 Ventura Blvd., Encino, 91316
AMERON INC. (I): 400 S. Atlantic Blvd., Monterey Park, 91754
AMPEX CORP. (I): 401 Broadway, Redwood City, 94063
ANADITE, INC. (I): 10647 Garfield Ave., South Gate, 90280
APPLIED TECHNOLOGY DIV. (I): 3410 Hillview Ave., Palo Alto, 94304
ARCATA NATIONAL CORP. (I): 2750 Sand Hill Rd., Menlo Park, 94025
ARGONAUT INSURANCE CO. (LI): 250 Middlefield Rd., Menlo Park, 94025
ASTRODATA, INC. (I): 240 E. Palais Rd., Anaheim, 92803
GUY F. ATKINSON CO. (I): 10 W. Orange Ave., South San Francisco, 94080
AVERY PRODUCTS CORP. (I): 415 Huntington Dr., San Marino, 91108
BALFOUR, GUTHRIE & CO., LTD.: One Maritime Plaza, San Francisco, 94111
GORDON H. BALL, INC. (S): 300 Camille Ave., Danville, 94526
BANK OF AMERICA NATIONAL TRUST & SAVINGS ASSN. (B): Bank of America Center, San Francisco, 94120
BANK OF CALIFORNIA NATIONAL ASSOC. (B): 400 California St., San Francisco, 94120
BECHTEL CORP. (I): 50 Beale St., San Francisco, 94119
BECKMAN INSTRUMENTS, INC. (I): 2500 Harbor Blvd., Fullerton, 92632
BLUE GOOSE GROWERS, INC. (I): 332 E. Commonwealth Ave., Fullerton, 92632
BOHEMIAN DISTRIBUTING CO.: 11428 Sherman Way, North Hollywood, 91605
BOURNS INC. (I): 1200 Columbia Ave., Riverside, 92607
C. F. BRAUN & CO. (S): 1000 S. Fremont Ave., Alhambra, 91802
JOHN BREUNER CO. (M): 2201 Broadway, Oakland, 94612
BUZZA-CARDOZO − DIV. GIBSON GREETING CARDS, INC. (I): 1500 S. Anaheim Blvd., Anaheim, 92803
CALIFORNIA ALMOND GROWERS EXCHANGE (I): 1802 C St., Sacramento, 95808
CALIFORNIA CANNERS & GROWERS (I): Ferry Bldg., San Francisco, 94106
CALIFORNIA AND HAWAIIAN SUGAR CO. (I): One California St., San Francisco, 94106
CALIFORNIA-WESTERN STATES LIFE INSURANCE CO. (LI): 2020 L. Street, Sacramento, 95804
CAPITOL INDUSTRIES, INC. (I): 1750 N. Vine St., Hollywood, 90028
CAPITOL RECORDS, INC. (I): 1750 N. Vine St., Hollywood, 90028
CAPTECH INC. (S): 2444 Wilshire Blvd., Santa Monica, 90403
CHEVRON ASPHALT CO. (I): 555 Market St., San Francisco, 94105

CHEVRON CHEMICAL CO. (I): 200 Bush St., San Francisco, 94104
CHEVRON OIL COMPANY (I): 225 Bush St., San Francisco, 94120
CITY NATIONAL BANK (B): 400 N. Roxbury Dr., Beverly Hills, 90210
CLOROX CO. (I): 7901 Oakport St., Oakland, 94621
CONSOLIDATED FREIGHTWAYS, INC. (T): International Bldg., San Francisco, 94108
CROCKER NATIONAL BANK (B): One Montgomery St., San Francisco, 94104
CROWN ZELLERBACH CORP. (I): One Bush St., San Francisco, 94104
DEL MONTE CORP. (I): 215 Fremont St., San Francisco, 94119
DENNY'S RESTAURANTS, INC. (M): 14256 E. Firestone Blvd., La Mirada, 90638
DI GIORGIO CORP.: One Maritime Plaza, San Francisco, 94111
WALT DISNEY PRODUCTIONS (I): 500 S. Buena Vista St., Burbank, 91505
ELECTRONIC SPECIALTY CO.: 80 S. Lake Ave., Pasadena, 91101
THE EMPORIUM CAPWELL CO. (M): 835 Market St., San Francisco, 94103
EQUITY FUNDING CORP. OF AMERICA (S): 9601 Wilshire Blvd., Beverly Hills, 90210
FMC CORPORATION (I): 1105 Coleman Ave., San Jose, 95110
MAX FACTOR & CO. (I): 1655 N. McCadden Pl., Hollywood, 90028
FAIRCHILD CAMERA & INSTRUMENT: 464 Ellis, Mountain View, 94040
FEDERAL LAND BANK OF BERKELEY (S): 2180 Milvia St., Berkeley, Calif. 94701
FED-MART CORP. (M): 8001 Othello St., San Diego, 92111
FIBREBOARD CORP. (I): 475 Brannan St., San Francisco, 94107
FIREMAN'S FUND INSURANCE CO. (LI): 3333 California St., San Francisco, 94120
FIRST CHARTER FINANCIAL CORP. (S): 9465 Wilshire Blvd., Beverly Hills, 90212
FLEETWOOD ENTERPRISES, INC. (I): 3125 Myers St., Riverside, 92503
FOREMOST-MC KESSON, INC. (I): 111 Pine St., San Francisco, 94111
GENERAL TELEPHONE CO. OF CALIFORNIA (U): 2020 Santa Monica Blvd., Santa Monica, 90404
GIBRALTAR FINANCIAL CORP. OF CAL. (S): 9111 Wilshire Blvd., Beverly Hills, 90213
GLASS CONTAINERS CORP. (I): 535 N. Gilbert Ave., Fullerton, 92634
GLOBAL ASSOCIATES (S): 2010 Webster St., Oakland, 94612
GRANITE CONSTRUCTION CO. (S): P.O. Box 900, Watsonville, 95076
GREAT WESTERN FINANCIAL CORP. (S): 9601 Wilshire Blvd., Beverly Hills, 90210
HARVEY ALUMINUM INC. (I): 19200 S. Western Ave., Torrance, 90509
HEWLETT-PACKARD CO. (I): 1501 Page Mill Rd., Palo Alto, 94304
HILLS BROS. COFFEE, INC. (I): 2 Harrison St., San Francisco, 94105
HITCO: 533 S. Fremont, Los Angeles, 90017
HOLMES-NARVER, INC. 400 E. Orangethorpe Ave., Anaheim, 92801
HONIA-COOPER & HARRINGTON (AA): 55 Francisco St., San Francisco, 94133
HUGHES AIRCRAFT (I): Centinela Ave. & Teale, Culver City 90230
HYATT CORP. (I): 1338 Bayshore Hwy., Burlingame, 94010
IMPERIAL CORP. OF AMERICA (I): 2320 Fifth Ave., San Diego, 92101
KAISER ALUMINUM & CHEMICAL CORP. (I): 300 Lakeside Dr., Oakland, 94604
KAISER CEMENT & GYPSUM CORP. (I): 300 Lakeside Dr., Oakland, 94604
KAISER INDUSTRIES CORP. (I): 300 Lakeside Dr., Oakland, 94604
KAISER STEEL CORP. (I): 300 Lakeside Dr., Oakland, 94612
KORACORP INDUSTRIES, INC. (I): 611 Mission St., San Francisco, 94105
LEAR SIEGLER INC. (I): 3171 S. Bundy Dr., Santa Monica, 90406
LEVI STRAUSS & CO. (I): 98 Battery St., San Francisco, 94106
ALFRED M. LEWIS, INC. (M): 3021 Franklin, Riverside, 92507
LITTON INDUSTRIES, INC. (I): 360 N. Crescent Dr., Beverly Hills, 90210
LOCKHEED AIRCRAFT CORP. (I): 2555 Hollywood Way, Burbank, 91503
MCA INC.: 100 Universal City Plaza, Universal City, 91608

MANNING'S INC. (S): 901 Battery St., San Francisco, 94111
MATSON NAVIGATION CO. (T): 100 Mission St., San Francisco, 94105
MATTEL INC. (I): 5150 Rosecrans Ave., Hawthorne, 90250
MEMOREX CORP. (I): San Tomas at Central Expressway, Santa Clara, 95052
MENASCO MFG. CO. (I): 805 S. San Fernando Blvd., Burbank, 91505
METRO-GOLDWYN-MAYER INC.: 10202 W. Washington Blvd., Culver City, 90230
NATIONAL STEEL & SHIPBUILDING CO. (I): 28th & Harbor, San Diego, 92112
NORTH AMERICAN ROCKWELL CORP. (I): 1700 East Imperial Hwy. El Segundo, 90245
NORTHROP CORP. (I): 1800 Century Park E., Los Angeles, 90067
PACIFIC AUTOMATION PRODUCTS, INC.: 626 Sonora, Glendale, 91201
PACIFIC GAS & ELECTRIC CO. (U): 245 Market St., San Francisco, 94106
PACIFIC INTERMOUNTAIN EXPRESS CO. (T): 1417 Clay, Oakland, 94612
PACIFIC TELEPHONE & TELEGRAPH CO. (U): 140 New Montgomery St., San Francisco, 94105
PACIFIC VEGETABLE OIL CORP. (I): World Trade Center, San Francisco, 94111
PETROLANE INC. (I): 1600 E. Hill St., Long Beach, 90801
POTLATCH FORESTS, INC., P.O. Box 3591, San Francisco, 94119
PUREX CORP. LTD. (I): 5101 Clark Ave., Lakewood, 90712
PURITY STORES, INC. (M): 15 Bovet Rd., San Mateo, 94402
RAYCHEM CORP. (I): 300 Constitution Dr., Menlo Park, 94025
REPUBLIC CORP.: 1900 Ave. of the Stars, Century City, 90067
ROHR CORP. (I): Foot of "H" St., Chula Vista, 92010
ROYAL INDUSTRIES: 980 S. Arroyo Pkwy., Pasadena, 91103
RUCKER CO. (I): 1330 Broadway, Oakland, 94612
S&W FINE FOODS, INC. (I): 333 Schwerin St., San Francisco, 94134
SAFEWAY STORES INC. (M): 4th & Jackson Sts., Oakland, 94604
SAGA ADMINISTRATIVE CORP. (S): One Sage Lane, Menlo Park, 94025
SAN DIEGO GAS & ELECTRIC CO. (U): 101 Ash St., San Diego, 92112
SANTA FE INTERNATIONAL CORP.: P.O. Box 1401, Orange, 92668
SIERRA PACIFIC INDUSTRIES (I): 822 G St., Arcata, 95521
SOUTHERN CALIFORNIA EDISON CO.: P.O. Box 800, Rosemead, 91770
SOUTHERN CAL. FIRST NAT. BANK (B): Box 1311, San Diego, 92112
SOUTHERN PACIFIC CO. (T): One Market St., San Francisco, 94105
STANDARD BRANDS PAINT CO. (I): 4300 W. 190th St., Torrance, 90509
STANDARD OIL CO. OF CALIFORNIA (I): 225 Bush St., San Francisco, 94104
STATHAM INSTRUMENTS INC. (I): 2230 Statham Blvd., Oxnard, 93030
SUNKIST GROWERS, INC.,: P.O. Box 7888, Valley Annex, Van Nuys, 91409
SUPERSCOPE, INC. (I): 8150 Vineland Ave., Sun Valley, 91353
SYSTRON-DONNER CORP.: 1 Systron Dr., Concord, 94520
TECHNICOLOR, INC. (I): 6311 Romaine St., Hollywood, 90038
TRANSAMERICA TITLE INSURANCE COMPANY (LI): 1330 Broadway, Oakland, 94612
UNITED STATES NATIONAL BANK OF SAN DIEGO (B): 190 Broadway, San Diego, 92101
UNITED VINTNERS INC. (I): 601 Fourth St., San Francisco, 94107
URS SYSTEMS CORP.: 155 Bovet Rd., San Mateo, 94402
U.S. FINANCIAL: 1250 Sixth Ave., San Diego, 92101
UTAH INTERNATIONAL INC.: 550 California St., San Francisco, 94104
VARADYNE INC. (I): 3223 Wilshire Blvd., Santa Monica, 90403
VARIAN ASSOCIATES (I): 611 Hansen Way, Palo Alto, 94303
VON'S GROCERY CO. (M): 10150 Lower Azusa Rd., El Monte, 91731
VSI CORP. (I): 600 N. Rosemead Blvd., Pasadena, 91107
WATKINS-JOHNSON CO. (I): 3333 Hillview Ave., Palo Alto, 94304
WELLS FARGO BANK (B): 464 California St., San Francisco, 94120
WESTERN GEAR CORP. (I): Box 182, Lynwood, 90262
WESTERN PACIFIC RR CO. (T): 526 Mission St., San Francisco, 94105

WESTGATE-CALIFORNIA CORP.: 1010 Second Ave., San Diego, 92101
WORLD AIRWAYS INC. (T): Oakland Intl. Airport, Oakland, 94614
WYLE LABORATORIES INC.: 128 Maryland St., El Segundo, 90245

COLORADO

ADOLPH COORS CO. (I): Golden, 80401
AMERICAN CRYSTAL SUGAR CO. (I): 600 Boston Bldg., Denver, 80202
COLORADO INTERSTATE CORP. (I): Box 1087, Col. Springs, 80901
COLORADO OIL & GAS CORP. (I): P.O. Box 1819, Colorado Springs, 80901
DENVER & RIO GRANDE WESTERN RR (T): 1531 Stout St., Denver, 80202
FRONTIER AIRLINES, INC. (T): 8250 Smith Rd., Denver, 80207
GATES RUBBER CO. (I): 999 S. Broadway, Denver, 80217
GREAT WESTERN UNITED CORP. (I): Equitable Bldg., Denver, 80202
HOLLY SUGAR CORP. (I): Holly Sugar Bldg., Col. Springs, 80902
ICX (T): 510 E. 51st Ave., Denver, 80216
IDEAL BASIC INDUSTRIES INC. (I): 821 17th St., Denver, 80202
KING RESOURCES CO.: Security Life Bldg., Denver, 80202
THE MOUNTAIN STATES TELEPHONE & TELEGRAPH CO. (U): 931 14th St., Denver, 80202
NATIONAL CITY LINES INC. (T): Security Life Bldg., Denver, 80202
PUBLIC SERVICE CO. OF COLORADO (U): 550 15th St., Denver, 80202
SAMSONITE CORP. (I): 11200 E. Forty-fifth Ave., Denver, 80217
STEARNS-ROGERS CORP.,: P.O. Box 5888, Denver, 80217
UNITED-BUCKINHAM FREIGHT LINES, INC. (T): 5773 S. Prince, Littleton, 80120

CONNECTICUT

ABRAMS BERNARD ASSOCIATES, INC.: P.O. Box 1110, Hartford, 06101
ADLEY CORP. (T): 900 Chapel St., New Haven, 06510
AEROSOL TECHNIQUES, INC. (I): Old Gate Lane, Milford, 06460
AETNA LIFE & CASUALTY (LI): 151 Farmington Ave., Hartford, 06115
ALLIED THERMAL CORP. (I): 215 Warren St., New Britain, 06050
AMERICAN CAN CO.: American Lane, Greenwich, 06830
AMERICAN THREAD CO.: High Ridge Park, Stamford, 06905
AMES DEPARTMENT STORES, INC. (M): 3580 Main St., Hartford, 06112
ANACONDA AMERICAN BRASS CO. (I): 414 Meadow St., Waterbury, 06720
ARBOR ACRES FARM, INC. (I): Marlborough Rd., Glastonbury, 06033
ARMSTRONG RUBBER CO. (I): 500 Sargent Dr., New Haven, 06507
ARNOLD BAKERS INC. (I): Hamilton Ave., Greenwich, 06830
ARROW-HART, INC. (I): 103 Hawthorn St., Hartford, 06105
ASSOCIATED SPRING CORP. (I): 18 Main St., Bristol, 06010
ATLANTIC CEMENT CO., INC.: P.O. Box 30, Stamford, 06904
AVCO CORP.: 1275 King St., Greenwich, 06830
BANGOR PUNTA CORP.: One Greenwich Plaza, Greenwich, 06830
BANGOR PUNTA OPERATIONS, INC.: One Greenwich Plaza, Greenwich, 06830
BARDEN CORP. (I): 200 Park Ave., Danbury, 06810
WALLACE BARNES (I): 18 Main St., Bristol, 06010
BENRUS CORP. (I): Benrus Center, Ridgefield, 06877
BRAND-REX COMPANY (I): P.O. Box 498, Willimantic, 06226
BRIDGEPORT BRASS CO. (I): 30 Grand St., Bridgeport, 06602
BRISTOL BRASS CORP. (I): 580 Broad St., Bristol, 06010
BURNDY CORP. (I): Richards Ave., Norwalk, 06856
CALDOR, INC. (M): 20 Glover Ave., Norwalk, 06852
CHASE BAG CO.: 2 Greenwich Plaza, Greenwich, 06830
CITIZENS UTILITIES CO. (U): High Ridge Park, Stamford, 06905
COLECO INDUSTRIES, INC. (I): 945 Asylum Ave., Hartford, 06105
CONDEC CORPORATION (I): Old Greenwich, 06870
CONNECTICUT GENERAL LIFE INSURANCE CO. (LI): Hartford, 06115
CONNECTICUT LIGHT & POWER CO. (U): P.O. Box 2010, Hartford, 06101

CONNECTICUT MUTUAL LIFE INSURANCE CO. (LI): 140 Garden St., Hartford, 06115
CONNECTICUT NATIONAL BANK (B): 888 Main St., Bridgeport, 06603
DORR-OLIVER INC. (I): Havemeyer Lane, Stamford, 06904
DRESSER INDUSTRIAL VALVE & INSTRUMENT DIVISION (I): 250 E. Main St., Stratford, 06497
EMHART CORP.: 950 Cottage Grove Rd., Bloomfield, 06002
FAFNIR BEARING CO. (I): Booth St., New Britain, 06050
GREAT NORTHERN PAPER CO.: 75 Prospect St., Stamford, 06901
HARTFORD ACCIDENT & INDEMNITY CO. (LI): Hartford Plaza, Hartford, 06115
HARTFORD FIRE INSURANCE CO. (LI): Hartford Plaza, Hartford, 06115
HARTFORD NAT. BANK & TRUST CO. (B): 777 Main St., Hartford, 06115
HEUBLEIN INC. (I): 330 New Park Ave., Hartford, 06101
HARVEY HUBBELL, INC. (I): State St. & Bostwick Ave., Bridgeport, 06605
HOWMET CORP.: 475 Steamboat Rd., Greenwich, 06830
INGRAHAM INDUSTRIES (I): Redstone Hill Rd., Bristol, 06010
KAMAN CORP. (I): Old Windsor Rd., Bloomfield, 06002
MICRODOT INC.: 475 Steamboat Rd., Greenwich, 06830
NATIONAL UNION ELECTRIC CORP. (I): 66 Field Point Rd., Greenwich, 06830
OLIN CORP.: 120 Long Ridge Rd., Stamford, 06904
PEPPERIDGE FARM, INC. (I): Westport Ave., Norwalk, 06852
PERKIN-ELMER, CORP. (I): Main Ave., Norwalk, 06852
PHOENIX MUTUAL LIFE INSURANCE CO. (LI): One America Row, Hartford, 06115
PITNEY-BOWES INC. (I): Walnut & Pacific Sts., Stamford, 06904
PRATT & WHITNEY INC. (I): Charter Oak Blvd., W. Hartford, 06107
RAYBESTOS-MANHATTAN, INC.: 205 Middle St., Bridgeport, 06603
REMINGTON ARMS CO., INC. (I): 939 Barnum Ave., Bridgeport, 06602
ROYAL TYPEWRITER CO.: 150 New Park Ave., Hartford, 06106
SCOVILL MFG. CO. (I): 99 Mill St., Waterbury, 06720
SOUTHERN NEW ENGLAND TELEPHONE CO. (U): 227 Church St., New Haven, 06506
THE STANLEY WORKS (I): 195 Lake St., New Britain, 06050
TORRINGTON CO. (I): 59 Field St., Torrington, 06790
TIMEX CORP. (I): Waterbury, 06720
TRAVELERS CORP.: One Tower Sq., Hartford, 06115
UNITED AIRCRAFT CORP. (I): 400 Main St., East Hartford, 06118
UNITED STATES TOBACCO COMPANY (I): 100 West Putnam Ave., Greenwich, 06830
VCA CORP. (I): 2 Greenwich Plaza, Greenwich, 06830
VEEDER INDUSTRIES, INC. (I): 799 Main St., Hartford, 06102
WARNACO INC. (I): 325 Lafayette St., Bridgeport, 06602
XEROX CORP.,: Stamford, 06904

DELAWARE

AMERICAN FINANCE SYSTEM (S): Wilmington Trust Bldg., Wilmington, 19801
AMERICAN WATER WORKS CO., INC. (U): 3908 Kennett Pike, Wilmington, 19807
ATLAS CHEMICAL INDUSTRIES, INC. (I): Atlas Bldg., Wilmington, 19899
JOSEPH BANCROFT & SONS CO.: P.O. Box 245, Wilmington, 19899
BENEFICIAL CORPORATION (S): Benficial Bldg., Wilmington, 19899
CENTRAL & SOUTH WEST CORP. (U): 300 Delaware Ave., Wilmington, 19899
E. I. DU PONT DE NEMOURS & CO.: Du Pont Bldg., Wilmington, 19898
DELMARVA POWER & LIGHT CO., (U): 600 Market St., Wilmington, 19899
HAVEG INDUSTRIES, INC. (I): Box 5225, Wilmington, 19808
HERCULES INCORPORATED (I): 910 Market St., Wilmington, 19899
MERCANTILE STORES CO., INC. (M): 100 W. 10th St., Wilmington, 19801
NVF COMPANY (I): Wilmington, 19899
PHOENIX STEEL CORP. (I): Claymont, 19703
WILMINGTON TRUST CO. (B): Tenth and Market Sts., Wilmington, 19801

DISTRICT OF COLUMBIA (WASHINGTON, D.C.)

ACACIA MUTUAL LIFE INSURANCE CO. (LI): 51 Louisiana Ave., 20001
AIR AMERICA, INC. (S): 1725 K St., N.W., 20006
ALLEGHENY AIRLINES, INC. (T): National Airport, 20001
AMERICAN SECURITY & TRUST CO. (B): 15th St. & Pennsylvania N.W., 20013
BLAKE CONSTRUCTION CO. (I): 1120 Connecticut Ave., N.W., 20036
CAPITAL CREDIT CORP. (S): 7600 Georgia Ave., N.W., 20012
CENTRAL CHARGE SERVICE, INC. (S): 1215 E. St., N.W., 20004
CHESAPEAKE & POTOMAC TELEPHONE CO. (U): 930 H. St., N.W., 20001
COMMUNICATIONS SATELLITE CORP. (I): 950 L'Enfant Plaza South S.W., 20024
D.C. TRANSIT SYSTEM, INC. (T): 1420 New York Ave., N.W., 20005
FEDERAL NATIONAL MORTGAGE ASSO., (S): 1133 Fifteenth St., N.W., 20005
GARFINCKEL, BROOKS BROS., MILLER & RHOADS, INC. (M): 1401 F St., N.W., 20004
GOVERNMENT EMPLOYEES INSURANCE CO. (LI): Government Employees Insurance Bldg., 20015
GOVERNMENT SERVICES, INC. (S): 1135 21st St., N.W., 20036
INTERNATIONAL BANK FOR RECONSTRUCTION & DEVELOP-MENT (B): 1818 H St., N.W., 20433
MARRIOTT CORP. (S): 5161 River Rd., N.W., 20016
NATIONAL BANK OF WASHINGTON (B): 619 14th St., N.W., 20005
PACIFIC CORP. (S): 1725 K St., N.W., 20006
PEOPLES DRUG STORES, INC. (M): 60 Florida Ave., N.E. 20002
POTOMAC ELECTRIC POWER CO. (U): 929 E. St., N.W., 20004
RIGGS NATIONAL BANK (B): 1503 Pennsylvania Ave., N.W., 20013
SOUTHERN RY. CO. (T): 920 15th St., N.W., 20005
WASHINGTON GAS LIGHT CO. (U): 1100 H St., N.W., 20005
WOODWARD & LOTHROP, INC. (M): 11th, F & G Sts., N.W., 20013

FLORIDA

AERODEX, INC. (S): Box 123, International Airport Br., Miami, 33148
AMERICAN AGRONOMICS CORP.: 3830 W. Flagler St., Miami, 33134
AIRPAX ELECTRONICS INC. (I): P.O. Box 8488, Ft. Lauderdale, 33310
ALL TECH INDUSTRIES, INC. (I): 14000 N.W. 57th Court, Miami Lakes, 33014
AMERICAN FIRE & CASUALTY CO. (LI): 307 S. Orange Ave., Orlando, 32802
AO INDUSTRIES INC. (I): 4601 Ponce de Leon Blvd., Coral Gables, 33146
ASSOCIATED COCA-COLA BOTTLING CO., INC. (I): 320 Orange Ave., Daytona Beach, 32015
ASSOCIATED GROCERS OF FLORIDA INC. (M): 6695 N.W. 36th Ave., Miami, 33152
BARNETT BANK OF JACKSONVILLE, N.A. (S): 100 Laura St., Jacksonville, 32202
BELCHER OIL CO. (I): Box 1751, Miami, 33101
CAIN & BULTMAN (I): 60 Copeland St., Jacksonville, 32202
CELOTEX CORP. (I): 1500 N. Dale Mabry, Tampa, 33607
CHRIS-CRAFT CORP.: P.O. Box 860, Pompano Beach, 33061
ECKERD (JACK) CORP. (I): 2120 U.S. 19, S., Clearwater, 33518
FLORIDA POWER CORP. (U): 101 5th St., S., St. Petersburg, 33733
FLORIDA POWER &LIGHT CO. (U): P.O. Box 3100, Miami, 33101
GEN. DEVELOPMENT CORP. (S): 1111 S. Bayshore Dr., Miami, 33131
GENERAL TELEPHONE CO. OF FLORIDA (U): 610 Morgan St., Tampa, 33602
GIFFEN INDUSTRIES, INC. (I): 3235 N.W. 62nd St., Miami, 33147
GULF AMERICAN CORP. (S): 7880 Biscayne Blvd., Miami, 33138
GULF LIFE INSURANCE CO. (LI): 1301 Gulf Life Dr., Jacksonville, 32207
HAVATAMPA CIGAR CORP. (I): 609 Cumberland, Tampa, 33602
INDEPENDENT LIFE & ACCIDENT INS. CO. (LI): 233 West Duval St., Jacksonville, 32202
JIM WALTER CORP. (I): 1500 N. Dale Mabry Hwy., Tampa, 33607
KELLER INDUSTRIES, INC. (I): 18000 State Rd. 9, Miami, 33162
LEWIS BUSINESS FORMS, INC.: 243 N. Lane Ave., Jacksonville, 32203

LYKES BROS. INC. (M): P.O. Box 1690, Tampa, 33601
NATIONAL AIRLINES INC. (T): Box 2055, Airport Mail Facility, Miami, 33159
RADIATION INC. (I): P.O. Box 37, Melbourne, Fla. 32902
RYDER SYSTEM, INC. (S): 2701 S. Bayshore Dr., Miami, 33133
RYDER TRUCK RENTAL, INC. (S): 2701 S. Bayshore Dr., Miami, 33133
SAV-A-STOP, INC. (M): 7660 Gainesville Ave., Jacksonville, 32208
SEABOARD COAST LINE RR CO. (T): 500 Water St., Jacksonville, 32202
SOUTHEAST BANKING CORP. (B): 100 S. Biscayne Blvd., Miami, 33131
STORER BROADCASTING CO. (BR): 1177 Kane Concourse, Miami Beach, 33154
TAMPA ELECTRIC CO. (I): P.O. Box 111, Tampa, 33601
TROPICANA PRODUCTS INC.: P.O. Box 338, Brandeton, 33505
WACKENHUT CORP. (S): 3280 Ponce de Leon Blvd., Coral Gables, 33134
WINN-DIXIE STORES INC' (M): 5050 Edgewood Ct., Jacksonville, 32202
WOMETCO ENTERPRISES, INC. (S): 316 N. Miami Ave., Miami, 33128

GEORGIA

ALTERMAN FOODS, INC.(M): 933 Lee St., S.W., Atlanta, 30310
AMERICAN CRYOGENICS, INC. (I): 1819 Peachtree Rd., N.E., Atlanta, 30309
ASSOCIATED GROCERS CO-OP, INC. (M): 1285 Milledge St., East Point, 30044
ATLANTA GAS LIGHT CO. (U): 235 Peachtree St., Atlanta, 30303
ATLANTA NEWSPAPERS, INC. (P): 10 Forsyth St., N.W., Atlanta, 30303
ATLANTIC STEEL CO. (I): 1300 Mecaslin St., N.W., Atlanta, 30318
E. T. BARWICK INDUSTRIES, INC. (I): 5025 New Peachtree Rd., Chamblee, 30341
BATSON-COOK CO. (S): 116 Fourth Ave., West Point, 31833
BIBB MFG. CO. (I): 237 Coliseum Dr., Macon, 31208
WILLIAM L. BONNELL CO. (I): 25 Bonnell St., Newnan, 30263
BRUNSWICK MFG. CO., INC., 1601 2nd St., Brunswick, 31520
BUTLER'S SHOE CORP. (M): 204 Brookwood Dr., N.E., Atlanta, 30309
CENTRAL OF GEORGIA RY. (T): 227 W. Broad St., Savannah, 31401
CITIZENS & SOUTHERN NATIONAL BANK (B): 35 Broad St., N.W., Atlanta, 30301
THE COCA-COLA COMPANY: 310 North Ave., N.W., Atlanta, 30313
COLONIAL PIPELINE CO. (I): 3390 Peachtree Rd., N.E., Atlanta, 30326
COLONIAL STORES INC.(M): 2251 N. Sylvan Rd., East Point, 30344
CORONET INDUSTRIES, INC. (I): Cleveland Rd., Dalton, 30720
DELTA AIR LINES INC. (T): Atlanta Airport, Atlanta, 30320
FIRST NATIONAL BANK OF ATLANTA (B): P.O. Box 4148, Atlanta, 30302
FULTON NATIONAL BANK (B): 55 Marietta St., N.W., Atlanta, 30303
FUQUA INDUSTRIES, INC. (I): First National Bank Tower, Atlanta, 30303
GENUINE PARTS CO. (M): 299 Piedmont Ave., N.E., Atlanta, 30312
GEORGIA MARBLE CO. (I): 11 Pryor St., S.W., Atlanta, 30303
GEORGIA POWER CO. (U): 270 Peachtree St., N.W., Atlanta, 30303
LIFE INSURANCE CO. OF GEORGIA (LI): 600 W. Peachtree St., N.E., Atlanta, 30308
MC CANN-ERICKSON (AA): 615 Peachtree, N.E., Atlanta, 30308
NATIONAL SERVICE INDUSTRIES, INC. (I): 1180 Peachtree St., N.E., Atlanta, 30309
OXFORD INDUSTRIES INC. (I): 222 Piedmont Ave., N.E., Atlanta, 30312
RETAIL CREDIT CO. (S): 1600 Peach St., N.W., Atlanta, 30302
RICH'S INC. (M): Broad, Alabama, Forsyth & Hunter Sts., Atlanta, 30302
ROLLINS, INC. (I): 2170 Piedmont Rd., N.E., Atlanta, 30324
ROYAL CROWN COLA CO. (I): 10th St. & 10th Ave., Columbus, Ga. 31901
SCRIPTO, INC.: 423 Houston St., N.E., Atlanta, 30302
SOUTHERN BELL TELEPHONE & TELEGRAPH CO. (U): 67 Edgewood Ave., S.E., Atlanta, 30303

SOUTHERN CO. (U): 64 Perimeter Center E., Atlanta, Ga. 30346
THOMASTON COTTON MILLS (I): Thomaston, Ga. 30286
WEST POINT-PEPPERELL INC. (I): Box 71, West Point, 31833

HAWAII

AMFAC INC. (I): P.O. Box 3230, Honolulu, 96801

IDAHO

ALBERTSON'S INC. (M): 1623 Washington St., Boise, 83707
BOISE CASCADE CORP. (I): P.O. Box 200, Boise, 83701
GARRETT FREIGHTLINES, INC.(T): 2055 Garrett Way, Pocatello, 83201
IDAHO FIRST NATIONAL BANK (B): 10th & Idaho Sts., Boise, 83702
IDAHO POWER CO. (U): 1220 Idaho St., Boise, 83701
MORRISON-KNUDSEN CO., INC. (S): P.O. Box 7808, Boise, 83707
ORE-IDA FOODS CO., INC. (I): P.O. Box 10, Boise, 83707

CHICAGO, ILLINOIS

ABBOTT LABORATORIES (I): Abbott Park, North Chicago, 60064
ACE HARDWARE CORP. (M): 6501 W. 65th St., 60638
ADMIRAL CORP. (I): 3800 Cortland St., 60647
AGAR FOOD PRODUCTS CO. (I): 700 W. 41st St., 60609
ALDENS, INC. (M): 5000 Roosevelt Rd., 60650
ALL AMERICAN LIFE & FINANCIAL CORP. (LI): 8501 W. Higgins Rd., 60631
ALLIED MILLS INC. (I): 110 N. Wacker Dr., 60606
ALLIED PRODUCTS CORP. (I): 5700 W. Roosevelt Rd., 60650
ALLIED RADIO CORP. (I): 100 N. Western Ave., 60680
AMERICAN BAKERIES CO. (I): 10 S. Riverside Plaza, 60606
AMERICAN CASUALTY CO. OF READING PENNSYLVANIA (LI): 310 Michigan Ave., 60604
AMERICAN MOTORISTS INSURANCE CO. (LI): Sheridan Rd. at Lawrence Ave., 60640
AMERICAN GAGE & MACHINE CO.: 5200 W. Kinzie St., 60644
AMERICAN NATIONAL BANK & TRUST CO. OF CHICAGO (B): 33 N. La Salle St., 60690
AMERICAN OIL CO. (I): 910 S. Michigan Ave., 60680
AMERICAN STEEL FOUNDRIES (I): Prudential Plaza, 60601
AMOCO CHEMICALS CORP. (I): 130 E. Randolph Dr., 60601
AMSTED INDUSTRIES INC. (I): Prudential Plaza, 60601
APPLETON ELECTRIC CO. (I): 1701 W. Wellington Ave., 60657
ARMOUR & CO. (I): 111 E. Wacker Dr., 60601
ARMOUR-DIAL, INC. (I): 111 E. Wacker Dr., 60601
ARTHUR MEYERHOFF ASSOC. (AA): No. Michigan Ave., 60611
ARVEY CORP. (I): 3450 N. Kimball Ave., 60618
ATCHISON TOPEKA & SANTA FE RAILWAY CO. (T): 80 E. Jackson Blvd., 60604
BANKERS LIFE & CASUALTY CO. (LI): 4444 W. Lawrence Ave., 60630
BARTON BRANDS, INC. (I): 200 S. Michigan Ave., 60604
BEATRICE FOODS CO. (I): 120 S. La Salle St., 60603
BELDEN CORP. (I): 415 S. Kilpatrick Ave., 60644
BELL & HOWELL CO. (I): 7100 McCormick Rd., 60645
BINKS MFG. CO. (I): 3114 W. Carroll Ave., 60612
BOOZ, ALLEN & HAMILTON INTERNATIONAL (N.V.) (MC): 135 S. La Salle St., 60603
BORG-WARNER INTERNATIONAL CORP.: 36 S. Wabash Ave., 60603
BRADNER CENTRAL CO. (I): 333 S. Des Plaines St., 60606
BRINK'S INC. (S): 234 E. 24th St., 60616
BROOK MOTOR CORP. (I): 7400 N. Croname Rd., 60648
BRUNSWICK CORP. (I): 69 W. Washington St., 60602
LEO BURNETT CO. (AA): Prudential Plaza, 60601
CNA FINANCIAL CORP. (S): 310 S. Michigan Ave., 60604
CANTEEN CORP. (M): 1430 Merchandise Mart, 60654
CARSON PIRIE SCOTT & CO. (M): One S. State St., 60603
CECO CORP. (I): 5601 W. 26th St., 60650
CENCO INSTRUMENTS CORP. (I): 2600 S. Kostner Ave., 60623
CENTRAL MEAT CO. (M): 824 W. 38th Pl, 60609
CENTRAL NATIONAL BANK (B): 120 S. La Salle St., 60603
CENTRAL SOLVENTS & CHEMICALS CO. (M): 7050 W. 71st St., 60638

CENTRAL STEEL & WIRE CO. (I): 3000 W. 51st St., 60632
CERTIFIED GROCERS OF ILLINOIS, INC. (M): 4800 S. Central Ave., 60638
CHEMETRON CORP. (I): 840 N. Michigan Ave., 60611
CHICAGO MILWAUKEE ST. PAUL & PACIFIC RAILROAD CO. (T): 516 W. Jackson Blvd., 60606
CHICAGO RAWHIDE MFG. CO. (I): 1301 Elston Ave., 60622
CHICAGO ROCK ISLAND & PACIFIC RAILROAD CO. (T): 139 W. Van Buren St., 60605
CHICAGO TRIBUNE (P): 435 N. Michigan Ave., 60611
CHICKEN UNLIMITED ENTERPRISES, INC.: 11300 S. Halsted St., 60628
H. C. CHRISTIANS CO. (M): 1325 W. 15th St., 60608
COMBINED INSURANCE CO. OF AMERICA (LI): 5050 Broadway, 60640
COMMERCIAL DISCOUNT CORP. (S): 105 W. Adams St., 60603
COMMONWEALTH EDISON CO.: P.O. Box 767, 60690
CONSOLIDATED FOODS CORP. (I): 135 S. La Salle St., 60603
CONTAINER CORP. OF AMERICA (I): 38 S. Dearborn St., 60603
CONTINENTAL ASSURANCE CO. (LI): 310 S. Michigan Ave., 60604
CONTINENTAL ILLINOIS NATIONAL BANK & TRUST CO. OF CHICAGO (B): 231 S. La Salle St., 60604
DARLING-DELAWARE CO., INC. (I): 4201 S. Ashland Ave., 60609
A. B. DICK CO. (I): 5700 W. Touhy Ave., 60648
R. R. DONNELLEY & SONS CO.: 2223 Martin Luther King Dr., 60616
A. EPSTEIN & SONS, INC. (S): 2011 W. Pershing Rd., 60609
FEDERAL RESERVE BANK OF CHICAGO (B): 230 S. LaSalle St., 60604
THE FIRST NATIONAL BANK OF CHICAGO (B): One First National Plaza, 60670
CLINTON E. FRANK, INC.: 120 S. Riverside Plaza, 60606
GENERAL AMERICAN TRANSPORTATION CORP. (I): 120 South Riverside Plaza, 60680
GOLDBLATT BROS., INC. (M): 333 S. State St., 60604
GOSS CO. (I): 5601 W. 31st St., 60650
GRANT ADVERTISING (AA): 10 S. Riverside Plaza, 60606
GREYHOUND CORP. (S), 111 E. Wacker Dr., 60001
GREYHOUND LINES INC. (T): 10 S. Riverside Plaza, 60606
W. F. HALL PRINTING CO. (P): 4600 Diversey Ave., 60639
HARRIS TRUST & SAVINGS BANK (B): 111 W. Monroe St., 60690
HART SCHAFFNER & MARX (I): 36 S. Franklin St., 60606
HAWTHORN-MELLODY, INC. (I): 4201 W. Chicago Ave., 60651
WALTER E. HELLER INTERNATIONAL CORP. (S): 105 W. Adams St., 60690
HILTON HOTELS CORP. (S): 720 S. Michigan Ave., 60605
EDWARD HINES LUMBER CO. (S): 200 S. Michigan Ave., 60604
HOTPOINT BUSINESS OPER. MAJOR APPLIANCE & HOTPOINT DIV. (I): 5600 W. Taylor St., 60644
HOUSEHOLD FINANCE CORP. (S): Prudential Plaza, 60601
ILLINOIS BELL TELEPHONE CO. (U): 225 W. Randolph St., 60606
ILLINOIS CENTRAL RR. CO. (T): 135 E. Eleventh Pl., 60605
ILLINOIS TOOL WORKS INC. (I): 8501 W. Higgins Rd., 60631
INLAND-RYERSON CONSTRUCTION PRODUCTS CO. (I): Box 5532, 60680
INLAND STEEL CO. (I): 30 W. Monroe St., 60603
INTERLAKE, INC. (I): 310 S. Michigan Ave., 60604
INTERNATIONAL HARVESTER CO. (I): 401 N. Michigan Ave., 60611
INTERSTATE UNITED CORP. (S): 120 S. Riverside Plaza, 60606
JEWEL COMPANIES, INC.: 5725 E. River Rd., 60631
JOSLYN MFG. & SUPPLY CO. (I): 155 N. Wacker Dr., 60606
JOSLYN STAINLESS STEELS (I): 155 N. Wacker Dr., 60606
JUPITER INDUSTRIES INC. (I): 400 E. Randolph St., 60601
A. T. KEARNEY & CO. INC. (MC): 100 S. Wacker Dr., 60606
LESTER B. KNIGHT & ASSOCIATES INC. (MC): 549 W. Randolph St., 60606
LIBBY, MC NEILL & LIBBY (I): 200 S. Michigan Ave., 60604
LIQUID CARBONIC CORP. (I): 135 S. La Salle St., 60603
MAREMONT CORP. (I): 168 N. Michigan Ave., 60601
MARMON GROUP, INC. (I): 39 S. La Salle St., 60603
MARQUETTE CEMENT MFG. CO. (I): 20 N. Wacker Dr., 60606
MARSH & MC LENNAN, INC. (LI): 231 La Salle St., 60604
MARSHALL FIELD & CO. (M): 111 N. State St., 60602
MASONITE CORP. (I): 29 N. Wacker Dr., 60606
MC DONALD'S CORP. (S): 221 N. La Salle St., 60601
F. W. MEANS & CO. (S): 35 E. Wacker Dr., 60601
MIDDLE WEST SERVICE CO. (MC): 69 W. Washington St., 60602

MIEHLE-GOSS-DEXTER INC. (I): 3100 S. Central Ave., 60650
MONTGOMERY WARD & CO., INC. (M): 619 W. Chicago Ave., 60607
JOHN MORRELL & CO. (I): 208 S. La Salle St., 60604
MORTON CHEMICAL CO.: 110 N. Wacker Dr., 60606
MSL INDUSTRIES, INC.: 6330 N. Pulaski Rd., 60646
MUTUAL TRUST LIFE INSURANCE CO. (LI): 77 S. Wacker Dr., 60606
THE L. E. MYERS CO. (S): 550 W. Jackson Blvd., 60606
NALCO CHEMICAL CO. (I): 180 N. Michigan Ave., 60601
NATIONAL CAN CORP. (I): Midway Center, 60638
NATIONAL TEA CO. (M): 8303 W. Higgins Rd., 60631
NATURAL GAS PIPELINE CO. OF AMERICA (S): 122 S. Michigan Ave., 60603
A. C. NIELSEN CO. (S): 2101 W. Howard St., 60645
NORTH AMERICAN LIFE INSURANCE CO. OF CHICAGO (LI): 35 E. Wacker Dr., 60601
NORTHERN TRUST CO. (B): 50 S. La Salle St., 60603
OPELIKA MFG. CORP. (I): 361 W. Chestnut St., 60610
PEOPLES GAS CO. (U): 122 S. Michigan Ave., 60603
PEOPLES GAS LIGHT & COKE CO. (U): 122 S. Michigan Ave., 60603
PETTIBONE MERCURY CORP. (I): 4700 W. Division St., 60651
POST-KEYES-GARDNER INC. (AA): 875 N. Michigan Ave., 60611
PULLMAN INCORPORATED (I): 200 S. Michigan Ave., 60604
QUAKER OATS CO. (I): Merchandise Mart Plaza, 60654
ALBERT RAMOND & ASSOCIATES, INC. (MC): Tribune Tower, 60611
RAULAND CORP.: 5600 W. Jarvis Ave., 60648
JOSEPH T. RYERSON & SON, INC. (I): 2558 W. 16th St., 60608
SARGENT & LUNDY (S): 140 S. Dearborn St., 60603
SCHOLL INC. (I): 213 W. Schiller St., 60610
SCOT LAD FOODS, INC. (M): 1500 E. 97th St., 60628
G. D. SEARLE & CO. (I): Box 5110, 60680
SEARS, ROEBUCK AND CO. (M): 925 S. Homan Ave., 60607
SEEBURG CORP. OF DELAWARE (S): 1500 N. Dayton St., 60622
SIGNODE CORP. (I): 2600 N. Western Ave., 60647
SKIL CORP. (I): 5033 Elston Ave., 60630
SPECTOR FREIGHT SYSTEM, INC. (T): 205 W. Wacker Dr., 60606
SPIEGEL, INC. (M): 2511 W. 23rd St., 60608
STANDARD ALLIANCE, INDUSTRIES, INC. (I): 1211 W. 22nd St., 60521
STANDARD OIL CO. (INDIANA) (I): 910 S. Michigan Ave., 60605
STANRAY CORP. (I): 200 S. Michigan Ave., 60604
STATISTICAL TABULATING CORP. (S): 104 S. Michigan Ave., 60603
STEWART-WARNER CORP. (I): 1826 Diversey Parkway, 60614
STONE CONTAINER CORP. (I): 360 N. Michigan Ave., 60601
SUN ELECTRIC CORP. (I): 6323 Avondale Ave., 60631
SUNBEAM CORP. (I): 5400 W. Roosevelt Rd., 60650
SWIFT & CO. (I): 115 W. Jackson Blvd., 60604
TATHAM-LAIRD & KUDNER, INC. (AA): 625 N. Michigan Ave., 60611
TFI COMPANIES INC. (M): 1200 No. Homan Ave., 60651
JOHN R. THOMPSON CO. (S): 29 W. Randolph, 60601
TRIBUNE CO. (P): 435 N. Michigan Ave., 60611
UNION TANK CAR CO. (I): 111 W. Jackson Blvd., 60604
UNITED AIR LINES, INC.: P.O. Box 66100, 60666
UNITED STATES GYPSUM CO. (I): 101 S. Wacker Dr., 60606
VICTOR COMPTOMETER CORP. (I): 3900 N. Rockwell St., 60618
WALGREEN CO. (M): 4300 Peterson Ave., 60646
WARWICK ELECTRONICS INC. (I): 7300 N. Lehigh Ave., 60648
EDWARD H. WEISS & CO. (AA): 360 N. Michigan Ave., 60601
WELLS LAMONT CORP. (I): 6640 W. Touhy Ave., 60648
WIEBOLDT STORES, INC. (M): 1 North State St., 60602
WILSON & CO., INC. (I): Prudential Plaza, 60601
WOLF MANAGEMENT SERVICES (MC): 7 S. Dearborn St., 60603
WM. WRIGLEY JR. CO. (I): 410 N. Michigan Ave., 60611
WURLITZER CO. (I): 105 W. Adams St., 60603
ZENITH RADIO CORP. (I): 1900 N. Austin Ave., 60639

ILLINOIS

ALBERTO-CULVER CO. (I): 2525 Armitage Ave., Melrose Pk., 60160
ALLIED VAN LINES, INC.: 25th & Roosevelt, Broadview, 60153
ALLSTATE INSURANCE CO.: Allstate Plaza, Northbrook, 60062
ALL-STEEL EQUIPMENT INC. (I): Box 871, Aurora, 60507
ALTON BOX BOARD CO. (I): Box 276, Alton, 62002
AMERICAN GAGE & MACHINE CO.: 853 N. Dundee, Elgin, 60120

AMERICAN HOSPITAL SUPPLY CORP. (I): 1740 Ridge Ave., Evanston, 60201
ANIXTER BROS, INC.: 2230 Brummel Pl., Evanston, 60202
APECO CORPORATION (I): 2100 W. Dempster St., Evanston, 60202
ARCHER-DANIELS-MIDLAND CO.: 4666 Faries Pkwy., Decatur, 62525
BARBER-COLMAN CO. (I): 1300 Rock St., Rockford, 61101
BARBER-GREENE CO. (I): 400 N. Highland Ave., Aurora, 60507
BAXTER LABORATORIES, INC. (I): 6301 Lincoln Ave., Morton Grove, 60053
BEELINE FASHIONS, INC. (I): 375 Meyer Rd., Bensenville, 60106
BEKINS VAN LINES CO.: 333 S. Center St., Hillside, 60162
P. A. BERGNER & CO. (M): 200 S. Adams St., Peoria, 61602
BLISS & LAUGHLIN INDUSTRIES, INC. (I): 122 W. 22nd St., Oak Brook, 60523
BUNKER-RAMO CORP. (I): 1200 Harger Rd., Oakbrook North, Oak Brook, 60521
A. M. CASTLE & CO. (I): 3400 N. Wolf Rd., Franklin Park, 60131
CATERPILLAR TRACTOR CO. (I): 100 N.E. Adams St., Peoria, 61602
CENTRAL ILLINOIS LIGHT CO. (U): 300 Liberty St., Peoria, 61602
CENTRAL ILLINOIS PUBLIC SERVICE CO. (U): 607 E. Adams St., Springfield, 62701
CHAMBERLAIN MANUFACTURING CORP. (I): 845 Larch Ave., Elmhurst, 60126
CHICAGO BRIDGE & IRON CO. (I): 901 W. 22nd St., Oak Brook, 60521
CHICAGO MUSICAL INSTRUMENT CO. (I): 7373 N. Cicero Ave., Lincolnwood, 60646
CHICKEN DELIGHT, INC. (M): 1515 S. Mt. Prospect Rd., Des Plaines, 60018
CITY PRODUCTS CORP. (M): 1700 S. Wolf Rd., Des Plaines, 60018
CLOW CORP.: 1211 W. 22nd St., Oak Brook, 60521
THE COPLEY PRESS, INC. (P): 434 Downer Pl., Aurora, 60506
DEAN FOODS CO. (I): 3600 N. River Rd., Franklin Park, 60131
DEERE & CO. (I): John Deere Rd., Moline, Ill. 61265
DE SOTO, INC. (I): 1700 S. Mt. Prospect Rd., Des Plaines, 60018
ELECTRO-MOTIVE (I): 9301 55th St., La Grange, 60525
EUREKA WILLIAMS CO. (I): 1201 E. Bell St., Bloomington, 61701
F S SERVICES, INC. (I): 1701 Towanda Ave., Bloomington, 61702
BEN FRANKLIN (S): Wolf & Oakton, Des Plaines, 60018
FRANKLIN LIFE INSURANCE CO. (LI): Franklin Square, Springfield, 62705
GALE PRODUCTS (I): Monmouth Blvd., Galesburg, 61401
GARDNER-DENVER CO. (I): Gardner Expressway, Quincy, 62301
GENERAL FINANCE CORP. (S): 1301 Central St., Evanston, 60201
GENERAL TELEPHONE CO. OF ILLINOIS (U): 1312 E. Empire St., Bloomington, 61701
GRANITE CITY STEEL CO. (I): 20th & State Sts., Granite City, 62040
HAMMON CORP. (I): 100 Wilmot Rd., Deer Field, 60015
ILLINOIS POWER CO. (U): 500 S. 27th St., Decatur, 62525
INTERNATIONAL MINERALS & CHEMICAL CORP. (I): Old Orchard Rd., Skokie, 60076
JEWEL COMPANIES INC. (M): 1955 W. North Ave., Melrose Park, 60160
KATY INDUSTRIES, INC.: 853 Dundee Ave., Elgin, 60120
KEEBLER COMPANY (I): 677 Larch Ave., Elmhurst, 60126
KEYSTONE CONSOLIDATED INDUSTRIES, INC. (I): 411 Hamilton Blvd., Peoria, 61602
KROEHLER MFG. CO. (I): 222 E. Fifth Ave., Naperville, 60540
MC DONALD'S CORP.: One Mc Donald Plaza, Oak Brook, 60521
MC GRAW-EDISON CO. (I): 333 W. River Rd., Elgin, 60120
MOORMAN MFG. CO. (I): 1000 N. 30th St., Quincy, 62301
MOTOROLA INC. (I): 9401 W. Grand Ave., Franklin Park, 60131
MUELLER CO. (I): 500 W. Eldorado St., Decatur, 62522
NATIONAL LOCK DIV. (I): 1902 7th St., Rockford, 61101
NORTHERN ILLINOIS GAS CO. (U): Box 190, Aurora, 60507
NORTHWESTERN STEEL & WIRE CO. (I): Avenue B & Wallace St., Sterling, 61081
OAK ELECTRO-NETICS CORP. (I): Crystal Lake, 60014
PACKAGING CORP. OF AMERICA (I): 1603 Orrington Ave., Evanston, 60204
PROCON INCORPORATED. (S): 30 UOP Plaza, Des Plaines, 60016
RAND MCNALLY & CO. (S): 8255 Central Park Ave., Skokie, 60076
RICHARDSON COMPANY (I): 2400 E. Devon Ave., Des Plaines, 60018
ROPER CORPORATION (I): 1905 W. Court St., Kankakee, 60901

SANGAMO ELECTRIC CO. (I): 11th & Converse, Springfield, 62708
SARGENT-WELSH SCIENTIFIC CO. (I): 7300 N. Linden, Skokie, 60076
SQUARE D CO. (I): Executive Plaza, Park Ridge, 60068
A. E. STALEY MFG. CO. (I): Eldorado at 22nd St., Decatur, 62525
STANDARD ALLIANCE INDUSTRIES, INC.: 1211 W. 22nd St., Oakbrook, 60521
STANDARD KOLLSMAN INDUSTRIES, INC. (I): 2085 N. Hawthorne Ave., Melrose Park, 60160
STATE FARM LIFE INSURANCE CO. (LI): 112 E. Washington St., Bloomington, 61701
STATE FARM MUTUAL AUTOMOBILE INSURANCE CO. (LI): 112 E. Washington St., Bloomington, 61701
SUNDSTRAND CORP. (I): 4751 Harrison Ave., Rockford, 61101
SZABO FOOD SERVICE, INC. (S): 4242 S. First Ave., Lyons, 60534
TELETYPE CORP. (I): 5555 Touhy Ave., Skokie, 60076
UARCO INC. (I): West County Line Rd., Barrington, 60010
UNIVERSAL OIL PRODUCTS CO. (I): 30 Algonquin Rd., Des Plaines, 60016
VOLNEY FELT MILLS (I): 5818 Archer Rd., Summit, 60501
WASHINGTON NATIONAL INSURANCE CO. (LI): 1630 Chicago Ave., Evanston, 60201

INDIANA

ACME EVANS CO. (I): 902 W. Washington Ave., Indianapolis, 46222
ALLIED STRUCTURAL STEEL CO. (I): 1435 - 165th St., Hammond, 46320
ALTAMIL CORP. (I): 1736 N. Meridian St., Indianapolis, 46202
AMERICAN FLETCHER NAT. BANK & TRUST CO. (B): 101 Monument Circle, Indianapolis, 46204
AMERICAN STATES LIFE INSURANCE CO. (LI): 542 N. Meridian St., Indianapolis, 46206
AMERICAN UNITED LIFE INSURANCE CO. (LI): 30 W. Fall Creek Pkwy., Indianapolis, 46206
ARVIN INDUSTRIES, INC. (I): 1531 E. 13th St., Columbus, 47201
ASSOCIATES CORP. OF NORTH AMERICA (LI): 1700 Mishawaka Ave., South Bend, 46624
L. S. AYERS & CO. (M): 1 W. Washington St., Indianapolis, 46204
BALL CORPORATION (I): 1509 S. Macedonia Ave., Muncie, 47302
BIO-DYNAMICS, INC. (I): 9115 Hague Rd., Indianapolis, 46250
BRYANT AIRCONDITIONING CO.: 7310 W. Morris St., Indianapolis, 46231
BURGER CHEF SYSTEMS, INC. (I): 1348 W. 16th St., Indianapolis, 46202
CTS CORP. (I): 905 N. West Blvd., Elkhart, 46514
CENTRAL SOYA COMPANY, INC. (I): 1300 Ft. Wayne National Bank Bldg., Ft. Wayne, 46802
CREDITTHRIFT FINANCIAL CORP. (S): 601 N. W. Second St., Evansville, 47701
CUMMINS ENGINE COMPANY INC. (I): 1000 Fifth St., Columbus, 47201
DELCO-REMY DIVISION (I): 2401 Columbus Ave., Anderson, 46011
DIVCO-WAYNE CORP. (I): Industries Rd., Richmond, 47374
ESSEX INTERNATIONAL INC. (I): 1601 Wall St., Fort Wayne, 46804
FOOD MARKETING CORP. OF MINNESOTA, INC. (I): 4815 Executive Blvd., Fort Wayne, 46808
GENERAL TELEPHONE CO. OF IND. (U): P.O. Box 1201, Fort Wayne, Ind. 46801
GUIDE LAMP DIVISION (I): 2915 Pendleton Ave., Anderson, 46013
HAMILTON COSCO, INC. (I): 2525 State St., Columbus, 47201
INDIANA BELL TELEPHONE CO. (U): 240 N. Meridian St., Indianapolis, 46204
INDIANA FARM BUREAU CO-OPERATIVE ASSN., INC. (I): 47 S. Pennsylvania St., Indianapolis, 46204
INDIANA & MICHIGAN ELECTRIC CO. (U): 2101 Spy Run Ave., Fort Wayne, 46801
INDIANA NATIONAL BANK (B): One Indiana Sq., Indianapolis, 46204
INDIANAPOLIS LIFE INSURANCE CO. (LI): 2960 N. Meridian St., Indianapolis, 46208
INDIANAPOLIS POWER & LIGHT CO. (U): 25 Monument Circle, Indianapolis, 46206
INLAND CONTAINER CORP. (I): 120 E. Market St., Indianapolis, 46206
ELI LILLY & CO.: 307 E. McCarty St., Indianapolis, 46206
LINCOLN NATIONAL LIFE INSURANCE CO., (LI): 1301 S. Harrison St., Fort Wayne, 46801

LINCOLN NATIONAL CORP. (S): 1301 S. Harrison St., Fort Wayne, 46802

P. R. MALLORY & CO. INC. (I): 3029 E. Washington St., Indianapolis, 46206

MARSH SUPERMARKETS, INC. (M): Yorktown, 47396

MERCHANTS NAT. BANK & TRUST CO. (B): 11 S. Meridian St., Indianapolis, 46204

MIDWESTERN UNITED LIFE INSURANCE CO. (LI): 7551 U.S. Highway 24 W., Fort Wayne, 46804

MILES LABORATORIES INC. (I): 1127 Myrtle St., Elkhart, 46514

MISHAWAKA RUBBER CO., INC. (I): 312 N. Hill St., Mishawaka, 46544

NATIONAL HOMES CORP. (S): Earl & Wallace, Lafayette, 47902

NORTHERN INDIANA PUBLIC SERVICE CO. (U): 5265 Hohman Ave., Hammond, 46320

THE O'BRIEN CORP. (I): 2001 W. Washington Ave., South Bend, 46621

POTTER & BRUMFIELD (I): 1200 E. Broadway, Princeton, 47570

PUBLIC SERVICE CO. OF INDIANA, INC. (U): 1000 E. Main St., Plainfield, 46168

SKYLINE CORP. (I): 2520 By-Pass Road, Elkhart, 46514

STOKELY-VAN CAMP INC. (I): 941 N. Meridian St., Indianapolis, 46206

TARZIAN SARKES, INC. (I): E. Hillside Dr., Bloomington, 47401

WABASH MAGNETICS INC.: 810 N. Cass St., Wabash, 46992

WEIL-MC LAIN CO., INC. (I): 723 Franklin Sq., Michigan City, 46360

IOWA

AMF WESTERN TOOL DIVISION (I): 3811 McDonald Ave., Des Moines, 50313

AMANA REFRIGERATION, INC. (I): Amana, 52203

AMERICAN MUTUAL LIFE INSURANCE CO. (LI): Liberty Bldg., Des Moines, 50307

BANDAG, INC. (I): 1056 Hershey Ave., Muscatine, 52761

BANKERS LIFE CO. (I): 711 High St., Des Moines, 50307

CENTRAL LIFE ASSURANCE CO. (LI): 611 5th Ave., Des Moines, 50309

DUBUQUE PACKING CO. (I): 16th & Sycamore, Dubuque, 52001

EQUITABLE LIFE INSURANCE CO. OF IOWA (LI): P.O. Box 1635, Des Moines, 50306

LENNOX INDUSTRIES INC. (I): 200 S. 12th Ave., Marshalltown, 50158

MASSEY-FERGUSON INC. (I): 1901 Bell Ave., Des Moines, 50315

MAYTAG CO. (I): 403 W. 4th St., Newton, 50208

MEREDITH CORP. (S): 1716 Locust St., Des Moines, 50303

NEEDHAM PACKING CO. (I): Badgerow Bldg., Sioux City, 51101

RATH PACKING CO. (I): Elm & Sycamore, Waterloo, 50703

SPENCER FOODS INC. (I): Spencer, 51301

YOUNKER BROS., INC. (M): 7th & Walnut Sts., Des Moines, 50306

KANSAS

ASSOCIATED WHOLESALE GROCERS, INC. (M): 1601 Fairfax Trafficway, Kansas City, 66115

BEECH AIRCRAFT CORP. (I): 9709 E. Central Ave., Wichita, 67206

CESSNA AIRCRAFT CO. (I): 5800 Pawnee Rd., Wichita, 67218

COLEMAN CO., INC. (I): 250 N. St. Francis Ave., Wichita, 67201

DILLON COMPANIES (M): 2700 E. Fourth St., Hutchinson, 67501

FLEMING CO., INC.: Garlinghouse Bldg., Topeka, 66612

KOCH ENGINEERING CO., INC.: 4111 E. 37th St., N., Wichita, 67204

H. D. LEE CO., INC. (I): Johnson Drive at State Line, Shawnee Mission, 66201

KENTUCKY

AMERICAN AIR FILTER CO., INC. (I): 215 Central Ave., Louisville, 40208

ANACONDA ALUMINUM CO.: 1251 S. 4th St., Louisville, 40203

ASHLAND OIL, INC. (I): 1409 Winchester Ave., Ashland, 41101

BROWN-FORMAN DISTILLERS CORP. (I): 850 Dixie Hwy., Louisville, 40210

BROWN & WILLIAMSON TOBACCO CORP. (I): 1600 W. Hill St., Louisville, 40201

CELANESE COATINGS CO. (I): 224 E. Broadway, Louisville, 40202

CITIZENS FIDELITY BANK & TRUST CO. (B): 437 W. Jefferson St., Louisville, 40202

C&I/GIRDLER INC.,: 1721 S. 7th St., Louisville, 40208

COMMONWEALTH LIFE INSURANCE CO. (LI): Commonwealth Bldg., Louisville, 40202

FISCHER PACKING CO. (I): Box 1138, Louisville, 40201

GLENMORE DISTILLERIES CO. (I): 660 S. 4th St., Louisville, 40202

GUERDON INDUSTRIES, INC. (S): P.O. Box 1259, Louisville, 40201

KENTUCKY FRIED CHICKEN CORP., P.O. Box 13331, Louisville, 40213

LOUISVILLE GAS & ELECTRIC CO. (U): 311 W. Chestnut St., Louisville, 40201

LOUISVILLE & NASHVILLE RR. (T): 908 W. Broadway, Louisville, 40203

MASON & HANGER — SILAS MASON CO.: 200 E. Main St., Lexington, 40507

NATIONAL INDUSTRIES, INC. (I): 510 W. Broadway, Louisville, 40202

TEXAS GAS TRANSMISSION CORP. (S): 3800 Frederica St., Owensboro, 42301

THOMAS INDUSTRIES INC. (I): 207 E. Broadway, Louisville, 40202

TITAN GROUP, INC., 222 Executive Park, Louisville, 40207

UNIVERSAL CONTAINER CORP. (I): 8318 Grande Lane, Louisville, 40219

VERMONT AMERICAN CORP.,: 500 E. Main St., Louisville, 40202

LOUISIANA

ARKANSAS LOUISIANA GAS CO. (I): Slattery Bldg., Shreveport, 71102

ARKLA CHEMICAL CORP. (I): Slattery Bldg., Shreveport, 71102

AVONDALE SHIPYARDS, INC. (I): Box 50280, New Orleans, 70150

BILLUPS WESTERN PETROLEUM CO. (M): Box 1000, Hammond, 70401

BOH BROS. CONSTRUCTION CO., INC. (S): 730 S. Tonti St., New Orleans, 70119

CENTRAL LOUISIANA ELECTRIC CO. (U): 415 Main St., Pineville, 71360

D. H. HOLMES CO., LTD. (M): 819 Canal St., New Orleans, 70112

LYKES-YOUNGSTOWN CORP.: 821 Gravier St., New Orleans, 70112

LOUISIANA LAND & EXPLORATION CO. (S): 225 Baronne St., New Orleans, 70112

LOUISIANA POWER & LIGHT CO. (U): 142 Delaronde St., New Orleans, 70114

J. RAY MC DERMOTT & CO.: 1010 Common St., New Orleans, 70160

NEW ORLEANS PUBLIC SERVICE INC. (U): 317 Baronne St., New Orleans, 70160

PAN-AMERICAN LIFE INSURANCE CO. (LI): 2400 Canal St., New Orleans, 70119

STANDARD FRUIT & STEAMSHIP CO. (I): 2 Canal St., New Orleans, 70130

TIDEWATER MARINE: 3308 Tulane Ave., New Orleans, 70119

MAINE

BATES MFG. CO. (I): Box 591, Lewiston, 04240

BATH IRON WORKS CORP. (I): 700 Washington St., Bath, 04530

CENTRAL MAINE POWER CO. (U): 9 Green St., Augusta, 04330

MARYLAND

AALCORP. (I): Box 6767, Baltimore, 21204

ALLEGHENY BEVERAGE CORP.: 2216 N. Charles St., Baltimore, 21218

ANCHOR POST PRODUCTS, INC. (I): 6500 Eastern Ave., Baltimore, 21224

ARUNDEL CORP. (I): 501 St. Paul Pl., Baltimore, 21202

A. S. ABELL CO. (P): Calvert & Center Sts., Baltimore, 21203

BALTIMORE GAS & ELECTRIC CO. (U): Gas & Electric Bldg., Baltimore, 21203

BALTIMORE & OHIO RR. CO. (T): 2 N. Charles St., Baltimore, 21201

BATA SHOE CO. (I): Belcamp, 21017

THE BLACK & DECKER MFG. CO. (I): 701 E. Joppa Rd., Towson, 21204

CHESAPEAKE & POTOMAC TELEPHONE CO. OF MARYLAND (U): 320 St. Paul Pl., Baltimore, 21202

COMMERCIAL CREDIT CO. (S): 300 St. Paul Place, Baltimore, 21202

EASCO CORP. (I): 201 North Charles St., Baltimore, 21201

EQUITABLE TRUST CO. (B): Calvert & Fayette Sts., Baltimore, 21201

FIRST NATIONAL BANK (B): Light & Redwood Sts., Baltimore, 21202

GIANT FOOD INC. (M): 6900 Sheriff Rd., Landover, Md. 20784

HOCHSCHILD, KOHN & CO. (M): Howard & Lexington, Baltimore, 21201

HUTZLER BROTHERS CO. (M): Howard, Saratoga & Clay, Baltimore, 21201

KELLY-SPRINGFIELD TIRE CO. (I): Kelly Blvd., Cumberland, 21502

LONDONTOWN MFG. CO. (I): 3600 Clipper Mile Rd., Baltimore, 21211

MACKE CO. (THE) (S): 1 Macke Circle, Cheverly, 20781

MARYLAND CASUALTY CO. (LI): Keswick Rd. & 40th St., Baltimore, 21203

MARYLAND CUP CORP. (I): Owings Mills, 21117

MARYLAND NATIONAL BANK (B): 10 Light St., Baltimore, 21203

MARYLAND SHIPBUILDING & DRYDOCK CO. (S): P.O. Box 537, Baltimore, 21203

MC CORMICK & CO., INC. (I): 11350 McCormick Rd., Cockeysville, 21030

PRESTON TRUCKING CO. (T): 151 Easton Blvd., Preston, 21655

QUALITY COURTS MOTELS, INC. (S): 11161 New Hampshire Ave., Silver Spring, 20904

SERVOMATION MATHIAS, INC. (S): 803 Gleneagles Ct., Towson, 21204

SUBURBAN TRUST (B): 6495 New Hampshire Ave., Hyattsville, 20783

SUN LIFE INSURANCE CO. OF AMERICA (LI): Sun Life Bldg., Charles Center, 21201

U.S. FIDELITY & GUARANTY CO. (LI): Calvert & Redwood Sts., Baltimore, 21203

UNION TRUST (B): Baltimore & St. Paul, Baltimore, 21203

WESTERN MARYLAND RY. (T): 201 N. Charles St., Baltimore, 21201

MASSACHUSETTS

ABERTHAW CONSTRUCTION CO. (I): 28 State St., Boston, 02109

ACUSHNET CO.: 744 Belleville Ave., New Bedford, 02715

ADAMS-RUSSELL CO. INC. (I): 1380 Main St., Waltham, 02154

AEROVOX CORP.: 740 Belleville Ave., New Bedford, 02741

AITS, INC. (S): 210 Boylston St., Chestnut Hill, 02167

ALGONQUIN GAS TRANSMISSION CO. (I): 1284 Soldiers Field Rd., Boston, 02135

ALPHA INDUSTRIES INC. (I): 20 Sylvan Rd., Woburn, Mass. 01801

AMERICAN BILTRITE RUBBER CO., INC. (I): 575 Technology Sq., Cambridge, 02139

AMERICAN EMPLOYER'S INSURANCE CO. (LI): 110 Milk St., Boston, 02107

AMERICAN MUTUAL LIABILITY INSURANCE CO. (LI); Wakefield, 01880

AMERICAN OPTICAL CORP. (I): Pleasant St. Connector, Framingham Center, 01701

AMERICAN RESEARCH & DEVELOPMENT CORP. (I): John Hancock Bldg., 200 Berkeley St., Boston, 02116

BADGER COMPANY, INC. (I): One Broadway, Cambridge, 02142

L. G. BALFOUR CO. (I): 25 County St., Attleboro, 02703

BAY STATE MILLING CO. (I): 4700 Prudential Center, Boston, 02199

BAYSTATE CORP. (S): 77 Franklin St., Boston, 02110

BERKSHIRE HATHAWAY INC. (I): 97 Cove St., New Bedford, 02744

BERKSHIRE LIFE INSURANCE CO. (LI): 700 South St., Pittsfield, 01202

BIRD & SON, INC. (I): Washington St., EAst Walpole, 02032

BOLTA PRODUCTS (I): 70 Garden St., Lawrence, 01841

BOSTON EDISON CO. (U): 800 Boylston St., Boston, 02199

BOSTON GAS CO.: Prudential Tower, Boston, 02199

BOSTON HERALD-TRAVELER CORP. (P): 300 Harrison Ave., Boston, 02118

BOSTON & MAINE CORP. (T): 150 Causeway St., Boston, 02114

BOSTON MUTUAL LIFE INSURANCE CO. (LI): 156 Stuart St., Boston, 02116

A. A. BRUNELL ELECTROPLATING CORP. (I): 41 Sutton Lane, Worcester, 01603

CABOT CORP. (I): 125 High St., Boston, 02110

CADILLAC AUTOMOBILE CO. OF BOSTON (M): 808 Commonwealth Ave., Boston, 02215

CARLING BREWING CO., INC. (I): 610 Lincoln St., Waltham, 02154

WILLIAM CARTER CO. (I): 963 Highland Ave., Needham Heights, 02194

COURIER CITIZEN CO. (S): 165 Jackson St., Lowell, 01852

CRAMER ELECTRONICS, INC. (I): 85 Wells Ave., Newton, 02159

DENNISON MFG. CO. (I): 300 Howard St., Framingham, 01701

DEWEY & ALMY CHEMICAL DIVISION (I): 62 Whittemore Ave., Cambridge, 02140

DIGITAL EQUIPMENT CORP. (I): 146 Main St., Maynard, 01754

EG & G, INC. (I): Crosby Dr., Bedford, 01730

EASTERN GAS & FUEL ASSOCIATES (I): 2900 Prudential Tower, Boston, 02199

WM. FILENE'S SONS CO. (M): 426 Washington St., Boston, 02108

FIRST NATIONAL BANK OF BOSTON (B): 100 Federal St., Boston, 02110

FIRST NATIONAL STORES INC. (M): 5 Middlesex Ave., Somerville, 02143

THE FOXBORO CO. (I): 38 Neponset Ave., Foxboro, 02035

GENERAL CINEMA CORP. (I): 500 Boylston St., Boston, 02116

THE GILLETTE CO. (I): Prudential Tower Bldg., Boston, 02199

GORTON CORP. (I): 327 Main St., Gloucester, 01930

HEYWOOD-WAKEFIELD CO. (I): 206 Central St., Gardner, 01440

JOHN HANCOCK MUTURAL LIFE INSURANCE CO. (LI): 200 Berkeley St., Boston, 02116

HOWARD JOHNSON CO. (S): One Howard Johnson Plaza, Boston, 02125

ITEK CORP. (I): 10 Maguire Rd., Lexington, 02173

THE KENDALL CO. (I): 225 Franklin St., Boston, 02110

KEYSTONE CUSTODIAN FUNDS, INC. (S): 99 High St., Boston, 02110

KING'S DEPT. STORES, INC. (M): 150 California St., Newton, 02158

KNAPP KING-SIZE CORP.: One Knapp Centre, Brockton, 02401

A. C. LAWRENCE LEATHER CO. (I): 10 Sawyer St., Peabody, 01960

LIBERTY MUTUAL INSURANCE (LI): 175 Berkeley St., Boston, 02117

LUDLOW CORP. (I): 145 Rosemary St., Needham Heights, 02194

MAMMOTH MART, INC. (M): 321 Manley St., West Bridgewater, 02379

MASSACHUSETTS ELECTRIC CO. (U): 20 Turnpike Rd., Westborough, 01581

MASSACHUSETTS MUTUAL LIFE INSURANCE CO. (LI): 1295 State St., Springfield, 01101

THE MITRE CORP.: Burlington Rd., Bedford, 01730

MOORE DROP FORGING CO. (I): 38 Walter St., Springfield, 01107

MORSE SHOE INC. (I): 555 Turnpike St., Canton, 02021

NEW ENGLAND ELECTRIC SYSTEM (U): 20 Turnpike Rd., Westboro, 01581

NEW ENGLAND MERCHANTS NAT. BANK (B): Prudential Center, Boston, 02199

NEW ENGLAND MUTUAL LIFE INSURANCE CO. (LI): 501 Boylston St., Boston, 02117

NEW ENGLAND POWER CO. (U): 20 Turnpike Rd., Westboro, 01581

NEW ENGLAND TELEPHONE & TELEGRAPH CO. (U): 185 Franklin St., Boston, 02107

NORTON CO. (I): 1 New Bond St., Worcester, 01606

PHOTON, INC. (I): 355 Middlesex Ave., Wilmington, 01887

POLAROID CORPORATION (I): 549 Technology Sq., Cambridge, 02139

H. K. PORTER, INC. (I): 74 Foley St., Somerville, 02143

RATH & STRONG, INC. (MC): 21 Worthen Rd., Lexington, 02173

RAYTHEON CO. (I): 141 Spring St., Lexington, 02173

RILEY STOKER CORP. (I): 9 Neponset St., Worcester, 01613

RUST CRAFT GREETING CARDS, INC. (I): Dedham, 02026

SEABOARD ALLIED MILLING CORP. (M): 200 Boylston St., Newton, 02167

SHAWMUT ASSOCIATION INC. (B): 82 Devonshire St., Boston, 02109

SONESTA INTERNATIONAL HOTELS CORP.: 390 Commonwealth Ave., Boston, 02215

A. G. SPALDING & BROS. INC. (I): Meadow St., Chicopee, 01013

SPENCER COMPANIES, INC. (M): 450 Summer St., Boston, 02210
SPRAGUE ELECTRIC CO.: 87 Marshall St., North Adams, 01247
C. H. SPRAGUE & SON CO. (I): 125 High St., Boston, 02110
STANDARD INTERNATIONAL CORP. (I): Elm Square, Andover, 01810
STANLEY HOME PRODUCTS, INC. (I): 333 Western Ave., Westfield, 01085
STAR MARKET CO. (M): 625 Mt. Auburn St., Cambridge, 02138
STATE MUTUAL LIFE ASSURANCE COMPANY OF AMERICA (LI): 440 Lincoln St., Worcester, 01605
STATE STREET BANK & TRUST CO. (B): 225 Franklin St., Boston, 02110
STOP & SHOP INC. (M): 393 D St., Boston, 02110
SWANK, INC. (I): 6 Hazel St., Attleboro, 02703
TRANSITRON ELECTRONIC CORP. (I): 168 Albion St., Wakefield, 01880
TYCO LABORATORIES, INC. (I): 16 Hickory Dr., Waltham, 02154
USM CORP. (I): 140 Federal St., Boston, 02107
UNITED FRUIT CO. (I): Prudential Center, Boston, 02199
U.S. ENVELOPE CO. (I): Memorial Industrial Pk., Springfield, 01101
USM CORP.: 140 Federal, Boston, 02107
VANCE, SANDERS & CO. (S): 111 Devonshire St., Boston, 02109
WANG LABORATORIES INC. (I): 836 North St., Tewksbury, 01876
WHITIN MACHINE WORKS (I): Main St., Whitinsville, 01588
WYMAN-GORDON CO. (I): 105 Madison St., Worcester, 01601
XTRA, INC. (I): 150 Causeway St., Boston, 02114
ZAYRE CORP.: Framingham, 01701

MICHIGAN

AC SPARK PLUG (I): 1300 N. Dort Highway, Flint, 48556
ABITIBI CORP. (I): 1400 N. Woodward Ave., Birmingham, 48011
ACME PRECISION PRODUCTS INC. (I): 3750 East Outer Dr., Detroit, 48234
ACME QUALITY PAINTS, INC. (I): 8250 St. Aubin Ave., Detroit, 48211
ACM INDUSTRIES INC. (I): 450 Union Bank Bldg., Grand Rapids,
AEROQUIP CORPORATION (I): 300 S. East Ave., Jackson, 49203
ALLEN INDUSTRIES, INC. (I): 17515 W. Nine Mile Rd., Southfield, 48015
ALLIED PAPER INCORPORATED (I): 1608 Lake St., Kalamazoo, 49003
ALLIED SUPERMARKETS INC. (M): 8711 Meadowdale Ave., Detroit, 48228
AMERICAN MOTORS CORP. (I): 14250 Plymouth Rd., Detroit, 48232
AMERICAN MOTORS SALES CORP. (I): 14250 Plymouth Rd., Detroit, 48232
AMERICAN MUSIC STORES, INC. (I): 1515 Woodward Ave., Detroit, 48226
AMERICAN SEATING CO. (I): 901 Broadway, Grand Rapids, 49502
AMWAY CORP. (I): 7575 E. Fulton Rd., Ada, 49301
ASSOCIATED BREWING CO. (I): 3740 Bellevue Ave., Detroit, 48207
ASSOCIATED TRUCK LINES, INC. (T): Vandenberg Center, Grand Rapids, 49502
AUTO SPECIALTIES MFG. CO. (I): St. Joseph, 49085
AUTO-OWNERS INSURANCE CO. (LI): 303 W. Kalamazoo St., Lansing, 48903
BANK OF THE COMMONWEALTH: Fort & Griswold Sts., Detroit, 48231
BARTON MALOW CO. (S): Box 5200, Detroit, 48235
BENDIX CORP. (I): Bendix Center, Southfield, 48076
BORMAN'S INC. (M): 12300 Mark Twain Ave., Detroit, 48227
BUICK MOTOR DIVISION (I): 902 E. Hamilton Ave., Flint, 48550
BUNDY CORPORATION (I): 333 W. Fort St., Detroit, 48226
BURROUGHS CORPORATION (I): Burroughs Pl., Detroit, 48232
J. P. BURROUGHS & SON, INC. (I): P.O. Box 1928, Saginaw, 48605
CADILLAC MOTOR CAR (I): 2860 Clark Ave., Detroit, 48232
CADILLAC PLASTIC & CHEMICAL CO. (I): 15111 Second Ave., Detroit, 48203
CAMPBELL-EWALD CO.: General Motors Bldg., Detroit, 48202
CAMPBELL, WYANT & CANNON FOUNDRY CO. (I): Henry St., Muskegon, 49441
CENTRAL FOUNDRY DIVISION (I): 77 W. Concord St., Saginaw, 48605
CHAMPION HOME BUILDERS CO. (I): 5573 E. North St., Dryden, 48428

CHEVROLET MOTOR (I): General Motors Bldg., Detroit, 48202
CHRYSLER CORP. (I): 341 Massachusetts Ave., Detroit, 48231
CITY NATL. BANK OF DETROIT (B): Penobscot Bldg., Detroit, 48226
CLARK EQUIPMENT CO. (I): 324 E. Dewey, Buchanan, 49107
CONSUMERS POWER CO. (U): 212 W. Michigan Ave., Jackson, 49201
DETROIT BANK & TRUST CO.: P.O. Box 59, Detroit, 48231
DETROIT DIESEL ALLISON DIVISION (I): 13400 W. Outer Dr., Detroit, 48228
DETROIT EDISON CO. (U): 2000 Second Ave., Detroit, 48226
DIESEL EQUIPMENT (I): 2100 Burlingame Ave., S.W., Grand Rapids, 49509
DOW CHEMICAL CO. (I): Midland, 48640
DOW CORNING CORP. (I): Box 592, Midland, 48640
EX-CELL-O CORP. (I): P.O. Box 386, Detroit, 48232
FEDERAL-MOGUL CORP. (I): Box 1966, Detroit, 48235
FEDERAL'S INC. (M): 1200 E. McNichols Rd., Detroit, 48203
FORD MOTOR CO. (I): The American Road, Dearborn, 48121
FORD MOTOR CREDIT CO. (S): American Road, Dearborn, 48121
FORD TRACTOR OPERATIONS (I): 2500 E. Maple Rd., Troy, 48084
FRUEHAUF CORP. (I): 10900 Harper Ave., Detroit, 48213
GMC TRUCK & COACH (I): 660 South Blvd., E., Pontiac, 48053
GENERAL MOTORS CORP. (I): General Motors Bldg., Detroit, 48202
GENERAL TELEPHONE CO. OF MICH. (U): 455 E. Ellis Rd., Muskegon, 49443
GERBER PRODUCTS CO. (I): 445 State St., Fremont, 49412
GIBSON PRODUCTS CORP. (I): 515 W. Gibson Dr., Greenville, 48838
GRAND TRUNK WESTERN RAILROAD CO. (T): 131 W. Lafayette Blvd., Detroit, 48226
HANDLEMAN COMPANY (I): 670 Woodbridge, Detroit, 48226
HAYES-ALBION CORP. (I): 437 Fern Ave., Jackson, 49202
HOLLEY INC. CARBURETOR DIVISION (I): 11955 E. Nine Mile Rd., Warren, 48089
HOOVER BALL & BEARING CO. (I): Box 1003, Ann Arbor, 48106
THE J. L. HUDSON CO. (S): 1206 Woodward Ave., Detroit, 48226
HYGRADE FOOD PRODUCTS CORP. (I): 26300 Northwestern Hwy., Southfield, 48075
INTERSTATE MOTOR FREIGHT SYSTEM (T): 134 Grandville Ave., S.W., Grand Rapids, 49502
KAWNEER CO. (I): 1105 N. Front St., Niles, 49120
KELLOGG CO. (I): 235 Porter St., Battle Creek, 49016
KELSEY-HAYES CO. (I): 38481 Huron River Dr., Romulus, 48174
KING-SEELEY THERMOS CO.: 3989 Research Park Dr., Ann Arbor, 48104
S.S. KRESGE CO. (M): 2727 Second Ave., Detroit, 48232
MAC MANUS, JOHN & ADAMS INC. (AA): 10 W. Long Lake Rd., Bloomfield Hills, 48013
MANUFACTURERS NATIONAL BANK OF DETROIT (B): 151 W. Fort St., Detroit, Mich. 48226
MASCO CORP. (I): 21001 Van Born Rd., Taylor, 48180
MC CORD CORP.: 2850 W. Grand Blvd., Detroit, 48202
MEIJER, INC.: 2727 Walker N.W., Grand Rapids, 49504
MICHIGAN BELL TELEPHONE CO. (U): 1365 Cass Ave., Detroit, 48226
MICHIGAN CONSOLIDATED GAS CO. (U): One Woodward Ave., Detroit, 48226
MICHIGAN NATIONAL BANK: Lansing, 48904
MICHIGAN-WISCONSIN PIPE LINE CO. (I): One Woodward Ave., Detroit, 48226
MOTOR WHEEL CORP. (I): 1600 N. Larch St., Lansing, 48914
NATIONAL BANK OF DETROIT (B): Woodward & Fort, Detroit, 48232
NATIONAL-STANDARD CO. (I): Niles, 49120
NATIONAL TWIST DRILL & TOOL CO.: Rochester, 48063
OLD KENT BANK & TRUST CO.: 1 Vandenberg Center, Grand Rapids, 49502
OLDSMOBILE DIVISION (I): 920 Townsend St., Lansing, 48921
PARKE, DAVIS & CO. (I): P.O. Box 118, Detroit, 48232
R. L. POLK & CO. (S): 431 Howard St., Detroit, 48231
PONTIAC MOTOR DIVISION (I): One Pontiac Plaza, Pontiac, 48053
ROSS ROY INC. (AA): 2751 E. Jefferson Ave., Detroit 48207
SAGINAW STEERING GEAR DIVISION (I): 3900 Holland Ave., Saginaw, 48605
SEALED POWER CORP. (I): 2001 Sanford St., Muskegon Heights, 49444

SPARTAN STORES, INC. (M): 1111 44th St., S.E., Grand Rapids, 49508

SPARTON CORP. (I): 2400 E. Ganson St., Jackson, 49202

THE STROH BREWERY CO. (I): 909 E. Elizabeth St., Detroit, 48226

TECUMSEH PRODUCTS CO. (I): Ottawa & Patterson Sts., Tecumseh, 49286

UPJOHN CO. (I): 7000 Portage Rd., Kalamazoo, 49001

VICKERS DIVISION (I): P.O. Box 302, Troy, 48084

W. B. DOVER & CO. (AA): 1060 First National Bldg., Detroit, 48226

WHIRLPOOL CORPORATION (I): Lake Shore & Monte Rd., Benton Harbor, 49022

WICKES CORP. (M): 515 N. Washington Ave., Saginaw, 48607

WOLVERINE WORLD WIDE INC. (I): 9341 Courtland Dr., Rockford, 49341

WYANDOTTE PAINT PRODUCTS (I): 1430 Sycamore St., Wyandotte, 48192

MINNESOTA

ADMIRAL-MERCHANTS/COLE-DIXIE MOTOR FREIGHT INC. (T): 2625 Territorial Rd., St. Paul, 55114

AMERICAN HARDWARE MUTUAL INSURANCE CO. (LI): P.O. Box 435, Minneapolis, 54450

AMERICAN HOIST & DERRICK CO. (I): 63 S. Robert St., St. Paul, 55107

AMERICAN LINEN SUPPLY CO. (I): 47 S. 9th St., Minneapolis, 55402

ANDERSEN CORP. (I): Bayport, 55003

APACHE CORP. (I): 1800 Foshay Tower, Minneapolis, 55402

APPLEBAUM'S FOOD MARKETS, INC. (M): 860 Vandalia, St. Paul, 55114

W. H. BARBER OIL CO. (I): 825 Thornton St., S.E., Minneapolis 55414

BEMIS COMPANY, INC. (I): 800 Northstar Center, Minneapolis, 55402

BROWN & BIGELOW (I): 450 N. Syndicate St., St. Paul, 55104

BUCKBEE MEARS CO. (I): 245 E. 6th St., St. Paul, 55101

CAMPBELL-MITHUN INC. (AA): North Star Center, Minneapolis, 55402

CARGILL, INC. (I): Cargill Bldg., Minneapolis, 55402

CONTROL DATA CORP. (I): 8100 34th Ave., Minneapolis, 55440

DAYTON-HUDSON CORP.: 700 Nicollet Mall, Minneapolis, 55402

DELUXE CHECK PRINTERS, INC. (S): 2199 N. Pascal Ave., St. Paul, 55113

FIRST BANK SYSTEM INC. (S): 1400 First National Bank Bldg., Minneapolis, 55402

GAMBLE-SKOGMO, INC.: 5100 Gamble Dr., St. Louis Park, Minneapolis, 55416

GENERAL MILLS INC. (I): 9200 Wayzata Blvd., Minneapolis, 55440

GRAIN BELT BREWERIES, INC.: P.O. Box 599, Grain Belt Park, Minneapolis, 55440

GREEN GIANT CO. (I): 1200 Commerce St., Le Sueur, 56058

THEODORE HAMM CO. (I): 720 Payne Ave., St. Paul, 55101

HOERNER-WALDORF CORP. (I): 2250 Wabash Ave., St. Paul, 55114

HONEYWELL INC. (I): 2701 4th Ave. S., Minneapolis, 55408

GEO. A. HORMEL & CO. (I): 501 16th Ave., Austin, 55912

INVESTORS DIVERSIFIED SERVICES, INC. (S): Investors Bldg., Minneapolis, 55402

INVESTORS MUTUAL, INC. (S): Roanoke Bldg., Minneapolis, 55402

INVESTORS SYNDICATE OF AMERICA (LI): Investors Bldg., Minneapolis, 55402

AL JOHNSON CONSTRUCTION CO. (I): Investors Bldg., Minneapolis, 55402

JOSTEN'S, INC. (S): 7851 Metro Office Park, Minneapolis, 55420

LAND O'LAKES CREAMERIES, INC. (I): 614 McKinley Pl., Minneapolis, 55413

MC CAFFREY ADVERTISING AGENCY (AA): 318 Baker Bldg., Minneapolis, 55402

MEDTRONIC, INC. (I): 3055 Old Highway 8, Minneapolis, 55418

MIDLAND COOPERATIVES, INC. (I): 739 Johnson St., N.E., Minneapolis, 55413

MINNEAPOLIS STAR AND TRIBUNE CO. (P): 425 Portland Ave., Minneapolis, 55415

MINNESOTA MINING & MFG. CO. (I): 3M Center, St. Paul, 55101

MINNESOTA MUTUAL LIFE INSURANCE CO. (LI): 345 Cedar St., St. Paul, 55101

MUNSINGWEAR, INC. (I): 718 Glenwood Ave., Minneapolis, 55405

NASH-FINCH CO. (M): 3381 Gorham Ave., Minneapolis, 55426

NATIONAL FOOD STORES INC. (M): Excelsior & Interlachen, Hopkins, 55343

NORTH CENTRAL AIRLINES, INC. (T): 7500 Northliner Dr., Minneapolis, 55450

NORTHERN PACIFIC TRANSPORT CO. (T): 176 E. 5th St., St. Paul, 55101

NORTHERN STATES POWER CO. (U): 414 Nicollet Mall, Minneapolis, 55401

NORTHWEST AIRLINES INC. (T): Minneapolis-St. Paul International Airport, St. Paul, 55111

NORTHWEST BANCORPORATION (S): 1200 Northwestern Bank Bldg., Minneapolis, 55480

NORTHWEST PAPER CO. (I): Avenue C & Arch, Cloquet, 55720

NORTHWEST PUBLICATIONS, INC. (P): 55 E. 4th St., St. Paul, 55101

NORTHWESTERN NATIONAL BANK OF MINNEAPOLIS (B): Minneapolis, 55480

NORTHWESTERN NATIONAL LIFE INSURANCE CO. (LI): 20 Washington Ave., So., Minneapolis, 55440

PILLSBURY CO. (I): 608 Second Ave., S., Minneapolis, 55402

PREMIUM SERVICE CORP. (S): 12715 B State Hwy. 55, Minneapolis, 55427

RED OWL STORES, INC.: 215 E. Excelsior Ave., Hopkins, 55343

ST. PAUL COMPANIES, INC. (LI): 385 Washington St., St. Paul, 55102

SOO LINE RR CO. (T): Soo Line Bldg., Minneapolis, 55440

STUDEBAKER CORP.: 1400 73rd Ave., N.E., Minneapolis, 55432

SUPER VALU STORES, INC. (M): 101 Jefferson Ave., Hopkins, 55343

TONKA CORP. (I): 9901 Wayzata Blvd., Minneapolis, 55426

THE TORO COMPANY (I): 8111 Lyndale Ave. So., Minneapolis, 55420

THE U.S. BEDDING CO. (I): Wabash & Vandalia, St. Paul, 55114

THE VALSPAR CORP. (I): 1101 South Third St., Minneapolis, 55415

MISSISSIPPI

ALODEX CORP., One Office Park Plaza, Southhaven, 38671

M P I INDUSTRIES (I): P.O. Box 492, Jackson, 39205

MISSOURI

J. S. ALBERICI CONSTRUCTION CO., INC. (S): 2150 Kienlen Ave., St. Louis, 63121

AMERICAN INVESTMENT CO. (S): 8251 Maryland Ave., St. Louis, 63105

AMERICAN ZINC CO. (I): 20 S. Fourth St., St. Louis, 63102

ANGELICA CORP. (I): 700 Rosedale Ave., St. Louis, 63112

ANHEUSER-BUSCH INC. (I): 721 Pestalozzi St., St. Louis, 63118

AUTOMATIQUE, INC. (M): 3225 Roanoke Rd., Kansas City, 64111

BANK BUILDING & EQUIPMENT CORP. OF AMERICA (I): 1130 Hampton Ave., St. Louis, 63139

BEATY GROCERY CO.: 424 Mitchell Ave., St. Joseph, 64501

BROWN SHOE CO., INC. (I): 8400 Maryland Ave., St. Louis, 63105

BUSINESS MEN'S ASSURANCE CO. OF AMERICA (LI): BMA Tower, Kansas City, 64141

BUTLER MFG. CO. (I): BMA Tower, Kansas City, 64141

CENTURY ACCEPTANCE CORP. (S): 1003 Walnut St., Kansas City, 64106

CENTURY ELECTRIC CO. (I): 1806 Pine St., St. Louis, 63166

A. B. CHANCE CO. (I): 210 N. Allen St., Centralia, 65240

COMMERCE BANCSHARES, INC. (S): 911 Main St., Kansas City, 64199

CONCHEMCO, INC. (I): 18th & Garfield, Kansas City, 64127

CONTINENTAL TELEPHONE CORP. (U): 222 S. Central Ave., St. Louis, 63105

D'ARCY ADVERTISING CO.: 1 Memorial Dr., St. Louis, 63102

DIVERSIFIED INDUSTRIES, INC. (I): 7701 Forsyth Blvd., Clayton, 63105

EDISON BROTHERS STORES, INC. (M): P.O. Box 14020, St. Louis, 63178

EMERSON ELECTRIC CO. (I): 8100 Florissant Ave., St. Louis, 63136

FALSTAFF BREWING CORP. (I): 5050 Oakland Ave., St. Louis, 63166

FAMOUS BARR CO. (M): 6th & Olive Sts., St. Louis, 63101

FARMLAND INDUSTRIES INC. (I): 3315 N. Oak Trafficway, Kansas City, 64116

FIRST NATIONAL BANK OF KANSAS CITY, 14 W. 10th St., Kansas City, 64105
FIRST NATIONAL BANK IN ST. LOUIS (B): 510 Locust St., St. Louis, 63101
GARDNER ADVERTISING CO. (AA): 10 Broadway, St. Louis, 63102
GAS SERVICE CO. (U): 700 Scarritt Bldg., Kansas City, 64142
GENERAL AMERICAN LIFE INSURANCE CO. (LI): 1501 Locust St., St. Louis, 63103
GENERAL BANCSHARES CORP. (S): 720 Olive St., St. Louis, 63166
GENERAL DYNAMICS CORP.: Pierce Laclede Center, St. Louis, 63105
GENERAL STEEL INDUSTRIES, INC. (I): One Memorial Dr., St. Louis, 63102
A. P. GREEN REFRACTORIES CO. (I): Green Blvd., Mexico, 65265
INTERCO INC. (I): Ten Broadway, St. Louis, 63102
KANSAS CITY LIFE INSURANCE CO. (LI): 3520 Broadway, Kansas City, 64111
KANSAS CITY POWER & LIGHT CO. (U): 1330 Baltimore Ave., Kansas City, 64141
KANSAS CITY SOUTHERN RY. (T): 114 W. 11th St., Kansas City, 64105
KATZ DRUG CO. (M): 1130 Walnut St., Kansas City, 64106
KELLWOOD CO. (I): 9909 Clayton Rd., St. Louis, 63124
LACLEDE GAS CO. (U): 720 Olive St., St. Louis, 63101
LACLEDE STEEL CO. (I): Arcade Bldg., St. Louis, 63101
LIBERTY LOAN CORP. (S): 7438 Forsyth, St. Louis, 63105
MACY'S MISSOURI-KANSAS (M): 1030 Main St., Kansas City, 64105
MALLINCKRODT CHEMICAL WORKS (I): 3600 N. Second St., St. Louis, 63160
MARION LABORATORIES, INC. (I): 10236 Bunker Ridge Rd., Kansas City, 64137
MAY DEPARTMENT STORES CO. (M): 6th & Olive Sts., St. Louis, 63101
MC DONNELL DOUGLAS CORP. (I): Box 516, St. Louis, 63166
MERCANTILE TRUST CO., N.A.: 721 Locust St., St. Louis, 63101
MISSISSIPPI RIVER CORP. (I): 9900 Clayton Rd., St. Louis, 63124
MISSOURI PACIFIC RR: Missouri Pacific Bldg., St. Louis, 63103
MONSANTO COMPANY (I): 800 N. Lindbergh Blvd., St. Louis, 63166
NATIONAL BELLAS HESS, INC. (M): 715 Armour Rd., North Kansas City, 64116
PARKVIEW-GEM, INC. (M): 6000 Manchester Trafficway Terr., Kansas City, 64130
PEABODY COAL CO. (I): 310 N. Memorial Dr., St. Louis, 63102
PERMANEER CORP.: 145 Weldon Pkwy., Maryland Heights, 63043
PET INCORPORATED (I): 400 S. Fourth St., St. Louis, 63166
PRICE CANDY CO. (I): 2 W. 39th St., Kansas City, 64111
PULITZER PUBLISHING CO. (P): 1133 Franklin Ave., St. Louis, 63101
RALSTON PURINA CO. (I): 835 S. Eighth St., St. Louis, 63102
RUSSELL STOVER CANDIES INC. (I): 1221 Baltimore Ave., Kansas City, 64105
ST. LOUIS-SAN FRANCISCO RY. (T): 906 Olive St., St. Louis, 63101
SOUTHWESTERN BELL TELEPHONE CO. (U): 1010 Pine St., St. Louis, 63101
THE SEVEN-UP COMPANY (I): 121 So. Meramec, St. Louis, 63105
STIX, BAER & FULLER (M): 603 Washington Ave., St. Louis, 63101
TERMINAL RR ASSOCIATION OF ST. LOUIS (T): 18th & Market Sts., St. Louis, 63103
TRI-STATE MOTOR TRANSIT CO. (T): E. 7th St., Joplin, 65801
UNION ELECTRIC CO.: One Memorial Dr., St. Louis, 63166
UNITED UTILITIES, INC. (U): Box 11315, Plaza Sta., Kansas City, 64112
VENDO CO. (I): 7400 E. 12th St., Kansas City, 64126
WAGNER ELECTRIC CORP. (I): 6400 Plymouth Ave., St. Louis, 63133
WESTERN AUTO SUPPLY CO. (M): 2107 Grand Ave., Kansas City, 64108
WETTERAU FOODS, INC. (I): 8400 Pershall Rd., Hazelwood, 63042
WOHL SHOE CO. (M): 8350 Maryland Ave., St. Louis, 63105
YELLOW FREIGHT SYSTEM, INC. (T): 92nd St. & State Line, Kansas City, 64114

MONTANA

MONTANA POWER CO. (U): 40 E. Broadway, Butte, 59701

NEBRASKA

AMERICAN BEEF PACKERS INC.: 7000 West Center Rd., Omaha, 68106
AMERICAN COMMUNITY STORES CORP. (M): 4206 S. 108th St., Omaha, 68137
BANKERS LIFE INSURANCE CO. OF NEBRASKA (LI): Cotner & O, Lincoln, 68501
CENTRAL TELEPHONE CO. (M): 1201 N. St., Lincoln, 68508
CENTRAL TELEPHONE & UTILITIES CORP. (Y): 1201 N. St., Lincoln, 68508
COMMODORE CORP.: 8712 W. Dodge Rd., Omaha, 68114
FAIRMONT FOODS CO. (I): 3201 Farnam St., Omaha, 68101
IOWA BEEF PROCESSORS, INC. (I): Dakota City, 68731
MUTUAL OF OMAHA INSURANCE CO. (LI): Dodge at 33rd St., Omaha, 68131
NORTHERN NATURAL GAS CO. (U): 2223 Dodge St., Omaha, 68102
NORTHWESTERN BELL TELEPHONE CO. (U): 100 S. 19th St., Omaha, 68102
UNITED BENEFIT LIFE INSURANCE CO. (LI): Dodge at 33rd, Omaha, 68131

NEW HAMPSHIRE

ASSOCIATED GROCERS OF NEW HAMPSHIRE, INC. (M): Gold St., Manchester, 03102
INTERNATIONAL PACKINGS CORP. (I): Pleasant St., Bristol, 03222
J. F. MC ELWAIN CO. (I): 12 Murphy Dr., Nashua, 03060
NASHUA CORP. (I): 44 Franklin St., Nashua, 03060
SANDERS ASSOCIATES INC. (I): Daniel Webster Hwy. S., Nashua 03060

NEW JERSEY

ALLSTATES DESIGN & DEVELOPMENT CO. (S): 25 N. Warren St., Trenton, 08608
AMERICAN CYANAMID CO. (I): Wayne, 07470
AMERICAN HOECHST CORP. (I): Box 2500 Somerville, 08876
ARWOOD CORP. (I): Rockleigh Industrial Park, Rockleigh, 07647
ATHLONE INDUSTRIES, INC.: 200 Webro Rd., Parsippany, 07054
ATLANTIC CITY ELECTRIC CO. (U): 1600 Pacific Ave., Atlantic City, 08404
AUTOMATIC DATA PROCESSING, INC. (S): 405 Route 3, Clifton, 07015
P. BALLANTINE & SONS (I): 57 Freeman St., Newark, 07101
BAMBERGER'S, 131 Market St., Newark, 07102
C. R. BARD INC. (M): 731 Central Ave., Murray Hill, 07974
BECTON, DICKINSON & CO. (I): Stanley St., East Rutherford, 07073
BEECHAM INC. (I): 65 Industrial South, Clifton, 07012
BELL TELEPHONE LABORATORIES, INC. (U): Mountain Ave., Murray Hill, 07971
BERGEN DRUG CO. (M): 138 Johnson Ave., Hackensack, 07601
BERMEC CORP.: 40 Bennett Rd., Englewood, 07631
BISHOP INDUSTRIES INC. (I): 2345 Vauxhall Rd., Union, 07083
BREEZE CORPORATIONS, INC. (I): 700 Liberty Ave., Union, 07083
BRO-DART INDUSTRIES (I): 56 Earl St., Newark, 07114
FRED J. BROTHERTON, INC. (S): 185 Atlantic St., Hackensack, 07601
BUTLER AVIATION INTL. INC.: 600 Sylvan Ave., Englewood Cliffs, 07632
CAMPBELL SOUP CO. (I): 375 Memorial Ave., Camden, 08101
CHICOPEE MFG. CO. (I): 303 George St., New Brunswick, 08901
CIBA PHARMACEUTICAL CO. (I): 556 Morris Ave., Summit, 07901
COLONIAL LIFE INSURANCE CO. OF AMERICA (LI): Box 191, East Orange, 07019
CONGOLEUM INDUSTRIES INC. (I): 195 Belgrove Dr., Kearny, 07032
CPC CORP. (I): International Plaza, Englewood Cliffs, 07632
CURTISS-WRIGHT CO.: One Passaic St., Wood Ridge, 07075
DE LAVAL TURBINE INC. (I): P.O. Box 2072, Princeton, 08540
ENGELHARD MINERALS & CHEMICALS CORP. (I): 113 Astor St., Newark, 07114
ETHICON, INC. (I): U.S. Highway 22, Somerville, 08876
FEDDERS CORP. (I): Woodbridge Ave., Edison, 08817

FEDERAL PACIFIC ELECTRIC CO. (I): 150 Ave. L, Newark, 07101
FEDERAL PAPER BOARD CO., INC. (I): 75 Chestnut Ridge Rd., Montvale, 07645
FIDELITY UNION TRUST CO. (B): 765 Broad St., Newark, 07102
FIRST JERSEY NATL. BANK (B): One Exchange Pl., Jersey City, 07302
FIRST NATIONAL STATE BANK OF N.J. (B): 550 Broad St., Newark, 07102
FOSTER WHEELER CORP. (I): 110 S. Orange Ave., Livingston, 07039
GRAND UNION CO. (M): 100 Broadway, East Paterson, 07407
GULTON INDUSTRIES, INC. (I): Metuchen, 08840
H. A. ASTLETT & CO.: 20 New Dutch Lane, Fairfield, 07006
HARVARD INDUSTRIES, INC. (I): Box 527, Farmingdale, 07727
HOFFMAN-LA ROCHE INC. (I): 340 Kingsland St., Nutley, 07110
THE HOOPER-HOLMES BUREAU, INC. (S): 170 Mt. Airy Rd., Basking Ridge, 07920
J. M. HUBER CORP.: P.O. Box 414, Rumson, 07760
INGERSOLL-RAND CO.: Woodcliff, 07675
INTERNATIONAL CONTROLS CORP.: 200 Fairfield Rd., Fairfield, 07006
JERSEY CENTRAL POWER & LIGHT CO. (U): Madison at Punchbowl, Morristown, 07960
JOHNSON & JOHNSON (I): 501 George St., New Brunswick, 08903
JONATHAN LOGAN INC. (I): 3901 Liberty Ave., North Bergen, 07047
WALTER KIDDE & CO., INC. (I): 9 Brighton Rd., Clifton, 07012
THOMAS J. LIPTON INC. (I): 800 Sylvan Ave., Englewood Cliffs, 07632
MC LEAN INDUSTRIES INC. (T): Corbin & Fleet Sts., Elizabeth, 07207
MENNEN COMPANY (I): East Hanover Ave., Morristown, 07960
MERCK & CO. INC. (I): 126 E. Lincoln Ave., Rahway, 07065
MUTUAL BENEFIT LIFE INSURANCE CO. (LI): 520 Broad St., Newark, 07101
NATIONAL NEWARK & ESSEX BANK (B): 744 Broad St., Newark, 07101
NEW JERSEY BANK N.A. (B): 1184 Main Ave., Clifton, 07015
NEW JERSEY BELL TELEPHONE CO. (U): 540 Broad St., Newark, 07102
NEW JERSEY NATURAL GAS CO. (I): 601 Bangs Ave., Asbury Park, 07712
OLLA INDUSTRIES (I): 4810 Broadway, Union City, 07087
PEOPLES TRUST OF NEW JERSEY (B): 210 Main St., Hackensack, 07602
PRENTICE-HALL, INC.: Englewood Cliffs, N.J. 07632
PRUDENTIAL INSURANCE CO. OF AMERICA (LI): Prudential Plaza, Newark, 07101
PUBLIC SERVICE COORDINATED TRANSPORT (T): 180 Boyden Ave., Maplewood, 07040
PUBLIC SERVICE ELECTRIC & GAS CO. (U): 80 Park Pl., Newark, 07101
PUROLATOR, INC. (I): 970 New Brunswick Ave., Rahway, 07065
RONSON CORP. (I): 1 Ronson Rd., Woodbridge, 07095
SCHERING CORP. (I): 60 Orange St., Bloomfield, 07003
SEA-LAND SERVICE, INC. (S): Box 1050, Elizabeth, 07207
SHULTON, INC. (I): 697 Route 46, Clifton, 07015
STERNCO INDUSTRIES, INC. (I): 722 Cross St., Harrison, 07029
SUBURBAN PROPANE GAS CORP. (I): Mt. Pleasant Ave., Whippany, 07981
ALEXANDER SUMMER MORTGAGE CO. (S): 222 Cedar Lane, Teaneck, 07666
SUPERMARKETS GENERAL CORP. (M): 301 Blair Rd., Woodbridge, 07015
TRIANGLE INDUSTRIES (I): 550 Broad St., Newark, 07102
UNION CAMP CORP.: 1600 Valley Rd., Wayne, 07470
UNISHOPS, INC. (M): 21 Cavan Point Ave., Jersey City, 07305
UNITED STATES REALTY & INVESTMENT CO.: 972 Broad St., Newark, 07102
VIKON TILE CORP. (I): 130 N. Taylor St., Washington, 07882
VOLKSWAGEN OF AMERICA, INC. (S): 818 Sylvan Ave., Englewood, Cliffs, 07632
VORNADO INC. (M): 174 Passaic St., Garfield, 07026
WARNER-LAMBERT COMPANY (I): 201 Tabor Rd., Morris Plains, 07950
WESTERN UNION CORP.: 85 McKee Dr., Mahwah, 07430

WESTON INSTRUMENTS, INC. (I): 614 Frelinghuysen Ave., Newark 07114
WORTHINGTON CORP. (I): 270 Sheffield St., Mountainside, 07092

NEW YORK CITY, NEW YORK

ACF INDUSTRIES INC. (I): 750 Third Ave., 10017
AFIA (LI): 110 William St., 10038
AMF INC. (I): 261 Madison Ave., 10016
ABACUS FUND INC.: 76 Beaver St., 10005
ABERDEEN MFG. CORP. (I): 16 E. 34th St., 10016
ABEX CORP. (I): 530 Fifth Ave., 10036
ABRAHAM & STRAUS (M): 422 Fulton St., Brooklyn, 11201
AEOLIAN CORP. (I): 33 W. 57th St., 10019
AFFILIATED FUND, INC. (S): 63 Wall St., 10005
AIKEN INDUSTRIES INC. (I): 200 Park Ave., 10017
AILEEN,INC. (I): 331 E. 38th St., 10016
AIR REDUCTION CO. (I): 150 E. 42nd St., 10017
ALBERT FRANK-GUENTHER LAW INC. (AA): 61 Broadway, 10006
ALEXANDER & ALEXANDER INC. (LI): 225 Broadway, 10007
ALEXANDER'S, INC. (M): 500 Seventh Ave., 10018
ALLEGHANY CORPORATION (LI)(B)(Leasing): 350 Park Ave.
ALLEGHENY POWER SYSTEM INC. (U): 320 Park Ave., 10022
ALLIED CHEMICAL CORP. (I): 1411 Broadway, 10018
ALLIED MAINTENANCE CORP. (S): 2 Pennsylvania Plaza, 10001
ALLIED STORES MARKETING CORP. (M): 401 Fifth Ave., 10016
AL PAUL LEFTON CO. (AA): 71 Vanderbilt St., 10017
ALTMAN, VOS & REICHBERG (AA): 485 Madison Ave., 10022
AMERACE ESNA CORP. (I): 245 Park Ave., 10017
AMERADA HESS CORP. (I): 51 W. 51st St., 10019
AMERICAN AIRLINES INC. (T): 633 Third Ave., 10017
AMERICAN BOOK STRATFORD PRESS INC.: 75 Varick St., 10013
AMERICAN BRANDS (I): 245 Park Ave., 10017
AMERICAN BROADCASTING CO. (BR): 1330 Ave. of the Americas, 10019
AMERICAN BROADCASTING COMPANIES, INC. (BR): 1330 Ave. of the Americas, 10019
AMERICAN CONSUMER INDUSTRIES, INC. & SUBS. (I): 375 Park Ave., 10022
AMERICAN DISTILLING CO. (I): 245 Park Ave., 10017
AMERICAN ELECTRIC POWER SERVICE CORP. (U): 2 Broadway, 10004
AMERICAN EXPORT INDUSTRIES INC. (T): 26 Broadway, 10004
AMERICAN EXPRESS CO. (T/S): 65 Broadway, 10004
AMERICAN HOME ASSURANCE CO. (LI): 102 Maiden Lane, 10005
AMERICAN HOME PRODUCTS CORP. (I): 685 Third Ave., 10017
AMERICAN INTERNATIONAL INSURANCE CO. (LI): 80 Maiden Lane, 10038
AMERICAN MAIZE — PRODUCTS CO. (I): 250 Park Ave., 10017
AMERICAN METAL CLIMAX INC. (I): 1270 Ave. of the Americas, 10020
AMERICAN NATURAL GAS CO. (U): 30 Rockefeller Plaza, 10020
AMERICAN PETROFINA INC. (I): 50 Rockefeller Plaza, 10020
AMERICAN RE-INSURANCE CO. (LI): 99 John St., 10038
AMERICAN SMELTING & REFINING CO. (I): 120 Broadway, 10005
AMERICAN STANDARD INC. (I): 40 W. 40th St., 10018
AMERICAN TELEPHONE & TELEGRAPH CO. (U): 195 Broadway, 10007
AMERICAN TRANSPORTATION ENTERPRISES, INC. (T): 14 E. 75th St., 10021
AMETEK, INC. (I): 233 Broadway, 10017
AMSTAR CORP.: 1251 Ave. of the Americas, 10020
ANACONDA CO. (I): 25 Broadway, 10004
ANACONDA WIRE & CABLE CO. (I): 605 Third Ave., 10016
ANCORP NATIONAL SERVICES INC. (S): 131 Varick St., 10013
ANGLO-LAUTARO NITRATE CO. LTD. (I): 120 Broadway, 10005
ARLAN'S DEPARTMENT STORES INC. (M): 393 Seventh Ave., 10001
GEORGE S. ARMSTRONG CO., INC.: 2 Park Ave., 10016
ASIATIC PETROLEUM CORP. (I): One Rockefeller Plaza, 10020
ASSOCIATED DRY GOODS CORP. (M): 417 5th Ave., 10016
ASSOCIATED FOOD STORES, INC. (M): 179-45 Brinkerhoff Ave., Jamaica, 11433
ASSOCIATED MERCHANDISING CORP. (M): 1440 Broadway, 10018
ASSOCIATED PRODUCTS, INC. (I): 445 Park Ave., 10022
ASSOCIATED TRANSPORT INC. (T): 380 Madison Ave., 10017
ATALANTA CORP. (M): 17 Varick St., 10013

ATLANTIC RICHFIELD CO.: 717 Fifth Ave., 10022
AUSTIN NICHOLS & CO., INC. (I): 58th & 55th Dr., Maspeth, 11378
AVNET, INC. (I): 767 Fifth Ave., 10022
AVON PRODUCTS INC. (I): 30 Rockefeller Plaza, 10020
BABCOCK & WILCOX CO. (I): 161 E. 42nd St., 10017
BALDWIN PAPER CO. INC. (I): 161 Ave. of the Americas, 10013
BANK OF NEW YORK (B): 48 Wall St., 10015
BANKERS TRUST CO. (B): 16 Wall St., 10005
BANKERS TRUST NEW YORK CORP. (B): 280 Park Ave., 10017
BARBARA LYNN STORES, INC. (M): 330 W. 34th St., 10001
BARTELL MEDIA CORP. (S): 205 E. 42nd St., 10017
TED BATES & CO. INC. (AA): 666 5th Ave., 10019
BATTEN, BARTON, DURSTINE & OSBORN INC. (AA): 383 Madison Ave., 10017
BAUMRITTER CORP. (I): 205 Lexington Ave., 10016
BEAUNIT CORP. (I): 261 Madison Ave., 10016
BECK INDUSTRIES, INC. (I): 28 W. 44th St., 10036
BELCO PETROLEUM CORP. (I): 630 Third Ave., 10017
BELDING HEMINWAY CO., INC. (I): 1430 Broadway, 10018
BERKEY PHOTO INC. (I): 842 Broadway, 10003
BEST COAT & APRON MFG. CO., INC. (I): 408 E. 59th St., 10022
BIGELOW-SANFORD, INC. (I): 140 Madison Ave., 10016
BINNEY & SMITH INC. (I): 380 Madison Ave., 10017
BLACK-CLAWSON CO. (I): 200 Park Ave., 10017
JOHN BLAIR & CO. (S): 717 Fifth Ave., 10022
BLITMAN CONSTRUCTION CORP. (I): 101 Park Ave., 10017
BLOOMINGDALE BROS. (M): 59th & Lexington, 10022
BOHACK CORP. (M): 4828 Metropolitan Ave., Brooklyn, 11237
BOND INDUSTRIES, INC. (M): Fifth & 35th, 10001
BORDEN, INC. (I): 277 Park Ave., 10003
BOTANY INDUSTRIES, INC. (I): 1290 Ave. of the Americas, 10019
BOYLE-MIDWAY DIVISION (I): 685 Third Ave., 10017
BOZELL & JACOBS (AA): 505 Park Ave., 10021
BRANCH INDUSTRIES (T): 114 Fifth Ave., 10011
BRISTOL-MYERS CO. (I): 345 Park Ave., 10022
THE BROOKLYN UNION GAS CO. (U): 195 Montague St., Brooklyn, 11201
BROWN CO. (I): 277 Park Ave., 10017
FRANK C. BROWN & CO. INC. (MC): 30 Rockefeller Plaza, 10020
BUCKEYE PIPE LINE CO. (I): 30 Rockefeller Plaza, 10020
BULOVA WATCH CO. INC. (I): 630 Fifth Ave., 10020
BUNGE CORP. (M): 1 Chase Manhattan Plaza, 10005
WILLIAM J. BURNS INTERNATIONAL DETECTIVE AGENCY, INC. (S): 235 E. 42nd St., 10017
CF & I STEEL CORP.: 300 Park Ave., 10022
C. I. T. FINANCIAL CORP. (S): 650 Madison Ave., 10022
CANADA DRY CORP. (I): 100 Park Ave., 10017
CARISTO CONSTRUCTION CORP. (S): 26 Court St., Brooklyn, 11201
CARL ALLY INC. (AA): 437 Madison Ave., 10022
CARTER WALLACE, INC. (I): 767 Fifth Ave., 10022
CASE & CO., INC. (MC): 30 Rockefeller Plaza, 10020
CASUAL SPORTSWEAR CO. (I): 135 W. 50th St., 10020
CELANESE CORP. (I): 522 5th Ave., 10036
CENTURY FACTORS, INC. (S): 444 Fifth Ave., 10018
CERRO CORP. (I): 300 Park Ave., 10022
CERRO DE PASCO CORP. (I): 300 Park Ave., 10022
CERRO SALES CORP. (I): 300 Park Ave., 10022
CERRO WIRE & CABLE CO. (I): 5500 Maspeth Ave., Maspeth, 11378
CHARTER NEW YORK CORP. (S): One Wall St., 10005
CHASE MANHATTAN BANK (B): 1 Chase Manhattan Plaza, 10015
CHEMICAL BANK (B): 20 Pine St., 10015
CHESEBROUGH-POND'S INC. (I): 485 Lexington Ave., 10017
CHICAGO PNEUMATIC TOOL CO. (I): 6 E. 44th St., 10017
CHILE COPPER CO. (I): 25 Broadway, 10004
CHILE EXPLORATION CO. (I): 25 Broadway, 10004
CHOCK FULL O'NUTS CORP. (I): 425 Lexington Ave., 10017
CHRIS-CRAFT INDUSTRIES, INC.: 600 Madison Ave., 10022
CHROMALLOY AMERICAN CORPORATION (I): 120 Broadway, 10005
CITIES SERVICE CO. (I): 60 Wall St., 10005
CITY INVESTING CO.: 767 Fifth Ave., 10022
CITY STORES CO. (M): 500 5th Ave., 10036
CITY TITLE INSURANCE CO. (LI): 32 Broadway, 10004
CLAIROL INC. (I): 345 Park Ave., 10022

COLT INDUSTRIES INC. (I): 430 Park Ave., 10022
CLYNE MAXON INC. (AA): 245 Park Ave., 10017
COATS & CLARK, INC. (I): 430 Park Ave., 10022
THE COCA-COLA BOTTLING CO. OF N.Y., INC. (I): 425 E. 34th St., 10016
COLGATE-PALMOLIVE CO. (I): 300 Park Ave., 10022
COLLINS & AIKMAN CORP. (I): 210 Madison Ave., 10016
COLONIAL SAND & STONE CO., INC. (I): 1740 Broadway, 10019
COLONIAL SUGARS CO. (I): 500 Fifth Ave., 10036
COLT INDUSTRIES INC. (I): 430 Park Ave., 10022
COLUMBIA BROADCASTING SYSTEM, INC. (BR): 51 W. 52nd St., 10019
COLUMBIA GAS SYSTEM INC. (U): 120 E. 41st St., 10017
COLUMBIA PICTURES CORP. (I): 711 Fifth Ave., 10022
COMBUSTION ENGINEERING INC. (I): 277 Park Ave., 10017
COMMERCIAL ALLIANCE CORP. (S): 770 Lexington Ave., 10021
COMMERCIAL SOLVENTS CORP. (I): 245 Park Ave., 10017
COMPTON ADVERTISING INC. (AA): 625 Madison Ave., 10022
CONDE NAST PUBLICATIONS INC. (I): 420 Lexington Ave., 10017
CONSOLIDATED CIGAR CORP. (I): One Gulf & Western Plaza, 10023
CONSOLIDATED EDISON CO. OF NEW YORK (U): 4 Irving Pl., 10003
CONSOLIDATED NATURAL GAS CO. (U): 30 Rockefeller Plaza, 10020
CONSULTANTS & DESIGNERS, INC. (MC): 55 Fifth Ave., 10003
CONTINENTAL CAN CO. INC. (I): 633 Third Ave., 10017
CONTINENTAL CORP.: 80 Maiden Lane, 10038
THE CONTINENTAL INSURANCE CO. (LI): 80 Maiden Lane, 10038
CONTINENTAL OIL CO. (I): 30 Rockefeller Plaza, 10020
CONTINENTAL ORE CORP. (I): 245 Park Ave., 10017
COORDINATED COMMUNICATIONS, INC. (AA): 1901 Ave. of the Americas, 10019
COWLES COMMUNICATIONS INC. (P): 488 Madison Ave., 10022
CRANE CO. (I): 300 Park Ave., 10022
CRESAP, MC CORMICK & PAGET (MC): 245 Park Ave., 10017
CROMPTON & KNOWLES CORP.: 345 Park Ave., 10022
CROWELL-COLLIER & MACMILLAN, INC. (I): 866 Third Ave., 10022
CRUM & FORSTER (LI): 110 William St., 10038
CUNNINGHAM & WALSH INC. (AA): 260 Madison Ave., 10016
DAIRYLEA COOPERATIVE INC.: (I): 1250 Broadway, 10001
DAITCH CRYSTAL DAIRIES, INC. (M): 400 Walnut Ave., Bronx, 10454
DANCER-FITZGERALD SAMPLE INC. (AA): 347 Madison Ave., 10017
DEERING MILLIKEN, INC.: 1045 6th Ave., 10018
DELLA FEMINA, TRAVISANO & PARTNERS (AA): 625 Madison Ave., 10022
DIAMOND INTERNATIONAL CORP. (I): 733 Third Ave., 10017
DINERS' CLUB, INC. (S): 10 Columbus Circle, 10019
THE REUBEN H. DONNELLEY CORP.: 825 Third Ave., 10022
DOREMUS & CO. (AA): 120 Broadway, 10005
DOUBLEDAY & COMPANY, INC.: 277 Park Ave., 10017
DOVER CORPORATION (I): 277 Park Ave., 10017
DOW JONES & CO. (S): 30 Broad St., 10004
DOYLE DANE BERNBACH INC. (AA): 20 W. 43rd St., 10036
DRAKE SHEAHAN/STEWART DOUGALL INC. (MC): 330 Madison Ave., 10017
DREW CHEMICAL CORP. (I): 522 Fifth Ave., 10036
DUN & BRADSTREET, INC. (S): 99 Church St., 10007
DYNAMICS CORPORATION OF AMERICA (I): 501 Fifth Ave., 10017
THE DYSON-KISSNER CORP. (S): 230 Park Ave., 10017
EASTERN AIRLINES, INC. (T): 10 Rockefeller Plaza, 10020
ELECTRONIC COMPUTER PROGRAMMING INSTITUTE, INC. (S): 350 5th Ave., 10001
ELTRA CORPORATION (I): 2 Pennsylvania Plaza, 10001
THE EMERSON CONSULTANTS INC. (MC): 30 Rockefeller Plaza, 10020
EQUITABLE LIFE ASSURANCE SOCIETY OF THE UNITED STATES (LI): 1285 Avenue of the Americas, 10019
WILLIAM ESTY CO. (AA): 100 East 42nd St., 10017
ETHYL CORP. (I): 100 Park Ave., 10017
FIDELITY & CASUALTY INSURANCE CO. OF N.Y. (LI): 80 Maiden Lane, 10038

FIRST BOSTON CORP. (S): 20 Exchange Place, 10005
FIRST NATIONAL CITY BANK (B): 399 Park Ave., 10022
FISCHBACH & MOORE, INC. (S): 545 Madison Ave., 10022
FOOTE, CONE & BELDING COMMUNICATIONS, INC.
(AA): 200 Park Ave., 10017
FORD, BACON & DAVIS, INC. (MC): 2 Broadway, 10004
CLINTON E. FRANK, INC. (AA): 666 Third Ave., 10017
FREEPORT MINERALS CO. (I): 161 E. 42nd St., 10017
L. W. FROHLICH & CO./INTERCON INT'L (AA): 34 E. 51st St.,
10022
FULLER & SMITH & ROSS INC. (AA): 666 5th Ave., 10019
FUND OF AMERICA, INC. (S): 90 Park Ave., 10016
GAF CORP. (I): 140 W. 51st St., 10020
GARDNER ADVERTISING CO. (AA): 90 Park Ave., 10016
GENERAL CABLE CORP. (I): 730 Third Ave., 10017
GENERAL CIGAR CO., INC. (I): 605 Third Ave., 10016
GENERAL ELECTRIC CO. (I): 570 Lexington Ave., 10022
GENERAL ELECTRIC CREDIT CORP. (S): 570 Lexington Ave.,
10022
GENERAL HOST CORP. (I): 245 Park Ave., 10017
GENERAL INSTRUMENT CORP.: 1775 Broadway, 10019
GENERAL MOTORS ACCEPTANCE CORP. (S): 767 Fifth Ave.,
10022
GENERAL PUBLIC UTILITIES CORP. (U): 80 Pine St., 10005
GENERAL REINSURANCE CORP. (LI): 400 Park Ave., 10022
GENERAL SIGNAL CORP. (I): 280 Park Ave., 10017
GENERAL TELEPHONE & ELECTRONICS CORP. (I): 730 Third
Ave., 10017
B. GERTZ, INC. (M): 162-10 Jamaica Ave., Jamaica, 11432
GIMBEL BROS. INC. (M): 1275 Broadway, 10001
GLEN ALDEN CORP. (I): 888 Seventh Ave., 10019
W. R. GRACE & CO. (I): 7 Hanover Sq., 10005
W. T. GRANT CO. (M): 1441 Broadway, 10018
GRAYBAR ELECTRIC CO., INC. (M): 420 Lexington Ave., 10017
GREAT AMERICAN INSURANCE CO. (LI): 99 John St., 10038
GREAT ATLANTIC & PACIFIC TEA CO. INC. (M): 420 Lexington
Ave., 10017
GREAT LAKES CARBON CORP. (I): 299 Park Ave., 10017
GREENWOOD MILLS INC. (I): 111 W. 40th St., 10018
GREY ADVERTISING INC. (AA): 777 Third Ave., 10017
GROLIER INCORPORATED (I): 575 Lexington Ave., 10022
GUARDIAN LIFE INSURANCE CO. OF AMERICA (LI): 201 Park
Ave., 10003
GULF & WESTERN INDUSTRIES, INC. (I): 1 Gulf & Western
Plaza, 10023
HANDY & HARMAN (I): 850 Third Ave., 10022
HARTFIELD-ZODYS, INC. (M): 441 Ninth Ave., 10001
THE HEARST CORP.: 57th & 8th Ave., 10019
HELME PRODUCTS, INC. (I): 9 Rockefeller Plaza, 10020
HERTZ CORP. (S): 660 Madison Ave., 10021
HERTZ INTERNATIONAL, LTD. (S): 660 Madison Ave., 10021
WILLIAM E. HILL & CO. INC. (MC): 640 Fifth Ave., 10019
HILTON INTERNATIONAL CO. (S): The Waldorf-Astoria, 10022
HOME INSURANCE CO. (LI): 59 Maiden Lane, 10008
HOME LIFE INSURANCE CO. (LI): 253 Broadway, 10007
HORN & HARDART CO. (M): 600 W. 50th St., 10019
HOWARD STORES CORP. (I): 40 Flatbush Ave. Ext., Brooklyn,
11201
HUBBARD, WESTERVELT & MOTTELAY, INC. (S): 60 E. 42nd
St., 10017
HUDSON PULP & PAPER CORP. (I): 477 Madison Ave., 10022
IBM WORLD TRADE CORP. (I): 821 United Nations Plaza, 10017
ITT CONSUMER SERVICES CORP. (S): 320 Park Ave., 10022
ITT RAYONIER, INC. (S): 161 E. 42nd St., 10017
IMPERIAL READING CORP. (I): 1290 Ave. of the Americas, 10019
INDIAN HEAD INC. (I): 111 W. 40th St., 10018
INGERSOLL-RAND CO. (I): 11 Broadway, 10004
INTERNATIONAL BASIC ECONOMY CORP. (I): 1271 Ave. of the
Americas, 10020
INTERNATIONAL FLAVORS & FRAGRANCES INC. (I): 521 W.
57th St., 10019
INTERNATIONAL PAPER CO. (I): 220 E. 42nd St., 10017
INTERNATIONAL STANDARD ELECTRIC CORP. (S): 320 Park
Ave., 10022
INTERNATIONAL TELEPHONE AND TELEGRAPH CORP. (I): 320
Park Ave., 10022

THE INTERPUBLIC GROUP OF COMPANIES, INC. (S): 1271 Ave.
of the Americas, 10020
INTERSTATE SECURITY SERVICE INC. (S): 316 W. 53rd St.,
10019
IRVING TRUST CO. (B): 1 Wall St., 10015
WILLIAM ISELIN & CO., INC. (S): 357 Park Ave., S., 10010
KLM ROYAL DUTCH AIRLINES (T): 609 Fifth Ave., 10017
KANE-MILLER CORP.: 355 Lexington Ave., 10017
KAYSER-ROTH CORP. (I): 640 5th Ave., 10019
KEARNY-NATIONAL INC. (I): 250 Park Ave., 10017
KENNECOTT COPPER CORP. (I): 161 E. 42nd St., 10017
KENYON & ECKHARDT ADVERTISING INC. (AA): 200 Park Ave.,
10017
KINNEY SERVICES, INC. (S): 10 Rockefeller Plaza, 10020
KNOTT HOTELS CORP. (S): 575 Madison Ave., 10022
KRAFTCO (I): 260 Madison Ave., 10016
LANE BRYANT, INC. (M): 1501 Broadway, 10036
LANVIN-CHARLES OF THE RITZ, INC. (I): 730 Fifth Ave., 10019
LEHIGH VALLEY INDUSTRIES, INC.: 200 East 42nd St., 10017
LENNEN & NEWELL INC. (AA): 380 Madison Ave., 10017
LERNER STORES CORP. (M): 460 W. 33rd St., 10001
LESLIE FAY INC. (I): 1400 Broadway, 10018
LEVER BROTHERS COMPANY (I): 390 Park Ave., 10022
LEVITON MFG. CO. (I): 236 Greenpoint Ave., Brooklyn, 11222
LIGGETT & MYERS INCORPORATED (I): 630 Fifth Ave., 10020
LITTON BUSINESS SYSTEMS, INC.: 850 Third Ave., 10022
LOEW'S CORPORATION (S): 666 Fifth Ave., 10019
JONATHAN LOGAN: 1411 Broadway, 10018
LOIS HOLLAND CALLAWAY (AA): 745 Fifth Ave., 10022
LONG ISLAND RR. (T): Jamaica Station, Jamaica, 11435
LORD ELECTRIC CO., INC. (S): 45 Rockefeller Plaza, 10020
LORD & TAYLOR (M): 424 Fifth Ave., 10018
LORILLARD CORP. (I): 200 E. 42nd St., 10017
M. LOWENSTEIN & SONS INC. (I): 1430 Broadway, 10018
M & T CHEMICALS, INC. (I): 100 Park Ave., 10017
R. H. MACY & CO. INC. (M): 151 W. 34th St., 10001
MAGMA COPPER CO. (I): 300 Park Ave., 10022
MAGNAVOX CO.: 345 Park Ave., 10022
MANGEL STORES CORP. (M): 115 W. 18th St., 10011
MANHATTAN INDUSTRIES; 1271 Ave. of the Americas, 10020
MANHATTAN LIFE INSURANCE CO. (LI): 111 W. 57th St., 10019
MANUFACTURERS HANOVER TRUST CO. (B): 350 Park Ave.,
10022
MARINE MIDLAND BANK — N.Y. (B): 140 Broadway, 10015
MARLENE INDUSTRIES CORP. (I): 1370 Broadway, 10018
MARSCHALK CO. (AA): 1345 Ave. of the Americas, 10019
MARTIN-MARIETTA CORP. (I): 277 Park Ave., 10017
J. W. MAYS, INC. (M): 510 Fulton St., Brooklyn, 11201
MC CALL PUBLISHING CO. (I): 230 Park Ave., 10017
MC CANN-ERICKSON INC. (AA): 485 Lexington Ave., 10017
MC CRORY CORP. (M): 360 Park Ave., 10010
MC GRAW-HILL INC. (I): 330 W. 42nd St., 10036
MC GREGOR-DONIGER INC. (I): 666 Fifth Ave., 10019
MEINHARD-COMMERCIAL CORP. (S): 9 E. 59th St., 10022
MELVILLE SHOE CORPORATION (I): 25 W. 43rd St., 10036
METROMEDIA INC. (BR): 277 Park Ave., 10017
METROPOLITAN LIFE INSURANCE CO. (LI): 1 Madison Ave.,
10010
MIDDLE SOUTH UTILITIES INC. (U): 280 Park Ave., 10017
MILLER-WOHL CO., INC.: 1372 Broadway, 10023
MITSUBISHI INTERNATIONAL CORP. (M): 277 Park Ave., 10017
MOBIL OIL CORP. (I): 150 E. 42nd St., 10017
MOORE AND MC CORMACK CO. INC. (T): 2 Broadway, 10004
MOORE-MC CORMACK LINES, INC. (T): 2 Broadway, 10004
MORGAN GUARANTY TRUST CO. OF NEW YORK (B): 23 Wall
St., 10015
JOHN F. MURRAY ADVERTISING (AA): 685 Third Ave., 10017
MUTUAL OF NEW YORK (LI): 1740 Broadway, 10019
NAREMCO SERVICES INC. (MC): 555 Fifth Ave., 10017
NATIONAL DISTILLERS & CHEMICAL CORP. (I): 99 Park Ave.,
10016
NATIONAL FUEL GAS CO. (U): 30 Rockefeller Plaza, 10020
NATIONAL STARCH & CHEMICAL CORP. (I): 750 Third Ave.,
10017
THE NATIONAL SUGAR REFINING CO. (I): 2 Pennsylvania Plaza,
10001

NEEDHAM, HARPER & STEERS INC. (AA): 909 Third Ave., 10022
NEPTUNE METER CO. (I): 630 Fifth Ave., 10020
NEW YORK LIFE INSURANCE CO. (LI): 51 Madison Ave., 10010
NEW YORK STOCK EXCHANGE (S): 11 Wall St., 10005
NEW YORK TELEPHONE CO. (U): 140 West St., 10007
THE NEW YORK TIMES COMPANY (P): 229 W. 43rd St., 10036
J. J. NEWBERRY CO. (M): 245 Fifth Ave., 10016
NEWMONT MINING CORP. (I): 300 Park Ave., 10022
NICHIMEN CO., INC. (M): 60 Broad St., 10004
NORMAN, CRAIG & KUMMEL (AA): 919 Third Ave., 10022
NORTH AMERICAN PHILIPS COMPANY, INC. (M): 100 E. 42nd
    St., 10017
NORTON SIMON, INC.: 230 Park Ave., 10017
NOVO CORP. (I): 733 Third Ave., 10017
N. W. AYER & SON (AA): 1345 Ave. of the Americas, 10019
OGDEN CORP. (I): 161 E. 42nd St., 10017
OGILVY & MATHER, INC. (AA): Two E. 48th St., 10017
OHRBACHS, INC. (M): 5 W. 34th St., 10001
OLIVETTI CORPORATION OF AMERICA (I): 500 Park Ave., 10022
ORIGINALA, INC. (I): 512 Seventh Ave., 10018
OTIS ELEVATOR CO. (I): 260 11th Ave., 10001
PAN AMERICAN WORLD AIRWAYS, INC. (T): Pan Am Bldg.,
    10017
PANTASOTE CO. (I): 277 Park Ave., 10017
PARAMOUNT PICTURES CORP. (I): 1501 Broadway, 10036
PARENTS' MAGAZINE ENTERPRISES, INC. (P): 52 Vanderbilt
    Ave., 10017
PARKSON ADVERTISING AGENCY (AA): 767 Fifth Ave., 10022
PARSONS & WHITTEMORE, INC. (M): 200 Park Ave., 10017
PENN-DIXIE CEMENT CORP. (I): 1345 Ave. of Americas, 10019
J. C. PENNEY CO. INC. (M): 1301 Ave. of the Americas, 10019
PEPSICO INC. (I): 500 Park Ave., 10022
PERKINS-GOODWIN CO., INC. (M): 1 Rockefeller Plaza, 10020
PFIZER INC. (I): 235 E. 42nd St., 10017
PHELPS DODGE CORP. (I): 300 Park Ave., 10022
PHILADELPHIA & READING CORP. (I): 1290 Ave. of the Americas,
    10019
PHILIP MORRIS INC. (I): 100 Park Ave., 10017
PHILLIP BROTHERS DIVISION (I): 299 Park Ave., 10017
PHILLIPS VAN HEUSEN CORP. (I): 417 Fifth Ave., 10016
PICKWICK INTERNATIONAL, INC. (I): Pickwick Bldg., L.I. City,
    11101
PINKERTON'S INC. (S): 100 Church St., 10007
PIONEER SYSTEMS, INC. (I): 375 Park Ave., 10022
PITTSTON CO. (I): 250 Park Ave., 10017
PRUDENTIAL BUILDING MAINTENANCE CORP. (S): 1430
    Broadway, 10018
PUBLIX SHIRT CORP. (I): Empire State Bldg., 10016
RCA COMMUNICATIONS, INC.: 60 Broad St., 10004
RCA INTERNATIONAL STAFF (I/BR): 30 Rockefeller Plaza, 10020
RADIO CORP. OF AMERICA (I/BR): 30 Rockefeller Plaza, 10020
RAPID-AMERICAN CORP. (M): 711 Fifth Ave., 10022
RAYMOND INTERNATIONAL INC. (I): 2 Pennsylvania Plaza, 10001
REACH, MC CLINTON & CO. (AA): 505 Park Ave., 10022
REEVES BROS., INC. (I): 1271 Ave. of the Americas, 10020
REMINGTON RAND (I): 1290 Ave. of the Americas, 10019
RESTAURANT ASSOCIATES, INC. (S): 1540 Broadway, 10036
RESTAURANT ASSOCIATES INDUSTRIES INC. (S): 1540
    Broadway, 10036
REVERE COPPER & BRASS, INC. (I): 605 3rd Ave., 10016
REVLON INC. (I): 767 Fifth Ave., 10022
RHEEM MFG. CO. (I): 400 Park Ave., 10022
RHEINGOLD CORP. (I): 41 E. 42nd St., 10017
RICHARDSON-MERRELL INC. (I): 122 E. 42nd St., 10017
RIEGEL PAPER CORP. (I): 260 Madison Ave., 10016
RIEGEL TEXTILE CORP. (I): 260 Madison Ave., 10016
ROGERS, SLADE & HILL INC. (MC): 30 East 42nd St., 10017
SYDNEY ROSS CO.: 90 Park Ave., 10016
RUSS TOGS, INC. (I): 1372 Broadway, 10018
SCM CORP. (I): 299 Park Ave., 10017
SSC & B (AA): 575 Lexington Ave., 10022
ST. REGIS PAPER CO. (I): 150 E. 42nd St., 10017
SAKS & CO. (M): 611 Fifth Ave., 10022
SALANT CORP. (I): 330 Fifth Ave., 10001
SANDERSON & PORTER INC. (MC): 25 Broadway, 10004
SAXON INDUSTRIES, INC. (I): 450 Seventh Ave., 10001
F & M SCHAEFER BREWING CO. (I): 430 Kent Ave., Brooklyn, 11211

SCHENLEY INDUSTRIES, INC. (I): 888 7th Ave., 10019
SCHLUMBERGER LTD. (S): 277 Park Ave., 10017
SCRIPPS HOWARD NEWSPAPERS: 200 Park Ave., 10017
JOSEPH E. SEAGRAM & SONS INC. (I): 375 Park Ave., 10022
SEAGRAVE CORP. (I): 350 Fifth Ave., 10001
SEARS INDUSTRIES INC. (S): 300 E. 42nd St., 10017
SEATRAIN LINES, INC.: 1 Chase Manhattan Plaza
SELIGMAN & LATZ, INC. (S): 666 Fifth Ave., 10019
SERVOMATION CORP. (I): 777 Third Ave., 10017
FRANK G. SHATTUCK CO. (I/S): 50 W. 23rd St., 10010
SHELL OIL CO. (I): 50 W. 50th St., 10020
HENRY I. SIEGEL CO. (I): 16 E. 34th St., 10016
SIMMONS CO. (I): 280 Park Ave., 10022
SIMON & SCHUSTER, INC. (P): 630 Fifth Ave., 10020
SIMPLICITY PATTERN CO., INC. (I): 200 Madison Ave., 10016
SINCLAIR VENEZUELAN OIL COMPANY (I): 277 Park Ave., 10017
SINGER CO. (I): 30 Rockefeller Plaza, 10020
SKY CHEFS, INC. (S): 605 Third Ave., 10016
SPARTANS INDUSTRIES INC. (M): 450 W. 33rd St., 10001
SPERRY & HUTCHINSON CO. (S): 330 Madison Ave., 10017
SPERRY RAND CORP. (I): 1290 Ave. of the Americas, 10019
SQUIBB CORP. (I): 460 Park Ave., 10022
STANDARD BRANDS INC. (I): 625 Madison Ave., 10022
STANDARD OIL CO. (NEW JERSEY) (I): 30 Rockefeller Plaza,
    10020
STANDARD PRUDENTIAL CORP. (I): 277 Park Ave., N.Y. 10017
STANDARD RESEARCH CONSULTANTS INC. (MC): 345 Hudson
    St., 10014
STAUFFER CHEMICAL CO. (I): 299 Park Ave., 10017
STERLING DRUG INC. (I): 90 Park Ave., 10016
J. P. STEVENS & CO., INC. (I): 1185 Avenue of the Americas,
    10036
STUDEBAKER WORTHINGTON INC. (I): 530 Fifth Ave., 10036
SU CREST CORP. (I): 120 Wall St., 10005
SUDLER & HENNESSEY (AA): 130 E. 59th St., 10022
SUN CHEMICAL CORP. (I): 750 Third Ave., 10017
SUNSHINE BISCUITS, INC. (I): 245 Park Ave., 10017
SWINGLINE INC. (I): 3200 Skillman Ave., L.I. City, 11101
TAMPAX, INC. (I): 161 E. 42nd St., 10017
TEACHERS INSURANCE & ANNUITY ASSN. OF AMERICA (LI):
    730 Third Ave., 10017
TENNECO CHEMICALS, INC. (I): 280 Park Ave., 10017
TEXACO INC. (I): 135 E. 42nd St., 10017
TEXAS GULF SULPHUR CO. (I): 200 Park Ave., 10017
J. WALTER THOMPSON CO. (AA): 420 Lexington Ave., 10017
TIME, INC. (P): Time & Life Bldg., 10020
TODD SHIPYARDS CORP. (I): 1 State St. Plaza, 10004
RUSS TOGS, INC. (I): 1411 Broadway, 10018
TRANS WORLD AIRLINES INC. (T): 605 Third Ave., 10016
TWENTIETH CENTURY-FOX FILM CORP.: 444 W. 56th St., 10019
"21" BRANDS, INC. (I): 23 W. 52nd St., 10019
UMC INDUSTRIES (I): 72 Wall St., 10005
UNION CARBIDE CORP. (I): 270 Park Ave., 10017
UNION PACIFIC RR. (T): 345 Park Ave., 10022
UNIROYAL INC. (I): 1230 Ave. of the Americas, 10020
UNITED ARTISTS CORP. (I): 729 Seventh Ave., 10019
UNITED ARTISTS THEATRE CIRCUIT, INC. (S): 1700 Broadway,
    10019
UNITED BRANDS (I): 245 Park Ave., 10017
UNITED INDUSTRIAL CORP. (I): 660 Madison Ave., 10021
UNITED INDUSTRIAL SYNDICATE, INC. (I): 45 Rockefeller Plaza,
    10020
UNITED MERCHANTS & MANUFACTURERS INC. (I): 1407
    Broadway, 10018
U.S. FREIGHT CO. (T): 711 Third Ave., 10017
U.S. INDUSTRIAL CHEMICALS CO. (I): 99 Park Ave., 10016
U.S. INDUSTRIES INC. (I): 250 Park Ave., 10017
U.S. LIFE CORP. (LI): 125 Maiden Lane, 10038
UNITED STATES LINES INC. (T): One Broadway, 10004
U.S. PLYWOOD-CHAMPION PAPERS INC. (I): 777 Third Ave.,
    10017
UNITED STATES SMELTING REFINING & MINING CO. (I):
    235 E. 42nd St., 10017
UNITED STATES STEEL CORP. (I): 71 Broadway, 10006
U.S. TRUST CO. OF NEW YORK (B): 45 Wall St., 10005
UNIVERSAL AMERICAN CORP. (I): 200 Park Ave., 10017
UNIVERSAL CARLOADING DISTRIBUTING CO., INC. (T): 345
    Hudson St., 10014

UNIVERSAL PICTURES (I): 445 Park Ave., 10022
VOLT INFORMATION SCIENCES, INC. (S): 640 W. 40th St., 10018
VOLUME MERCHANDISE, INC. (I): 75 Ninth Ave., 10011
VAN RAALTE CO., INC. (I): 417 5th Ave., 10016
WALCO NATIONAL CORP. (I): 743 Fifth Ave., 10022
WALLACE-MURRAY CORP. (I): 299 Park Ave., 10017
WALSH CONSTRUCTION CO. (I): 711 Third Ave., 10017
WALTHAM INDUSTIRES CORP. (I): 345 Park Ave., 10022
WARD FOODS INC. (I): 2 Pennsylvania Plaza, 10001
WARREN, MULLER, DOLOBOWSKY (AA): 711 Third Ave., 10017
WARWICK & LEGLER INC. (AA): 375 Park Ave., 10022
WEIGHT WATCHERS INC. (S): 99-11 Queens Blvd., Forest Hills, 11375
WELBILT CORP (I): 57-18 Flushing Ave., Maspeth, 11378
WELLS, RICH, GREENE, INC. (AA): 767 Fifth Ave., 10022
WESTAVCO CORP. (I): 299 Park Ave., 10017
WESTERN ELECTRIC CO. INC. (I): 195 Broadway, 10007
WESTERN UNION TELEGRAPH CO. (U): 60 Hudson St., 10013
WHEELABRATOR-FRYE INC. (I): 299 Park Ave., Suite 500, 10017
WHITE PINE COPPER CO. (I): 630 Fifth Ave., 10020
JULIUS WILE SONS & CO., INC. (I): 320 Park Ave., 10022
WILLCOX & GIBBS INC. (I): 1040 Ave. of the Americas, 10018
WILLIAM DOUGLAS MC ADAMS INC. (AA): 110 E. 59th St., 10022
WILLIAMHOUSE-REGENCY INC. (I): 28 West 23rd St., 10010
WINTHROP LABORATORIES (I): 90 Park Ave., 10016
WITCO CHEMICAL CO. (I): 277 Park Ave., 10017
F. W. WOOLWORTH CO. (M): Woolworth Bldg., 10007
WUNDERMAN, RICOTTA & KLINE (AA): 575 Madison Ave., 10022
YOUNG & RUBICAM INC. (AA): 285 Madison Ave., 10017

NEW YORK (OTHER THAN NEW YORK CITY)

A.I.C. PHOTO INC. (S): 168 Glen Cove Rd., Carle Place, 11514
APL CORP. (M): 1 Linden Pl., Great Neck, 11021
ADAM MELDRUM & ANDERSON CO. (M): 389 Main St., Buffalo, 14203
AGWAY, INC. (I): Box 1333, Syracuse, 13201
ALBANY FELT CO. (I): 1373 Broadway, Albany, 12201
ALBANY INTERNATIONAL CORP. (I): 1373 Broadway, Albany, 12201
ALLEN ELECTRIC & EQUIPMENT CO.: 534 Broadhollow Rd., 11746
AMBAC INDUSTRIES INC. (I): 900 Old Country Rd., Garden City, 11530
AMERICAN MANUFACTURING CO. (I): Noble & West, Brooklyn, 11222
AMERICAN PRECISION IND. (I): 2777 Walden Ave., Buffalo, 14225
ART METAL (I): Jamestown, 14701
AVIS RENT A CAR SYSTEM, INC.: 900 Old Country Rd., Garden City, 11530
BAUSCH & LOMB INC. (I): 635 St. Paul St., Rochester, 14602
BIG V SUPERMARKETS, INC. (M): 176 N. Main St., Florida, 10921
BIRDS EYE DIVISION (I): 250 North St., White Plains, 10625
BUFFALO FORGE CO. (I): 490 Broadway, Buffalo, 14204
BURNS INTERNATIONAL SECURITY SERVICES, INC.: 320 Old Briarcliff Rd., Briarcliff Manor, 10510
CARBORUNDUM CO. (I): Buffalo Ave., Niagara Falls, 14302
CARRIER CORP. (I): Carrier Parkway, Syracuse, 13201
CENTRAL HUDSON GAS & ELECTRIC CORP. (U): 284 S. Road Ave., Poughkeepsie, 12602
CENTRAL MARKET OPERATING CO. (U): 501 Duanesburg Rd., Schnectady, 12306
CITY INVESTING CO. (S): Box 777, Tuxedo, 10987
CORNING GLASS WORKS (I): Corning, 14830
COUNTRY TRUST CO. (B): 235 Main St., White Plains, 10601
DELCO PRODUCTS (I): 1555 Lyell Ave., Rochester, 14606
DUNLOP TIRE & RUBBER CORP. (I): River Rd. & Sheridan Dr., Buffalo, 14240
EASTMAN KODAK CO. (I): 343 State St., Rochester, 14650
E. W. EDWARDS & SON (M): 200 S. Salina St., Syracuse, 13202
ENDICOTT JOHNSON CORP. (I): 1100 E. Main St., Endicott, 13760
FERROXCUBE CORP. OF AMERICA (I): Mt. Marion Rd., Saugerties, 12477
S. M. FLICKINGER CO., INC. (M): 45 Azalea Dr., Buffalo, 14240
FLINTKOTE CO. (I): 400 Westchester Ave., White Plains, 10604
FRANKLIN NEW YORK CORP. (B): 199 Second St., Mineola, 11501
GANNETT CO., INC. (S): 55 Exchange St., Rochester, 14614

GARLOCK INC. (I): Midtown Tower, Rochester, 14604
GEIGY CHEMICAL CORP. (I): Ardsley, 10502
GENERAL FOODS CORP. (I): 250 North St., White Plains, 10625
GENERAL FOODS INTERNATIONAL (I): 250 North St., White Plains, 10625
GENESEE BREWING CO., INC. (I): 445 St. Paul St., Rochester, 14605
GENUNG'S INCORPORATED (M): 535 Old Tarrytown Rd., White Plains, 10603
GLEASON WORKS (I): 1000 University Ave., Rochester, 14607
GRUMMAN AIRCRAFT ENGINEERING CORP. (I): South Oyster Bay Rd., Bethpage, 11714
HAMILTON WATCH CO.: 4 Corporate Park, Harrison, 10528
HARRISON RADIATOR DIVISION (I): 200 Upper Mountain Rd., Lockport, 14094
HOMELITE (I): 70 Riverdale Ave., Port Chester, 10573
HOUDAILLE INDUSTRIES INC. (I): One M & T Plaza, Buffalo, 14203
ITT AETNA CORP.: 1900 Hempstead Tpke., East Meadow, 11554
IDEAL TOY CORP (I): 184-10 Jamaica Ave., Hollis, 11423
INTERNATIONAL BUSINESS MACHINES CORP (I): Old Orchard Rd., Armonk, 10504
IROQUOIS GAS CORP. (U): 10 Lafayette Sq., Buffalo, 14203
JELL—O DIVISION (I): GENERAL FOODS CORP.: 250 North St., White Plains, 10625
KOLLSMAN INSTRUMENT CORP. (I): 575 Underhill Blvd., Syosset, 11791
LAFAYETTE RADIO ELECTRONICS CORP.: 111 Jericho Tpke.: Syosset, 11791
LEASCO CORP. (S): 280 Park Ave., New York, 10017
LIBERTY NATIONAL BANK & TRUST (B): Main, Court & Pearl Sts., Buffalo, 14240
LINCOLN FIRST BANKS INC. (B): P.O. Box 1939, Rochester, 14603
LOBLAW, INC. (M): 678 Bailey Ave., Buffalo, 14240
LONG ISLAND LIGHTING CO. (U): 250 Old Country Rd., Mineola, 11501
MANUFACTURERS AND TRADERS TRUST CO. (B): One M & T Plaza, Buffalo, 14240
MARINE MIDLAND BANKS, INC. (B): 241 Main St., Buffalo, 14203
MARINE MIDLAND BANK — WESTERN (B): 237 Main St., Buffalo, 14205
MARLIN-ROCKWELL (I): 402 Chandeler St., Jamestown, 14701
MC CORMICK & CO. (MC): Park Bldg., Yonkers, 10701
MOHASCO INDUSTRIES INC. (I): 57 Lyon St., Amsterdam, 12010
PAUL B. MULLIGAN & CO. INC. (MC): 2 Overhill Rd., Scarsdale, 10583
NATIONAL BANK OF WESTCHESTER (B): 31 Mamaroneck Ave., White Plains, 10601
NATIONAL COMMERCIAL BANK & TRUST (B): 60 State St., Albany, 12207
NATIONAL BANK OF NORTH AMERICA (B): 60 Hempstead Ave., West Hempstead, 11552
NATIONAL GYPSUM CO. (I): 325 Delaware Ave., Buffalo, 14202
NEISNER BROTHERS, INC. (M): 49 East Ave., Rochester, 14604
THE NESTLE COMPANY, INC. (I): 100 Bloomingdale Rd., White Plains, 10605
NEW YORK STATE ELECTRIC & GAS CORP. (U): Box 287, Ithaca, 14850
NIAGARA MOHAWK POWER CORP. (U): 300 Erie Blvd., W., Syracuse, 13202
ONEIDA LTD. (I): Kenwood Station, Oneida, 13421
PEPSICO, INC. (I): Purchase, 10577
POLORON PRODUCTS, INC. (I): 165 Huguenot St., New Rochelle, 10801
R F COMMUNICATIONS INC. (I): 1680 University Ave., Rochester, 14610
READER'S DIGEST ASSN., INC.: Pleasantville, 10570
RED STAR EXPRESS LINES OF AUBURN, INC. (T): 24 Wright Ave., Auburn, 13021
REICHHOLD CHEMICALS, INC. (I): RCI Bldg., White Plains, 10602
ROBLIN INDUSTRIES INC. (I): 290 Main St., Buffalo, 14202
ROCHESTER GAS & ELECTRIC CORP. (U): 89 East Ave., Rochester, 14604
ROCHESTER PRODUCTS DIVISION (I): 1000 Lexington Ave., Rochester, 14603
ROCHESTER TELEPHONE CORP. (U): 100 Midtown Plaza, Rochester, 14604

SATTLER'S INC. (M): 998 Broadway, Buffalo, 14212
SEABROOK FOODS INC.: 175 Great Neck Rd., Great Neck, 11021
SECURITY NATIONAL BANK (B): 350 Main St., Huntington, 11743
SENECA FOODS CORP.: 74 Seneca St., Dundee, 14837
SIBLEY, LINDSAY & CURR CO. (M): 228 Main St., E., Rochester, 14604
SIMMONDS PRECISION PRODUCTS, INC. (I): 105 Martling Ave., Tarrytown, 10591
SOLITRON DEVICES INC. (I): 256 Oak Tree Rd., Tappan, 10983
STATE BANK OF ALBANY (B): 69 State St., Albany, 12201
SYBRON CORP. (I): 1100 Midtown Tower, Rochester, 14604
TAMPAX, INC.: 5 Dakota Dr., Lake Success, 11040
TOBIN PACKING CO., INC.(I): 900 Maple St., Rochester, 14602
TRICO PRODUCTS CORP. (I): 817 Washington St., Buffalo, 14203
UNITED NUCLEAR CORP. (I): Elmsford, 10523
VERNITRON CORP. (I): 175 Community Dr., Great Neck, 11020
VIEWLEX, INC. (I): Broadway Ave. & Veterans Memorial Hwy., Holbrook, 11741
WEIGHT WATCHERS INTERNATIONAL INC.: 175 E. Shore Rd., Great Neck
WEST CHEMICAL PRODUCTS INC.: 42-16 West, Long Island, 11101

NORTH CAROLINA

AKZONA INC.: Asheville, 28802
ALBA WALDENSIAN INC. (I): Valdese, 28690
AMERICAN & EFIRD MILLS, INC. (I): Box 507, Mount Holly, 28120
BLUE BELL INC. (I): 335 Church St., Greensboro, 27401
BURLINGTON INDUSTRIES INC. (I): 301 N. Eugene St., Greensboro, 27401
CANNON MILLS CO. (I): Box 7, Kannapolis, 28081
CAROLINA FREIGHT CARRIERS CORP. (T): Cherryville, 28021
CAROLINA MILLS, INC. (I): P.O. Box 157, Maiden, 28650
CAROLINA POWER & LIGHT CO. (U): 336 Fayetteville St., Raleigh, 27602
CAROLINA TELEPHONE & TELEGRAPH CO. (U): 122 E. St. James St., Tarboro, 27886
CHADBOURN, INC. (I): 2417 N. Davidson St., Charlotte, 28205
CHATHAM MFG. CO. (I): Elkin, 28621
CONE MILLS CORP. (I): 4th & Maple Sts., Greensboro, 27405
DUKE POWER CO. (U): 422 S. Church St., Charlotte, 28202
FIBER INDUSTRIES, INC. (I): Box 10038, Charlotte, 28201
FIELDCREST MILLS, INC. (I): Eden, 27288
GENERAL TELEPHONE CO. OF THE SOUTHEAST (U): 3632 Roxboro Rd., Durham, 27704
GLEN RAVEN MILLS, INC. (I): Glen Raven, 27215
B. F. GOODRICH FOOTWEAR CO.: Goodrich Dr., Charlotte, 28201
HANES CORP. (I): P. O. Box 1413, Winston-Salem
J. B. IVEY & CO. (M): 127 N. Tryon St., Charlotte, 28201
JEFFERSON STANDARD LIFE INSURANCE CO. (LI): Box 21008, Greensboro, 27420
J. A. JONES CONSTRUCTION CO.: P.O. Box 966, Charlotte, 28201
LANCE, INC. (I): Pineville Rd., Charlotte, 28201
MC LEAN TRUCKING CO. (T): P.O. Box 213, Winston-Salem, 27102
NORTH CAROLINA NATIONAL BANK (B): 200 S. Tryon St., Charlotte, 28202
NORTHWESTERN BANK (B): North Wilkesboro, 28659
OCCIDENTAL LIFE INSURANCE CO. OF NORTH CAROLINA (LI): 1001 Wade Ave., Raleigh, 27605
PIEDMONT AVIATION, INC. (T): Smith-Reynolds Airport, Winston-Salem, 27102
PILOT LIFE INSURANCE CO. (LI): Box 20727, Greensboro, 27420
R. J. REYNOLDS TOBACCO CO. (I): Winston-Salem, 27101
ROBERTS CO. (I): Box 250, Sanford, 27330
ROSE'S STORES, INC. (M): 218-220 Garnett St., Henderson, 27536
THOMASVILLE FURNITURE INDUSTIRES, INC. (I): 401 E. Main St., Thomasville, 27360
THE WACHOVIA CORP.: 301 N. Main St., Winston-Salem, 27101

OHIO

A-T-O INC.: 4420 Sherwin Rd., Willoughby, 44094
ACME CLEVELAND CORP. (I): 170 E. 131st St., Cleveland, 44101
ADDRESSOGRAPH-MULTIGRAPH CORP. (I): Tower East, Shaker Heights, Ohio 44120

ALCAN ALUMINUM CORP. (I): 100 Erieview Plaza, Cleveland, 44114
ALLOYS & CHEMICALS CORP. (I): 4365 Bradley Rd., Cleveland, 44109
AMERICAN AUTOMATIC VENDING CORP. (S): 31100 Solon Rd., Solon, 44139
AMERICAN FINANCIAL CORP.: 3955 Montgomery Rd., Cincinnati, 45212
AMERICAN GREETING CORP. (I): 10500 American Rd., Cleveland, 44144
AMERICAN SHIP BUILDING CO. (I): Investment Plaza, Cleveland, 44114
ANCHOR HOCKING CORP. (I): 109 N. Broad St., Lancaster, 43130
ANCHOR MOTOR FREIGHT, INC. (T): 21111 Chagrin Blvd., Cleveland, 44122
ARMCO STEEL CORP. (I): 703 Curtis St., Middletown, 45042
ARO CORP. (I): Bryan, 43506
AUSTIN CO. (S): 3650 Mayfield Rd., Cleveland, 44121
AUTOMATION & MEASUREMENT (I): 721 Springfield St., Dayton, 45403
AVCO ELECTRONICS (S): 2630 Glendale & Milford Rd., Cincinnati, 45241
D. H. BALDWIN CO. (I): 1801 Gilbert Ave., Cincinnati, 44109
BANCOHIO CORP.(S): 51 N. High St., Columbus, 43216
BASIC INC. (I): Hanna Bldg., Cleveland, 44115
BATTELLE MEMORIAL INSTITUTE (S): 505 King Ave., Columbus, 43201
BEARINGS, INC. (M): 3634 Euclid Ave., Cleveland, 44115
BENDIX-WESTINGHOUSE AUTOMOTIVE AIR BRAKE CO. (I): 901 Cleveland St., Elyria, 44035
L. M. BERRY & CO. (AA): P.O. Box 6000, 3170 Kettering Blvd., Dayton, 45401
BIG BEAR STORES CO. (M): 770 W. Goodale Blvd., Columbus, 43212
E. W. BLISS CO. (I): 217 Second St., N.W., Canton, 44702
BUCKEYE INTERNATIONAL, INC. (I): 2211 Parsons Ave., Columbus, 43207
BURGER BREWING CO. (I): Central Parkway & Liberty St., Cincinnati, 45214
PHILIP CAREY CORP. (I): 320 S. Wayne, Cincinnati, 45215
CARLISLE CORP.: 511 Walnut St., Cincinnati, 45202
CENTRAL MUTUAL INSURANCE CO. (I): 800 S. Washington St., Van Wert, 45891
CENTRAL NATIONAL BANK OF CLEVELAND (B): 800 Superior Ave., Cleveland, 44114
CENTRAL TRUST CO. (B): Fourth & Vine, Cincinnati, 45202
CHAMPION SPARK PLUG CO. (I): 900 Upton Ave., Toledo, 43607
CHESAPEAKE & OHIO RAILWAY CO. (T): Terminal Tower, Cleveland, 44101
CINCINNATI GAS & ELECTRIC CO. (U): 4th & Main Sts., Cincinnati, 45201
CINCINNATI MILACRON INC. (I): 4701 Marburg Ave., Cincinnati, 45209
CLEVELAND-CLIFFS IRON CO. (I): Union Commerce Bldg., Cleveland, 44115
CLEVELAND ELECTRIC ILLUMINATING CO. (U): 55 Public Sq., Cleveland, 44101
CLEVELAND PNEUMATIC TOOL CO. (I): 3781 E. 77th St., Cleveland, 44105
CLEVELAND TRUST CO. (B): 900 Euclid Ave., Cleveland, 44101
CLEVELAND TWIST DRILL CO. (I): 1242 E. 49th St., Cleveland, 44101
CLEVITE CORP. (I): 17000 St. Clair Ave., Cleveland, 44110
CLIMALENE CO. (I): 1022 9th St., S.W., Canton, 44707
COLUMBIA GAS OF OHIO, INC. (U): 99 N. Front St., Columbus, 43215
COLUMBUS MUTUAL LIFE INSURANCE CO. (LI): 303 E. Broad St., Columbus, 43216
COLUMBUS & SOUTHERN OHIO ELECTRIC CO. (U): 215 N. Front St., Columbus, 43215
COOK UNITED, INC. (M): 16501 Rockside Rd., Maple Heights, Cleveland, 44137
DANA CORP. (I): 4500 Dorr St., Toledo, 43601
DAYCO CORP. (I): 333 W. First St., Dayton, 45402
DAYTON POWER AND LIGHT CO. (U): 25 N. Main St., Dayton, 45401
DIAMOND SHAMROCK CORP. (I): Union Comm. Bldg., Cleveland, 44115
DIEBOLD, INCORPORATED (I): 818 Mulberry Rd., S.E., Canton, 44709

EAGLE-PICHER INDUSTRIES INC. (I): American Bldg., Cincinnati, 45202

EAST OHIO GAS CO. (U): 1717 E. Ninth St., Cleveland, 44114

EATON CORP. (I): 100 Erieview Plaza, Cleveland, 44114

EPKO SHOES, INC. (I): 1401 Summit St., Toledo, 43604

ERIE LACKAWANNA RY. CO.: Midland Bldg., Cleveland

FEDERATED DEPARTMENT STORES INC. (M): 222 W. 7th St., Cincinnati, 45202

FERRO CORP.: One Erieview Plaza, Cleveland, 44114

FIFTH THIRD BANK (B): 38 Fountain Sq. Plaza, Cincinnati, 45201

FIRST NATIONAL BANK OF CINCINNATI (B): Fourth & Walnut Sts., Cincinnati, 45202

FIRESTONE SYNTHETIC RUBBER & LATEX CO. (I): P.O. Box 2786, Akron, 44301

FIRESTONE TIRE & RUBBER CO. (I): 1200 Firestone Pkwy., Akron, 44317

FISHER FOODS, INC. (M): 5300 Richmond Rd., Bedford Heights, 44105

GENERAL TELEPHONE CO. OF OHIO (U): P.O. Box 519, Marion, 43302

GENERAL TIRE & RUBBER CO. (I): One General St., Akron, 44309

GIBSON GREETING CARDS, INC. (I): 2100 Section Rd., Cincinnati, 45237

B. F. GOODRICH CHEMICAL CO. (I): 3135 Euclid Ave., Cleveland, 44115

THE B. F. GOODRICH CO. (I): 500 S. Main St., Akron, 44318

GOODYEAR TIRE & RUBBER CO. (I): 1144 E. Market St., Akron, 44316

GRAY DRUG STORES, INC. (M): 666 Euclid Bldg., Cleveland, 44114

GREIF BROS. CORP.: 621 Pennsylvania Ave., Delaware, 43015

GRISWOLD-ESHLEMAN CO. (AA): 55 Public Sq., Cleveland, 44113

HANNA MINING CO. (I): 100 Erieview Plaza, Cleveland, 44114

HARRIS-INTERTYPE CORP. (I): 55 Public Sq., Cleveland, 44113

HARSHAW CHEMICAL CO. (I): 1945 E. 97th St., Cleveland, 44106

HAUSERMAN INC. (I): 5711 Grant Ave., Cleveland, 44105

HIGBEE CO. (M): 100 Public Sq., Cleveland, 44113

HIRSCH GUSTAV ORGANIZATION, INC. (S): 1347 W. Fifth Ave., Columbus, 43212

HOBART BROTHERS CO. (I): Hobart Sq., Troy, 45373

HOBART MANUFACTURING CO.: World Headquarters Ave., Troy, 45373

HOOVER CO. (I): 101 E. Maple St., North Canton, 44720

ISLAND CREEK COAL CO. (I): 1501 Euclid Ave., Cleveland, 44115

JOSEPH & FEISS CO. (I): P.O. Box 5968, Cleveland, 44101

KROGER CO. (M): 1014 Vine St., Cincinnati, 45202

LAMSON & SESSIONS CO. (I): 5000 Tiedeman Rd., Cleveland, 44144

LEASEWAY TRANSPORTATION CORP. (T): 21111 Chagrin Blvd., Cleveland, 44122

LIBBEY-OWENS-FORD CO. (I): 811 Madison Ave., Toledo, 43624

LILY-TULIP DIVISION: P.O. Box 1035, Toledo, 43601

THE LUBRIZOL CORP. (I): P.O. Box 3057, Cleveland, 44117

M T D PRODUCTS INC. (I): 5389 W. 130th St., Cleveland, 44111

E. F. MAC DONALD CO. (S): 129 S. Ludlow St., Dayton, 45402

MANSFIELD TIRE & RUBBER CO. (I): 515 Newman St., Mansfield, 44902

MARATHON OIL CO. (I): 539 S. Main St., Findlay, 45840

MARION POWER SHOVEL CO. (I): 617 W. Center St., Marion, 43302

MC NEIL CORP. (I): 96 E. Crosier St., Akron, 44311

MEAD CORP. (I): 118 W. 1st St., Dayton, 45402

MID CONTINENT TELEPHONE CORP.: 100 Executive Pkwy., Hudson, 44236

MIDLAND-ROSS CORP. (I): 55 Public Sq., Cleveland, 44113

THE MOSLER SAFE CO. (I): 1561 Grand Blvd., Hamilton, 45012

MUTUAL INVESTING FOUNDATION (S): 246 N. High St., Columbus, 43216

NATIONAL CASH REGISTER CO. (I): Main & K Sts., Dayton, 45409

NATIONAL CITY BANK OF CLEVELAND (B): 623 Euclid Ave., Cleveland, 44114

NATIONAL SCREW & MFG. CO. (I): 8100 Tyler Blvd., Mentor, 44060

NATIONWIDE LIFE INSURANCE CO. (LI): 246 N. High St., Columbus, 43216

NATIONWIDE MUTUAL INSURANCE CO. (LI): 246 N. High St., Columbus, 43216

NORTH ELECTRIC CO. (I): 553 S. Market St., Galion, 44833

NUTONE DIVISION (I): Madison & Red Bank, Cincinnati, 45227

OGLEBAY NORTON CO. (I): Hanna Bldg., Cleveland, 44115

OHIO BELL TELEPHONE CO. (U): 100 Erieview Plaza, Cleveland, 44114

OHIO BRASS CO. (I): 380 N. Main St., Mansfield, 44902

OHIO CASUALTY INSURANCE CO. (LI): 136 N. Third St., Hamilton, 45025

OHIO EDISON CO. (U): 47 N. Main St., Akron, 44308

OHIO NATIONAL LIFE INSURANCE CO. (LI): William Howard Taft Rd. at Highland Ave., Cincinnati, 45201

OHIO POWER CO. (U): 301 Cleveland Ave., S.W., Canton, 44702

OHIO RUBBER CO. (I): Willoughby, 44094

OLDBERG MFG. CO. (I): 1801 Spielbusch Ave., Toledo, 43601

M. O'NEIL CO. (M): 226-250 S. Main St., Akron, 44308

OWENS-CORNING FIBERGLAS CORP. (I): Fiberglass Tower, Toledo, 43659

OWENS-ILLINOIS INC. (I): Box 1035, Toledo, 43601

PALM BEACH CO. (I): 400 Pike St., Cincinnati, 45202

PARKER ADVERTISING (AA): 333 W. First St., Dayton, 45402

PARKER-HANNIFIN CORP. (I): 17325 Euclid Ave., Cleveland, 44112

PARK-OHIO INDUSTRIES, INC. (I): 777 E. 79th St., Cleveland, 44103

PHILIPS INDUSTRIES, INC. (I): 4801 Springfield St., Dayton, 45401

PNEUMO-DYNAMICS CORP. (I): 3781 E. 77th St., Cleveland, 44105

PROCTOR & GAMBLE CO. (I): 301 E. Sixth St., Cincinnati, 45202

QUESTOR CORP. (I): 1801 Spielbusch Ave., Toledo, 43601

RANCO INC. (I): 601 W. Fifth Ave., Columbus, 43201

RANDALL CO. (I): 10179 Commerce Park Dr., Cincinnati, 45246

RELIANCE ELECTRIC CO. (I): 24701 Euclid Ave., Cleveland, 44117

REPUBLIC STEEL CORP. (I): Republic Bldg., Cleveland, 44101

ROADWAY EXPRESS, INC. (T): 1077 Gorge Blvd., Akron, 44309

ROBBINS & MYERS, INC. (I): 1345 Lagonda Ave., Springfield, 45501

RUBBERMAID INC. (I): 1255 E. Bowman St., Wooster, 44691

SCOTT & FETZER CO. (I): 14701 Detroit Ave., Cleveland, 44107

SHELLER GLOBE CORP. (I): 1505 Jefferson Ave., Toledo, 43624

SHERWIN-WILLIAMS CO. (I): 101 Prospect Ave., N.W., Cleveland, 44115

JOHN SHILLITO CO. (M): 7th & Race Sts., Cincinnati, 45202

SOCIETY CORP. (S): 127 Public Sq., Cleveland, 44114

STANDARD OIL CO. (I): Midland Bldg., Cleveland, 44115

STANDARD PRODUCTS CO. (I): 2130 W. 110th St., Cleveland, 44102

STANDARD REGISTER CO. (I): 626 Albany St., Dayton, 45401

STOUFFER RESTAURANT & INN CORP. (S): 1375 Euclid Ave., Cleveland, 44115

SUPER FOOD SERVICES, INC. (M): 3185 Elbee Rd., Dayton, 45439

SUPERIOR COACH CORP. (T): 1200 E. Kibby St., Lima, 45802

TRW INC. (I): 23555 Euclid Ave., Cleveland, 44117

TAFT BROADCASTING CO. (BR): 1906 Highland Ave., Cincinnati, 45219

TAPPAN CO. (I): 180 Park Ave., W. Mansfield, 44902

TIMKEN COMPANY (I): 1835 Dueber Ave., S.W., Canton, 44706

TOLEDO TRUST (B): 245 Summit St., Toledo, 43603

TOWMOTOR CORP. (I): 16100 Euclid Ave., Cleveland, 44112

TRUNDLE CONSULTANTS INC. (MC): 5500 South Marginal Rd., Cleveland, 44103

W. S. TYLER, INC. (I): 3615 Superior Ave., Cleveland, 44114

UNION CENTRAL LIFE INSURANCE CO. (LI): Mill & Waycross, Cincinnati, Ohio 45240

UNION COMMERCE BANK (B): 917 Euclid Ave., Cleveland, 44101

U. S. SHOE CORP. (I): 1658 Herald Ave., Cincinnati, 45207

U. S. TRUCK LINES, INC. OF DELAWARE (T): Union Commerce Bldg., Cleveland, 44114

UNITED TELEPHONE CO. OF OHIO (U): 665 Lexington Ave., Mansfield, 44907

VLN CORP.: 1374 E. 51st St., Cleveland, 44103

VULCAN CORP. (I): 6 E. 4th St., Cincinnati, 45202

WARNER & SWASEY CO. (I): 11000 Cedar Ave., Cleveland, 44106

WEAN INDUSTRIES, INC. (S): 3805 Henricks Rd., Youngstown, 44515

WEATHERHEAD CO. (I): 300 E. 131st St., Cleveland, 44108

WESTERN & SOUTHERN LIFE INS. CO. (LI): 400 Broadway, Cincinnati, 45201

WHITE CASTLE SYSTEM, INC. (S): 555 W. Goodale St., Columbus, 43216

WHITE CONSOLIDATED INDUSTRIES INC. (I): 11770 Berea Rd., Cleveland, 44111

WHITE MOTOR CORP. (I): 100 Erieview Plaza, Cleveland, 44114

WINTERS NATIONAL BANK & TRUST CO. (B): 40 N. Main St., Dayton, 45401

WORK WEAR CORP. (I): 1768 E. 25th St., Cleveland, 44114

YOUNGSTOWN SHEET & TUBE CO. (I): 7655 Market St., Youngstown, 44501

OKLAHOMA

AMERICAN POTASH & CHEMICAL CORP.: Kerr-McGee Bldg., Oklahoma City, 73102

C. R. ANTHONY CO. (M): 701 N. Broadway, Oklahoma City, 73102

APCO OIL CORP. (I): P.O. Box 1841, Oklahoma City, 73101

CCI CORPORATION (I): 4111 S. Darlington, Tulsa, 74135

CENTRAL MERCHANDISE CO. (M): 11 N.W. 37th St., Oklahoma City, 73118

CITIES SERVICE GAS CO. (I): First Natl. Bldg., Oklahoma City, 73125

CITIES SERVICE OIL CO. (DELAWARE) (I): Oil Center Bldg., Tulsa, 74102

FIRST NATIONAL BANK & TRUST CO. OF TULSA: Mid-Continent Bldg., Tulsa, 74103

FIRST OKLAHOMA BANCORPORATION, INC. (B): 120 N. Robinson Ave., Oklahoma City, 73102

KERR-MC GEE CORP. (I): Kerr-McGee Bldg., Oklahoma City, 73102

LEE WAY MOTOR FREIGHT CO. (T): 3000 W. Reno, Oklahoma City, 73108

OKLAHOMA GAS & ELECTRIC CO. (U): 321 N. Harvey Ave., Oklahoma City, 73101

OKLAHOMA NATURAL GAS CO.: P.O. Box 871 Tulsa, 74102

OKLAHOMA TIRE & SUPPLY CO. (I): P.O. Box 885, Tulsa, 74102

PHILLIPS PETROLEUM CO. (I): Phillips Bldg., Bartlesville, 74003

PUBLIC SERVICE CO. OF OKLA. (U): P.O. Box 201, Tulsa, 74102

SCRIVNER-BOOGAART, INC. (M): P.O. Box 26146, Oklahoma City, 73126

SEISMOGRAPH SERVICE CORP. (I): 6200 E. 41st St., Tulsa, 74102

SKELLY OIL CO. (I): Oil Center Bldg., Tulsa, 74102

T G & Y STORES CO.: P.O. Box 25967, Oklahoma City, 73125

THE TELEX CORP. (C): 41st & Sheridan Rd., Tulsa, 74135

UNION EQUITY COOPERATIVE EXCHANGE (I): 10th & Willow, Enid, 73701

WILLIAMS BROTHERS PIPE LINE CO.: P.O. Drawer 3448, Tulsa, 74101

WOODS CORP.: 4900 N. Santa Fe, Oklahoma City

OREGON

AUTOMOTIVE EQUIPMENT CO. (M): 5411 N. Lagoon Swan Island, Portland, 97217

BAZA'R INC. (M): 1845 S.E., 3rd Ave., Portland, 97214

BLITZ-WEINHARD CO. (I): 1133 W. Burnside St., Portland, 97209

BUMBLE BEE SEAFOODS (I): P.O. Box 60, Astoria, 97103

EVANS PRODUCTS CO. (I): 1121 S.W. Salmon St., Portland, 97205

FIRST NATIONAL BANK OF OREGON (B): P.O. Box 3131, Portland, 97208

GEORGIA-PACIFIC CORP. (I): 900 S.W. 5th Ave., Portland, 97204

HYSTER CO. (I): Lloyd Bldg., Portland, 97232

JANTZEN INC.: P.O. Box 3001, Portland, 97208

FRED MEYER, INC. (M): 3800 S.E. 22nd, Portland, 97202

OMARK INDUSTRIES, INC. (I): 2100 S.E. Milport Rd., Portland, 97222

PACIFIC POWER & LIGHT CO. (U): 920 S.W. 6th Ave., Portland, 97204

PUBLISHERS PAPER CO. (I): 419 Main St., Oregon City, 97045

SPOKANE, PORTLAND & SEATTLE RY. (T): 1101 N.W. Hoyt St., Portland, 97209

SPROUSE-REITZ CO., INC. (M): 2175 N.W. Upshur St., Portland, 97210

STANDARD INSURANCE CO. (LI): 1100 S.W. Sixth Ave., Portland, 97204

TEKTRONIX, INC. (I): Box 500, Beaverton, 97005

U.S. NATIONAL BANK OF OREGON (B): 321 S.W. 6th Ave., Portland, 97204

WILLAMETTE INDUSTRIES, INC. (I): Executive Bldg., Portland, 97204

PENNSYLVANIA

A M P INC. (I): Eisenhower Blvd., Harrisburg, 17111

A R A SERVICES INC. (M): 6th & Walnut St., Philadelphia, 19106

A V M CORP.: 123 S. Broad St., Philadelphia, 19109

ACME MARKETS, INC. (M): 124 N. 15th St., Philadelphia, 19101

ACTION INDUSTRIES INC. (I): 460 Nixon Rd., Cheswick, 15024

AERO SERVICE CORP. (S): 4219 Van Kirk St., Philadelphia, 19135

AIR PRODUCTS & CHEMICALS INC. (I): P.O. Box 538, Allentown, 18105

ALAN WOOD STEEL CO. (I): Box 112, Conshohocken, 19428

ALCAN CABLE (I): 610 Washington Ave., Jersey Shore, 17740

ALCO STANDARD CORP.: Valley Forge, 19481

ALDON INDUSTRIES, INC.: Concordville, 19331

ALLEGHENY LUDLUM INDUSTRIES, INC. (I): Oliver Bldg., Pittsburgh, 15222

ALPHA PORTLAND CEMENT CO. (I): 15 S. Third St., Easton, 18042

ALUMINUM CO. OF AMERICA (I): 1501 Alcoa Bldg., Pittsburgh, 15219

ANCHEM PRODUCTS, INC. (I): Brookside Ave., Ambler, 19002

AMERICAN CHAIN & CABLE CO., INC.: 454 E. Princess St., York, 17403

AMERICAN ELECTRONIC LABORATORIES INC.: Box 552, Lansdale, 19446

AMERICAN HARDWARE SUPPLY CO. (M): P.O. Box 1549, Butler, 16001

AMERICAN INSTITUTIONAL DEVELOPERS, INC.: 351 E. Conestoga Rd., Stafford-Wayne, 19087

AMERICAN MEDICORP INC.: Bala-Cynwyd, 19004

AMERICAN METER CO. (I): 13500 Philmont Ave., Philadelphia, 19116

AMERICAN STERILIZER CO. (I): 2424 West 23rd St., Erie, 16506

AMPCO-PITTSBURG CORP.: 700 Porter Bldg., Pittsburg, 15219

AMSCO, AMER. STERILIZER CORP.: 2222 W. Grandview Blvd., Erie, 16509

ARMSTRONG CORK CO. (I): Liberty & Charlotte St., Lancaster, 17604

ASPLUNDH TREE EXPERT CO. (S): 505 York Rd., Jenkintown, 19046

N. W. AYER & SON INC. (AA): W. Washington Sq., Philadelphia, 19106

THE BALLINGER CO. (S): 1625 Race St., Philadelphia, 19103

BAYUK CIGARS INC. (I): 9th & Columbia, Philadelphia, 19122

BECKWITH MACHINERY CO.: Rte. 22, E., Pittsburg

BELL TELEPHONE CO. OF PA. (U): One Parkway, Philadelphia, 19102

BETHLEHEM STEEL CORP. (I): 701 E. 3rd St., Bethlehem, 18016

BIRDSBORO CORP. (I): Birdsboro, 19508

BONNEY FORGE & FOUNDRY DIV.: P.O. Box 1755, Allentown, 18105

BOOK-OF-THE-MONTH CLUB, INC.: Camp Hill, 17011

BOWEN-MC LAUGHLIN-YORK CO. (I): P.O. Box 1512, York, 17405

BROCKWAY GLASS CO., INC. (I): McCullough Ave., Brockway, 15824

BUDD CO. (I): 2450 Hunting Park Ave., Philadelphia, 19132

BULLETIN CO. (S): 30th & Market, Philadelphia, 19101

A. M. BYERS CO.: Ambridge, 15003

CALGON CORPORATION (I): Rte. 60 & Campbells Run Rd., Pittsburgh, 15230

CALORIC CORP. (I): Topton, 19562

CARNEGIE-MELLON UNIVERSITY (S): 5000 Forbes Ave., Pittsburgh, 15213

CARPENTER TECHNOLOGY CORP.: 101 W. Bern St., Reading, 19601

JOHN F. CASEY CO. (S): Box 1888, Pittsburgh, 15230

CATALYTIC INC. (S): 1528 Walnut St., Philadelphia, 19102

CENTRAL PENN NATIONAL BANK (B): Barclay Bldg., Bala Cynwyd, 19004

CERTAIN-TEED PRODUCTS CORP. (I): Valley Forge, 19481

CHEMICAL LEMAN TANK LINES, INC. (T): 520 E. Lancaster Ave., Downingtown, 19335

COLUMBIA GAS OF PENNSYLVANIA, INC. (U): Union Trust Bldg., Pittsburgh, 15219

CONTINENTAL BANK (B): Main & Swede Sts., Norristown, 19401

COPPERWELD STEEL CO.: Frick Bldg., Pittsburgh, 15219

CROWN CORK & SEAL COMPANY INC. (I): 9300 Ashton Rd., Philadelphia, 19136

CRUCIBLE INC. (I): P.O. Box 88, Pittsburgh, 15230

CURTIS PUBLISHING CO. (P): Independence Sq., Philadelphia, 19106

H. DAROFF & SONS, INC. (I): 2320 Walnut St., Philadelphia, 19103

DAY & ZIMMERMANN, INC. (S): 1700 Sansom St., Philadelphia, 19103

DECORATOR INDUSTRIES, INC. (I): 1401 Forbes Ave., Pittsburgh, 15219

DRAVO CORP. (I): One Oliver Plaza, Pittsburgh, 15222

DUQUESNE BREWING CO. OF PITTSBURGH (I): S. 22nd & Mary Sts., Pittsburgh, 15203

DUQUESNE LIGHT CO. (U): 435 Sixth Ave., Pittsburgh, 15219

ESB INCORPORATED (I): 5 Penn Center Plaza, Philadelphia, 19103

EASTERN ASSOCIATED COAL CORP. (M): Koppers Bldg., Pittsburgh, 15219

FABRICATED METALS (I): Porter Bldg., Pittsburgh, 15219

THE FIDELITY BANK (B): 1200 E. Lancaster Ave., Rosemont, 19010

FIDELITY MUTUAL LIFE INSURANCE CO. (LI): Parkway at Fairmount, Philadelphia, 19101

FIRST PENNSYLVANIA BANKING & TRUST CO. (B): 15th & Chestnut Sts., Philadelphia, 19101

FOOD FAIR STORES, INC. (M): 3175 John F. Kennedy Blvd., Philadelphia, 19104

GAC FINANCE INC. (I): 1105 Hamilton St., Allentown, 18101

GENERAL ACCIDENT, FIRE & LIFE ASSURANCE CORP., LTD. (LI): 414 Walnut St., Philadelphia, 19106

GENERAL BATTERY CORP. (I): P.O. Box 1262, Reading

GENERAL REFRACTORIES CO. (I): 1520 Lucust St., Philadelphia, 19102

GENERAL TELEPHONE CO. OF PA. (U): 150 W. Tenth St., Erie, 16512

GIRARD BANK (B): One Girard Plaza, Philadelphia, 19101

GULF OIL CORP. (I): Gulf Bldg., Pittsburgh, 15219

HALL'S MOTOR TRANSIT CO. (T): 1151 S. 21st St., Harrisburg, 17111

HAMMERMILL PAPER CO. (I): 1453 East Lake Rd., Erie, 16507

HARSCO CORP. (I): Camp Hill, 17011

H. J. HEINZ CO. (I): 1062 Progress St., Pittsburgh, 15230

HERSHEY FOODS CORP. (I): 19 E. Chocolate Ave., Hershey, 17033

JOSEPH HORNE CO. (S): 501 Penn Ave., Pittsburgh, 15222

I—T—E IMPERIAL CORP. (I): 1900 Hamilton St., Philadelphia, 19130

INDUSTRIAL VALLEY BANK & TRUST CO. (B): Old York & West, Jenkintown, 19046

INSURANCE CO. OF NORTH AMERICA (LI): 1600 Arch St., Philadelphia, 19103

INTERNATIONAL SALT CO. (I): Clarks Summit, 18411

CHARLES JACQUIN ET CIE, INC. (I): 2633 Trenton Ave., Philadelphia, 19125

JESSUP STEEL CO. (I): 500 Green St., Washington, 15301

JONES & LAUGHLIN STEEL CORP. (I): 3 Gateway Center, Pittsburgh, 15230

JONES MOTOR CO. (T): Bridge & Schuykill, Spring City, 19475

JOY MFG. CO. (I): Oliver Bldg., Pittsburgh, 15222

KAWECKI BERYLCO INDUSTRIES, INC.: Box 1462, Reading, 19603

KENNAMETAL INC. (I): 1 Lloyd Ave., Latrobe, 15650

KETCHUM, MACLEOD & GROVE (AA): 4 Gateway Center, Pittsburgh, 15222

KOPPERS CO., INC. (I): Koppers Bldg., Pittsburgh, 15219

LEEDS & NORTHRUP CO. (I): Sumneytown Pike, North Wales, 19454

LEES CARPETS DIVISION,: 1000 Adams Ave., Valley Forge Industrial Park, Norristown, 19401

LEHIGH PORTLAND CEMENT CO. (I): Young Bldg., 718 Hamilton St., Allentown, 18105

LEHIGH VALLEY RR. (T): 415 Brighton St., 18015

LIFE INSURANCE CO. OF NORTH AMERICA (LI): 1600 Arch St., Philadelphia, 19103

LUKENS STEEL CO. (I): Coatesville, 19320

MACK TRUCKS INC. (I): Box M, Allentown, 18105

MAGEE CARPET CO. (I): Fifth St., Bloomsburg, 17815

H. B. MAYNARD & CO. INC. (MC): 2040 Ardmore Blvd., Pittsburgh, 15221

MELLON NATIONAL BANK & TRUST CO. (B): Mellon Sq., Pittsburgh, 15230

MESTA MACHINE CO. (I): Box 1466, Pittsburgh, 15230

METROPOLITAN EDISON CO.: P.O. Box 542, Reading, 19603

MINE SAFETY APPLIANCE CO. (I): 201 N. Braddock Ave., Pittsburgh, 15208

G. C. MURPHY CO. (M): 531 Fifth Ave., McKeesport, 15132

NATIONAL STEEL CORP.: 2800 Grant Bldg., Pittsburgh, 15219

NEW HOLLAND (I): Franklin & Roberts Sts., New Holland, 17557

NEW JERSEY ZINC CO.: 2045 City Line Rd., Bethlehem, 18017

OPTICAL SCANNING CORP. (I): Box 40, Route 332 E., Newtown, 18940

PPG INDUSTRIES, INC. (I): 1 Gateway Center, Pittsburgh, 15222

PENN CENTRAL TRANSPORTATION CO. (T): 6 Penn Center Plaza, Philadelphia, 19104

PENN FRUIT CO., INC. (M): Grant & Bluegrass, Philadelphia, 19115

PENN MUTUAL LIFE INSURANCE CO. (LI): 530 Walnut St., Philadelphia, 19105

PENNSYLVANIA ELECTRIC CO. (U): 1001 Broad St., Johnstown, 15907

PENNSYLVANIA POWER & LIGHT CO. (U): 901 Hamilton St., Allentown, 18101

PENNWALT CORP.: Pennwalt Bldg., Philadelphia, 19102

PHILADELPHIA BULLETIN (P): 30th & Market Sts., Philadelphia, 19101

PHILADELPHIA ELECTRIC POWER CO. (U): 1000 Chestnut St., Philadelphia, 19105

PHILADELPHIA GAS WORKS (U): 1401 Arch St., Philadelphia, 19102

PHILADELPHIA NATIONAL BANK (B): Broad & Chestnut, Philadelphia, 19101

PHILCO-FORD CORP. (I): Tioga & C Sts., Philadelphia, 19134

PIPER AIRCRAFT CORP. (I): 820 E. Bald Eagle St., Lock Haven, 17745

PITTSBURGH COKE & CHEMICAL CO. (I): Grant Bldg., Pittsburgh, 15219

PITTSBURGH-DES MOINES STEEL CO. (I): Neville Island, Pittsburgh, 15225

PITTSBURGH FORGINGS CO. (I): Gateway 3, 401 Liberty Ave., Pittsburgh, 15222

PITTSBURGH & LAKE ERIE RR. (T): 6 Penn Plaza, Philadelphia, 19104

PITTSBURGH NATIONAL BANK (B): Fifth Ave. at Wood, Pittsburgh, 15230

PITTSBURGH PRESS (P): Box 566, Pittsburgh, 15230

PROVIDENT MUTUAL LIFE INSURANCE CO. OF PHILADELPHIA (LI): 4601 Market St., Philadelphia, 19139

PROVIDENT NATIONAL BANK (B): Broad & Chestnut Sts., Philadelphia, 19101

PUBLICKER INDUSTRIES INC. (I): 1429 Walnut St., Philadelphia, 19102

READING CO. (T): Reading Terminal, Philadelphia, 19107

RELIANCE INSURANCE CO. (LI): 4 Penn Center Plaza, Philadelphia, 19103

H. H. ROBERTSON CO. (I): Two Gateway Center, Pittsburgh, 15222

ROCKWELL MFG. CO. (I): Rockwell Bldg., 410 Lexington Ave., Pittsburgh, 15208

ROHM & HAAS CO. (I): Independence Mall West, Philadelphia, 19105

ROSENAU BROTHERS INC. (I): Fox & Roberts, Philadelphia, 19129

RUST ENGINEERING CO. (S): 930 Fort Duquesne Blvd., Pittsburgh, 15222

S K F INDUSTRIES, INC. (I): P.O. Box 6731, Philadelphia, 19132

SAFEGUARD INDUSTRIES, INC.: 630 Park Ave., King of Prussia, 19406

C. SCMIDT & SONS, INC. (I): 127 Edward St., Philadelphia, 19123

SCOTT PAPER CO. (I): Scott Plaza, Philadelphia, 19113

SHARON STEEL CORP. (I): Box 291, Sharon, 16146

THE SHENANGO FURNACE CO. (I): One Oliver Plaza, Pittsburgh, 15230

SMITH KLINE & FRENCH LABORATORIES (I): 1500 Spring Garden St., Philadelphia, 19130

SPANG & CO. (I): Brugh Ave., Butler, Pa. 16001

SPECTRO INDUSTRIES, INC. (I): Jenkintown Plaza, Suite 302, Jenkintown, 19046

STACKPOLE CARBON CO. (I): St. Marys, 15857

STANDARD PRESSED STEEL CO. (I): The Benson-East, Jenkintown, 19046

STRAWBRIDGE & CLOTHIER (M): 801 Market St., Phila., 19105

SUN OIL CO. (I): 1608 Walnut St., Philadelphia, 19103

SUN SHIPBUILDING & DRY DOCK CO.: Chester, 19013

TALON, INC. (I): 626 Arch St., Meadville, 16335

TASTY BAKING CO.: 2801 Hunting Park Ave., Philadelphia, 19129

THERMOID (I): Porter Bldg., Pittsburgh, 15219

THIOKOL CHEMICAL CORP. (I): Newportville Rd., Bristol, 19007

THOROFARE MARKETS, INC. (M): Meadowbrook Rd., Murrysville, 15668

THRIFT DRUG CO.: 615 Alpha Dr., Pittsburgh, 15238

TRIANGLE PUBLICATIONS, INC. (P): 250 King of Prussia Rd., Radnor, 19088

UGI CORP. (I): 1401 Arch St., Philadelphia, 19105

THE UNION CORP.: Jones St., Verona, 15147

UNION NATIONAL BANK OF PITTSBURGH (B): Fourth at Wood, Pittsburgh, 15222

UNION RR. CO.: 4 Gateway Center, Pittsburgh, 15222

UNITED ENGINEERING & FOUNDRY CO. (I): 948 Fort Duquesne Blvd., Pittsburgh, 15222

UNITED ENGINEERS & CONSTRUCTORS INC. (S): 1401 Arch St., Philadelphia, 19105

UNIVAC DIVISION (I): P.O. Box 500, Blue Bell, 19422

U.S. STEEL CORP.: 600 Grant St., Pittsburg, 15219

VILLAGER INDUSTRIES, INC. (I): Richmond & Allegheny, Philadelphia, 19139

WALWORTH CO.: One Decker Sq., Bala Cynwyd, 19004

WARNER COMPANY (I): 1721 Arch St., Philadelphia, 19103

WEIS MARKETS, INC. (M): 1000 S. Second St., Sunbury, 17801

WELLING & WOODARD INC. (MC): Wyncote House, Box 29, Jenkintown, 19046

WESTERN PENNSYLVANIA NATIONAL BANK (B): Fifth & Smithfield, Pittsburgh, 15230

WEST PENN POWER CO. (U): Cabin Hill, Greensburg, 15601

WESTINGHOUSE AIR BRAKE CO. (I): 3 Gateway Center, Pittsburgh, 15222

WESTINGHOUSE ELECTRIC CORP. (I): 3 Gateway Center, Pittsburgh, 15222

WHEELING-PITTSBURGH STEEL CORP.: 4 Gateway Center, Pittsburgh, 15222

WHITE CROSS STORES, INC. (I): 339 Haymaker Rd., Monroeville, 15146

WYETH LABORATORIES: Radnor, 19088

YELLOW CAB CO. OF PHILADELPHIA (S): 105 S. 12th St., Philadelphia, 19130

ZURN INDUSTRIES, INC. (S): 2214 W. 8th St., Erie, 16512

RHODE IDLAND

AMTEL INC. (I): 40 Westminster St., Providence, 02903

BROWN & SHARPE MFG. CO. (I): Precision Park, North Kingstown, 02852

GILBANE BUILDING CO.: 90 Calverley St., Providence, 02908

GORHAM (I): 333 Adelaide Ave., Providence, 02907

GRINNELL CORP. (I): 260 W. Exchange St., Providence, 02903

LEESONA CORP. (I): 333 Strawberry Field Rd., Warwick, 02887

NICHOLSON FILE CO. (I): 667 Waterman Ave., East Providence, 02914

TEXTRON INC. (I): 10 Dorrance St., Providence, 02903

SOUTH CAROLINA

ABNEY MILLS (I): Jordan St., Greenwood, 29646

CRYOVAC (I): Box 464, Duncan, 29334

GRANITEVILLE CO. (I): Graniteville, 29829

GREENWOOD MILLS, (I): Greenwood, 29646

LIBERTY LIFE INSURANCE CO. (LI): Liberty Life Bldg., Greenville, 29602

MOUNT VERNON MILLS, INC.: Daniel Bldg., Greenville, 29602

SHAKESPEARE COMPANY (I): P.O. Box 246, Columbia, 29202

SONOCO PRODUCTS CO. (I): N. 2nd St., Hartsville, 29550

SOUTH CAROLINA ELECTRIC & GAS CO. (U): 328 Main St., Columbia, 29202

SOUTH CAROLINA NATIONAL BANK (B): P.O. Box 168, Columbia, 29202

SPARTAN MILLS (I): 436 Howard St., Spartanburg, 29303

SPRINGS MILLS INC. (I): Fort Mill, 29715

STONE MANUFACTURING CO. (I): P.O. Box 3725 Park Place, Greenville, 29608

TENNESSEE

ALLEN & O'HARA, INC. (MC): 3385 Airways Blvd., Memphis, 38130

ALLENBERG COTTON CO. (I): 104 S. Front St., Memphis, 38101

ASSOCIATES CAPITAL CORP. (S): 601 Broadway, Nashville, 37203

CAPITOL INTERNATIONAL AIRWAYS, INC. (T): P.O. Box 325, Smyrna Airport, Smyrna

FIRST AMERICAN NATIONAL BANK (B): Fourth Ave. & Union St., Nashville, 37202

FIRST NATIONAL BANK OF MEMPHIS (B): 165 Madison Ave., Memphis, 38103

GENESCO INC. (I): 111 7th Ave., N., Nashville, 37203

HOLIDAY INNS INC. (S): 3742 Lamar Ave., Memphis, 38118

INTERSTATE LIFE & ACCIDENT INSURANCE CO. (LI): Interstate Life Bldg., Chattanooga, 37402

KENTUCKY FRIED CHICKEN CORP.: 3901 Atkinson Dr., Louisville, 40213

KINGSPORT PRESS, INC.: Press St., Kingsport, 37662

KUHN'S BIG K STORES CORP.: 3040 Sidco Drive, Nashville, 37204

LIFE & CASUALTY INSURANCE CO. OF TENNESSEE (LI): Life & Casualty Tower, Nashville, 37219

LINCOLN AMERICAN LIFE INSURANCE CO. (LI): 60 N. Main St., Memphis, 38101

MALONE & HYDE, INC. (M): 1451 Union Ave., Memphis, 38104

MASON & DIXON LINES, INC. (T): Eastman Rd., Kingsport, 37664

MURRAY OHIO MFG. CO. (I): 635 Thompson Lane, Nashville, 37204

NATIONAL LIFE AND ACCIDENT INSURANCE CO. (LI): 301 7th Ave., Nashville, 37219

PLOUGH, INC. (I): Box 377, Memphis, 38101

PROVIDENT LIFE & ACCIDENT INSURANCE CO. (LI): Fountain Sq., Chattanooga, 37402

SKYLAND INTERNATIONAL CORP. (I): 2001 Wheeler Ave., Chattanooga, 37406

STANDARD-COOSA THATCHER CO. (I): 18th & Watkins Sts., Chattanooga, 37401

STANDARD KNITTING MILLS, INC. (I): Washington & Mitchell, Knoxville, 37901

TENNESSEE EASTMAN CO. (I): Eastman Rd., Kingsport, 37662

THIRD NATIONAL BANK IN NASHVILLE (B): Fourth & Church, Nashville, 37202

UNION PLANTERS NATIONAL BANK (B): 67 Madison Ave., Memphis, 38101

WAYNE-GOSSARD CORP. (I): N. 22nd St., Humboldt, 38343

TEXAS

A D A OIL COMPANY: 6910 Fannin, Houston, 77025

A L D INC. (I): 2002 Gaisford, Dallas, 75210

AFFILIATED FOOD STORES, INC. (M): 9001 Ambassador Row, Dallas, 75247

ALASKA INTERSTATE CO. (I): 5051 Westheimer, Houston, 77027

ALCON LABORATORIES INC.: 6201 S. Freeway, Ft. Worth, 76134

ALLEN PARKER CO. (S): 3701 Kirby Dr., Houston, 77006

ALLIED FINANCE CO. (S): 2808 Fairmont St., Dallas, 75201

AMARILLO HARDWARE CO. (I): 600 Grant St., Amarillo, 79101

AMERICAN-AMICABLE LIFE INS. CO. (LI): Alico Center, Waco, 76703

AMERICAN COMMERCIAL LINES INC. (T): 2919 Allen Pkwy., Houston, 77019

AMERICAN GENERAL LIFE INSURANCE CO. (LI): 2727 Allen Pkwy., Houston, 77019

AMERICAN NATIONAL INSURANCE CO. OF GALVESTON (LI): Moody & Market, Galveston, 77550

AMERICAN PETROFINA CO. OF TEXAS (I): P.O. Box 2159, Dallas, 75221

ANDERSON, CLAYTON & CO. (I): Tennessee Bldg., Houston, 77002
AUSTIN BRIDGE CO. (I): 1000 Singleton Blvd., Dallas, 75212
J. W. BATESON CO. (S): 10150 Monroe Dr., Dallas, 75220
BELL HELICOPTER CO. (I): P.O. Box 482, Fort Worth, 76101
W. S. BELLOWS CONSTRUCTION CORP. (S): 716 N. York St., Houston
T. J. BETTES CO. (S): 201 Main St., Houston, 77002
BIG THREE INDUSTRIES INC. (I): 3602 W. Eleventh St., Houston, 77008
BLACK SIVALLS & BRYSON, INC.: 2727 Allen Pkwy., Houston, 77019
BRANIFF AIRWAYS, INC. (T): Exchange Park, Dallas, 75235
BURRUS MILLS, INC. (I): Mercantile Securities Bldg., Dallas, 75221
WM. CAMERON & CO. (I): Drawer 889, Waco, 76703
CAMERON IRON WORKS, INC. (I): Box 1212, Houston, 77001
CAMPBELL TAGGART, INC. (I): 6211 Lemmon Ave., Dallas, 75209
CENTRAL POWER & LIGHT CO. (U): 120 N. Chaparral St., Corpus Christi, 78401
CHAMPLIN PETROLEUM CO. (I): P.O. Box 9365, Fort Worth, 76107
CITY PUBLIC SERVICE BOARD (U): 145 Navarro St., San Antonio, 78206
COASTAL STATES GAS PRODUCING CO.: Petroleum Tower, Corpus Christi, 78401
COLLINS RADIO CO. (I): 1200 N. Alma Rd., Dallas, 75207
COLUMBIA GULF TRANSMISSION CO. (S): 3805 W. Alabama Ave., Houston, 77027
COMMERCIAL METALS CO. (I): 3000 Diamond Park Dr., Dallas, 75247
COOPER INDUSTRIES INC. (I): First City National Bank Bldg., Houston, 77002
DR PEPPER CO. (I): 5523 E. Mockingbird Lane, Dallas, 75222
DRESSER INDUSTRIES, INC. (I): Republic Natl. Bank Bldg., Dallas, 75201
EL PASO NATURAL GAS CO. (U): P.O. Box 1492, El Paso, 79978
FARAH MFG. CO., INC. (I): 8889 Gateway Blvd., W., El Paso, 79985
FIRST CITY NATIONAL BANK OF HOUSTON (B): 1001 Main St., Houston, 77002
FIRST NATIONAL BANK OF DALLAS (B): 1401 Elm St., Dallas, 75202
FIRST NATIONAL BANK OF FORT WORTH (B): 1 Burnett Plaza, Fort Worth, 76102
FORT WORTH NATIONAL BANK (B): P.O. Box 2050, Ft. Worth, 76101
FOLEY'S (M): Box 1971, Houston, 77001
FOX-STANLEY PHOTO PRODUCTS, INC. (I): 1734 Broadway, San Antonio, 78206
FRITO-LAY, INC. (I): Frito-Lay Tower, Dallas, 75235
GENERAL AMERICAN OIL COMPANY OF TEXAS (I): Meadows Bldg., Dallas, 75206
GENERAL PORTLAND CEMENT CO. (I): 4400 Republic Bank Tower, Dallas, 75201
GLENN ADVERTISING (AA): 4700 Republic Bank Tower, Dallas, 75201
GOOD PASTURE, INC. (I): 900 W. Broadway, Brownfield, 79316
GORDON JEWELRY CORP.: Gordon Bldg., Houston, 77002
GULF STATES UTILITIES CO. (U): 285 Liberty Ave., Beaumont, 77701
HALLIBURTON CO. (S): 3211 Southland Center, Dallas, 75201
HOUSTON CONTRACTING CO. (I): 2807 Buffalo Speedway, Houston, 77006
HOUSTON LIGHTING & POWER CO. (U): 611 Walker Ave., Houston, 77002
HOUSTON NATURAL GAS CORP. (U): 1200 Travis St., Houston, 77001
HUGHES TOOL CO.: 5425 Polk Ave., Houston, 77023
HUMBLE OIL & REFINING CO. (I): 800 Bell Ave., Houston, 77002
INTERNATIONAL SYSTEMS & CONTROLS CORP. (I): 2727 Allen Pkwy., Houston, 77001
KIMBELL, INC. (I): 1929 S. Main St., Fort Worth, 76101
LTV AEROSPACE CORP. (I): P.O. Box 5003, Dallas, 75222
LTV ELECTROSYSTEMS, INC. (I): Box 6030, Dallas, 75222
R. G. LETOURNEAU, INC. (I): P.O. Box 2307 Longview, 75601
LEVINE DEPT. STORE DIVISION (N): 3000 Diamond Park, Dallas, 75247
LIFSON, WILSON, FERGUSON & WINICK, INC. (MC): 7616 LBJ Freeway, Dallas, 75240
LING-TEMCO-VOUGHT INC. (I): Box 5003, Dallas, 75222

LONE STAR BREWING CO. (I): 600 Lone Star Blvd., San Antonio, 78204
LONE STAR GAS CO. (I): 301 S. Harwood St., Dallas, 75201
CURTIS MATHES MFG. CO. (I): 2220 Young St., Dallas, 75201
MERCANTILE NATIONAL BANK OF DALLAS (B): 1704 Main St., Dallas, 75201
MISSOURI BEEF PACKERS, INC.: Amarillo Bldg., Amarillo, 79105
MISSOURI-KANSAS-TEXAS RR. CO. (T): Katy Bldg., Dallas, 75202
G. W. MURPHY INDUSTRIES, INC. (I): 6501 Navigation Blvd., Houston, 77011
NATIONAL CHEMSEARCH CORP. (I): 2730 Carl Rd., Irving, 75060
NEIMAN-MARCUS CO. (M): Main & Ervay Sts., Dallas, 75201
OILWELL DIVISION (I): 2001 N. Lamar St., Dallas, 75221
PANHANDLE EASTERN PIPE LINE CO. (U): P.O. Box 1642, Houston, 77001
PEARL BREWING CO. (I): 312 Pearl Pkwy., San Antonio, 78215
PENNZOIL UNITED, INC. (I): 900 Southwest Tower, Houston, 77002
PLAINS COTTON CO-OPERATIVE ASSN. INC. (I): 3301 E. 50th St., Lubbock, 79408
RAINBO BAKING CO. OF BEAUMONT (I): 2695 Laurel St., Beaumont, 77702
REPUBLIC NATIONAL BANK OF DALLAS (B): Pacific, Ervay & Bryan Sts., Dallas, 75201
SHOP RITE FOODS, INC.: 1106 Hwy. 360, Grand Prairie, 75050
ST. LOUIS SOUTHWESTERN RY. (T): 1517 W. Front St., Tyler, 75703
SOUTHERN UNION GAS CO. (U): Fidelity Union Tower, Dallas, 75201
THE SOUTHLAND CORP. (M): 2828 N. Haskell Ave., Dallas, 75204
SOUTHLAND LIFE INSURANCE CO. (LI): Southland Center, Dallas, 75201
SOUTHWESTERN INVESTMENT CO. (B): 205 East 10th Ave., Amarillo
SOUTHWESTERN LIFE INSURANCE CO. (LI): P.O. Box 2699, Dallas, 75221
SOUTHWESTERN PUBLIC SERVICE CO. (U): Mercantile Dallas Bldg., Dallas, 75201
STERLING ELECTRONICS (I): 4201 Southwest Freeway, Houston, 77001
SUPERIOR OIL CO. (THE) (I): First City National Bank Bldg., Houston, 77002
TCO INDUSTRIES, INC. (T): 315 Continental Ave., Dallas, 75207
T.I.M.E.-DC, INC. (T): 2598 74th St., Lubbock, 79408
TANDY CORP. (I): 2727 W. Seventh St., Fort Worth, 76107
TENNECO INC. (I): Tenneco Bldg., Houston, 77002
TENNECO OIL CO. (I): P.O. Box 2511, Houston, 77001
TEXAS EASTERN TRANSMISSION CORP. (U): Box 2521, Houston, 77001
TEXAS ELECTRIC SERVICE CO. (U): 7th & Lamar Sts., Ft. Worth, 76102
TEXAS INDUSTRIES, INC. (I): 8100 Carpenter Freeway, Dallas, 75247
TEXAS INSTRUMENTS INC. (I): P.O. Box 5475, Dallas, 75222
TEXAS OIL & GAS CORP. (I): Fidelity Union Tower, Dallas, 75201
TEXAS & PACIFIC RY. (T): Fidelity Union Tower, Dallas,75201
TEXAS POWER & LIGHT CO. (U): Fidelity Union Life Bldg., Dallas, 75201
TEXAS UTILITIES CO. (U): 1506 Commerce St., Dallas, 75201
TRACOR INC. (I): 6500 Tracor Lane, Austin, 78721
TRACY-LOCKE, INC. (AA): 1407 Main St., Dallas, 75202
TRANSCONTINENTAL GAS PIPE LINE CORP. (S): 3100 Travis St., Houston, 77001
TEXAS INTERNATIONAL AIRLINES, INC. (T): 8451 Lockheed St., Houston, 77017
TRINITY INDUSTRIES, INC. (I): 4001 Irving Blvd., Dallas, 75207
TRUNKLINE GAS CO. (U): 3000 Bissonnet Ave., Houston, 77005
TYLER PIPE INDUSTRIES, INC.: Lindale Rd., Swan, 75701
UNITED GAS PIPE LINE CO.: 1500 Southwest Tower, Houston, 77002
UNIVERSITY COMPUTING CO. (S): P.O. Box 6228, Dallas 75222
VARO INC. (I): Garland Bank & Tr. Bldg., Garland, 75040
WAPLES-PLATTER CO. (I): 7133 Burns, Ft. Worth, 76101
WEINGARTEN, INC. (M): 600 Lockwood Dr., Houston, 77011
WILLIAMSON-DICKIE MFG. CO. (I): 509 W. Vickery Blvd., Fort Worth, 76104
ZALE CORP. (M): 3000 Diamond Park Dr., Dallas, 75247
ZAPATA NORNESS INC.: 2000 Southwest Tower, Houston, 77002

UTAH

THE AMALGAMATED SUGAR CO. (I): 801 First Security Bank Bldg., Ogden, 84401.
ASSOCIATED FOOD STORES, INC. (I): 1812 S. Empire Rd., Salt Lake City, 84104
FIRST SECURITY CORP.: P.O. Box 390, Salt Lake City, 84110
IML FREIGHT, INC. (T): 2175 South 3270 West, Salt Lake City, 84110
SKAGGS COMPANIES, INC. (I): 1467 South Main, Salt Lake City, 84110
STEINER AMERICAN CORP. (S): 505 E. South Temple St., Salt Lake City, 84102
UTAH-IDAHO SUGAR CO.: 47 W. South Temple, Salt Lake City

VERMONT

NATIONAL LIFE INSURANCE CO. (LI): National Life Dr., Montpelier, 05602
VERMONT MARBLE CO.: Proctor, 05765

VIRGINIA

AMERICAN FURNITURE CO., INC. (I): Martinsville, 24112
APPALACHIAN POWER CO. (U): 40 Franklin Rd., Roanoke, 24009
BASSETT FURNITURE INDUSTRIES, INC. (I): Bassett, 24055
BINSWANGER GLASS CO. (I): 3300 W. Leigh St., Richmond, 23230
THE CHESAPEAKE CORP. OF VA. (I): West Point, 23181
CHESAPEAKE & POTOMAC TELEPHONE CO. OF VA. (U): 703 E. Grace St., Richmond, 23219
CRADDOCK-TERRY SHOE CORP. (I): 3100 Albert Lankford Dr., Lynchburg, 24505
DAN RIVER INC. (I): Danville, 24541
DOMINION BANKSHARES CORP. (B): 201 S. Jefferson St., Roanoke, 24011
DRUG FAIR, INC. (M): 6315 Bren Mar Dr., Alexandria, 22312
FIRESTONE SYNTHETIC FIBERS CO. (I): Hopewell, 23860
FIRST & MERCHANTS NATIONAL BANK (B): Ninth & Main St., Richmond, 23219
FIRST VIRGINIA BANK SHARES CORP. (B): 2924 Columbus Pike, Arlington, 22204
HOME BENEFICIAL LIFE INSURANCE CO. (LI): 3901 W. Broad St., Richmond, 23209
LANE CO., INC. (I): Altavista, 24517
LIFE INSURANCE CO. OF VIRGINIA (LI): 914 Capitol St., Richmond, 23219
MILLER & RHOADS DIVISION: Sixth & Broad St., Richmond, 23217
NEWPORT NEWS SHIPBUILDING & DRY DOCK CO. (I): 4101 Washington Ave., Newport News, 23607
NORFOLK SHIPBUILDING & DRYDOCK CORP. (I): P.O. Box 2100, Norfolk, 23501
OVERNITE TRANSPORTATION CO. (T): 1100 Commerce Rd., Richmond, 23224
OXFORD PAPER CO.: 330 S. Fourth St., Richmond, 23217
REYNOLDS METALS CO. (I): 6601 Broad St. Rd., Richmond, 23230
RICHMOND CORP.: 914 Capitol St., Richmond, 23209
ROBERTSHAW CONTROLS CO. (I): 1701 Byrd Ave., Richmond, 23226
ROBINS, A. H. CO., INC. (I): 1407 Cummings Dr., Richmond, 23220
SALE KNITTING CO., INC.: Moss St., Martinsville, 24112
SOUTHERN RAILWAY COMPANY (I): 14th & Canal St., Richmond, 23219
SOUTHERN STATES COOPERATIVE, INC. (I): Southern States Bldg., Richmond, 23213
THE SUSQUEHANNA CORP. (I): Shirley Hwy. & Edsall Rd., Alexandria, 22314
TIDEWATER CONSTRUCTION CORP. (I): Box 57, Norfolk, 23501
UNITED VIRGINIA BANKSHARES INC. (B): 900 E. Main St., Richmond, 23219
UNIVERSAL LEAF TOBACCO CO. (I): Hamilton St., at Broad, Richmond, 23230
VIRGINIA COMMONWEALTH BANKSHARES (B): 800 E. Main St., Richmond, 23219
VIRGINIA ELECTRIC & POWER CO. (U): 700 E. Franklin St., Richmond, 23216
VIRGINIA NATIONAL BANK (B): 1 Commercial Pl., Norfolk, 23510

WASHINGTON

ASSOCIATED GROCERS, INC. (M): 3301 S. Norfolk, Seattle, 98118
BOEING CO. (I): 7755 E. Marginal Way, Seattle, 98124
BON MARCHE (M): 3rd & Pine Sts., Seattle, 98101
GENERAL INSURANCE CO. OF AMERICA (LI): Safeco Insurance Bldg., Seattle, 98105
HEATH TECNA CORP. (I): 19819 84th, S., Kent, 98031
LONGVIEW FIBER CO. (I): Longview, 98632
OLYMPIA BREWING CO. (I): Box 947, Olympia, 98501
PACIFIC CAR & FOUNDRY CO. (I): 777 106th Ave., N.E., Bellevue, 98004
PACIFIC GAMBLE ROBINSON CO.: P.O. Box 3687, Seattle, 98124
PACIFIC NORTHWEST BELL TELEPHONE CO. (U): 821 Second Ave., Seattle, 98104
PEOPLES NATIONAL BANK OF WASHINGTON (B): 1414 4th Ave., Seattle, 98111
SAFECO CORP.: Safeco Insurance Bldg., Seattle, 98105
SAFECO INSURANCE CO. OF AMERICA (LI): Safeco Insurance Bldg., Seattle, 98105
SEATTLE-FIRST NATIONAL BANK (B): Box 3586, Seattle, 98124
VWR UNITED CORP. (I): 1600 Norton Bldg., Seattle, 98104
WASHINGTON NATURAL GAS CO. (U): 815 Mercer St., Seattle, 98111
WEYERHAEUSER CO. (I): Tacoma, 98401

WEST VIRGINIA

BLUEFIELD SUPPLY CO. (I): Bluefield, 24701
CHESAPEAKE & POTOMAC TELEPHONE CO. OF W. VA. (U): 1500 MacCorkle Ave., S.E., Charleston, 25314
MONONGAHELA POWER CO. (U): Monongahela Power Bldg., Fairmont, 26554
WEIRTON STEEL DIVISION (I): Weirton, 26062

WISCONSIN

ALLIS-CHALMERS CORP.: 1126 S. 70th St., Milwaukee, 53201
ALUMINUM SPECIALTY CO. (I): S. 16th & Wollmer St., Manitowoc, 54220
AMERICAN FAMILY MUTUAL INSURANCE CO. (LI): 3099 E. Washington Ave., Madison, 53704
APPLIED POWER INDUSTRIES INC. (I): P.O. Box 3100, Milwaukee, 53218
GEORGE BANTA CO. (S): Curtis Reed Plaza, Menasha, 54952
BATH INDUSTRIES, INC.: 2100 N. Mayfair Rd., Milwaukee, 53226
BELOIT CORP. (I): 1 St. Lawrence Ave., Beloit, 53511
BRIGGS & STRATTON CORP. (I): 3300 N. 124th St., Wauwatosa, 53201
BUCYRUS-ERIE CO.: South Milwaukee, 53172
BUTLER PAPER CO. (M): 100 Wisconsin River Dr., Port Edwards, 54469
J. I. CASE CREDIT CORP. (I): 700 State St., Racine, 53404
CLARK OIL & REFINING CORP. (I): 8530 W. National Ave., Milwaukee, 53227
CONSOLIDATED PAPERS, INC. (I): Wisconsin Rapids, Wisc., 54494
CUTLER-HAMMER INC. (I): 4201 N. 27th St., Milwaukee, 53216
EMPLOYERS MUTUAL LIABILITY INSURANCE CO. OF WISCON-SIN (LI): 2000 Westwood Dr., Wausau, 54401
FIRST WISCONSIN BANKSHARES CORP. (B): 735 N. Water St., Milwaukee, 53202
FIRST WISCONSIN NATIONAL BANK OF MILWAUKEE (B): 743 N. Water St., Milwaukee, 53202
GATEWAY TRANSPORTATION CO. (T): 2130 South Ave., La Crosse, 54601
GIDDINGS & LEWIS, INC. (I): 142 Doty St., Fond du Lac, 54935
GLOBE-UNION INC. (I): 5757 N. Green Bay Ave., Milwaukee, 53201
HAMILTON MFG. CO. (I): 1316 18th St., Two Rivers, 54241
HARNISCHFEGER CORP. (I): 4400 W. National Ave., Milwaukee, 53246
G. HEILEMAN BREWING CO., INC. (I): 925 S. Third St., La Crosse, 54601
S. C. JOHNSON & SON, INC. (I): 1525 Howe St., Racine, 53403
JOHNSON SERVICE CO. (I): 507 E. Michigan St., Milwaukee, 53201
KEARNEY & TRECKER CORP. (I): 11000 Theodore Trecker Way, Milwaukee, 53214

KIMBERLY-CLARK CORP. (I): N. Lake St., Neenah, 54956
KOEHRING CO.: 780 N. Water St., Milwaukee, 53202
KOHL CORP.: 11100 W. Burleigh St., Milwaukee, 53201
KOHLER CO. (I): Kohler, Wisc., 53044
MANPOWER, INC. (S): 820 N. Plankinton Ave., Milwaukee, 53201
MARINE CORP.: One Marine Plaza, Milwaukee, 53201
MARSHALL & ISLEY BANK STOCK CORP. (B): 770 N. Water St., Milwaukee, 53201
MEDALIST-INDUSTRIES, INC.: 111 E. Wisconsin Ave. — 1870 Marine Plaza, Milwaukee, 53202
GEO. J. MEYER MFG. CO. (I): Box 452, Milwaukee, 53201
MILLER BREWING CO. (I): 4000 W. State St., Milwaukee, 53208
MILPRINT INC. (I): 4200 N. Holton St., Milwaukee, 53201
MIRRO ALUMINUM CO. (I): 1512 Washington St., Manitowoc, 54220
MODINE MANUFACTURING CO. (I): 1500 De Koven Ave., Racine, 53403
NATIONAL PRESTO INDUSTRIES, INC. (I): Eau Claire, 54701
NEKOOSA EDWARDS PAPER CO., INC. (I): 100 Wisconsin River Dr., Port Edwards, 54469
NORDBERG MFG. CO. (I): 3073 S. Chase Ave., Milwaukee, 53207
OLD LINE LIFE INSURANCE CO. OF AMERICA (LI): 707 N. 11th St., Milwaukee, 53233
OSCAR MAYER & CO.: 910 Mayer Ave., Madison, 53701
JOHN OSTER MANUFACTURING CO. (I): 5055 N. Lydell Ave., Milwaukee, 53217
PABST BREWING CO. (I): 917 W. Juneau, Milwaukee, 53233
PARKER PEN CO. (I): 219 E. Court St., Janesville, 53546
R T E CORP. (I): 1900 E. North St., Waukesha, 53186

REX CHAINBELT INC. (I): 111 E. Wisconsin Ave., Milwaukee, 53201
JOS. SCHLITZ BREWING CO. (I): 235 W. Galena St., Milwaukee, 53201
SCHWERMAN TRUCKING CO. (T): 611 S. 28th St., Milwaukee, 53246
A. O. SMITH CORP. (I): 3533 N. 27th St., Milwaukee, 53216
SOLA BASIC INDUSTRIES, INC.: P.O. Box 753, Milwaukee, 53201
STA-RITE INDUSTRIES, INC. (I): 234 S. 8th St., Delavan, 53115
TRANE CO. (I): 3600 Pammel Creek Rd., La Crosse, 54601
TWIN DISC. INC. (I): 1328 Racine St., Racine, 53403
WALKER MFG. CO. (DEL.) (I): 1201 Michigan Blvd., Racine, 53402
WAUKESHA MOTOR CO. (I): W. St. Paul Ave., Waukesha, 53186
WESTERN PUBLISHING CO. (I): 1220 Mound Ave., Racine, 53404
WEYENBERG SHOE MFG. CO. (I): 234 E. Reservoir Ave., Milwaukee, 53201
WILL ROSS, INC. (I): P.O. Box 2012, Milwaukee, 53201
WISCONSIN ELECTRIC POWER CO. (U): 231 W. Michigan St., Milwaukee, 53201
WISCONSIN TELEPHONE CO. (U): 722 N. Broadway, Milwaukee, 53202

WYOMING

HUSKY OIL LTD. (I): Box 380, Cody, 82414
HUSKY OIL CO. (I): Box 380, Cody, 82414

7.

PERSONNEL AGENCIES

&

EXECUTIVE SEARCH FIRMS

YOUR USE OF PERSONNEL AGENCIES

The Types of Personnel Agencies

There will be many personnel agencies who have listings for jobs between $8,000 and $30,000. These firms can generally be divided into three categories; single industry agencies, functional agencies, and multi-industry agencies. Regardless of the particular category into which they fall, they will be of interest to the job hunter if they handle fee paid positions. These are the firms who accept listings for jobs to be filled on a contingency basis. They receive their fee from the companies when the firm hires an individual based upon the agency's referral.

Avoid Early Reliance on Agencies

You will definitely be able to generate interviews through personnel agencies. However, we recommend that you normally avoid contacting them until your campaign is under way. This is a particularly significant point and is actually the exact opposite of the approach taken by most job hunters. When many people decide to look for a new job, the first thing they will do is contact agencies. The immediate result is generally a discouragement about their own marketability. There are situations where these firms will actively represent job candidates. However, these types of situations are normally quite rare. Since job applicants are transients, these firms work at building long term client relationships and they concentrate on placing the most easily marketed candidates. If an individual happens to be available at a bargain price almost any agency will work hard to place him. However, most tend to give lip service to the individuals who seek a position offering substantially greater income.

Contact Agencies Only if You Seek $30,000 or Less

If your're in middle management and your salary requirements are not in excess of $30,000, you should consider contacting 3 to 5 of the better agencies when your campaign has been underway for over a month. (Note: A relatively small percentage of all agencies are effective for positions over $20,000, and even less for positions with salaries over $30,000.)

The delay of one month will enable you to refine your objectives and gain a much better understanding of your marketability. You may also be fortunate enough to find that you already have more interviews than your time schedule will permit.

The reason for contacting a number of agencies is simply to improve your chances of being submitted for attractive positions. It is generally quite unusual for agencies to get exclusive listings on an available position. While one agency may refuse to submit your resume to an employer, another may submit it immediately. Also remember that regardless of an agency's apparent enthusiasm over your qualifications, they usually like to submit a group of candidates to an employer. At the same time you should be extremely cautious of any decision to shot-gun your resume to dozens of agencies within one city. If you are not fortunate enough to rapidly land a position, this kind of action will probably eliminate any chances you have through them.

Be Selective in Choosing Agencies

In choosing agencies, it is important to be as selective as possible. Unfortunately, we can only suggest that you rely on what you can find out about other people's experiences with specific firms. Of course, an effective agency for one person can be the least effective for another. In any event you should be able to find out which agencies are most active in your specialty and have a good reputation in general. Despite licensing requirements, the agency firms in many areas have attracted a number of people of questionable ability. Some individuals have had experiences where their resumes ended up in the hands of their friends, their present employers, and sometimes their subordinates.

If you are unfamiliar with the agencies in a given city you might try contacting the major metropolitan newspaper. Since agencies are consistent advertisers, newspapers will frequently have a directory available which gives names and addresses, along with the agency areas of emphasis. In addition, personnel at the newspaper may give you some qualitative advice based on the experiences of others.

Some Agency People Can Greatly Assist You

In every city there is usually a group of truly fine personnel agencies. Among the top agencies there are exceptionally knowledgeable men and women with very broad contacts. If you can locate them (and this can be a problem) they can be of invaluable assistance if you develop a friendly relationship. In fact, while you are in junior management it will pay you to develop and maintain a good relationship over the years. In working with them it will pay you to be frank and honest, but to always project great confidence in your own worth. When you're actively job hunting be sure to maintain contact and follow-up weekly as the top people are likely to be very busy.

Contact Agencies by Mail

If you are on a fairly high level, you should be able to explore positions and quickly line-up interviews via phone. However, in most cases we suggest that you contact agencies by sending a letter and resume in answer to a specific listing. This way you will be less likely to spend time finding out that they did not have positions where you met the requirements. If possible, direct it by name to an individual or the president of the agency. When you send your material be sure to avoid having it arrive at the beginning of the week. Agencies are deluged with both mail and business at that time. Also insist that the agency contact you prior to forwarding your resume (or facts about your availability) to any company. There will be firms with employees to whom you do not wish to make your availability known.

Avoid Agency Forms

If you are at a senior level and only desire a fee-paid position, you should attempt to avoid completing too many agency forms. Completing these forms can be quite time consuming. In addition, some agencies have a very high turnover and the personal information in their files may come back to haunt you. At a more senior level you will probably find that agencies will not ask you to complete their application and sign their contract. However, if your letter does bring such a form in the mail, you can just write on it that they should see the resume and that you will consider fee-paid positions only. If your resume does not contain the complete information an agency needs, you should of course, write in the pertinent facts which are missing.

Summary Comments on Personnel Agencies

Personnel agencies can generally be of assistance if you seek a position at less than $30,000. A number of them should be selected with discretion and contacted only after your campaign is well under way. At junior levels, your actual contact should generally be made by mail, and in reference to a specific position they advertised. If possible, your correspondence should be directed by name and preferably to the agency president. If your salary improvement goals are modest, you will probably find them earnestly enthusiastic. However, if you seek a substantial increase, personnel agencies are not going to be the best vehicle for achieving your goal.

LIST OF MAJOR PERSONNEL AGENCIES

As previously indicated we strongly urge that you do not make blind selections of agencies to contact. As we have also pointed out we feel it is most wise to contact agencies in relation to a specific position which they advertised.

However, for the benefit of individuals who are out of the United States, and for those who seek to relocate great distances, we have listed major personnel agencies by geographical areas. This listing is not intended as an endorsement. It has been prepared through the courtesy of the National Employment Association which maintains an even more extensive listing covering their entire membership.

The listing produced here is far from all-inclusive. Nevertheless, it does provide the name, address, and owner of a significant number of agencies. The names of the individuals who are listed are either the owner, partner, or a manager of a given firm. They are included so that you may have a specific person to either write or phone.

Almost all of the listed agencies handle fee-paid positions in most professional areas. Those agencies serving limited occupational fields can be identified by their name. The codes which appear next to the agencies indicate that they are interested in candidates in the following areas:

AD = ADVERTISING
Account executives, art directors, copywriters, artists, graphic arts, radio and tv, publishing, sales promotion, market research, public relations, editorial, etc.

COMP = COMPUTER OPERATIONS
Electronic data processing, software development, software specialists, hardware specialists, programmers, computer operators, etc.

ED = EDUCATIONAL
Educational administrators, teachers, librarians, etc.

F = FINANCIAL
Controllers, accountants, purchasing agents, costs, credits and collection, banking, brokerage, etc.

FS = FULL SERVICE
All types of placements.

LEG = LEGAL
Attorneys, legal secretaries, legal assistants, etc.

MED = MEDICAL
Medical, pharmaceutical, nurses, nurses' aids, orderlies, therapists, technicians, etc.

NR = NURSES' REGISTRY
Private duty nursing, temporary nursing and other temporary hospital personnel

OFF ADM = OFFICE ADMINISTRATION
Administrators, executives, office managers, personnel administrators, insurance, etc.

OS = OVERSEAS

RE = RETAIL
Retail management, supervisors, and buyers, etc.

S = SALES
Merchandising, sales trainees, salesmen, sales managers, sales engineers, etc.

TE = TECHNICAL & ENGINEERING
Engineers, chemists, physicists, designers, draftsmen, technicians, plant managers, plant superintendents, etc.

ALABAMA

BIRMINGHAM

BIRMINGHAM JOB CENTER
1926 - 4th Ave., N., Room 209 35203
(205) 323-3455
Shelby J. Nelson/D. Walker
FS

DUNHILL OF BIRMINGHAM, INC.
2207 - 1st National - Sou. Nat. Bldg.
 35203
(205) 323-4471
Dudley E. Morgan
AD,COMP,F,LEG,MED,OFF ADM,RE,S,TE

SNELLING AND SNELLING
421 City Federal Bldg. 35203
(205) 328-5350
Ruth McDonald
COMP,F,FS,LEG,MED,RE,S,TE

SOUTHERN EMPLOYMENT AGENCY
801 Frank Nelson Bldg., 205 N. 20th St.
 35203
(205) 322-0646
Jo Ross
AD,COMP,F,FS,LEG,MED,OFF ADM,
 RE,S,TE

SP PERSONNEL ASSOCIATES OF
 BIRMINGHAM
1314 Central Bank Bldg. 35233
(205) 252-6171
Jackson C. Coker/William P. Simril
AD,COMP,F,OFF ADM,S,TE

HUNTSVILLE

DARRELL WALKER PERSONNEL
104 State National Bank Bldg. 35801
(205) 539-4136
Darrell Walker
AD,COMP,ED,F,FS,LEG,MED,OFF ADM,
 RE,S,TE

MOBILE

CAREER MANAGEMENT OF MOBILE,
 INC.
Suite 101, 1509 Government St. 36604
(205) 471-1471
John Malpas
AD,COMP,ED,F,FS,LEG,MED,OFF ADM,
 RE,S,TE

C/M WORLDWIDE PERSONNEL
 CONSULTANTS, INC.
Suite 2207, First National Bank Bldg.
 36602
(205) 433-7448
H. A. Peters, III

LONG'S PERSONNEL SERVICE, INC.
Suite 304, Commerce Bldg., 118 N. Royal
 St. 36602
(205) 433-9521
W. T. Long, CEC/G. F. Montiel
FS

SNELLING AND SNELLING OF MOBILE
1400 First National Bank Bldg. 36602
(205) 438-3695
P. R. Millner
AD,COMP,ED,F,LEG,MED,OFF ADM,
 RE,S,TE

MONTGOMERY

CAREER EMPLOYMENT AGENCY
Room 300, 125 Washington Bldg. 36104
(205) 269-2341
Katherine T. Thames
AD,COMP,F,LEG,MED,OFF ADM,
 RE,S,TE,

DARRELL WALKER PERSONNEL
7 Turner Pl. 36109
(205) 272-8590
Darrell H. Walker
AD,COMP,F,LEG,MED,OFF ADM,RE,
 S,TE

JOB CENTER
134 Dexter Ave. 36104
(205) 263-0203
FS

SNELLING AND SNELLING
312 Montgomery St. 36104
(205) 263-0581
J. Robert Thompson,
AD,COMP,ED,F,LEG,MED,OFF ADM,
 RE,S,TE

ALASKA

ANCHORAGE

H B EMPLOYMENT AGENCY
326 H St., Suite 1, 99501
(907) 279-5713, (907) 279-7823
Richard Hall
AD,COMP,F,FS,LEG,MED,Off ADM,
 RE,S,TE

NORTH EMPLOYMENT AGENCY,INC.
440 W. 5th Ave. 99501
(907) 279-6488
(Mrs.) Naomi L. Bowen/Robert O. Bowen
AD,COMP,F,FS,LEG,MED,OFF ADM,
 RE,S,TE

ARIZONA

PHOENIX

ABLE PERSONNEL CONSULTANTS
5108-C North 7th St. 85014
(602) 264-9561
George V. Rowe
AD,COMP,F,FS,ED,LEG,MED,OFF ADM,
 RE,S,TE

B & B EMPLOYMENT
Suite 512, 3550 N. Central Ave. 85012
(602) 277-3381
Robert L. Eno
AD,FS,LEG,MED,OFF ADM,RE,S

DOCTOR'S OFFICE PLACEMENT BUREAU
2025 North Central Ave. 85004
(602) 254-7069
(Mrs.) Elizabeth Hanley
MED,OFF ADM

DUNHILL OF PHOENIX, INC.
3550 N. Central Ave. 85012
(602) 264-1166
Robert D. Urquhart
COMP,F,LEG,OFF ADM,S,TE

FANNING PERSONNEL OF PHOENIX,
 INC.
3550 N. Central Ave., Suite 423 85012
(602) 263-5656
Clinton W. Petersen
AD,COMP,ED,F,LEG,MED,OFF ADM,
 RE,S,TE

FAR WESTERN PLACEMENT BUREAU
812 N. 1st St. 85004
(602) 252-1441
Vera B. Grady
AD,COMP,F,LEG,OFF ADM,RE,S,TE

PROFESSIONAL PLACEMENT, INC.
112 N. Central Ave., Suite #400 85004
(602) 254-7358
M. J. "Chic" Reistad
AD,COMP,ED,F,FS,LEG,MED,OFF ADM,
 OS,RE,S,TE

SNELLING AND SNELLING
111 W. Monroe St., Suite 320 85003
(602) 254-5151
Paul P. Payne/Robert Graef
AD,COMP,ED,F,FS,LEG,MED,OFF ADM,
 OS,RE,S,TE

SNELLING AND SNELLING
3424 N. Central Ave. 85012
(602) 264-9955
William C. Conover/Kathryn Ford
AD,COMP,ED,F,LEG,MED,OFF ADM,
 RE,S,TE

WESTERN PERSONNEL ASSOCIATES
3800 N. Central Ave., Suite 604 85012
(602) 279-5301
Ted Stump/Bob MacDonald
COMP,F,LEG,MED,OFF ADM,S,TE

SCOTTSDALE

SCOTTSDALE EMPLOYMENT AGENCY
7220 E. 1st Ave. (PIMA Plaza) 85251
(602) 947-7578
Richard A. Hutchinson/Walt Dahlman
AD,COMP,F,LEG,MED,OFF ADM,RE,
 S,TE

SNELLING AND SNELLING PERSONNEL
77 Third Ave. West 85251
(602) 947-5456
Leslie J. Harness
AD,COMP,ED,F,FS,LEG,MED,OFF ADM,
 RE,S,TE

ARIZONA—Continued

TUCSON

HALLMARK PERSONNEL CONSULTANTS, INC.
5648 E. Broadway 85711
(602) 885-2345
Roy J. Miller/Lou Carlin
AD,COMP,F,FS,OFF ADM,RE,S,TE

PERSONNEL SYSTEMS
2343 E. Broadway, Suite 114 85719
(602) 623-4260
James N. Coco
AD,COMP,ED,F,FS,LEG,MED,OFF ADM,
RE,S,TE

PROFESSIONAL PLACEMENT, INC.
2030 E. Broadway, Suite 220 85719
(602) 792-0382
M. J. "Chic" Reistad
AD,COMP,ED,F,FS,LEG,MED,OFF ADM,
OS,RE,S,TE

SNELLING AND SNELLING
1016 E. Broadway 85719
(602) 792-0622
Paul P. Payne/Eugene C. Stuessy
AD,COMP,ED,F,FS,LEG,MED,OFF ADM,
OS,RE,S,TE

SNELLING AND SNELLING
2227 E. Broadway 85719
(602) 623-3405
Paul P. Payne/Rosemary Linsley
AD,COMP,ED,F,FS,LEG,MED,OFF ADM,
OS,RE,S,TE

ARKANSAS

LITTLE ROCK

AMERICAN EMPLOYMENT AGENCY,INC.
719 University Tower Bldg. 72204
(501) 664-0729
Margaret Lucas
FS

CONTINENTAL EMPLOYMENT AGENCY, INC.
285 Tower Building 72201
(501) 375-9121
Roy E. Meadows
AD,COMP,ED,F,FS,LEG,MED,OFF ADM,
RE,S,TE

RICE EMPLOYMENT AGENCY
1408 Donaghy Bldg. 72201
(501) 372-5201
Peyton E. Rice, CEC
FS

CALIFORNIA

ALHAMBRA

ALHAMBRA EMPLOYMENT AGENCY
106 S. Chapel St. 91801
(213) 283-3691
Mabel Erpelding
F,IND,MED,S

ALHAMBRA PHYSICIANS & NURSES REGISTRY
1041 S. Garfield 91801
Gertrude Levasseur
FS

THE TOWER PERSONNEL AGENCY
100 E. Huntington Dr., Suite 204 91801
(213) 289-5025
Claire Towery
FS

BAKERSFIELD

KERN EMPLOYMENT AGENCY
Suite 216, 1522 18th St. 93301
(805) 327-8433
Betty Jo Cox
COMP,F,FS,LEG,MED,OFF ADM,RE,
S,TE

KOLB PERSONNEL AGENCY
Great Western Savings Bldg. 1415 - 18th St.
93301
(805) 327-7251
Robert N. Kolb
FS

BERKELEY

ALTA PERSONNEL AGENCY
809 American Trust Bldg., 2140 Shattuck
Ave. 94704
(415) 843-2491
Charm Brown
AD,COMP,F,LEG,MED,OFF ADM,RE,
S,TE

BEVERLY HILLS

BEVERLY-CROSS AGENCY
9405 Brighton Way 90210
(213) 274-8931
Jean McCart/Shirley Robertson
AD,COMP,F,LEG,OFF ADM,S

MARDI MAY AGENCY
9363 Wilshire Blvd. 90210
(213) 272-0291
Marjorie M. May
AD,COMP,F,LEG,OFF ADM

FRESNO

RELIABLE AGENCY OF FRESNO, INC.
1015 Fulton Mall 93721
(209) 266-9777
(Mrs.) Sunny Shapiro
AD,COMP,ED,F,FS,LEG,MED,OFF ADM,
RE,S,TE

GLENDALE

COURTNEY NURSES REGISTRY
211-G East Broadway 91205
(213) 247-6233
Rhea Littrell/Carveta Laurie
NR

EMPLOYMENT RESEARCH AGENCY, INC.
946 North Brand Blvd. 91202
(213) 243-2154
Gordon Scott
AD,COMP,ED,F,FS,LEG,MED,OFF ADM,
RE,S,TE

HOLLYWOOD

FRANCES LEE AGENCY
1741 N. Ivar, Suite 108 90028
Grant Evans
FS

LONG BEACH

FLO BAILEY AGENCIES
4270 Long Beach Blvd., Suite C 90807
(213) 636-3372, (213) 422-0471
Flo Bailey/T. D. Bradbury
FS

PROSPECTORS EMPLOYMENT AGENCY
3413 E. 7th St. 90804 213-434-3401
John V. Johnson, Jr.
FS

SNELLING AND SNELLING LONG BEACH AGENCY
110 Pine Ave., Suite #308 90802
(213) 437-0911
Don Conger
FS

LOS ANGELES

A-1 NURSES REGISTRY
6430 Sunset Blvd. 90028
(213) 462-7293
John Patterson/K. T. Arnold
MED

ACADEMY AGENCY
610 S. Broadway 90014
(213) 626-8631
Ann Stephenson
AD

BRENTWOOD NURSES REGISTRY
1736 Westwood Blvd. 90024
(213) 474-3563
John H. Broders
NR

DUNHILL OF LOS ANGELES AGENCY, INC.
3670 Wilshire Blvd. 90005
(213) 385-5261
John M. Thompson
AD,F,S,TE

EXCLUSIVELY INSURANCE PERSONNEL AGENCY
1636 W. 8th St. 90017
(212) 381-5258
Will Cornell
OFF ADM,OS

CALIFORNIA—Continued

HELEN EDWARDS & STAFF AGENCY
3105 Wilshire Blvd. 90005
(213) 388-0493
Helen Edwards
AD,ED,F,FS,LEG,OFF ADM,RE,S,TE

JEAN KERR AGENCY
117 W. 9th St. 90015
(213) 627-2808
Leslie S. Victor
AD,F,LEG,OFF ADM,RE,S,TE

L. A. MEDICAL BUREAU AGENCY
756 S. Broadway 90014
(213) 627-5618
B. Linn Faylor
CL,F,MED,OFF ADM

LIFE AGENCY
412 W. 6th St., Suite 820 90014
(213) 628-7101
W. E. Lambright/F. R. Logan/William Taylor
AD,COMP,F,LEG,MED,OFF ADM,S,TE

LUCILLE COOK EMPLOYMENT AGENCY
633 Shatto Place, Suite #207 90005
(213) 386-4080
Lucile Cook Salas/Lois C. Dewey
CL,F,LEG,OFF ADM

**NURSES REGISTRY OF WEST
  LOS ANGELES**
11753 Wilshire Blvd. 90025
(213) 479-5050
Gifford H. Ormes/Matilda S. Ormes
NR

J. R. PIERSE ASSOCIATES AGENCY, INC.
3960 Wilshire Blvd. 90010 213-386-1276
Arthur Forsman
TE,AD,COMP,ED,F,LEG,OFF ADM,RE,S

**ROTH YOUNG PERSONNEL SERVICE OF
  LOS ANGELES, INC.**
3960 Wilshire Blvd. 90010
(213) 386-6402
James Bright
COMP,LEG,AD,F,MED,OFF ADM,RE,
  S,TE

SAINT AGATHA NURSES REGISTRY
11600 Wilshire Blvd. 90025
(213) 478-0127
Monica Storie
NR

SALES CONSULTANTS, INC.
3550 Wilshire Blvd., Suite 920-926 90005
(213) 381-7021
E. E. Pearlman
S

**SMILE PERSONNEL AGENCY
  (R.E.L. ENTERPRISES, INC.)**
3850 Wilshire Blvd. 90010
(213) 384-2583
Richard Lewis
FS

SPECIALIZED PERSONNEL AGENCY
3960 Wilshire Blvd., Suite 502 90010
(213) 386-1310
Euna G. Whelan
F,OFF ADM

V.I.P. AGENCY, INC.
3960 Wilshire Blvd., Suite 301 90005
(213) 380-9990
Edwin H. Herzog
FS

YAMATO EMPLOYMENT AGENCY
312 E. First St., Suite 202 90012
(213) 624-2821
(Mrs.) Chiyo S. Yamato
AD,COMP,F,FS,LEG,MED,OFF ADM,
  S,TE

OAKLAND

BLOCK AGENCIES, INC.
436 - 14th St., Suite 414 94612
(415) 832-1561
E. Coffey Dildine
AD,COMP,F,LEG,OFF ADM,RE,S,TE

KRAFFT PERSONNEL AGENCY
436 - 14th St., 94612
(415) 835-9200
Richard H. Krafft
COMP,F,LEG,OFF ADM,RE,S,TE

LOCAL EMPLOYMENT SERVICE AGENCY
436 - 14th St., Suite 711 94612
(415) 893-7444
Betty Black
F,FS,LEG,MED,OFF ADM,S,TE

OAKLAND AGENCY
405 - 14th St. (Terrace) 94612
Richard H. Taher
COMP,F,LEG,MED,OFF ADM,RE,S,TE

**SNELLING AND SNELLING CAL-OAK
  AGENCY**
2150 Franklin St. 94612
(415) 835-8550
Robert E. Smith
AD,COMP,ED,F,LEG,MED,OFF ADM,
  OS,RE,S,TE

PALO ALTO

CHARLES EMPLOYMENT AGENCY
495 Calif. Ave. 94306
(415) 326-5340
Charles Cinegran
AD,COMP,F,FS,IND,MED,OFF ADM,
  RE,S

**PALO ALTO SNELLING AND SNELLING
  PERSONNEL AGENCY**
499 Hamilton Ave. 94301
(415) 324-2711
Wesley K. Graves
AD,F,FS,LEG,MED,OFF ADM,RE,S,TE

PEGGY ULRICH PERSONNEL AGENCY
467 Hamilton Ave. 94301
(415) 324-1361
Peggy Ulrich
AD,COMP,F,LEG,MED,OFF ADM,TE

PASADENA

CARVER AGENCY
1245 E. Walnut St. 91106
(213) 792-7187
(Miss) Marylu Uppinghouse
FS

EMPLOYMENT RESEARCH AGENCY, INC.
1470 E. Walnut St. 91106
(213) 795-8411
Fern Cawley
AD,COMP,ED,F,FS,LEG,MED,OFF ADM,
  RE,S,TE

EMPLOYMENT RESEARCH AGENCY, INC.
1000 E. Walnut St. 91106
(213) 795-8426
Ross W. Winans

J. R. PIERCE ASSOCIATES AGENCY, INC.
521 E. Green 91101
(213) 795-7721
J. R. Pierce
F,TE,COMP,ED,LEG,OFF ADM,RE,S,AD

PASADENA NURSES REGISTRY
1991 E. Villa St. 91107
(213) 792-2103
Jeanette C. Stuhr
COMP,F,FS,MED,NR

SACRAMENTO

NORTH AREA AGENCY
2720 Arden Way, Room 170 95825
(916) 482-8070
Vera May Richards
FS

SAN DIEGO

ACTION EMPLOYMENT AGENCY
3108 - 5th Ave. 92103
(714) 297-5027
M. C. "Keith" Keithley
COMP,F,FS,LEG,MED,OFF ADM,RE,
  S,TE

ADVANCE EMPLOYMENT AGENCY
Suite 703 Home Tower, 707 Broadway
  92101
(714) 232-2955
Esther P. Green
COMP,ED,F,LEG,MED,OFF ADM,S,TE

CHADWICK AGENCIES, INC.
P.O. Box 3608 92103
(714) 291-3500
James Chadwick/(Miss) Maureen O'Neill
FS

CALIFORNIA—Continued

DOCTORS SERVICE BUREAU, INC.
3427 Fourth Ave. 92103
(714) 298-8261
Charles E. Jackson
MED,NR

EXECUTIVE PERSONNEL AGENCY
964 Fifth Ave. 92101
(714) 239-1118
Sally Flaherty/Victor M. Flaherty
AD,COMP,ED,F,FS,LEG,MED,OFF ADM,
RE,S,TE

SNELLING AND SNELLING AGNECY
OF SAN DIEGO
1007 - 5th Ave. 92101
(714) 232-8941
Glen A. English
AD,COMP,F,LEG,MED,OFF ADM,RE,S

SAN FRANCISCO

A-1 NURSES REGISTRY
655 Sutter St. 94102
(415) 474-7005
Maxime Taylor/Elizabeth Price
NR

HARPER ASSOCIATES
44 Montgomery St. 94104
(415) 989-6111
R. A. Evans
COMP,F,OFF ADM,S,TE

NINA ATKINSON AGENCY
625 Market St. 94105
(415) 421-4070
Donald M. Holley
FS

NORTHERN CALIFORNIA
MANAGEMENT RECRUITERS
One California St., Suite 925 94111
(415) 981-5950
W. Lorin Parmalee/Thomas W. Brown
AD,COMP,F,LEG,OFF ADM,RE,S,TE

PRO-FIND COMPUTER PERSONNEL
AGENCY
444 Market St. 94111
(415) 434-3851
Leonard Nawak
FS

ROBERT HALF PERSONNEL AGENCIES
111 Pine St. 94111
(415) 434-1900
Frank Davidson
F,COMP

SALES CONSULTANTS, INC.
1 Maritime Plaza 94111
(415) 421-9540
Robert J. Hansen
S

SAN FRANCISCO PLACEMENT
AGENCY, INC.
593 Market St., Suite 800 94105
(415) 421-2043
James T. Rubey/Raye A. Murray/
Jane L. Rubey
AD,COMP,F,LEG,OFF ADM,RE,S,TE

TALENT PERSONNEL AGENCY
742 Market St. 94102
(415) 982-3858
Jo Eskridge Smith
AD,COMP,F,FS,LEG,MED,OFF ADM,
RE,S,TE

WESTERN EMPLOYERS SERVICE
870 Market St. 94102
(415) 362-4186
(Mrs.) Bette Oxborrow Root
FS

SAN JOSE

METRO EMPLOYMENT AGENCY
1760 The Alameda, Suite 200 95126
(408) 294-5684
Clive N. Ross
AD,COMP,F,FS,MED,OFF ADM,RE,S,TE

RESULTS EMPLOYMENT AGENCY
1654 The Alameda 95126
(408) 295-5647
Frederic A. Naglestad
AD,COMP,F,LEG,MED,OFF ADM,RE,S,TE

ROBERT HALF PERSONNEL AGENCIES
675 N. First St., 95112
(408) 293-9040
Stanley S. Ings
F,COMP

SAN JOSE SNELLING AND SNELLING,
INC.
111 West St. John St. 95113
(408) 286-0137
Joyce Gleeson
AD,COMP,F,LEG,OFF ADM,RE,S,TE

TREND PERSONNEL AGENCY
1671 The Alameda, Suite 206 95126
(408) 297-5153
(Mrs.) Lys Brinker
COMP,F,LEG,OFF ADM,S,TE

SANTA ANA

MAIN STREET EMPLOYMENT
AGENCY, INC.
215 S. Main St. 92701
835-5383
Eugene E. Sied
FS

SNELLING & SNELLING AGNECY
OF SANTA ANA
1666 N. Main, #330 92701
(714) 543-0190
Marilyn R. Ceiley/John P. Wenzelberger
FS

COLORADO

BOULDER

SNELLING AND SNELLING
1245 Pearl 80302
(303) 444-5770
Frederick D. Clark
FS

COLORADO SPRINGS

WESTERN PERSONNEL PLACEMENTS,
INC.
116 N. Tejon, Suite 302 80904
(303) 635-3531
James L. Oxford
AD,COMP,ED,F,FS,LEG,MED,OFF ADM,
RE,S,TE

DENVER

ACME EMPLOYMENT METHOD
711 - 17th St. 80202
(303) 825-2347
Robert P. Rickert
FS,MED

BUSINESS MEN'S CLEARING HOUSE, INC.
520 Midland Savings Bldg. 80202
(303) 534-0271
John E. Green
AD,COMP,F,OFF ADM,RE,S,TE

EMPIRE EMPLOYERS SERVICE, INC.
Suite 110 Capitol Life Center 80203
(303) 222-8646
Orise Gaudreault
AD,COMP,F,FS,LEG,OS,TE

HALLMARK PERSONNEL OF COLORADO,
INC.
1612 Tremont Pl. 80202
(303) 892-0422
Joe Sweeney
AD,COMP,F,LEG,OFF ADM,RE,S,TE

HIGHLAND PLACEMENT SERVICE
240 Josephine 80206
(303) 399-8044
Alan L. Detwiler
AD,COMP,ED,F,FS,LEG,MED,OFF ADM,
RE,S,TE

KEY PERSONNEL SERVICE, INC.
888 Federal Blvd. 80204
(303) 892-0273
Bill Wilderson/Frank Shissler
AD,F,OFF ADM,RE,S,TE

LARSON EMPLOYMENT SERVICE
490 Denver Club Bldg., 518 - 17th St. 80202
(303) 222-4621
John D. Travis, Jr./Elsie R. Travis
FS

MARGARET HOOK'S PERSONNEL, INC.
280 Columbine St. 80206
(303) 355-2308
Margaret Hook
AD,COMP,F,LEG,OFF ADM

COLORADO—Continued

**MARIE SMITH'S EMPLOYMENT
SERVICE, INC.**
1207 Broadway 80203
(303) 244-2424
Marie Smith
FS

MILE-HI EMPLOYMENT AGENCY, INC.
1505 Grant St. 80203
(303) 623-6156
(Miss) Rine Smith/Ann Williams
AD,COMP,F,LEG,MED,OFF ADM,S

MOUNTAIN STATES PLACEMENT
509 - 17th St., First Nat'l Bank Bldg.,
Suite 306 80202
(303) 266-2165
Robert H. Hyndman,
AD,COMP,F,LEG,OFF ADM,S,TE

OFFICE PLACEMENT SERVICE, INC.
116 Security Life Bldg. 80202
(303) 266-2373
Cora H. West/Joni Van Portfliet
AD,COMP,ED,F,LEG,MED,OFF ADM,S

OLYMPIA ASSOCIATES
4401 E. Yale Ave. 80222
(303) 757-3311
Thomas S. Dunn
FS

PETERSON EMPLOYMENT CONSULTANTS
710 Security Life Bldg. 80202
(303) 222-5749
A. E. "Pete" Peterson
F,OFF ADM,S

PHILLIPS PERSONNEL SERVICE
818 - 17th St., Suite 314 80202
(303) 292-1850
Phil Heinschel
AD,COMP,ED,F,FS,LEG,MED,OFF ADM,
RE,S,TE

PLACEMENTS, INC.
Western Federal Savings Bldg.
17th and California Sts. 80202
(303) 244-4133
Ted K. Cobb
AD,COMP,F,LEG,MED,OFF ADM,OS,
RE,S,TE

**ROBERT HALF PERSONNEL AGENCIES
OF DENVER, INC.**
1612 Court Place, Suite 534 80202
(303) 244-2925
Sig Levisohn
F,COMP,OFF ADM

SALES CONSULTANTS, INC.
909 - 17th St., Suite 533 80202
(303) 292-9400
Ronald D. Sampson
S,TE

**SNELLING AND SNELLING PERSONNEL
CONSULTANTS**
817 — 17th St. 80202
(303) 266-3581
A. Robert Strawn
AD,COMP,ED,F,LEG,OFF ADM,RE,
S,TE MED

STAFF EMPLOYMENT SERVICE
718 - 17th St., Suite 1550, Western Federal
Savings Bldg. 80202
(303) 266-3171
William G. Dale, Jr.
AD,COMP,F,LEG,MED,OFF ADM,S,TE

WELLEY BUSINESS PERSONNEL
810 Midland Savings Bldg. 80202
(303) 534-0186
Norman A. Welley/Lee Welley
AD,COMP,F,LEG,OFF ADM,S,TE

GREELEY

SNELLING AND SNELLING
316 Hested Bldg., 8th Ave. & 8th St. 80631
(303) 353-4743
Willene B. Venable
F,LEG,MED,OFF ADM,RE,S,TE

CONNECTICUT

BRIDGEPORT

AAA PERSONNEL ASSOCIATES
4695 Main St. 06606
(203) 374-5588
Louis C. Klein/Ellie Kay
AD,COMP,F,FS,LEG,MED,OFF ADM,
RE,S,TE

**DUNHILL OF BRIDGEPORT —
NEW HAVEN, INC.**
4695 Main St. 06606
(203) 374-5576
Herbert K. Wischow
AD,COMP,ED,F,FS,LEG,OFF ADM,RE,
S,TE

**ROBERT McGRATH PROFESSIONAL
STAFFING & DESIGN SERVICE**
49 Plaza 06603
Robert C. McGrath
FS

SNELLING & SNELLING-BRIDGEPORT
114 State St. 06603
(203) 333-6146
Harold J. Lemkin
AD,COMP,ED,F,LEG,MED,OFF ADM,RE,
S,TE

FAIRFIELD

**TAYLOR ASSOCIATES CAREER COUN-
SELING AND PLACEMENT SERVICE**
1424 Post Road 06430
(203) 255-4588
(Mrs.) Beth E. Taylor
FS

HARTFORD

BK ASSOCIATES
75 Pearl St. 06103
(203) 527-9107
Barbara S. Kupferschmid
FS

**DAVID BRUCE PERSONNEL SYSTEMS,
INC.**
179 Allyn St. 06103
(203) 549-4600
Edwin S. Ross/David V. Francis
FS

**ETHAN ALLEN PERSONNEL
PLACEMENT OF HARTFORD**
18 Asylum St. 06103
(203) 547-1950
David J. Levine
FS

**GILBERT LANE PERSONNEL AGENCY,
INC.**
750 Main St., Suite 1110 06103
(203) 278-7700
Howard Specter
FS

RICHARD P. RITA PERSONNEL SYSTEM
60 Washington St., Suite 1308 06106
(203) 278-0000
Richard P. Rita
AD,COMP,F,LEG,MED,OFF ADM,RE,
S,TE

SNELLING AND SNELLING
242 Trumbull St. 06103
(203) 527-2651
Albert W. Biondi
AD,COMP,F,LEG,OFF ADM,RE,S,TE

UNI/SEARCH OF HARTFORD, INC.
15 Lewis St. 06103
(203) 278-8040
Pierce Clayberger
AD,COMP,F,LEG,MED,OFF ADM,RE,
S,TE

WILSON AGENCY
11 Asylum St. 06103
(203) 246-8541
Charles J. Anthony
FS

NEW HAVEN

**SNELLING AND SNELLING OF
NEW HAVEN**
35 Center St. 06510
(203) 624-2101
Gilbert T. McCrea
COMP,F,LEG, OFF ADM,RE,S,TE

UNI/SEARCH OF NEW HAVEN, INC.
246 Church St. 06510
(203) 777-6601
Carl Kamphausen
AD,COMP,F,LEG,OFF ADM,RE,S,TE

CONNECTICUT—Continued

WALTER J. ZACKRISON ASSOCIATES OF NEW HAVEN, INC.
900 Chapel St. 06510
(203) 772-1070
Walter J. Zackrison
AD,CL,COMP,F,FS,IND,LEG,OFF ADM,
RE,S,TE

NORWALK

BAILEY EMPLOYMENT SERVICE OF NORWALK
83 Wall St. 06850
(203) 838-4845
John Mac Neil
FS

RICHARD P. RITA PERSONNEL SERVICES
71 East Ave. 06851 (203) 838-4181
Marilynn S. Anderson
AD,COMP,ED,F,LEG,MED, OFF ADM,OS,
RE,S,TE

SNELLING AND SNELLING
64 Wall St. 06850
(203) 853-1281
Barbara Gabrys
AD,COMP,ED,F,LEG,MED,OFF ADM,RE,
S,TE,

STAMFORD

MANAGEMENT RECRUITERS
111 High Ridge Rd. 06905
(203) 327-4770
Arthur S. High
AD,COMP,F,LEG,OFF ADM,S,TE

ROBERT HALF PERSONNEL AGENCIES OF STAMFORD, INC.
111 Prospect St.
Daniel K. Roberts
F,COMP

SNELLING AND SNELLING
695 Summer St. 06901
(203) 325-4187
Dorothy DuBow
AD,COMP,ED,F,LEG,MED,OFF ADM,RE,
S,TE

DELAWARE

DOVER

MID-DEL EMPLOYMENT SERVICE
205 Bank of Delaware Bldg., P.O. Box 82
 19901
(302) 734-5921
George P. Brett, III
FS

WILMINGTON

BERNARD & BERNARD
902 Orange St. 19801
(302) 655-4491
Al Bernard
AD,COMP,F,FS,LEG,OFF ADM,RE,S,TE

CASEY EMPLOYMENT SERVICE CORP.
820 West St. 19801
(302) 658-6461
Andrew Jack Casey
AD,COMP,ED,F,LEG,OFF ADM,RE,S,TE

SNELLING AND SNELLING
917 Washington St. 19801
(302) 652-3711
N. Norman Schutzman
AD,COMP,ED,F,FS,LEG,MED,OFF ADM,
RE,S,TE

DISTRICT OF COLUMBIA

WASHINGTON

ABART EMPLOYMENT CENTER
1841 - 14th St., N.W. 20009
(202) 462-7671
Thaddeus T. Jones
FS

ALBERS PERSONNEL, INC.
1735 K St., N.W. 20006
(202) 659-5791
Robert C. Graebner/Barbara A. Toms
AD,COMP,ED,F,LEG,MED,OFF ADM,
RE, S, TE

AMERICAN PERSONNEL SERVICES
1701 K St., N.W. 20006
(202)638-6404
Don E. Springer
AD,COMP,ED,F,FS,LEG,MED,OFF ADM,
RE,S,TE

ATLAS PERSONNEL AGENCY, INC.
1660 L St., N.W., Suite 309 20036
(202) 293-7210
Allen Kipnis/Benjamin Kipnis
AD,COMP,ED,F,LEG,OFF ADM,RE,S,TE

BETTY GRAY PERSONNEL
1730 K St., N.W., 1102 Riddell Bldg. 20006
(202) 659-9270
Ruth Osborne Arens, CEC/Robert C.
 Graebner
LEG, OFF ADM

BOB GRAY, INC.
839 - 17th St., N.W., Suite 200 20006
(202) 638-4277
Robert C. Graebner/Myra Lenard
AD,COMP,F,LEG,OFF ADM,RE,S,TE

CAREERS BY HOLIDAY
1120 Conn. Ave., N.W., Suite 1242 20036
(202) 833-9450
Doris Holiday (Rishty)
FS

DUNHILL PERSONNEL SYSTEM
1025 Vermont Ave., N.W. 20005
(202) 737-2315
Norman Rosenberg
AD,F,FS,OFF ADM,S,TE

EASTERN EMPLOYMENT SERVICE OF WASHINGTON
15th & H Sts., N.W., Suite 426
 Woodward Bldg. 20005
(202) 737-2513
Stephen A. Land/David S. Hoffman
AD,COMP,F,LEG,OFF ADM,RE,S,TE

FANNING PERSONNEL OF WASHINGTON, D.C., INC.
1430 K St., N.W. 20005
(202) 347-5716
Peter J. Accorti
F,OFF ADM

GILBERT PERSONNEL, INC.
1001 Conn. Ave., N.W. 20036
(202) 393-7977
Patrick W. Dyer/Robert C. Graebner
F,FS,OFF ADM,S

MANAGEMENT BUREAU, INC.
724 - 14th St., N.W. 20005
(202) 393-6500
David R. Harrison
FS

PRESS EMPLOYMENT SERVICE
1182 National Press Bldg. 20004
(202) 638-1232
Ben Hooten
AD

PROFESSIONAL PLACEMENT SERVICE
1835 Eye St., N.W. 20006
(202) 737-7633
Mario E. Zampiello
MED

PROFESSIONAL STAFFING SERVICES
919 - 18th St., N.W., Suite 620 20006
(202) 296-4571
William Oberfelder
AD,COMP,F,FS,LEG,OFF ADM,S,TE

SNELLING AND SNELLING OF WASHINGTON, INC.
1341 G St., N.W. 20005
(202) 783-6888
Spencer Wood
AD,COMP,ED,F,LEG,OFF ADM,OS,
S,TE

TOM McCALL & ASSOCIATES OF WASHINGTON
1750 Pennsylvania Ave., N.W. 20006
(202) 298-9086
Charley Greene/John Mulholland
S

TPC PERSONNEL
1030 - 15th St., N.W., Suite #752 20005
(202) 296-7210
Robert L. Philipson
AD,COMP,F,FS,LEG,OFF ADM,S,TE

DISTRICT OF COLUMBIA—
Continued

BETHESDA, MD.

FORREST PERSONNEL, INC.
7401 Wisconsin Ave. 20014
(301) 656-3812
Robert C. Graebner/Mary L. Williamson
AD,COMP,F,FS,LEG,MED,OFF ADM,RE,
S,TE

SILVER SPRING, MD.

ALLEN-O'BRIEN ASSOCIATES
2929 Beaverwood Lane 20906
(202) 347-7301
Kenneth A. Elbert, II
FS

**CARTER HILL PERSONNEL OF
SILVER SPRING**
8121 Georgia Ave. 20910
FS

GUARDIAN PERSONNEL, INC.
8605 Cameron St. 20910
(301) 588-3144
Robert C. Graebner/Barbara A. Toms/
Irene Dennis
AD,COMP,ED,F,LEG,MED,OFF ADM,
RE,S,TE

ALEXANDRIA, VA.

GUARANTY EMPLOYMENT AGENCY
4105 Duke St. 22304
(703) 751-0600
Murray W. Kliger
FS,AD,COMP,ED,F,LEG,MED,OFF ADM,
RE,S,TE

OLD DOMINION EMPLOYMENT AGENCY
121 N. Washington St. 22314
(703) 548-3311
(Mrs.) Tracy B. Diggs
AS,F,TE

POTOMAC EMPLOYMENT AGENCY, INC.
201 N. Washington St. 22314
(703) 549-5055
(Mrs.) Harold Greene
AD,COMP,ED,F,FS,LEG,MED,OFF ADM,
S,TE

**SNELLING AND SNELLING OF
ALEXANDRIA, VIRGINIA**
100 N. Pitt St. 22314
(703) 836-8100
W. H. Armstrong
FS

ARLINGTON, VA.

GUARANTY EMPLOYMENT AGENCY
704 N. Glebe Rd. 22203
(703) 525-5535
Murray W. Kliger
FS,AD,COMP,ED,F,LEG,MED,OFF ADM,
RE,S,TE

OLD DOMINION EMPLOYMENT AGENCY
2420 Wilson Blvd. 22201
(703) 522-3100
(Mrs.) Tracy B. Diggs
AD,COMP,ED,F,LEG,MED,OFF ADM,RE,
S,TE

POTOMAC EMPLOYMENT AGENCY, INC.
2440 Wilson Blvd. 22201
(703) 525-2000
(Mrs.) Harold Greene
AD,COMP,ED,F,FS,LEG,MED,OFF ADM,
S,TE

SNELLING AND SNELLING
927 S. Walter Reed Dr. 22204
(703) 521-3810
Howard Shiflett
FS

FLORIDA

CORAL GABLES

EMPLOYMENT BUREAU, INC.
2312 Salzedo St. 33134
(305) 448-7411
Donald L. Comstock
AD,COMP,ED,F,LEG,MED,OFF ADM,
OS,RE,S,TE

FORT LAUDERDALE

SNELLING AND SNELLING
305 S. Andrews Ave. 33301
(305) 525-8582
E. S. Goodrich
AD,COMP,ED,F,LEG,MED,OFF ADM,OS,
RE,S,TE

GAINESVILLE

PERSONNEL CENTER
West Side of Florida National Bank Building
11 N.W. 2nd St., Suite 3, P.O. Box 1111
32601
(904) 372-6377
(Mrs.) Marion Voyles
AD,CL,COMP,ED,F,LEG,MED,OFF ADM,
RE,S,TE

JACKSONVILLE

BRODEUR PERSONNEL SERVICE, INC.
2747 Art Museum Dr. 32207
(904) 396-6902
Walter P. Friend
AD,COMP,F,FS,LEG,OFF ADM,RE,S,TE

THE JOBFINDERS
1372 Cassat Ave. 32205
(904) 359-2564
Hal K. Johnson
FS

MIAMI

**AUTOMATED PERSONNEL
INTERNATIONAL OF MIAMI, INC.**
14 N.E. 1st Ave., Suite 700, Ainsley
Bldg. 33132
(305) 358-1141
Alex DeFonso/C. P. "Rusty" Phillips
AD,COMP,F,LEG,MED,OFF ADM,
OS,RE,S,TE

**OTT, HERTNER, OTT & ASSOCIATES,
INC.**
600 Brickell Ave., Suite 601 33131
(305) 373-3181
Herbert H. Hertner/Gene Hollander
AD,COMP,F,FS,LEG,OFF ADM,OS,
RE,S,TE

**ROBERT HALF PERSONNEL AGENCIES
OF MIAMI**
150 S. E. Second Ave. 33131
(305) 377-8728
Guy R. Tann
COMP,F

**ROTH, YOUNG PERSONNEL SERVICE
OF MIAMI, INC.**
1035 N.E. 125th St. 33161
(305) 891-3041
David R. Morton
AD,COMP,F,LEG,MED,OFF ADM,RE,
S,TE

ORLANDO

ACTION PERSONNEL CONSULTANTS
205 E. Colonial Dr. 32801
(305) 424-6561
Ace "Kinney" Zryd/Harry E. Pirtle
AD,COMP,F,FS,MED,OFF ADM,S,TE

SNELLING AND SNELLING
Suite 609, 100 S. Orange Ave. 32801
(305) 241-6511
John Fordham/Pat Zastrow
AD,COMP,F,FS,LEG,MED,OFF ADM,
RE,S,TE

PENSACOLA

BRENT PERSONNEL CONSULTANTS
117 W. Garden St., P.O. 2202 32503
(904) 434-2621
Sunny R. Thorn
AD,CL,COMP,CON,ED,F,IND,LEG,MED,
OFF ADM,RE,S,TE

LANDRUM PERSONNEL ASSOCIATES
21 S. Tarragona St. 32501
(904) 434-2565
H. Britt Landrum, Jr.
AD,COMP,F,LEG,MED,OFF ADM,RE,
S,TE

**SNELLING AND SNELLING (BENNETT
ENTERPRISES OF PENSACOLA)**
Suite 428, Plaza Bldg. 32505
Robert C. Bennett
FS

FLORIDA—Continued

TAMPA

A-1 CAREER POSITIONS
518 Tampa St. 33602
(813) 223-3751
William C. Wackerman/M. Kelley
AD,COMP,ED,F,LEG,MED,OFF ADM,RE
S,TE

ALERT PERSONNEL, INC.
412 Madison, Suite 102 33602
(813) 229-0465
William D. Hollar, Sr./Veston A. Taylor
COMP,F,FS,LEG,OFF ADM,RE,S,TE

ALLIED PERSONNEL OF TAMPA
1211 N. Westshore Blvd., Suite 512 33607
(813) 872-4895
William E. Scherrer
AD,COMP,ED,F,FS,LEG,MED,OFF ADM,
RE,S,TE

AVAILABILITY OF TAMPA
Suite 202, 1211 N. Westshore Blvd. 33607
(813) 872-2631
Thomas L. Maguire
AD,COMP,ED,F,FS,LEG,MED,OFF ADM,
RE,S,TE

FANNING PERSONNEL OF TAMPA, INC.
514 N. Franklin St., Suite 203 33602
(813) 229-7731
Robert J. Gordon
AD,COMP,ED,F,FS,LEG,MED,OFF ADM,
RE,S,TE

**HARPER ASSOCIATES, INC. S.W.
FLORIDA**
110 S. Hoover St. 33609
(813) 879-2741
Walter R. Comfort
FS

IPS OF TAMPA, INC.
1211 North West Shore Boulevard, Suite
100 33607
(813) 872-6696
Winston R. Wordsworth/A. Porter McFarland/
Robert F. Bolster
AD,COMP,F,LEG,MED,OFF ADM,RE,
S,TE

WM. FLOWERS ASSOCIATES
2401 W. Platt St. 33609
(813) 253-5311
W. C. Flowers/L. S. Flowers
CON,OS,TE

**MANAGEMENT RECRUITERS OF
TAMPA BAY, INC.**
Exchange Nat'l Bank Bldg., Suite 1120,
610 Florida Ave. 33601
(813) 229-2981
Fred Kaths/Millie Kaths
AD,COMP,ED,F,LEG,MED,OFF ADM,
RE,S,TE

PERSONNEL CONSULTANTS
5010 W. Kennedy Blvd., Allstate Bldg.,
Suite 206 33609
(813) 223-4228
Ruth L. Marr
FS

SALES CONSULTANTS OF TAMPA, INC.
5600 Mariner- Suite #213 33609
(813) 872-1538
M. K. "Bud" Baach/Seth Miller
AD,MED,RE,S,TE

SNELLING & SNELLING
415 Tampa St., Suite 336 33602
(813) 223-2701
James W. Clark
AD,COMP,ED,F,FS,LEG,MED,OFF ADM,
RE,S,TE

WEST PALM BEACH

SNELLING AND SNELLING
208 Clematis St. 33401
(305) 655-3671
David S. Wood/Ronald L. Larson
AD,COMP,ED,F,LEG,MED,OFF ADM,OS,
RE,S,TE

GEORGIA

ATLANTA

CLARK ASSOCIATES
400 Honeywell Bldg. - 6 W. Druid Hills Dr.,
N.E. 30329
(404) 636-3037
Robert E. Clark
F,OFF ADM,TE,S

DENNISSON PERSONNEL CONSULTANTS
3400 Peachtree Rd., N.W. 30326
(404) 261-4762
Spencer Lawton
COMP,ED,F,OFF ADM,S,TE

DUNHILL OF ATLANTA, INC.
Suite 1410, 235 Peachtree St. 30303
(404) 525-7756
Marvin I. Bearman
AD,COMP,F,OFF ADM,RE,S,TE

**HALLMARK PERSONNEL OF GEORGIA,
INC.**
3400 Peachtree Rd. N.E., Suite 1625 30326
(404) 261-8222
Charles McDicken
AD,CL,COMP,F,LEG,OFF ADM,RE,S,TE

**KEY PERSONNEL, INC. &
BETTY PARKER ASSOCIATES**
1024 Healey Bldg., 57 Forsyth St. 30303
(404) 577-7500
Betty C. Reaid/Don R. Williams
AD,COMP,ED,F,FS,LEG,MED,OFF ADM,
RE,S,TE

KING PERSONNEL CONSULTANTS
34 Peachtree St. N.W., Suite 2101 30303
(404) 577-4080
Neale T. Traves
AD,COMP,F,FS,LEG,OFF ADM,S,TE

**MANAGEMENT RECRUITERS OF
ATLANTA, INC.**
1111 First Federal Bldg. 30303
(404) 577-5454
Eric J. Lindberg
AD,COMP,ED,F,FS,LEG,OFF ADM,
RE,S,TE

MANAGEMENT RECRUITERS
Suite 909, Cities Service Bldg.
(404) 261-3850
Eric J. Lindberg
AD,COMP,ED,F,FS,LEG,OFF ADM,
RE,S,TE

MEDICAL PLACEMENT
1371 Peachtree St., N.E., Suite 724 30309
(404) 892-1822
Ruby H. Roberts
MED, OFF ADM

NORRELL PERSONNEL SERVICE, INC.
1510 Fulton Nat'l Bank Bldg. 30303
(404) 525-4214
Guy W. Millner/Edwin L. Garner
AD,COMP,F,LEG,MED,OFF ADM,RE,
S,TE

PEACHTREE PLACEMENT SERVICE, INC.
2970 Peachtree Rd., N.W. Suite 622
30309
(404) 233-8219
(Mrs.) Margaret Hutchison
F,LEG,OFF ADM,S

**ROBERT HALF PERSONNEL AGENCIES
OF ATLANTA, INC.**
235 Peachtree St. N.E. 30303
(404) 688-2300
Edward J. Rozhon
COMP,F

**SNELLING AND SNELLING OF
ATLANTA, N.E.**
2250 N. Druid Hills Rd., N.E. 30329
(404) 633-4461
George H. Roe/Lucille McElynn
COMP,F,LEG,OFF ADM,RE,S,TE

SNELLING & SNELLING
225 Peachtree St., Suite 1110 30303
(404) 688-4061
George Roe/Gene Bell
AD,COMP,F,LEG,MED,OFF ADM,
RE,S,TE

SOUTHEASTERN PERSONNEL, INC.
1216 Fulton National Bank Bldg. 30303
(404) 525-4931
Guy W. Millner
AD,COMP,F,OFF ADM,S,TE

GEORGIA—Continued

SPEER PERSONNEL CONSULTANTS
1115 Healey Bldg. 30303
(404) 523-2961
Carol Speer Shirley
AD,COMP,F,LEG,MED,OFF ADM,
RE,S,TE

AUGUSTA

JEROME PERSONNEL SERVICE
963 - 65 Greene St., P.O. Box 308 30903
(404) 724-7703
Nan Anderson/A. J. Connell
FS

COLUMBUS

CHARLESTON PERSONNEL BUREAU
500½ 9th St. 31902
(404) 322-7242
Clara E. Charleston
FS

SOUTHERN EMPLOYMENT SERVICE
233 - 12th St., Suite 704, Georgia Power
Bldg. 31901
(404) 327-6533
(Mrs.) Cleo J. Cox
AD,COMP,F,MED,OFF ADM,RE,S,TE

DECATUR

NORRELL PERSONNEL SERVICE, INC.
645 First Nat'l Bank Bldg., 315 W. Ponce
de Leon Ave. 30030
(404) 373-4436
Guy W. Millner/Edwin L. Garner
AD,COMP,F,LEG,MED,OFF ADM,RE,S,TE

MACON

CRANDALL & GOLDSMITH PERSONNEL SERVICE
830 Mulberry St. 31201
(912) 746-6241
Mary B. Crandall/Mary Jo Goldsmith
AD,COMP,F,LEG,MED,OFF ADM,
RE,S,TE

HARPER-GAY EMPLOYMENT AGENCY
209 Southern United Bldg. 31201
(912) 746-2744
(Mrs.) Helen Piers Browning/(Mrs.) Carolyn
Milner
AD,COMP,F,FS,LEG,MED,OFF ADM,
RE,TE,S

SNELLING AND SNELLING
544 Mulberry St. 31201
(912) 746-5671
Carl L. Christenson
AD,COMP,F,LEG,MED,OFF ADM,
RE,S,TE

SAVANNAH

SAVANNAH EMPLOYMENT SERVICE
705 Industrial Bldg. 31401
(912) 233-5747
Barbara O. Donnelly/Mable L. Clarke
AD,COMP,ED,F,LEG,MED,OFF ADM,
RE,S,TE

HAWAII

HONOLULU

ASSOCIATED SERVICES, LTD.
1023 Pensacola St. 96814
(808) 531-8963
Harold Yokoyama
FS

DATA PROCESSING & OFFICE PERSONNEL
700 Bishop St., Suite 300 96813
(808) 531-0547
Leslie Jackson
COMP,F,LEG,OFF ADM,S,TE

ILLINOIS

CHICAGO

ABC PERSONNEL
The Marshall Field Annex Bldg., 25 E.
Washington, Suite 806 60602
312-368-0525
(Mrs.) Elaine B. Lewin
AD,COMP,ED,F,LEG,MED,OFF ADM,
RE,S,TE

ADRIENNE GRIFFIN ASSOCIATES, INC.
16 N. Wabash, Suite 1300 60602
(312) 641-7150
Adrienne S. Griffin
FS

BELSON, HEMINGWAY & ASSOCIATES, INC.
327 So. La Salle 60604
(312) 939-6210
Bill Hemingway
FS

BRYANT ASSOCIATES, INC.
67 E. Madison 60603
(312) 726-5860
Richard D. Bryant
AD,COMP,F,TE

CAREER OAK PARK PERSONNEL, INC.
6742 W. North Ave. 60635
(312) 889-1333
Bill Stumbo
FS

DIVERSCO PERSONNEL, INC.
919 N. Michigan, Suite 3000 60611
(312) 751-0200
Jack O'Neil
FS

GAIL GREEN PERSONNEL SERVICE
7 S. Dearborn St. 60603
(312) 782-0680
Hilda Gail Green, CEC/Larry McKinley, CEC
F,OFF ADM,S,TE

GARLAND MEDICAL PLACEMENT
30 N. Michigan, #1010 60602
(312) 263-0145
Natalie Garland
MED

HALLMARK PERSONNEL, INC.
180 N. Michigan Ave. 60601
(312) 236-7117
Walter H. Ketel/Gary R. Clarke/
Patrick T. Prieb/Lee Randall
AD,COMP,F,FS,LEG,OFF ADM,RE,S,TE

HUNT PERSONNEL SERVICE
67 E. Madison 60603
(312) 641-6225
Ray Preden
FS

IVY EMPLOYMENT SERVICE, INC.
7215 W. Touhy 60648
(312) 774-8585
Al Bennet
FS

IVY PERSONNEL SERVICE, INC.
3223 N. Ashland 60657
(312) 935-6331
Ann Nathan/Virjean Ross
AD,COMP,F,FS,LEG,MED,OFF ADM,
S,TE

LASALLE PERSONNEL
7 W. Madison St. 60602
(312) 236-5688
Daniel Glickauf/Ronald Norris
AD,F,FS,LEG,OFF ADM,S,TE

MANAGEMENT RESOURCES
28 E. Jackson Blvd. 60604
(312) 922-6381
Michael Keeler
FS

McKEE ASSOCIATES, INC.
25 E. Washington 60602
(312) AN 3-1815
G. McKee Kirkpatrick
FS

MODERN EMPLOYMENT SERVICE, INC.
7 W. Madison St. 60602
(312) 782-3960
Joe Kelly
FS

ROBERT HALF PERSONNEL AGENCIES, INC.
333 N. Michigan Ave. 60601
(312) 782-6930
W. A. Robertson
COMP,F

ILLINOIS—Continued

SALES CONSULTANTS CHICAGO, INC.
332 S. Michigan Ave. 60604
(312) 922-7855
Norm Ellan
S

SKY PERSONNEL
22 W. Madison St. 60602
(312) 332-7398
Sid Robbins
AD,COMP,F,FS,LEG,MED,OFF ADM,
RE,S,TE

YARDLEY CONSULTANTS, INC.
32 W. Randolph 60601
(312) 263-3253
James F. Yardley
AD,COMP,ED,F,FS,LEG,MED,OFF ADM,
OS,RE,S,TE

ZENITH EMPLOYMENT SERVICE, INC.
202 S. State 60604
(312) HA7-1995
Ray Scully/Ted Moras
FS

DECATUR

HELEN COLLINS PERSONNEL, INC.
158 S. Water St. 62525
(217) 423-6909
Helen M. Collins/La Verne Berg
AD,COMP,ED,F,LEG,MED,OFF ADM,OS,
RE,S,TE

DES PLAINES

FORD EMPLOYMENT AGENCY
2400 E. Devon 60018
(312) 297-7160
Francis Kennedy
AD,F,LEG,MED,OFF ADM,S

VAN NOTE/ASSOCIATES
967 First Ave., Suite 3 60016
(312) 297-6360
Donald J. Peters/Richard J. Van Note
AD,COMP,F,FS,OFF ADM,RE,S,TE

EVANSTON

MURPHY EMPLOYMENT SERVICE, INC.
1612 Chicago Ave. 60201
(312) 273-2155
Rick Crisp
AD,COMP,F,LEG,MED,OFF ADM,
RE,S,TE

PEORIA

CAPITOL EMPLOYMENT AGENCY
1204 Jefferson Bldg. 61602
(309) 673-8247
Margaret S. Ryan/Mary Lee Taylor
AD,COMP,ED,F,FS,LEG,MED,NR,
OFF ADM,RE,S,TE

SNELLING AND SNELLING
109 S.W. Jefferson 61602
(309) 676-5581
Dale J. Alcorn
AD,COMP,F,FS,LEG,MED,OFF ADM,
RE,S,TE

INDIANA

ELKHART

HOUSE OF EMPLOYMENT, INC.
131 Tyler St., P.O. Box 1084 46514
(219) 522-4224
Janet M. Beatty/Betty Mack
AD,COMP,ED,F,LEG,MED,OFF ADM,
RE,S,TE

PERSONNEL BY PARRISH
401 Communicana Bldg. 46514
(219) 294-2432
Robert H. Parrish
AD,F,FS,OFF ADM,S,TE

SNELLING AND SNELLING PERSONNEL
810 -D W. Bristol St. 46514
(219) 293-4511
John S. Heise
AD,COMP,F,LEG,MED,OFF ADM,RE,
S,TE

FORT WAYNE

BONE PERSONNEL, INC.
2008 Ft. Wayne Bank Bldg. 46802
(219) 743-4423
Bruce Bone/Dale Mayhall/
Norb Workinger
AD,COMP,ED,F,FS,LEG,MED,OFF ADM,
RE,S,TE

METROPOLITAN PERSONNEL SERVICE
Suite 2204, Ft. Wayne National Bank Bldg.,
110 W. Berry St. 46802
(219) 743-5768
Eric S. Holmgren
AD,COMP,ED,F,LEG,MED,OFF ADM,
RE,S,TE

SNELLING AND SNELLING
Anthony Wayne Bank Bldg., Clinton &
Berry St. 46802
(219) 422-3544
C. Roger Harris
AD,COMP,ED,F,LEG,MED,OFF ADM,
RE,S,TE

TOWER PERSONNEL SERVICE, INC.
Suite 805-835 - Lincoln Tower 46802
(219) 742-5201
Althea Mann Asbury
AD,COMP,ED,F,LEG,MED,OFF ADM,
RE,S,TE

INDIANAPOLIS

ASSOCIATED NURSES REGISTRY
4002 N. New Jersey St.
(317) 283-5976, 283-2261
(Mrs.) Letitia N. Abramson
MED,NR

BRILL PERSONNEL, INC.
4000 Meadows Dr., Suite 102 46205
(317) 547-9595
John W. Brill/Sue Scott
AD,COMP,ED,F,FS,LEG,MED,OFF ADM,
RE,S,TE

JOBS INCORPORATED
3599 S. East St. 46227
(317) 783-9246
William H. Meyers
FS

SALES CONSULTANTS, INC.
2421 Willowbrook Pky., Suite 203 46205
(317) 257-5411
Stephen Anderson, Jr.
S

SNELLING AND SNELLING –
INDIANAPOLIS SOUTH
5305 Rt. #31 South, Turtle Creek, Suite 1A
46227
(317) 783-9381
Harry R. Zietz
FS

UNITED PERSONNEL SERVICE, INC.
5330 E. 38th St., Suite 3025 46218
(317) 545-6671
Robert L. Erbrich
FS

RICHMOND

HUMAN DYNAMICS ASSOCIATES
111 S. 10th St. 47374
(317) 966-5594
Margaret Higgins/Ken Bolen
COMP,F,LEG,OFF ADM,RE,S,TE

SOUTH BEND

MICHIANA PERSONNEL SERVICE
2309 American National Bank Bldg. 46601
(219) 232-3364
James E. Rudasics
FS

SNELLING AND SNELLING
224 W. Jefferson Blvd. 46601
(219) 234-9011
John R. Underhill
AD,COMP,ED,F,FS,LEG,MED,OFF ADM,
RE,S,TE

TERRE HAUTE

MEYER EMPLOYMENT AGENCY
112 N. 7th St. 47801
(812) 232-9671
E. R. Meyer
AD,COMP,ED,F,LEG,MED,OFF ADM,
RE,S,TE

MIRIAM BLACK PERSONNEL SERVICE
112 N. Seventh St., Suites 6-7-8 47801
(812) 232-1394
(Miss) Miriam Hamilton Black
AD,COMP,ED,F,LEG,MED,OFF ADM,
S,TE

IOWA

COUNCIL BLUFFS

JOBS BY CHAMBERS
215 Bennett Bldg. 51501
(712) 328-1503
Wendell S. Haack
AD,COMP,ED,F,FS,LEG,OFF ADM,S,TE

DAVENPORT

DEE SPRINGER PERSONNEL
216 W. Third St. 52801
(319) 326-4011
Dee Springer
AD,COMP,F,LEG,MED,OFF ADM,RE,
S,TE

DES MOINES

ACME EMPLOYMENT SERVICE, INC.
305 Kresge Bldg. 50309
(515) 244-9156
Katherine E. Moody/Kathryn B. Ward
AD,COMP,ED,F,FS,LEG,MED,OFF ADM,
RE,S,TE

CAPITAL PERSONNEL SERVICE
204 Securities Bldg. 50309
(515) 283-2545
Arthur N. Berven/Ruth Ruben
AD,COMP,F,FS,LEG,MED,OFF ADM,RE,
S,TE

DUBUQUE

FUTURE EMPLOYMENT SERVICE
470 Fischer Bldg. 52001
(319) 583-8900
Robert L. Luthro
AD,F,FS,OFF ADM,RE,S,TE

SIOUX CITY

**PRATT & YOUNGLOVE EMPLOYMENT
SERVICE**
625 Security Bank Bldg., 6th & Pierce Sts.
51101
(712) 255-7961
Earl D. Pratt, Jr. CEC/(Mrs.) Barbara L.
Currier
AD,COMP,ED,F,FS,LEG,MED,OFF ADM,
RE,S,TE

SNELLING AND SNELLING
435 Frances Bldg. 51101
(515) 281-5151
Bruce W. Wiese
AD,COMP,ED,F,FS,LEG,MED,OFF ADM,
RE,S,TE

WATERLOO

CITY & NATIONAL EMPLOYMENT
709 W. 3rd St., P.O. Box 83 50704
(319) 232-6641
Helen V. Moodie
AD,COMP,ED,F,FS,LEG,MED,OFF ADM,
RE,S,TE

KANSAS

TOPEKA

BOSSLER & ASSOCIATES, INC.
100 E. 9th Kansan Towers 66612
(913) 234-5626
Keith V. Bossler
AD,COMP,F,OFF ADM,RE,S,TE

KENTUCKY

LEXINGTON

SNELLING AND SNELLING
1220 S. Broadway 40504
(606) 233-0583
Gary A. Shaw
AD,COMP,ED,F,LEG,MED,OFF ADM,
RE,S,TE

LOUISVILLE

**AMERICAN EMPLOYMENT SERVICE,
DIVISION OF SWISHER PERSONNEL**
211 Speed Bldg. 40202
(502) 589-9164
Jack L. Swisher
AD,COMP,F,LEG,OFF ADM,RE,S,TE

DUNHILL OF LOUISVILLE, INC.
638 Lincoln Federal Bldg., Fourth &
Chestnut 40202
(502) 589-4740
Richard A. Berger
AD,F,IND,LEG,OFF ADM,S,TE

HARPER ASSOCIATES - LOUISVILLE
235 Starks Bldg. 40207
(502) 587-6583
Clark Beauchamp
AD,COMP,F,LEG,MED,OFF ADM,RE,
S,TE

**MANAGEMENT RECRUITERS OF
LOUISVILLE**
425 S. 4th St., Suite 433 40202
(502) 583-9701
Howard J. Markus
AD,COMP,F,FS,OFF ADM,RE,S,TE

**SNELLING AND SNELLING OF
LOUISVILLE, INC.**
312 South 4th St. 40202
(502) 585-5841
C. Bruce Culbreth
AD,COMP,F,OFF ADM,RE,S,TE

LOUISIANA

BATON ROUGE

**AMERICAN AGENCY OF EMPLOYMENT,
INC.**
2036 Wooddale Blvd., Suite H 70806
(504) 926-8150
Charles E. Rist, Sr.
FS

ANGEL EMPLOYMENT
3150 Florida Blvd. 70806
(504) 344-0453
William P. Jackson
FS

BADON'S EMPLOYMENT CENTER, INC.
1724 Dallas Dr., Suite 11 70806
(504) 927-7406
Barbara L. Badon
AD,COMP,ED,F,LEG,MED,OFF ADM,OS,
RE,S,TE

BOEKER'S EMPLOYMENT SERVICE
451 Florida St., Suite 730, LNB Bldg. 70801
(504) 348-5336
Catherine G. Boeker
AD,COMP,ED,F,LEG,MED,OFF ADM,OS,
RE,S,TE

DIXIE EMPLOYMENT SERVICE
506 Reymond Bldg. 70801
(504) 342-1625
(Mrs.) Helen S. Heath
AD,COMP,F,LEG,MED,OFF ADM,RE,
S,TE

**PORT CITY PLACEMENT EMPLOYMENT
SERVICE**
7400 Exchange Pl., Rm. 104, P.O. Box 66391
70806
(504) 927-5800
(Mrs.) Mary Lee Jackson
FS

**PROFESSIONAL PERSONNEL SERVICE,
INC.**
Republic Tower Bldg., 5700 Florida Blvd.,
Suite 504 70806
(504) 926-7350
W. K. Carlile
FS

NEW ORLEANS

A-1 EMPLOYMENT SERVICE
1409 National Bank of Commerce Bldg.
70112
(504) 524-8281
Lillian Lee Deslattes/Neil Cromiller
AD,COMP,F,LEG,OFF ADM,OS,RE,S,
TE,MED

ACCOUNTING PERSONNEL
912 National Bank of Commerce Bldg.
70112
(504) 581-9051
William A. Troth
FS

APEX EMPLOYMENT SERVICE, INC.
601 Carondelet Bldg. 70130
(504) 529-2304
Robert C. Hagen/Robert C. Fox
AD,COMP,F,FS,LEG,OFF ADM,OS,
RE,S,TE

LOUISIANA—Continued

**AUTOMATED PERSONNEL INTER-
NATIONAL OF NEW ORLEANS, INC.**
Carondelet Bldg., 226 Carondelet St.
70130
(504) 529-1681
Charles E. West
AD,COMP,F,FS,LEG,MED,OFF ADM,S,TE

**BEE ROBERTSON'S EMPLOYMENT
SERVICE, INC.**
301 Carondelet Bldg., 226 Carondelet St.
70130
(504) 524-2133
Floyd E. Robertson
AD,COMP,ED,F,LEG,MED,OFF ADM,OS,
RE,S,TE

BETTY BREAUX PERSONNEL SERVICE
226 Carondelet St., Room 502 70130
(504) 529-7628
Betty E. Breaux
COMP,F,LEG,OFF ADM,RE,S,TE

C/M OF NEW ORLEANS, INC.
600 Pere Marquette Bldg. 70112
(504) 524-3253
August H. Lentz
FS

COMMERCIAL EMPLOYMENT AGENCY
1001 National Bank of Commerce Bldg.
70112
(504) 525-5237
Lynn W. Cobena
AD,COMP,ED,F,LEG,OFF ADM,OS,
RE,S,TE

**DOT ROMER'S EMPLOYMENT SERVICE,
INC.**
234 Loyola Ave. 70112
(504) 522-1431
Dorothy Romer Carpenter/Stewart M.
Carpenter
AD,COMP,ED,F,LEG,MED,OFF ADM,OS,
RE,S,TE

ENGINEERING PERSONNEL
4948 Chef Menteur Highway 70126
(504) 949-3841
R. J. Abadie
FS

LAWRENCE PERSONNEL, INC.
200 Carondelet St. 70130
(504) 525-3171
Vic Lawrence
AD,COMP,F,LEG,OFF ADM,OS,RE,
S,TE,MED

**MEDICAL SERVICES PLACEMENT
BUREAU**
4121 Prytania St. 70115
(504) 895-4155
(Mrs.) Virginia B. Waldo
F,MED,OS

**NATIONWIDE EMPLOYMENT BUREAU,
INC.**
216 Carondelet Bldg., 226 Carondelet St.
70130
(504) 525-9071
Ruth S. Russell/Effie S. Bernard
AD,COMP,ED,F,LEG,MED,OFF ADM,
RE,S,TE

NUNES, INC., EMPLOYMENT SERVICES
231 Carondelet St., Suite 701-702 70130
(504) 529-4691
S. Vas Nunes
AD,COMP,ED,F,LEG,MED,OFF ADM,RE
S,TE

JOE RICH & ASSOCIATES, INC.
909 Carondelet Bldg. 70130
(504) 581-6333
Mary Farley
FS

SNELLING AND SNELLING
1110 Carondelet Bldg. 70130
(504) 529-5781
F. P. Clark
AD,COMP,ED,F,FS,LEG,MED,OFF ADM,
RE,S,TE

**SP PERSONNEL ASSOCIATES OF
NEW ORLEANS**
Suite 2036, International Trade Mart Bldg.
70130
(504) 523-5691
Donald M. Shiell
AD,COMP,F,MED,OFF ADM,S,TE

MARYLAND

BALTIMORE

ACTION PERSONNEL AGENCY
1125 Fidelity Bldg. 21201
(301) 539-8250
Ellie Howard
FS

EASTERN EMPLOYMENT SERVICE, INC.
Arlington Federal Bldg., 201 N. Charles St.
21201
(301) 837-0777
Jay A. Ford
AD,COMP,F,FS,LEG,OFF ADM,RE,
S,TE

FORD-ADAMS, INC.
812 One Charles Center Bldg. 21201
(301) 685-7220
Robert C. Graebner/Richard A. Sovero
AD,COMP,F,LEG,MED,OFF ADM,RE,
S,TE

GUILFORD PERSONNEL SERVICE, INC.
415 Equitable Bldg. 21202
(301) 685-4340
Daniel N. & Bernice Silver
AD,COMP,F,FS,LEG,OFF ADM,RE,S,
TE,MED

THE SCOTT AGENCIES
6305 York Rd. 21212
(301) 532-6300
Woody Scott
FS

SILVER EMPLOYMENT SERVICE, INC.
524 Dolphin St., 1221 W. North Ave. 21217
(301) 462-5600
Jerry Silverstein/Ronnie Silverstein
FS,MED

**SNELLING AND SNELLING OF
HIGHLANDTOWN, INC.**
3603 Eastern Ave. 21224
(301) 675-7110
Maynard Z. Drossner
AD,COMP,ED,F,LEG,MED,OFF ADM,
RE,S,TE

**SNELLING AND SNELLING OF
BALTIMORE, INC.**
312 Equitable Bldg. 21202
(301) 837-2860
Maynard Z. Drossner, CEC/George P. Bonar
AD,COMP,ED,F,LEG,MED,OFF ADM,
RE,S,TE

**TOM McCALL & ASSOCIATES OF
BALTIMORE**
One Charles Center 21201
(301) 539-0700
Charley Greene
AD,OFF ADM,S

TOWSON

**FANNING PERSONNEL AGENCY OF
TOWSON, INC.**
Investment Bldg., Suite A 21204
(301) 821-9650
(Miss) Marcie Norris
FS

**MANAGEMENT RECRUITERS OF
BALTIMORE, INC.**
Investment Bldg., Suite 1111 21204
(301) 823-9010
William Sweetser
FS

**SNELLING AND SNELLING OF
TOWSON, INC.**
500 York Rd. 21204
(301) 825-7610
Maynard Z. Drossner/Leonard R. Holmes
AD,COMP,ED,F,LEG,MED,OFF ADM,RE,
S,TE

MASSACHUSETTS

BOSTON

ADVANCE CAREERS CORPORATION
120 Boylston St., Suite 901 02116
(617) 482-8330
Stanley S. Herman
AD,COMP,F,OFF ADM,RE,S,TE

MASSACHUSETTS—Continued

BURTON PERSONNEL SERVICE, INC.
120 Boylston St. 02116
(617) 482-1950
Burton S. Adler/Morris Gallant
AD,COMP,ED,F,LEG,MED,OFF ADM,
OS,RE,S,TE

FANNING PERSONNEL OF BOSTON, INC.
585 Boylston St. 02116
(617) 261 8400
Stephen P. Flynn/Christine K. Flynn
AD,F,LEG,MED,OFF ADM,RE

HARPER & ASSOCIATES
80 Boylston St., Suite 850 02116
(617) 482-2336
Raymond Daniels/Irwin Goldstein
AD,ED,F,LEG,MED,OFF ADM,S,TE

MANAGEMENT RECRUITERS INC.
OF BOSTON
500 Boylston St. 02116
(617) 262-5050
Walter P. McLaughlin
FS

MASSACHUSETTS MEDICAL BUREAU
58 Winter St. 02108
(617) 426-5845
Basil Cass
F,MED,OFF ADM,S,TE

PUBLIC EMPLOYMENT SERVICE, INC.
37 Temple Pl., Suite 508 02111
(617) 482-9530
Martin M. Franklin/James F. Blaney
AD,COMP,F,OFF ADM,RE,S,TE

ROBERT HALF PERSONNEL AGENCIES
OF BOSTON, INC.
140 Federal St. 02110
(617) 423-6440
Herbert J. Myers
COMP,F

ROGERS AND SANDS INC.
PROFESSIONAL PLACEMENT
19 Temple Place 02111
(617) 426-4180
Lillian Rogers/Irving Sands
AD,ED,LEG,MED,OFF ADM,RE,S,TE

ROTH YOUNG PERSONNEL SERVICE
OF BOSTON, INC.
18 Oliver St. 02110
(617) 482-7377
Robert M. Derba/Peter J. Derba
AD,F,MED,OFF ADM,RE,S,TE

SNELLING AND SNELLING OF
BOSTON, INC.
500 Boylston St. 02116
(617) 262-2660
Jerome S. Bartzoff,CEC/Burton Bartzoff,CEC
AD,COMP,F,LEG,OFF ADM,RE,S,TE,MED

WHITE'S EMPLOYMENT SERVICE
18 Tremont St. 02108
(617) 523-6190
Walter F. Matson
DI,F,LEG,MED,OFF ADM,S

BROOKLINE

KEY PERSONNEL SERVICE
1330 Beacon St. 02146
(617) 731-6320
Joy Benjamin
AD,COMP,F,LEG,MED,OFF ADM,RE,S

CAMBRIDGE

CAPITOL PERSONNEL SERVICE, INC.
649 Massachusetts Ave. 02139
(617) 868-9800
Darrell C. Hoag/Dick Stevens
AD,COMP,F,FS,LEG,MED,OFF ADM,
RE,S,TE

SPRINGFIELD

BAILEY EMPLOYMENT SERVICE
145 State St. 01103
(413) 781-3191
Hubert V. Blackburn
AD,COMP,ED,F,FS,LEG,MED,OFF ADM,
RE,S,TE

G & M EMPLOYMENT SERVICE OF
WESTERN MASS.
145 State St. 01103
(413) 785-1533
Joseph Koneski
FS

NATIONWIDE BUSINESS SERVICE
145 State St. 01103
(413) 732-4104
Betty Leary
AD,COMP,ED,F,LEG,OFF ADM,RE,
S,TE

SNELLING AND SNELLING
135 State St. 01103
(413) 781-0235
Henry Parish
AD,COMP,ED,F,FS,LEG,MED,OFF ADM,
RE,S,TE

WORCESTER

AD HOC PERSONNEL SERVICE
101 Pleasant St. 01608
(617) 791-3281
Jane Menard
AD,COMP,ED,F,LEG,MED,OFF ADM,
RE,S,TE

G & M EMPLOYMENT SERVICE, INC.
340 Main St. 01608
(617) 799-2794
H. C. Goodwin, Jr.
AD,COMP,ED,F,LEG,MED,OFF ADM,
RE,S,TE

SCANNEL EMPLOYMENT AGENCY
306 Main St. 01608
(617) 752-3739
John T. Scannell
FS

MICHIGAN

DETROIT

ESSEX PERSONNEL SERVICE, INC.
1028 Penobscot Bldg. 48226
(313) 961-4300
Jay Fernstrum
AD,F,LEG,OFF ADM,S

GRAEBNER EMPLOYMENT SERVICE
1225 First National Bldg. 48226
(313) 965-6800
Herbert J. Graebner
FS

PERSONNEL BY RIGO
715 Ford Bldg. 48226
(313) 961-3060
Donna M. Rigo
AD,COMP,F,LEG,OFF ADM,S,TE

UNITED PERSONNEL, INC.
17800 Woodward 48203
(313) 869-9400
Emil Sundheimer
AD,F,OFF ADM,RE,S

EAST DETROIT

SNELLING AND SNELLING
18121 E. 8 Mile Rd. 48021
Doug Sharrow
FS

FLINT

MILLER CAREER CENTRE EMPLOY-
MENT SERVICE
502 Commerce Bldg., 114 W. Union St.
48502
(313) 239-5821
(Mrs.) Gerrie Davis
AD,COMP,ED,F,LEG,MED,OFF ADM,
RE,S,TE

SELECT EMPLOYMENT SERVICE
1603 Mott Foundation Bldg. 48502
(313) 238-0408
Helen A. Reed
AD,COMP,F,FS,LEG,MED,OFF ADM,
RE,S,TE

GRAND RAPIDS

GILBERT PERSONNEL
Waters Bldg., 301A 49502
(616) 451-2993
(Mrs.) Orimal Hudson
MED,RE,S,AD,CL,COMP,F,LEG,OFF ADM,
TE

MICHIGAN—Continued

HUDSON PERSONNEL SERVICE
820 Commerce Bldg. 49502
(616) 458-3614
(Mrs.) Orimal Hudson, CEC/Tom Williamson
AD,COMP,F,LEG,MED,OFF ADM,RE,S,TE

LANSING

EXECUTIVE RECRUITERS, INC.
601 S. Capitol Ave. 48933
(517) 371-1620
James Hoefer
AD,COMP,ED,F,FS,LEG,MED,OFF ADM,
RE,S,TE

SOUTHFIELD

DUNHILL OF DETROIT
29350 Southfield Rd. 48075
(313) 557-1100
Donald E. Dahlin
F,S,TE

EXECUTIVES' PERSONNEL SERVICE, INC.
24123 Greenfield, Suite 112 48075
(313) 557-9400
Charles S. Brooks
AD,COMP,F,LEG,MED,OFF ADM,RE,S,TE

SNELLING AND SNELLING
15565 Northland Dr., 201 E. Northland
   Towers 48075
(313) 353-6500
Norma Adair
FS

MINNESOTA

MINNEAPOLIS

ABC EMPLOYMENT SERVICE
436 Midland Bank Bldg. 55401
(612) 339-1453
Gerald H. Otten
FS

CAREERS, INC.
1433 Northwestern Bank Bldg., 7th &
   Marquette 55402
(612) 332-1406
Mel Hansen/Joseph Edeskuty
AD,COMP,F,LEG,OFF ADM,RE,S,TE

DER-KEL EMPLOYMENT SERVICE
628 Nicollet Mall 55402
(612) 338-0621
John L. Olson/Dorothy Touhey
   Donald Cook
AD,COMP,F,FS,LEG,MED,OFF ADM,S,TE

DUNHILL OF MINN./ST. PAUL, INC.
523 Marquette Ave., Suite 707 55402
(612) 335-6451
Kenneth E. Peters
AD,COMP,F,LEG,OFF ADM,RE,S,TE

ELLS EMPLOYMENT SERVICE
1129 Plymouth Bldg. 55402
(612) 335-1131
Richard E. Peterson
AD,COMP,F,LEG,OFF ADM,RE,S,TE

HALLMARK PERSONNEL INCORPORATED
601 F&M Bank Bldg., 88 S. 6th St. 55402
(612) 339-0031
Jim Suchecki
AD,COMP,F,LEG,OFF ADM,S,TE

JOB MASTERS, INC.
503 Syndicate Bldg. 55402
(612) 339-4503
John T. Sherman
AD,COMP,F,LEG,MED,OFF ADM,RE,S,TE

McNITT PERSONNEL BUREAU
602 Baker Bldg. 55402
(612) 339-5533
(Mrs.) Eunice P. Rognlie, CEC/(Mrs.)
   Jeanne Bleecker
AD,F,LEG,MED,OFF ADM,RE,S

MINNEAPOLIS EMPLOYMENT SERVICE
512 Nicollet Mall Bldg. 55402
(612) 332-6406
Alfred O. Mohr
AD,COMP,ED,F,LEG,MED,OFF ADM,TE

ROBERT HALF PERSONNEL AGENCIES OF MINNESOTA, INC.
822 Marquette Ave. 55402
(612) 336-8636
Stephen L. Ryter
COMP,F

SALES CONSULTANTS
7450 France Ave., So., Suite 111 55435
(612) 920-4505
H. Roger Koobs
S

UPPER MIDWEST EMPLOYMENT
Hennepin Ave. & 6th St., Suite 1035 55402
(612) 338-6748
Helen L. Deardorff
FS

ST. PAUL

ANGELL EMPLOYMENT
319 Hamm Bldg. 55102
(612) 227-8066
Jane Michaels/Beverly Boyer/Virginia Barnes
AD,COMP,ED,F,FS,LEG,MED,OFF ADM,
RE,S,TE

BUSINESS EMPLOYMENT SERVICE
W. 952 First National Bank Bldg. 55101
(612) 224-3394
Paul P. Wolfe/Mitch G. Rogers
AD,COMP,F,LEG,OFF ADM,RE,S,TE

COMMERCIAL EMPLOYMENT BUREAU
W. 2071 First Nat'l. Bank Bldg. 55101
(612) 224-7441
John J. Coffee/Genevieve G. Ness
AD,COMP,ED,F,LEG,OFF ADM,RE,S
TE

METROPOLITAN PERSONNEL
440 Hamm Bldg., 408 St. Peter St. 55102
(612) 224-9428
Lawrence C. Baker
AD,COMP,F,FS,LEG,OFF ADM,RE,S,TE

MIDWAY EMPLOYMENT SERVICE
1588 University Ave. 55104
(612) 645-0611
Willard W. Roepke
AD,COMP,ED,F,LEG,MED,OFF ADM,
S,TE

MISSISSIPPI

GULFPORT

SNELLING AND SNELLING
2320 14th St. 39501
(601) 864-6331
Geo. B. Huth
AD,COMP,ED,F,FS,LEG,MED,OFF ADM,
OS,RE,S,TE

JACKSON

EXECUTIVE SERVICE OF MISSISSIPPI
409 Bankers Trust Plaza Bldg. 39201
(601) 355-7476 to 355-7478
Henry P. Anderson
AD,COMP,ED,F,FS,LEG,MED,OFF ADM,
OS,RE,S,TE

RUDY TATUM PERSONNEL SERVICE, INC.
317 E. Capitol St. 39205
(601) 948-3344
Rudy D. Tatum/Emma Lee Tatum
FS

SNELLING AND SNELLING
121½ President St. 39201
John Hulsebosch
FS

MISSOURI

INDEPENDENCE

INDEPENDENCE EMPLOYMENT SERVICE
Katz Bldg., 203 N. Main St. 64050
(816) 252-5040
Harold Vince/Beth Haas
COMP,F,LEG,S,TE

KANSAS CITY

BRANDOM PERSONNEL
1006 Grand Ave. 64106
(816) 842-7131
Barbara A. Brandom
COMP,F,LEG,MED,OFF ADM,S,TE

CAREER CONSULTANTS
Suite 205 Altman Bldg. 64106
(816) 421-5030
Agnes V. Rochester
AD,COMP,ED,F,FS,OFF ADM,RE,
S,TE

MISSOURI—Continued

GLYNN-MULLEN PLACEMENT SERVICE
Commerce Tower, 911 Main 64105
(816) 421-7484
John W. Mullen/Joseph P. Glynn
AD,COMP,ED,F,LEG,MED,OFF ADM,RE,
S,TE

**LOEHR EMPLOYMENT SERVICE OF
K.C., INC.**
18 E. 11th 64106
(816) 221-5640
Louis Kram
AD,COMP,ED,F,FS,LEG,MED,OFF ADM,
RE,S,TE

McBRIDE PERSONNEL SERVICE
Suite 1127, Ten Main Center, 920 Main St.
64105
(816) 421-7711
Elmer G. Behrens
AD,COMP,ED,F,LEG,OFF ADM,RE,S,TE

ST. LOUIS

C & S PERSONNEL
915 Olive, Rm. 1011 63101
(314) 231-7300
H. Clinton Claiborne
AD,COMP,F,LEG,MED,OFF ADM,RE,S,TE

GENE WANNER PERSONNEL
418 Olive St. 63102
(314) 621-8588
(Mrs.) Gene Wanner
AD,COMP,ED,F,LEG,MED,OFF ADM,
RE,S,TE

**HALLMARK PERSONNEL OF
MISSOURI, INC.**
915 Olive St. 63101
(314) 621-3039
Ken Crittenden
FS

**ROTH YOUNG PERSONNEL SERVICE
OF ST. LOUIS**
8201 Maryland 63105
(314) 726-0500
Burt Ingersoll/Milt Bibko
AD,COMP,F,MED,OFF ADM,RE,S,TE

SALES CONSULTANTS, INC.
330 Mansion House Center, Suite 304 63102
(314) 241-0606
Joseph Knowles
S

SPRINGFIELD

DORSEY LOVE ASSOCIATES, INC.
1988 South Glenstone 65804
(417) 883-1212
Dorsey A. Love/Richard L. Gafner
AD,COMP,F,FS,LEG,OFF ADM,RE,S,TE

MEADOWMERE EMPLOYMENT AGENCY
1930 East Meadowmere 65804
(417) 869-1806
Ruby L. Letsch
AD,COMP,F,FS,LEG,MED,OFF ADM,
RE,S,TE

NEBRASKA

LINCOLN

BOOMERS
412 Sharp Bldg. 68508
(402) 432-8559
Sterling Maus
FS

DAN ROTH EMPLOYMENT
1213 M St. 68508
(402) 432-3381
Dan Roth
FS

SNELLING AND SNELLING
Suite 1012 Anderson Bldg. 68508
(402) 477-7151
Robert B. Shearer
AD,COMP,F,LEG,MED,OFF ADM,RE,S,TE

OMAHA

ACE CAREERS, INC.
6901 Dodge St. 68118
(402) 558-8222
Donald T. Faris
FS

CENTRALIZED PLACEMENT
Suite 304, Dodge Center Bldg. 68132
(402) 556-5716
Dan Fox
FS

CORNER STONES CAREERS, INC.
7301 Pacific 68114
(402) 397-0900
Frank F. Wood
FS

DUNHILL OF OMAHA, INC.
Suite 604, 1624 Douglas 68102
(402) 342-3502
James W. Eggers/Ed McDowell
AD,COMP,F,FS,LEG,MED,OFF ADM,
RE,S,TE

**THE JOB MART EMPLOYMENT
SERVICE**
9001 Arbor Bldg., Suite 206 68124
(402) 391-2460
Wallace G. Quest/Kathryn Buckley
CL,COMP,CON,F,FS,IND,LEG,MED,
OFF ADM,RE,S,TE,TEMP

**MANAGEMENT RECRUITERS OF
OMAHA, INC.**
1624 Douglas 68102
(402) 348-9550
Les Zanotti
AD,COMP,F,LEG,OFF ADM,RE,S,TE

MIDLAND PERSONNEL
206 Farm Credit Bldg. 68102
(402) 342-5275
Marvin Bradford/Janet Bradford
AD,COMP,ED,F,FS,LEG,MED,OFF ADM,
RE,S,TE

MUTUAL EMPLOYMENT SERVICE, INC.
2305 S. 103 St. 68124
(402) 346-6070
(Mrs.) Blanche C. Webber
AD,COMP,ED,F,LEG,OFF ADM,RE,S,TE

PERSONNEL COUNSELING SERVICE, INC.
130 W. Dodge Medical Bldg., 8300 Dodge St..
68114
(402) 397-6777
Gene R. Alloway
FS

PERSONNEL EXPERTS, INC.
540 Continental Bldg., 19th & Douglas
68102
(402) 342-6161
Tom Lane/Jean Knight
AD,COMP,F,FS,LEG,OFF ADM,RE,
S,TE

PERSONNEL SEARCH
1133 Redick Tower 68102
(402) 348-9083
Larry Courtnage
FS

**SNELLING AND SNELLING —
DOWNTOWN**
1100 Woodmen Tower 68102
(402) 344-7670
Wm. F. Sline
AD,COMP,ED,F,FS,LEG,OFF ADM,
RE,S,TE

NEW HAMPSHIRE

MANCHESTER

SNELLING AND SNELLING
815 Elm St. 03101
(603) 669-2011
Albert A. Barrows
AD,COMP,F,LEG,MED,OFF ADM,
RE,S,TE

NEW JERSEY

ASBURY PARK

**SNELLING AND SNELLING
PERSONNEL**
710 Cookman Ave. 07712
(201) 988-5000
Edward S. Granger/ Ronald
T. Nimick
AD,COMP,F,OFF ADM,RE,S,TE

BLOOMFIELD

—NATIONAL SEARCH ASSOCIATES
330 Glenwood Ave. 07003
(201) 429-9000
Norman Lee
FS

NEW JERSEY—Continued

**NORTH JERSEY MIDTOWN
EMPLOYMENT AGENCY**
39 Broad St. 07003
(201) 748-1345
Arthur Gartenlaub
FS

**PLACE MART PERSONNEL CON-
SULTANTS OF BLOOMFIELD, INC.**
622 Bloomfield Ave. 07003
(201) 429-9500
Donald J. Marletta
AD,COMP,F,OFF ADM,RE,S,TE

SNELLING AND SNELLING
15 Ward St. 07003
(201) 748-3050
George W. Menkes
AD,COMP,F,LEG,MED,OFF ADM,RE,S,TE

BURLINGTON

**SNELLING AND SNELLING OF
BURLINGTON, N.J. INC.**
9 E. Union St. 08016
(609) 387-2430
Marion Livezey
AD,COMP,F,FS,LEG,MED,OFF ADM,
RE,S,TE

CALDWELL

A-1 EMPLOYMENT SERVICE
115 Bloomfield Ave. 07006
(201) 228-1300
Audrey Hull/C. Borst
AD,COMP,F,FS,OFF ADM,RE,S,TE

ARTHUR PERSONNEL SERVICE
244 Bloomfield Ave. 07006
(201) 226-4555
Allen MacWright/Robert Fralley
COMP,F,OFF ADM,RE,S,TE

FANNING PERSONNEL OF WEST ESSEX
285 Bloomfield Ave. 07006
(201) 226-3024
Irwin West
AD,COMP,F,FS,LEG,OFF ADM,RE,S,TE

CAMDEN

**SNELLING AND SNELLING OF
CAMDEN, INC.**
519 Federal St. 08103
(609) 966-4230
George M. Mayock
AD,COMP,F,LEG,MED,OFF ADM,RE,
S,TE,FS

CHERRY HILL

A & H PERSONNEL SERVICES
One Cherry Hill 08034
(609) 667-2500
H. C. Mundt
AD,COMP,F,LEG,MED,OFF ADM,RE,S,TE

FANNING PERSONNEL OF CAMDEN,INC.
1 Cherry Hill (Mall) 08034
(609) 667-3885
Alan B. Taplow
AD,COMP,F,LEG,OFF ADM,RE,S,TE

**SIDNEY EVANS PERSONNEL
ASSOCIATES**
409 Bldg., Rt. 70 E. 08034
(609) 428-9300
Arlene Sidney/Lee Evans
AD,COMP,F,FS,LEG,MED,OFF ADM,S,TE

**SNELLING AND SNELLING OF
CHERRY HILL, INC.**
802 One Cherry Hill Bldg. 08034
(609) 667-4880
(Mrs.) M. Lyle Laird
AD,COMP,ED,F,LEG,MED,OFF ADM,
RE,S,TE

CLIFTON

BUFFINGTON AND WELLS INC.
1111 Clifton Ave. 07011
(201) 778-5858
Penny Surgent
FS

**RELIABLE PROGRAMMING
ASSOCIATES, INC.**
1096 Main Ave. 07011
(201) 478-0900
Vincent Ribortella
FS

CRANFORD

**SCE PERSONNEL SERVICES OF
CRANFORD**
10 Alden St. 07016
(201) 272-4943
Marjorie Lighthipe
AD,COMP,F,LEG,OFF ADM,RE,S,TE

EAST BRUNSWICK

**BAKER & BAKER EMPLOYMENT
SERVICE**
43A W. Prospect St. 08816
(201) 254-1989
James J. Donohue
COMP,F,LEG,MED,OFF ADM,RE,TE

EAST ORANGE

**SNELLING AND SNELLING
PERSONNEL**
24 Halsted St. 07018
(201) 674-6276
Stephen Holowack
AD,COMP,F,LEG,MED,OFF ADM,RE,S,TE

SUPER PLACEMENTS LTD.
160 Halsted St. 07018
(201) 674-3370
Albert I. Siegel/Selma (Red) Siegel
AD,COMP,ED,F,FS,LEG,OFF ADM,S,TE

EDISON

**SNELLING AND SNELLING PERSONNEL
SERVICE**
100 Menlo Park 08817
(201) 494-1200
Carroll H. Gardner
AD,COMP,F,LEG,OFF ADM,RE,S,TE

ELIZABETH

**GENERAL PERSONNEL AND
TECHNICAL SERVICES**
115 Broad St. 07201
(201) 289-7050
Don Ormsby/Joanne Gilligan
COMP,F,LEG,OFF ADM,OS,RE,S,TE

FORT LEE

SNELLING AND SNELLING
1625 Lemoine Ave. 07024
(201) 947-6700
David A. Levitt
AD,COMP,F,LEG,OFF ADM,RE,S,TE

HACKENSACK

ABBEY EMPLOYMENT AGENCY
240 Main Street 07601
(201) 343-7035
Albert Cancro/Marie A. Cancro
FS

ABC EMPLOYMENT AGENCY, INC.
241 Main St. 07601
(201) 487-5515
Gerre Jones/Arthur C. Maurello/Pat Bennett
AD,COMP,F,OFF ADM,S,TE

ABLE CAREER CENTERS
389 Main St. 07601
(201) 488-7888
Howard Cassel
AD,COMP,F,LEG,OFF ADM,RE,S,TE

A-1 EMPLOYMENT SERVICE
200 Main St. 07601
(201) 488-3500
Audrey Hull/J. Sabatini
AD,COMP,F,FS,OFF ADM,RE,S,TE

**FANNING PERSONNEL OF
BERGEN, INC.**
387 Main St. 07601
(201) 487-5766
Robert Modica/Joseph G. Malone
AD,COMP,F,LEG,OFF ADM,RE,S,TE

JOSEPH KEYES ASSOCIATES
241 Main St. 07601
(201) 489-1881
Joseph A. Keyes/Emil Kalka
COMP,CON,F,LEG,MED,OFF ADM,S,TE

LYN-ELL PERSONNEL, INC.
389 Main St. 07601
(201) 342-5935
Jay H. Dworkin/Milton Madison
COMP,F,LEG,OFF ADM,S,TE

NEW JERSEY—Continued

MICHAEL CRAIG PERSONNEL AGENCY OF BERGEN COUNTY, INC.
389 Main St. 07601
(201) 488-1910
Harvey Klein
FS

PROGRESS PERSONNEL AGENCY OF BERGEN, INC.
170 State St. 07601
(201) 487-4800
Hy Farber
COMP,F,OFF ADM,TE

HADDONFIELD

ALPHA PERSONNEL ASSOCIATES OF NEW JERSEY, INC.
No. 3 South Haddon Ave. 08033
(609) 428-0400
Harold N. Hoffer
AD,COMP,F,LEG,MED,OFF ADM,RE,S,TE

HIGHSTOWN

SWIFT & SWIFT OF HIGHSTOWN, INC.
Route 130 08520
(609) 448-6500
Sidney Swift
FS

JERSEY CITY

BERGEN SQUARE EMPLOYMENT AGENCY t/a BEST EMPLOYMENT
40 Journal Square 07306
(201) 656-6600
Phil Phillips/Marion Forbes
AD,COMP,F,FS,LEG,OFF ADM,
RE,S,TE

WELSH EMPLOYMENT AGENCY
26 Journal Square 07306
(201) 656-5900
Charles H. Howes/Louis A. Troisi
AD,COMP,F,FS,LEG,OFF ADM,S,TE

KEARNY

DEE OF KEARNY
232 Belleville Pike 07032
(201) 991-9080
D. Dee/J. Fay
AD,COMP,F,FS,LEG,OFF ADM,RE,S,TE

LINDEN

A-1 EMPLOYMENT SERVICE
101 N. Wood Ave. 07036
(201) 925-1600
Audrey Hull/C. Borst
AD,COMP,F,FS,OFF ADM,RE,S,TE

MADISON

FORBES PERSONNEL AGENCY
661 Shunpike Rd. 07940
(201) 822-0400
Otto W. Sticht
AD,COMP,F,LEG,OFF ADM,RE,S,TE

MAPLEWOOD

HALL EMPLOYMENT AGENCY, INC.
193 Maplewood Ave. 07040
(201) 763-8310
Evelyn M. Tully/David M. Hoffman/
Laverne Linton
AD,COMP,F,LEG,OFF ADM,OS,
RE,S,TE

METUCHEN

CLARKE EMPLOYMENT AGENCY, INC.
495 Main St. 08840
(201) 549-2020
(Mrs.) Marcelle Frey Clarke
AD,COMP,ED,F,FS,LEG,MED,OFF ADM,
RE,S,TE

MORRISTOWN

CLARKE EMPLOYMENT AGENCY INC.
123 Washington St. 07960
(201) 538-5400
R. H. Clarke/Marcelle F. Clarke
AD,COMP,F,FS,LEG,MED,OFF ADM,
RE,S,TE

FANNING PERSONNEL OF MORRIS COUNTY, INC.
20 Park Place 07960
(201) 538-8100
Christine Demetropolous
FS

PERSONNEL SPECIALISTS, INC.
10 Park Pl. 07960
(201) 267-7700
Blaise Conte
AD,COMP,F,FS,LEG,OFF ADM,OS,
RE,S,TE,MED,ED

SNELLING AND SNELLING PERSONNEL OF MORRISTOWN, INC.
10 Park Place 07960
(201) 539-6600
William H. Armstrong
AD,COMP,F,LEG,MED,OFF ADM,
RE,S,TE

NEW BRUNSWICK

A-1 EMPLOYMENT SERVICE
106 Albany St. 08901
(201) 249-8300
Audrey Hull/R. Purdy
AD,COMP,F,FS,OFF ADM,RE,S,TE

FANNING PERSONNEL OF NEW BRUNSWICK, INC.
124 Church St. 08902
(201) 846-7300
A. J. Ekstrom
AD,COMP,F,LEG,OFF ADM,RE,S,TE

SCE PERSONNEL SERVICES OF NEW BRUNSWICK
303 George St. 08901
(201) 246-2500
Walter E. Pfeifer
AD,COMP,F,LEG,MED,OFF ADM,RE,S,TE

NEWARK

EQUAL OPPORTUNITIES PERSONNEL SERVICES, INC.
24 Commerce St., Suite 431 07102
(201) 622-7963
Eugene M. Watson
FS

MARTIN PERSONNEL ASSOCIATES
1180 Raymond Blvd. 07102
(201) 642-0492
Martin Untermeyer
S,OFF ADM

McCABE PERSONNEL ASSOCIATES
790 Broad St. 07102
(201) 623-4787
Richard P. McCabe/Marie E. McCabe
AD,COMP,ED,F,LEG,OFF ADM,
RE,S,TE

ROBERT HALF PERSONNEL AGENCIES OF NEWARK, INC.
1180 Raymond Blvd. 07102
(201) 623-3661
L. J. Miller/M. M. Meisels
COMP,F

NORTH NEW BRUNSWICK

NOEL CRAM TECHNICAL PERSONNEL
424 George St. 08901
(201) 246-0603
Noel Cram
FS

NORTH PLAINFIELD

PLACE MART PERSONNEL SERVICE OF THE PLAINFIELDS
136 Somerset St. 07060
(201) 753-8676
Nathan Jacobs
AD,COMP,ED,F,FS,LEG,MED,OFF ADM,
OS,RE,S,TE

PARAMUS

NORMANN PERSONNEL CONSULTANTS
676 Winters Ave. 07652
(201) 261-1576
Gerd W. Normann/Catherine R. Normann
AD,COMP,F,FS,LEG,MED,OFF ADM,
RE,S,TE

PARSIPPANY

S-H-S PERSONNEL SERVICE OF PARSIPPANY, N.J.
1200 Rt. 46 07054
(201) 335-6100
A. Bruce Campbell
AD,COMP,F,FS,LEG,MED,OFF ADM,
RE,S,TE

SNELLING AND SNELLING
1180 Rt. 46 07054
(201) 335-8100
Robert C. Iseman
AD,COMP,ED,F,LEG,OFF ADM,RE,
S,TE

NEW JERSEY—Continued

PENNSAUKEN

F. R. WILLIAMS OFFICE SERVICES & PERSONNEL PLACEMENTS
2221 37th St. 08110
Florence R. Williams
FS

PENN-HILL ASSOCIATES
5434 King Ave. 08109
(609) 665-3980
Edward Verner
F,OFF ADM,RE,S,TE

PLAINFIELD

SNELLING AND SNELLING
40 Somerset St. 07060
(201) 753-7400
Leonard Marks
AD,COMP,F,OFF ADM,RE,S,TE

PRINCETON

A-1 EMPLOYMENT SERVICE
82 Nassau St. 08540
(609) 924-9200
Audrey Hull/G. Egert
AD,COMP,F,FS,OFF ADM,RE,S,TE

PRINCETON EMPLOYMENT AGENCY
352 Nassau St. 08540
(609) 924-3726
Mae A. Wainford/Marjorie M. Halliday/
  Philip J. Wainford
AD,COMP,ED,F,FS,LEG,OFF ADM,TE

PROFESSIONAL PLACEMENTS OF PRINCETON, INC.
29 Princeton Center, U.S. 206 N. 08540
(609) 924-1900
Stuart S. Gilbert
AD,COMP,F,LEG,MED,OFF ADM,RE,S,TE

SNELLING AND SNELLING OF PRINCETON, INC.
134 Nassau St. 08541
(609) 921-2021
Eileen Cobb
FS

RED BANK

MANAGEMENT RECRUITERS OF RED BANK, INC.
176 Riverside Ave. 07701
(201) 842-2405
Paul Shaktman/Alexander Shaktman
COMP,F,OFF ADM,RE,S,TE

RIDGEWOOD

SNELLING AND SNELLING
171 E. Ridgewood Ave. 07450
(201) 447-4200
H. D. Wolf
AD,COMP,F,LEG,MED,OFF ADM,RE,S,TE

SCOTCH PLAINS

A-1 EMPLOYMENT SERVICE
219 Park Ave. 07076
(201) 322-8300
Audrey Hull/L. Moser
AD,COMP,F,FS,OFF ADM,RE,S,TE

SUCCASUNNA

SNELLING AND SNELLING OF ROXBURY
21 Sunset Strip 07876
(201) 584-3200
Robert L. Jackson
AD,COMP,F,LEG,MED,OFF ADM,RE,S,TE

TRENTON

HAYES PERSONNEL
143 E. State St. 08608
(609) 394-8141
Andrew & Mary Hayes
FS

SWIFT AND SWIFT INC.
44 W. State St. 08608
(609) 396-3565
Sidney Swift/Arline Lambert
AD,COMP,F,LEG,OFF ADM,RE,S,TE

UNION

A-1 EMPLOYMENT SERVICE
1995 Morris Ave. 07083
(609) 964-1300
Audrey Hull/R. Wright
AD,COMP,F,FS,OFF ADM,RE,S,TE

COMPUTER RESOURCES, INC.
1519 Stuyvesant Ave. 07083
(201) 687-7622
James J. O'Donnell, Jr.
COMP,LEG

FANNING PERSONNEL OF UNION, INC.
1961 Morris Ave. 07083
(201) 687-0390
Richard R. Odierna
AD,COMP,F,LEG,OFF ADM,RE,S,TE

PERSONNEL SEARCH INC.
1416 Morris Ave. 07083
(201) 688-5180
Peter Santeusanio
AD,COMP,F,LEG,MED,OFF ADM,RE,S,TE

PERSONNEL SPECIALISTS, INC.
2424 Morris Ave. 07083
(201) 688-7440
Leonard Wolfe
AD,COMP,F,FS,LEG,OFF ADM,OS,
  RE,S,TE,MED,ED

SNELLING AND SNELLING
1961 Morris Ave. 07083
(201) 688-5700
Roy Lamendola
AD,COMP,F,LEG,OFF ADM,RE,S,TE

WAYNE

FANNING PERSONNEL OF WAYNE, INC.
1341 Hamburg Turnpike 07470
(201) 696-8502
Joseph Villani
FS

SNELLING AND SNELLING OF WAYNE
1341 Hamburg Turnpike 07470
(201) 696-2121
Roger H. Hammond/Lawrence P. Fagan
AD,COMP,F,LEG,OFF ADM,RE,S,TE

WOODBRIDGE

R. P. BARONE ASSOCIATES
73 Main St. 07095
(201) 634-4300
(Dr.) Ralph P. Barone/(Mrs.) JoAnn Yates
AD,COMP,F,MED,OFF ADM,RE,S,TE

NEW MEXICO

ALBUQUERQUE

NEW MEXICO EMPLOYMENT BUREAU, INC.
2206 Central Ave., S.E. 87106
(505) 265-6655
Sam B. Dunlap
AD,COMP,ED,F,FS,LEG,MED,OFF ADM,
  RE,S,TE

SNELLING AND SNELLING
150 Washington SE 87108
(505) 265-6411
John B. Murphy
AD,COMP,F,FS,LEG,MED,OFF ADM,RE,S,TE

NEW YORK

ALBANY

DUNHILL OF ALBANY INC.
Suite 607, 41 State St. 12201
(518) 462-6591
Robert J. McCabe/Clark R. Baker
AD,COMP,F,OFF ADM,RE,S,TE

MANAGEMENT RECRUITERS OF ALBANY, INC.
41 State St. 12207
(518) 462-7401
Gardner W. Hubbard/Gerald J. McCabe
AD,COMP,F,LEG,OFF ADM,RE,S,TE

BUFFALO

C/M AGENCY OF BUFFALO, INC.
420 Rand Bldg. 14203
(716) 853-3329
Henry P. Vogt
AD,COMP,F,LEG,OFF ADM,S,TE

DELAWARE EMPLOYMENT AGENCY
3024 Delaware Ave. 14217
(716) 875-9644
(Mrs.) Leola M. Berst
F,LEG,OFF ADM,S,TE

NEW YORK—Continued

FRONTIER PLACEMENT AGENCY AND FRONTIER TEMPORARIES
1333 Rand Bldg., 14 Lafayette Square 14203
(716) 856-4490
Leonard C. Gademsky, Jr.
AD,COMP,F,LEG,MED,OFF ADM,RE,S,TE

HALLORAN PLACEMENT SERVICE AGENCY INC.
430 Brisbane Bldg. 14203
(716) 856-3170
James F. Halloran, Jr.
COMP,F,FS,OFF ADM,S,TE

MALLEY PERSONNEL AGENCY
710 Genesee Bldg., 1 West Genesee St. 14202
(716) 852-4461
Edward R. Lord
AD,COMP,F,LEG,OFF ADM,S,TE

HEMPSTEAD, L.I.

CAREER PLACEMENTS INCORPORATED
320 Fulton Ave. 11550
(516) 485-5800
Edward Grant
COMP,F,LEG,OFF ADM,RE,S,FS

RALPH BROWN ASSO. INC.
250 Fulton Ave. 11550
(516) 485-7210
Ralph Brown/Shirley Brown
COMP,ED,F,FS,LEG,MED,OFF ADM,S,TE

SNELLING AND SNELLING
250 Fulton Ave. 11550
(516) 485-6810
David Mendel
COMP,F,FS,LEG,MED,OFF ADM,RE,S,TE

HICKSVILLE, L.I.

AMHERST EMPLOYMENT SERVICE INC.
82 N. Broadway 11801
(516) 433-7610
Charles J. Eibeler
F,MED,OFF ADM,RE,S

ARROW EMPLOYMENT AGENCY, INC.
320 N. Broadway 11802
(516) 931-4200
Norman T. Shapp, CEC/Burt Stone
AD,COMP,F,OFF ADM,RE,S,TE

IDEAL EMPLOYMENT SERVICE
79 Broadway 11801
(516) 931-1124
Martin Kane
FS

NEW YORK CITY

ABET EMPLOYMENT AGENCY
25 W. 14th St. #121 10011
(212) 242-4482
Irving Goldman
FS

ABLE PERSONNEL INC.
475 Fifth Ave. 10017
(212) 689-5500
Dan Gardner
AD,COMP,F,FS,LEG,OFF ADM,RE,S,TE

ACCOUNTANTS & AUDITORS AGENCY
30 East 42nd St. 10017
(212) 986-8785
Ira Stone
F

ACCURATE PERSONNEL SERVICE, INC. (AGENCY)
41 E. 42nd St. 10017
(212) 986-5805
William Steiner/Jerry Ferris
AD,COMP,F,FS,LEG,OFF ADM,RE,S,TE

ACORN EMPLOYMENT SERVICE, INC.
160 Broadway 10038
(212) 233-1891
Meredith Melke/Paul Brund
F,LEG,OFF ADM,OS,TE

ALBERTA SMYTH EMPLOYMENT AGENCY, INC.
170 Broadway 10038
(212) 732-8788
Edward A. Broderick/Lillian Kirkeby
FS

ALCOTT ASSOCIATES, INC.
485 Madison Ave. 10022
Howard Fader
FS

ALL-AMERICAN EMPLOYMENT SERVICE
16 E. 41st St. 10017
(212) 686-0200
Jason W. Small
AD,F,OFF ADM,RE

AMERICAN CAREER SERVICE AGENCY
330 Madison Ave. 10017
(212) 661-0800
(Miss) Leslie A. Granat/Sabatino A. Russo
CL,LEG,TEMP

ANN ANDERSON PERSONNEL AGENCY
274 Madison Ave., Suite 1301 10016
(212) 685-2178
Ann Anderson
AD,COMP,ED,F,FS,LEG,OFF ADM,S

ARCHER EAST ASSOCIATES, INC.
301 Madison Ave. 10017
(212) 986-7373
Scott Michaels/Diva Robinson
AD,COMP,F,MED,OFF ADM

ARDEN PERSONNEL SERVICE
11 East 47 St. 10017
(212) 751-0820
M. J. Levy/Wm. Rosenfeld
AD,ED,F,LEG,OFF ADM,S,TE

ARTISTS & ART DIRECTORS AGENCY
505 Fifth Ave. 10017
(212) 697-7477
(Miss) Ela Allen
AD

AUTOMATED PERSONNEL INTERNATIONAL, INC.
15 E. 40 St. 10017
(212) 697-0300
Hank Leeds/Sidney Davis
COMP,F,LEG

BEARMAN PERSONNEL SERVICE
147 W. 42nd St. 10036
Herbert Bearman
FS

BIL-LU PERSONNEL AGENCY
415 Lexington Ave. 10017
(212) 682-5740
(Mrs.) Lucy Bill
AD,COMP,F,LEG,OFF ADM,OS,S,TE

BING-CRONIN PERSONNEL, INC.
1 Rockefeller Plaza 10020
(212) 245-2525
(Miss) Bernice Jennings
FS

BOOKKEEPERS UNLIMITED AGENCY
505 Fifth Ave. 10017
(212) 697-7878
(Mrs.) Cherie Bernard
F,OFF ADM

BROMLY PERSONNEL INC.
41 E. 42 St. 10017
(212) 687-2230
Jay Bromly
AD,COMP,F,LEG,MED,OFF ADM,S,TE

THERESA M. BURKE EMPLOYMENT AGENCY
8 West 40th St. 10018
(212) 563-6075
Theresa M. Burke
AD,ED,F,LEG,MED,OFF ADM,TE

CAREER BLAZERS AGENCY, INC.
36 W. 44th St. 10036
(212) 986-1280
Adele Lewis
AD,ED,LEG,OFF ADM,RE

CAREER BUILDERS, INC.
501 Madison Ave. 10021
(212) 752-7640
Robert H. Gaines
AD,F,OFF ADM,RE,S,TE

CAREER GUIDES
415 Lexington Ave. 10017
(212) 697-3358
Sy Gellman/Charles A. Winston
F,S,TE

NEW YORK—Continued

CHANKO ASSOCIATES, INC.
527 Madison Ave. 10022
(212) 421-7190
James Chanko
COMP,F,OFF ADM

**CHARLES PRINCE PERSONNEL
 AGENCY, INC.**
40 East 49th St. 10017
(212) 486-9494
Charles H. Prince
AD,COMP,F,LEG,OFF ADM,OS,RE,S,TE

CHURCH EMPLOYMENT, INC.
270 Madison Ave., Suite 1805 10016
(212) 689-8610
Robert M. Bellinger/Frank J. Bambury
TE

**CLAREMONT MAJESTIC EMPLOYMENT
 SERVICE AGENCY, INC.**
80 Warren St. Room 303-307 10007
(212) 267-3692
George Zahler
FS

CO-ED PERSONNEL, INC.
2 E. 42nd St. 10017
(212) 686-8611
Gerald Vogel
FS

**COLUMBIA EDP EMPLOYMENT
 AGENCY, INC.**
342 Madison Ave. 10017
(212) 661-3434
Donald Kaye
COMP

CORINNE-DARBY INC.
50 E. 42nd St. 10017
(212) 682-3900
Corinne Reid/Darby Reid
AD,OFF ADM,OS

CORNWALL PERSONNEL AGENCY INC.
179 Broadway 10007
(212) 349-2520
J. P. Schader/Cora Parker
COMP,F,OFF ADM

CRIS ASSOCIATES, INC.
274 Madison Ave. 10016
(212) 679-0320
Helen Crismara
AD,COMP,F,LEG,OFF ADM,RE,S,TE

DEAN PERSONNEL AGENCY, INC.
535 Fifth Ave. at 44th St. 10017
(212) 986-3600
Edwin Bennett/Frederic Perlman
AD,COMP,ED,F,LEG,MED,OFF ADM,RE,S

JACK DILL ASSOCIATES, INC.
10 E. 40th St. 10016
Don Waldron/Jim Colt
AD,COMP,F,OFF ADM,OS,S,TE,FS

DON HOWARD PERSONNEL, INC.
179 Broadway 10007
(212) 227-9000
Don Howard
COMP,F,OFF ADM,S,TE

DUNHILL PERSONNEL SYSTEM
535 5th Ave. 10017
(212) 986-0100
Edward Kushell
FS

**ENGINEERING EMPLOYMENT
 SERVICE, INC.**
217 Broadway 10007
(212) 267-5640
Robert B. Duffy
TE

ENWOOD PERSONNEL AGENCY
6 E. 45th St. 10017
(212) 682-4080
Eunice Brill
F

ESSEX PERSONNEL AGENCY, INC.
507 Fifth Ave. 10017
(212) 661-6990
Robert Sharkey
F,TE

EXECUTIVE TALENT, INC.
21 W. 45th St. 10036
(212) 765-7300
Michael Cooper
FS

FANNING PERSONNEL AGENCY, INC.
105 E. 42nd St. 10017
(212) 349-3800
William Cass/Ron Morgan
COMP,F,LEG,OFF ADM,RE,TE,MED

FORD PERSONNEL AGENCY, INC.
11 John St. 10038
(212) 732-3115
Phyllis Yodice
FS

FORD EMPLOYMENT AGENCY, INC.
16 E. 42nd St. 10017
(212) 972-1710
Robert Williams
FS

FORTUNE PERSONNEL AGENCY
505 5th Ave. 10017
(212) 682-8600
Rudy Schott/Malcolm Lazinsk
AD,COMP,F,LEG,OFF ADM,RE,TE

GARDNER PERSONNEL, INC.
545 Fifth Ave. 10017
(212) 687-6616
Marvin Gardner
AD,F,OFF ADM,S,TE

GARNET ASSOCIATES, INC.
52 Vanderbilt Ave. 10017
(212) 889-3830
Mike Jacobs
AD,F,FS,LEG,OFF ADM,S,TE

GILBERT LANE INTERNATIONAL
505 5th Ave., 10017
(212) 867-8100
Jerry Gilbert/William S. Howe/
 Howard Specter
AD,COMP,F,LEG,OFF ADM,S,TE

THE HADLE AGENCY
501 Madison Ave. 10016
(212) 753-7578
Helen Hadle
FS

HARPER ASSOCIATES, INC.
22 W. 48th St. 10036
(212) 582-1700
Maxwell Harper/Arthur R. Pell
AD,COMP,F,LEG,MED,OFF ADM,S,TE

HARVARD CONSULTANTS, INC.
342 Madison Ave. 10017
(212) 986-9600
Edwin Wells
FS

**HELEN HUTCHINS PERSONNEL
 AGENCY**
767 Lexington Ave. 10021
(212) 838-3070
Helen Hutchins
TE

**HOTELMEN'S EXECUTIVE PERSONNEL,
 INC.**
25 W. 45th St. 10036
(212) 582-1400
Rudolph O. Weihl
INSTITUTIONAL, OFF ADM,LEG,TE,F,OS

**HOTEL WORLD REVIEW PERSONNEL
 SERVICE, INC.**
230 Park Ave. 10017
(212) 683-0059
Beatrice O'Brien
F,OFF ADM,OS,S

HUNT PERSONNEL, LTD.
10 East 44th St. 10017
(212) 687-9140
George Hunt
COMP,F,OS,TE

**J. G. KETCHAM EMPLOYMENT
 SERVICE**
150 Broadway 10038
(212) 277-0725
James G. Ketcham
F

JELLENIK AGENCY
141 E. 44th St. 10017
(212) 697-8745
George Jellenik, Jr.
AD,F,LEG,OFF ADM,OS,RE,S,TE

NEW YORK—Continued

JOB MART, INC.
280 Madison Ave. 10016
(212) 685-2611
Celia Mayer
AD,F,LEG,OFF ADM

JOHN MURRAY PERSONNEL AGENCY
18 East 48th St. 10017
(212) 752-9820
John Murray
AD,LEG,OFF ADM,OS,RE

JUDY WALD AGENCY, INC.
110 E. 59th St., 10022
(212) 421-6750
Judy Wald
FS

ANTHONY KANE PERSONNEL, INC.
160 Broadway 10038
(212) 227-1190
Anthony Kane
FS

K. B. WHITE PERSONNEL AGENCY
15 East 40th St. 10016
(212) 682-7050
Katharine B. White
AD,F,LEG,MED,OFF ADM,RE,S

KENT PERSONNEL AGENCY, INC.
485 - 5th Ave. 10017
(212) 697-9595
Donn Sand/Nancy Andrews
AD,COMP,F,LEG,OFF ADM,RE

KLING PERSONNEL AGENCY, INC.
180 Broadway 10038
(212) 964-3640
Anthony Price
COMP,F,FS,LEG,OFF ADM,RE,S,TE

LAWRENCE EMPLOYMENT AGENCY, INC.
341 Madison Ave. 10017
(212) 695-7000
Arnold Lewis
F,MED,OFF ADM,RE,S,AD,COMP,LEG

LIBERTY PERSONNEL AGENCY, INC.
11 John St. 10038
(212) 267-1033
Pieter C. Wyckoff
AD,COMP,F,LEG,RE,S

LORETTA BRODERICK PERSONNEL AGENCY, INC.
150 Broadway 10038
(212) 732-6055
Loretta Broderick
AD,COMP,F,LEG,OFF ADM,S,TE

LYNNE PALMER PUBLISHING PERSONNEL, INC.
75 East 55th St. 10022
(212) 759-9045
Lynne Palmer
FS

MAE DALY AGENCY, INC.
6 East 45th St., 10017
(212) 687-3911
George Menegus/Daniel E. Comiskey/ Rita Grady

MARY DIEHL PLACEMENT BUREAU, INC.
50 E. 42nd St. 10017
(212) MU 7-1632
Rose-Joan Grotta/Estelle L. Meyer
AD,ED,F,OFF ADM,RE,S

MASTER PERSONNEL AGENCY, INC.
11 John St. 10038
(212) 227-7310
Dan Sullivan
AD,COMP,F,LEG,OFF ADM,OS, RE,S

MEDICAL CAREERS AGENCY, INC.
342 Madison Ave. Room 722 10017
(212) 687-7065
(Mrs.) Virginia C. Thorp
MED,OFF ADM,ED,F,OS

MERIDIAN PERSONNEL ASSOCIATES, INC. AGENCY
25 W. 45th St. 10036
(212) 247-4300
Jack Berger/Joel Berger/Joseph Reese
AD,F,FS,LEG,MED,OFF ADM,OS, RE,S,TE

MICHAEL CRAIG PERSONNEL, INC.
150 Broadway 10038
(212) 267-6300
Irwin Dort
COMP,F,LEG,OFF ADM,TE

MICHAELS PERSONNEL AGENCY, INC.
2 West 45th St. 10036
(212) 697-4020
Carl Morgenbesser/Victor Kalos
AD,COMP,F,OFF ADM,S

MILLER-GREENE ASSOCIATES, INC.
501 Fifth Avenue 10017
(212) 986-3950
Albert H. Miller/Angela Greene
AD,COMP,F,OFF ADM,S,TE

MORAN AGENCY, INC.
9 East 47th St. 10017
(212) 751-2915
Matthew F. Moran
AD,OFF ADM

NASSAU MEDICAL EXCHANGE
11 W. 42nd St. 10036
(212) 244-8101
Ichabod Klasfeld/Pauline Klasfeld
MD,OFF ADM

NEW YORK MEDICAL EXCHANGE, INC.
25 W. 45th St. 10036
(212) 757-0662
(Miss) Patricia Edgerly
MED

OXFORD PERSONNEL, INC.
341 Madison Ave. 10017
(212) 695-0730
Bernard Lubliner
FS

PALMATEER PERSONNEL AGENCY
18 E. 41st St. 10017
(212) 532-1412
George R. Palmateer/Arthur J. Hansen
AD,F,LEG,OFF ADM,OS

QUALIFIED TECHNICAL EMPLOYMENT AGENCY
485 - 5th Ave. 10017
(212) 661-4844
Harold Cooper
ED,F,LEG,MED,OFF ADM,S,TE

REBECCA EHRINPRIES PERSONNEL, INC.
366 Fifth Ave. 10001
(212) 565-0655
Rebecca Ehrinpries
AD,F,OFF ADM,RE

RESEARCH EXECUTIVE PERSONNEL AGENCY, INC.
420 Madison Ave. 10017
(212) 755-3918
Ess Wein
AD

ROBERT HALF PERSONNEL AGENCIES, INC.
330 Madison Ave. 10017
(212) 986-1300
Bernard Wilens
COMP,F

ROBERTS-LUND PERSONNEL, LTD.
366 Madison Ave. 10017
(212) 490-3300
Paul A. Roberts/Michael P. Iserson
F,OFF ADM,S,TE

ROSE LESLIE PERSONNEL AGENCY, INC.
475 Fifth Ave. 10017
(212) LE 2-5120
(Mrs.) Rose H. Leslie
AD

ROTH YOUNG PERSONNEL SERVICE, INC.
18 E. 41st St. 10017
(212) 689-8020
David Roth/Ralph Young
AD,F,MED,OFF ADM,RE,S,TE

SALES CONSULTANTS EMPLOYMENT AGENCY, INC.
Penthouse 535 Madison Ave. 10022
(212) 421-4466
Benjamin M. Thomas, III
S

NEW YORK—Continued

SALESMEN UNLIMITED AGENCY, INC.
485 5th Ave. 10016
(212) 661-5800
Arthur R. Abrams/Joseph Schupler
FS

HENRY SCHAPPER AGENCY, INC.
101 Park Ave. 10017
(212) 683-8626
Henry Schapper/Robert Parrella/Cleo Phillips
AD

SIMMONS PERSONNEL SERVICE, INC.
25 W. 45th St. 10036
(212) 265-3320
Robert B. Simmons
AD,F,LEG,OFF ADM

**SMITH'S FIFTH AVENUE PERSONNEL
  AGENCY**
1472 Broadway 10036
(212) 564-1350
Arnold Milgaten/Marcia Fleschner
AD,ED,F,FS,OFF ADM,S

STANDARD EMPLOYMENT SERVICE
475 5th Ave. 10017
(212) 683-4070
D. Dyckman/Dorothy Randall
OS,TE

**STANTON PERSONNEL SERVICE,
  LTD.**
2 E. 42nd St. 10017
(212) 986-2913
Gerald Vogel
F,OFF ADM,RE,S

STITT ASSOCIATES AGENCY, INC.
52 Vanderbilt Ave. 10017
Ted Stitt
FS,RE

TAFT PERSONNEL AGENCY
341 Madison Ave. 10017
(212) 687-6640
Peter F. Gay/David West/David Lavine
AD,COMP,F,LEG,OS,RE,S,TE

VOGUE PERSONNEL AGENCY
2 E. 42nd St. 10017
Gerald Vogel
FS

WARD CLANCY ASSOCIATES
545 Fifth Ave. 10017
(212) 661-6490
Anthony C. Ward/John Clancy/
  Andrew Sherwood
AD,F,S,TE

WATSON PERSONNEL AGENCY
8 W. 40th St. 10018
(212) 524-1339
Charles R. Watson
F,S

WINSTON PERSONNEL AGENCY, INC.
18 E. 41st St. 10017
(212) 889-1700
Sy Kaye
AD,F,OFF ADM

XL PERSONNEL, INC.
11 W. 42nd St. 10036
(212) 279-8200, 594-3300
Warren S. Moss
AD,COMP,F,FS,OFF ADM,RE,S,TE

**YALE REGISTRY FOR NURSES &
  EMPLOYMENT AGENCY, INC.**
186 East 73rd St. 10021
(212) 288-0040
Mae E. Curtis
MED

ROCHESTER

**BAILEY EMPLOYMENT SERVICE OF
  ROCHESTER, INC.**
1053 Sibley Tower 14604
Harold J. Levy
FS

DUNHILL OF ROCHESTER, INC.
15 Prince St. 14607
(716) 442-5900
Jack J. Tanner
AD,COMP,F,LEG,OFF ADM,RE,S,TE

KRUPKA EMPLOYMENT AGENCY
Suite 1012, Sibley Tower Bldg.
  25 North Street 14604
(716) 325-4434
Marjorie M. Krupka
AD,COMP,ED,F,LEG,MED,OFF ADM,
  RE,S,TE

TALENT SEARCH, INC.
607 Temple Bldg. 14604
(716) 546-5595
B. C. Bush/Robert B. Snyder
AD,COMP,F,LEG,OFF ADM,S,TE

SYRACUSE

CAREER COUNSELORS AGENCY
412 State Tower Bldg., 109 S. Warren St. 13202
James H. O'Neill
FS

**COLLEGE AND PROFESSIONAL
  PLACEMENT SERVICE AGENCY**
600 E. Genesee St. 13202
(315) 475-6179
James P. Kinsella
AD,COMP,ED,F,LEG,MED,OFF ADM,OS,
  RE,S,TE

**GREATER SYRACUSE EMPLOYMENT
  AGENCY, INC.**
526 University Bldg., 120 E. Washington St.
  13202
(315) 472-6607
Bev Corteville
AD,COMP,ED,F,LEG,MED,OFF ADM,RE,
  S,TE

J. W. WILLARD ASSOCIATES, INC.
220 S. Warren St. 13202
(315) 422-5111
John W. Willard
AD,COMP,ED,F,LEG,MED,OFF ADM,
  RE,S,TE

THE PERSONNEL CENTER
405 Loew Bldg. 13202
(315) 472-4551
Wilhma K. D'Addario
AD,COMP,F,LEG,OFF ADM,RE,S,TE

**SNELLING AND SNELLING OF
  SYRACUSE, INC.**
224 Harrison St. 13202
(315) 479-6651
James Sweeney
AD,COMP,F,LEG,OFF ADM,RE,S,TE

WHITE PLAINS

**AUTOMATED PERSONNEL INTER-
  NATIONAL OF WESTCHESTER, INC.**
34 South Broadway 10601
(914) 428-1700
Gerald A. Bertisch
COMP,F,OFF ADM,RE

BRENNAN EMPLOYMENT AGENCY
47 Mamaroneck Ave. 10601
(914) 949-7770, 949-7771, 949-7772
(Mrs.) Jane B. Swanson/
  (Mrs.) Anne Nathanson
F,FS,LEG,MED,OFF ADM,S

**MANAGEMENT RECRUITERS OF
  WESTCHESTER INC.**
1 N. Broadway 10601
(914) 949-1800
Charles F. Cole
AD,COMP,F,LEG,OFF ADM,RE,S,TE

**SNELLING AND SNELLING
  PERSONNEL**
99 Mamaroneck Ave. 10601
(914) 948-2322
James G. Iorio/Fred Olson
AD,COMP,F,LEG,MED,OFF ADM,RE,S,TE

TRI-STATE STAFFING ASSOCIATES, INC.
180 E. Post Rd. 10601
(914) 946-1227
William H. Strawson/David L. Tait/
  Richard J. Sandor
AD,COMP,F,OFF ADM,OS,S,TE

WORK IN WESTCHESTER, INC.
170 E. Post Rd. 10601
(914) 946-8660
John J. Blanchfield
COMP,F,LEG,OFF ADM,S,TE

NORTH CAROLINA

ASHEVILLE

SNELLING AND SNELLING
603 First Union National Bank Bldg. 28801
(704) 254-0921
E. L. Davis, Jr.
FS,OFF ADM,F,TE,AD,S,MED,LEG,ED

NORTH CAROLINA—Continued

CHARLOTTE

AMERICAN PERSONNEL OF CHARLOTTE, INC.
Suite 205, 1051 E. Morehead St. 28204
(704) 334-2884
Carson L. Young
AD,COMP,ED,F,LEG,OFF ADM,RE,S,TE

DUNHILL OF CHARLOTTE
808 Baugh Bldg., 112 S. Tryon St. 28202
(704) 375-2511
Elwyn C. Hannan
AD,COMP,F,FS,OFF ADM,RE,S,TE

KOGEN PERSONNEL OF CHARLOTTE
237 S. Tryon 28202
(704) 372-6650
Carl Swan
AD,COMP,F,LEG,MED,OFF ADM,RE,S,TE

MANAGEMENT RECRUITERS, INC.
Suite 1206, Baugh Bldg, 112 S. Tryon St. 28202
(704) 372-3202
Gilbert N. Ketcham/Charles W. Lent
AD,COMP,F,LEG,OFF ADM,RE,S,TE

SNELLING AND SNELLING OF CHARLOTTE, INC.
222 S. Church St. 28202
(704) 375-2501
Charles G. Jones
COMP,F,LEG,MED,OFF ADM,RE,S,TE

UNIVERSAL EMPLOYMENT SERVICE, INC.
1103 Baugh Bldg. 28202
(704) 372-8740
Robert M. Brooks
AD,COMP,ED,F,LEG,MED,OFF ADM, RE,S,TE

DURHAM

PHILIP L. CEGLIA & ASSOCIATES, INC.
Suite 221, Office Area #2, Northgate Shopping Center, 1058 W. Club. Blvd. 27701
(919) 286-0721
Philip L. Ceglia
AD,COMP,ED,F,LEG,MED,OFF ADM,OS, RE,S,TE

SNELLING AND SNELLING
717 CCB Bldg. 27701
(919) 682-5751
Anne W. Kern
AD,COMP,ED,F,LEG,MED,OFF ADM, RE,S,TE

FAYETTEVILLE

NATIONWIDE PERSONNEL SERVICE, INC.
806 Elm St. (P.O. Box 5925) 28303
(919) 484-6174
George D. Shooter, Jr./H. Ronald Stone
AD,COMP,F,OFF ADM,OS,RE,S,TE

SNELLING AND SNELLING
P.O. Box 525, 5th Floor, First Citizens Bank 28302
(919) 483-3671
G. P. Morris
AD,COMP,ED,F,LEG,MED,OFF ADM, RE,S,TE

GREENSBORO

APPROVED PERSONNEL SERVICE, INC.
Suite 1025, Wachovia Bldg. 27401
(919) 275-8636
Thomas S. Bishop
AD,COMP,F,LEG,MED,OFF ADM,RE,S,TE

EMPLOYERS PREFERRED PERSONNEL, INC.
1425 Wachovia Bldg. 27401
(919) 273-9706
Dick Krick
AD,COMP,F,OFF ADM,TE

SCHNEIDER, HILL & SPANGLER OF GREENSBORO, INC.
201 N. Elm St. 27401
James H. Pate
FS

SNELLING AND SNELLING OF GREENSBORO, INC.
102 N. Elm St., Suite 400 27401
(919) 275-0231
Joe D. Kyle, Sr.
AD,COMP,F,LEG,MED,OFF ADM,RE,S,TE

RALEIGH

NATIONAL EMPLOYMENT SERVICE, INC.
P.O. Box 468/212 Raleigh Bldg., 5 W. Hargett St. 27602
(919) 828-0777
G. W. "Bill" Poole
AD,COMP,ED,F,FS,LEG,MED,OFF ADM, OS,RE,S,TE

SNELLING AND SNELLING PERSONNEL SERVICE
615 Oberlin Rd. 27605
(919) 834-3692
Robt. C. Greene, Sr., CEC/Joseph P. Wofford
FS

WINSTON-SALEM

PARK'S PERSONNEL INC.
725 First Union Bldg. 27101
(919) 722-1186
E. P. Winburn
FS

SNELLING AND SNELLING
Suite 624, First Union Bldg. 27101
(919) 723-8821
James L. Williams
AD,COMP,F,LEG,MED,OFF ADM,RE,S,TE

WINSTON PLACEMENT INC.
602 Pepper Bldg. 27101
(919) 725-5328
(Mrs.) Shirley D. Shouse
AD,COMP,F,LEG,MED,OFF ADM,RE,S,TE

OHIO

AKRON

BAIRD EMPLOYMENT SERVICE
Suite 1006, Akron Savings Bldg. 44308
(216) 762-7641
George C. Baird/Russell K. Carter
AD,COMP,F,OFF ADM,RE,S,TE

NELSON PERSONNEL CONSULTANTS
600 First National Tower 44308
(216) 376-6861
Louis B. Bokanyi/Charles L. Hensley
AD,COMP,F,FS,OFF ADM,TE

SALES CONSULTANTS OF AKRON, INC.
137 S. Main, Suite 211 44308
(216) 762-9891
David R. Slutzker/Ned F. Bauhof, Jr.
AD,COMP,OFF ADM,RE,S,TE

CANTON

BAIRD EMPLOYMENT SERVICE
1201 30th N.W. 44709
(216) 452-9785
George C. Baird
FS

GREAT FALLS EMPLOYMENT AGENCY OF CANTON, INC.
330 Cleveland Ave. N.W. 44702
(216) 456-2701
Earl E. Rayl
AD,COMP,ED,F,FS,LEG,MED,OFF ADM, RE,S,TE

KAVANAGH PERSONNEL
1201 - 30th St. N.W. 44709
(216) 492-6298
George R. Dawson
FS,AD,COMP,ED,F,LEG,MED,OFF ADM, RE,S,TE

NELSON PERSONNEL CONSULTANTS
514 Citizens Savings Bldg., 110 Central Plaza S. 44702
(216) 453-9168
Paul B. Blair/Victor J. Glenn
AD,COMP,F,LEG,MED,OFF ADM,RE,S,TE

SNELLING AND SNELLING OF CANTON
220 E. Tuscarawas St. 44702
(216) 456-4511
Howard S. Rubin/Richard Cord
AD,COMP,ED,F,FS,LEG,MED,OFF ADM, RE,S,TE

CINCINNATI

DUNHILL OF CINCINNATI INC.
Suite 602, Terrace Hilton, 15 W. 6th St. 45202
(513) 621-9905
Allan R. Soldwisch/Raymond Henson
AD,COMP,F,FS,LEG,OFF ADM,RE, S,TE

OHIO—Continued

EXECUTIVE CONSULTANTS
35 E. 7th St. 45202
(513) 621-5885
John A. Blum/Pauline M. Taylor
COMP,F,LEG,OFF ADM,TE

ROBERT HALF PERSONNEL AGENCIES OF CINCINNATI, INC.
606 Terrace Hilton 45202
(513) 621-7711
Gerald G. Gilberg
COMP,F

SALES CONSULTANTS
Enquirer Bldg., Suite 1020, 617 Vine St. 45202
(513) 621-8010
Robert Tanner
S

SNELLING AND SNELLING
7796 Montgomery Rd. 45236
(513) 793-5560
H. S. Sackett
FS,OFF ADM,S,TE

CLEVELAND

BELL PERSONNEL SERVICE, INC.
530 Williamson Bldg., 215 Euclid Ave. 44114
(216) 241-4500
Walter C. Mason
FS,F,LEG,OFF ADM,S,TE

BRUCKER, YAECKER, GIBSON AND RUSSELL
1301 Citizens Bldg. 44114
(216) 621-9686
Robert J. Brucker/
 Albert E. Yaecker
F,OFF ADM,TE

CHAMPION PERSONNEL SYSTEM, INC.
335 Euclid Ave. 44114
(216) 781-5900
Ralph A. Schepens
AD,COMP,F,FS,OFF ADM,RE,S,TE

CRETNEY AND ASSOCIATES, INC.
754 Hanna Bldg. 44116
(216) 771-2141
Wilfred T. Cretney
F,LEG,OFF ADM,S,TE

DREHER EMPLOYMENT SERVICE, INC.
Suite 682 Old Arcade, 401 Euclid Ave. 44114
(216) 861-1980
Harold A. Dreher/Frances K. Dreher
AD,COMP,F,FS,LEG,RE,S,TE

HOLBROOK & ASSOCIATES
21010 Center Ridge Rd. 44116
(216) 333-1810
M. Richard Holbrook
AD,COMP,F,LEG,OFF ADM,RE,S,TE

MAERKLE, FRENCH ASSOCIATES
944 Hanna Bldg., 1422 Euclid Ave. 44115
(216) 861-5865
Elmer H. French, Jr.
AD,COMP,F,LEG,OFF ADM,RE,S,TE

MANAGEMENT RECRUITERS INTERNATIONAL, INC.
1255 Euclid Ave. 5th Floor 44115
(216) 696-1122
Elton D. Marcus/Alan R. Schonberg/
 Marvin B. Basil
COMP,FS,OS,S

MARY L. FIELD ASSOCIATES
1801 E. 12th St., Chesterfield Suite 218 44114
(216) 522-1810
Mary L. Field
Exec. & Mgmt., Food & Hospitality

PERSONNEL ASSOCIATES
Ten-Ten Euclid Bldg., Suite 200 44116
(216) 861-2600
Donald A. Kingsbury
AD,COMP,F,OFF ADM,S,TE

ROBERT HALF PERSONNEL AGENCIES OF CLEVELAND, INC.
1367 East 6th St. 44114
(216) 621-0670
James R. Herbig
COMP,F

SALES CONSULTANTS, INC.
1001 Euclid Ave. 44115
(216) 623-1030
William C. Maxwell
S

WESTGATE PERSONNEL, INC.
20325 Center Ridge Rd. 44116
(216) 333-1344
Richard Gigax
F,OFF ADM,S,TE

COLUMBUS

ACCURATE EMPLOYMENT SERVICE
16 E. Broad St., Room 606 43215
(614) 224-8254
Charlotte R. Vought
AD,COMP,ED,F,LEG,MED,OFF ADM,
 RE,S,TE

DUNHILL OF COLUMBUS
Suite 345, 88 East Broad St. 43215
(614) 228-4576
Leo Salzman
AD,COMP,ED,F,LEG,OFF ADM,RE,S,TE

MANAGEMENT RECRUITERS
88 E. Broad St., Suite 1115 43215
(614) 221-1111
Jack R. Wolin
AD,COMP,ED,F,FS,LEG,MED,OFF ADM,
 RE,S,TE

NATIONWIDE CAREER CENTERS
21 E. State St. 43215
(614) 228-6501
James E. DeMaria/Nancy Clapper
AD,F,MED,OFF ADM,RE,S,TE

DAYTON

NATIONAL EMPLOYMENT SERVICE
4 S. Main St. 45402
(513) 222-8964
Samuel A. Mays/John C. Bunn/Duke Ayers
AD,COMP,F,FS,OFF ADM,RE,S,TE

SNELLING AND SNELLING
3 E. Second St.
(513) 224-1961
Edwin H. Gessel/Vern Frost/
 Joseph Andrasik
AD,COMP,F,FS,LEG,MED,OFF ADM,
 RE,S,TE

TOLEDO

AMERICAN PERSONNEL SERVICES
1025 Edison Bldg. 43604
(419) 248-3724
John William Jones
FS

CLAUS EMPLOYMENT SERVICE, INC.
520 Madison Ave. 43604
Peter Claus
FS

IMPERIAL PLACEMENT SERVICE
316 Gardner Bldg. 43604
(419) 243-2222
Albert J. Sprenger
FS

OTT & FORNI PERSONNEL SPECIALISTS
406 Madison Ave. 43604
(419) 243-9203
Robert B. Forni/Irene H. Ott
AD,COMP,F,OFF ADM,S,TE

R. G. HUDSON & CO.
Commodore Perry Arcade 43604
(419) 248-2651
Richard G. Hudson, Jr.
FS

SAUTTER EMPLOYMENT SERVICE
626 Madison Ave. 43604
(419) 243-4271
A. H. Sautter/R. L. Storck
AD,COMP,F,OFF ADM,S,TE

TOLEDO EMPLOYMENT SERVICE
2909 W. Central Ave. 43606
(419) 479-9684
Kenneth H. Robinson
AD,COMP,F,FS,OFF ADM,RE,S,TE

OHIO—Continued

YOUNGSTOWN

DAVIS PERSONNEL CONSULTANTS
500 Union National Bank Bldg. 44503
(216) 747-2621
Willard T. Davis/John G. Callos
AD,COMP,ED,F,FS,LEG,MED,OFF ADM,
OS,RE,S,TE

KOGEN PERSONNEL OF YOUNGSTOWN, INC.
Suite 415 Legal Arts Centre, 101 Market St.
44503
(216) 746-0571
John S. Goodridge
FS

WELLS VOCATIONAL SERVICE
1006 Realty Bldg. 44503
(216) 744-4174
(Mrs.) Marjorie Martin
AD,COMP,ED,F,LEG,MED,OFF ADM,
OS,RE,S,TE

OKLAHOMA

OKLAHOMA CITY

BEACON EMPLOYMENT SERVICE
460 Leininger Bldg., 3545 N.W. 58 73112
(405) 947-2387
Leonard Jay
AD,COMP,ED,F,FS,LEG,MED,OFF ADM,
RE,S,TE

UNIVERSAL EMPLOYMENT SERVICE
1013 Cravens Bldg. 73102
(405) 235-0475
Paul A. Ogle/Mary Lee Ogle
COMP,F,LEG,MED,OFF ADM,RE,S,TE

ZIP PERSONNEL, INC.
2452 N.W. 39th, Spanish Village Min-Mall
73112
(405) 528-2985
Mary McDaris Simons/Foye Story/
Ray Hawkins
AD,COMP,F,FS,LEG,MED,OFF ADM,
RE,S,TE

TULSA

CAREER SPECIALISTS
201 Thompson Bldg. 5th at Boston
74103
(918) 584-4771
(Mrs.) Margaret Olsen/(Mrs.) Lee Williams
AD,COMP,F,LEG,MED,OFF ADM,OS,
RE,S,TE

LLOYD RICHARDS EMPLOYMENT SERVICE
Plaza Bldg., 8 E. 3rd St. 74103
(918) 582-5251
Lloyd Richards
AD,COMP,ED,F,FS,LEG,MED,OFF ADM,
OS,RE,S,TE

SALES CONSULTANTS OF TULSA
1810 4th National Bank Bldg. 74119
(918) 583-1191
Max C. Nelson
AD,COMP,S,TE

TURNER/WICK PERSONNEL
2525 E. 21st St. 74114
(918) 743-7852
Margaret R. Wick/Jim Cumby
AD,COMP,F,LEG,MED,OFF ADM,OS,
RE,S,TE

OREGON

PORTLAND

BUSINESS MEN'S CLEARING HOUSE
900 S. W. 5th Ave. 97206
(503) 222-3537
Roger Johnson
FS

DUNHILL OF PORTLAND, INC.
618 S.W. 5th Ave. 97204
(503) 224-1850
Courtland F. Carrier/Betty Carrier
AD,COMP,F,OFF ADM,RE,S,TE

HARPER ASSOCIATES, INC.-PORTLAND
522 S.W. Fifth Ave. 97204
(503) 226-2621
J. K. Long
AD,COMP,F,FS,LEG,OFF ADM,
RE,S,TE

MANAGEMENT RECRUITERS OF PORTLAND
818 Executive Bldg., 811 S.W. 6th
97204
(503) 224-8870
Jack R. Stowell
AD,COMP,F,LEG,MED,OFF ADM,RE,S,TE

RIVERGATE PERSONNEL
3534 N. Lombard 97203
Kay Snow
FS

SNELLING AND SNELLING
711 S.W. Alder 97205
(503) 224-1925
Sheldon Barry
FS,OFF ADM,F,TE,AD,S

PENNSYLVANIA

ALLENTOWN

KOGEN PERSONNEL
11 N. 7th St. 18101
(215) 437-4805
S. David Davis/Marvin Lemisch
AD,COMP,F,LEG,OFF ADM,RE,
S,TE

LEHIGH EMPLOYMENT SERVICE
534 Hamilton St. 18101
(215) 433-7569, 433-7560
Elsie M. Yellis
AD,COMP,ED,F,LEG,OFF ADM,OS,
RE,S,TE

SNELLING AND SNELLING
1132 Hamilton St. 18101
(215) 437-9821
Murray A. E. Howden/Joseph Wroble
AD,COMP,ED,F,LEG,MED,OFF ADM,OS,
RE,S,TE

SNELLING AND SNELLING
672 Hanover Ave. 18103
(215) 435-4764
Joseph Wroble
AD,COMP,ED,F,LEG,MED,OFF ADM,OS,
RE,S,TE

BALA CYNWYD

LAWRENCE PERSONNEL
29 Bala Ave. 19004
(215) 839-1500
Larry A. Goldberg
AD,COMP,F,OFF ADM,OS,S,TE

SNELLING AND SNELLING
217 One Decker Square 19004
(215) 667-4222
George B. Hannay
AD,COMP,F,FS,LEG,MED,OFF ADM,S,TE

HARRISBURG

SNELLING AND SNELLING
123 Walnut St. 17101
(717) 233-4593
Robinson Stevens
AD,COMP,ED,F,LEG,MED,OFF ADM,
RE,S,TE

PHILADELPHIA

ALLEN & ALLEN
1411 Walnut St. 19102
(215) 568-4350
Mindy Allen
FS

AMES EMPLOYMENT SERVICE, INC.
1601 Walnut St., Suite 1010
(215) 569-3737
Roslyn Kaufman/Jerome L. Kaufman
CEC/Mollie Stern, CEC
F,FS,OFF ADM,S

ANDERSON-TAYLOR & ASSOCIATES
230 South 15th St. 19102
(215) 546-6333
Eugene G. Taylor
AD,COMP,F,LEG,MED,OFF ADM,S,TE

ATOMIC PERSONNEL, INC.
1518 Walnut St. 19102
(215) 735-4908
Arthur L. Krasnow
AD,COMP,LEG,MED,S,TE

PENNSYLVANIA—Continued

AUSTIN PERSONNEL CONSULTANTS
12 S. 12th St. 19107
(215) 925-3446
David D. Brown/Bert Blicher
AD,COMP,F,LEG,OFF ADM,S,TE

E. J. BETTINGER COMPANY
1510 Chestnut St. 19102
(215) 564-0700
E. J. Bettinger/H. Nicholson/C. Thorne/
  C. Berke
AD,COMP,ED,F,LEG,OFF ADM,RE,S,TE

**CAREER DEVELOPMENT ASSOCIATES,
  INC.**
1422 Chestnut St., Suite 415 19102
(215) 561-2100
Christopher P. Mooney/Robert H. Kindred
F,FS,OFF ADM,RE,S

CAREERS, INC.
830 Philadelphia National Bank Bldg.,
  Broad & Chestnut Sts. 19107
(215) 563-9005
Frank C. Trexler
AD,COMP,F,FS,OFF ADM,S,TE

EVERETT KELLY ASSOCIATES
121 S. Broad St., - Suite 1320 19107
(215) 546-5240
Everett Kelly
OFF ADM,F,TE,AD,S,MED,LEG,ED,OS,FS

**EXECUTIVE EMPLOYMENT SERVICE,
  INC.**
37 S. 13th St. 19107
(215) 567-2828
John Previti/John W. McLaughlin
AD,COMP,F,OFF ADM,S,TE

**F-O-R-T-U-N-E PERSONNEL AGENCY
  OF PHILA., INC.**
1528 Walnut St. 19102
(215) 546-9490
Joel S. Hatoff
FS

HAYES PERSONNEL SERVICE
259 S. 17th St. 19103
(212) PE5-3079
(Miss) Marion A. Hayes
FS

METROPOLITAN PERSONNEL, INC.
1700 Market St., Suite 2730 19103
(215) 561-5522
Lawrence J. La Boon/Robert B. Paul/
  Anne McAllister
AD,F,FS,LEG,OFF ADM,RE,S

O'SHEA SYSTEM OF EMPLOYMENT
1 E. Penn Square 19107
(215) LO 7-6000
Samuel Francis Maben
AD,COMP,F,LEG,OFF ADM,OS,TE

PAUL STEVENS & ASSOCIATES, INC.
1324 Walnut St. 19107
(215) 546-6354
Paul Stevens
F,OFF ADM,S,TE

PRESSLER EMPLOYMENT SERVICE
21 S. 12th St. 19107
(215) 564-1090
Eugene C. Pressler, Sr./E. C. Pressler, Jr.
AD,COMP,F,OFF ADM,TE

**ROBERT HALF PERSONNEL AGENCIES
  OF PHILADELPHIA**
2 Penn Center Plaza 19102
(215) 568-4580
A. S. Grishman
COMP,F

**ROTH YOUNG PERSONNEL SERVICE OF
  PHILADELPHIA INC.**
1015 Chestnut St. 19107
(215) 923-7200
C. C. Catacosinos
AD,COMP,F,OFF ADM,RE,S,TE

RUSHTON PERSONNEL SERVICE
121 S. Broad St. 19107
(215) 545-0140
(Miss) Mary E. Rushton/James A. Rushton
F,OFF ADM

SALES CONSULTANTS, INC.
Suburban Station Bldg., Suite 354,
  1617 J. F. Kennedy Blvd. 19103
(215) 569-1450
Stephen Berlin
S

SCHNEIDER, HILL & SPANGLER, INC.
121 S. Broad St. 19107
(215) 546-2804
Tom Megill
AD,COMP,F,LEG,OFF ADM,RE,S,TE

SCIENCE CENTER
8040 Roosevelt Boulevard 19152
(215) 333-9783
Robert J. Lynch
COMP,S,TE

SNELLING AND SNELLING
1530 Chestnut St. 19102
(215) 568-5900
John J. McBrearty
AD,COMP,F,FS,LEG,MED,OFF ADM,S,TE

STURM, BURROWS & COMPANY
1420 Walnut St. 19102
(215) 546-4111
Frederick C. Sturm, Jr./
  Garfield C. Burrows, Jr.
AD,COMP,F,LEG,OFF ADM,S,TE

PITTSBURGH

ROBERT J. BUSHEE & ASSOCIATES, INC.
300 Sixth Ave. Bldg. 15222
(412) 471-5750
Robert J. Bushee/Joseph F. Cornelius/
  Richard L. Phifer/Dorothea R. Crass
AD,COMP,F,FS,LEG,OFF ADM,OS,RE,S,TE

**CONSULTANT SERVICE ENTERPRISES,
  INC.**
708 Empire Building
  507 Liberty Ave. 15222
(412) 471-6133
Walter W. Armstead
AD,COMP,ED,F,LEG,OFF ADM,S,TE

**COSMOPOLITAN PROFESSIONAL
  PLACEMENT, INC.**
2007 Investment Bldg., 239 Fourth Ave.
  15222
(412) 261-1390
Mabel L. Anderson
AD,COMP,ED,F,LEG,MED,OFF ADM,
  RE,S,TE

DUNHILL OF PITTSBURGH, INC.
221 Oliver Bldg. 15222
(412) 261-6070
James C. Drumm/
  Richard L. Schweiger
AD,COMP,F,FS,OFF ADM,RE,S,TE

FISHER PERSONNEL SERVICES
1010 N. American Rockwell Bldg. 15205
(412) 391-1700
W. R. Chadwick
AD,COMP,ED,F,FS,LEG,MED,OFF ADM,RE
  S,TE

**GILBERT LANE PERSONNEL AGENCY
  OF PITTSBURGH**
903 N. American Rockwell Bldg. 15222
(412) 391-7300
Steven N. Brieger
AD,COMP,F,OFF ADM,S,TE

LEONARD PERSONNEL SERVICES
414 N. American Rockwell Bldg. 15222
(216) 281-2888
A. Barry Leonard
AD,COMP,F,S,OFF ADM,LEG

**LIKEN EMPLOYMENT AND PERSONNEL
  SERVICE**
4 Gateway Center 15222
(412) 391-1866
Dale E. Liken/Robert D. Liken
AD,COMP,ED,F,LEG,MED,OFF ADM,OS,
  RE,S,TE

**MEDICAL HOSPITAL PLACEMENT
  BUREAU**
3506 5th Ave. 15213
(412) 683-6570
Raymond W. Hussey, Jr.
AD,COMP,ED,F,MED,OFF ADM,S,TE

**MONTGOMERY EMPLOYMENT &
  SERVICE BUREAU**
5077 Jenkins Arcade 15222
(412) 471-2787
Robert P. Shaffer/June C. Shaffer
AD,COMP,F,LEG,OFF ADM,RE,S,TE

**ROBERT HALF PERSONNEL AGENCIES
  OF PITTSBURGH, INC.**
Gateway Towers 15222 (412) 471-5946
Thomas H. Hurst, Jr.
COMP,F

PENNSYLVANIA—Continued

SALES CONSULTANTS, INC.
1912 Clark Bldg., 717 Liberty Ave. 15222
(412) 281-6900
William R. Blume
S

STRAUSS PERSONNEL SERVICE
1523 Park Bldg., 305 Fifth Ave. 15222
(412) 281-8235
Lester H. Strauss/Jay K. Jarrell/
 Estelle M. Strauss
AD,COMP,ED,F,LEG,OFF ADM,RE,S,TE

TOMSETT ASSOCIATES, INC.
402 Frick Bldg. 15219
(412) 471-2050
Richard S. MacQuown
AD,COMP,F,LEG,OFF ADM,OS,RE,S,TE

TRIANGLE PERSONNEL SERVICE
1023 Park Bldg. 15222
(412) 471-6762
Edna A. Jaros, CEC/Margaret Kerr
FS

RHODE ISLAND

PROVIDENCE

**MANAGEMENT RECRUITERS OF
 RHODE ISLAND**
155 Westminster 02903
(401) 831-7050
Eugene W. Majewski
AD,COMP,F,LEG,OFF ADM,RE,S,TE

WARWICK

**MANAGEMENT RECRUITERS OF
 RHODE ISLAND**
1230 Greenwich Ave. 02886
(401) 739-8400
Eugene W. Majewski/Herb Fradin
FS

SCHATTLE AND STORTI, INC.
2845 Post Rd. 02886
(401) 739-0500
Michael A. Storti/Donald J. Schattle
AD,COMP,F,LEG,OFF ADM,RE,S,TE

SOUTH CAROLINA

CHARLESTON

SNELLING AND SNELLING
134 Meeting St. 29401
(803) 723-7816
R. B. Hamms, Jr.
AD,COMP,ED,F,LEG,MED,OFF ADM,OS,
 RE,S,TE

COLUMBIA

CONTINENTAL CONSULTANTS, INC.
2418 Devine St. 29205
(803) 779-4030
John S. Rinehart
F,TE

DATA SERVICES
P.O. Box 1355 29202
(803) 254-5467
F. E. Woods
COMP,F,OFF ADM,S,TE

**MANAGEMENT RECRUITERS OF
 COLUMBIA**
1801 Main St.
(803) 779-5660
Oneal Hightower
FS

PERSONNEL ASSISTANCE
301 Palmetto Bldg., 1440 Main St. 29201
Don Phillips
FS

SNELLING AND SNELLING
Suite 2-A, Jefferson Square 29202
(803) 779-3520
Charles A. Edwards
AD,COMP,F,FS,OFF ADM,RE,S,TE

TECHNICAL SERVICES
Suite 507, 1310 Lady Street
(803) 779-5088
Bill Tolleson
FS

FLORENCE

SNELLING AND SNELLING
615 Florence Trust Bldg. 29501
(803) 662-8471
Douglas Parsons/Monte Parsons
AD,COMP,F,LEG,OFF ADM,RE,S,TE

GREENVILLE

**AMERICAN PERSONNEL & EXECUTIVE
 PLACEMENT SERVICE**
712 Hudson Bldg., 135 S. Main St.
 29601
(803) 239-5381
E. G. Sinclair, Jr.
AD,ED,F,LEG,MED,OFF ADM,S,TE

DUNHILL OF GREENVILLE, INC.
12th Floor, SCN Bldg. 29601
(803) 232-7305
Duke Haynie
AD,COMP,ED,F,LEG,OFF ADM,RE
 S,TE

**GODSHALL & GODSHALL PERSONNEL
 CONSULTANTS, INC.**
Suite 1212, Daniel Bldg. 29602
(803) 242-3491
Wayne C. Godshall
AD,COMP,F,LEG,OFF ADM,OS,RE,S,TE

**SNELLING AND SNELLING OF
 GREENVILLE, INC.**
S. C. Nat'l Bank Bldg. 29601
(803) 232-5181
Joe E. Lambeth
AD,COMP,F,FS,LEG,MED,OFF ADM,RE
 S,TE

TENNESSEE

CHATTANOOGA

HILL EMPLOYMENT BUREAU
502 American National Bank Bldg. 37402
(615) 266-8185
Dorothy Holt
AD,COMP,ED,F,FS,LEG,MED,OFF ADM,
 OS,RE,S,TE

SNELLING AND SNELLING
521 Pioneer Bank Bldg. 37402
(615) 266-4851
W. W. Brunson/D. S. Hawxhurst
AD,COMP,ED,F,FS,LEG,MED,OFF ADM,
 RE,S,TE

SNELLING AND SNELLING
Suite 3200, 6100 Bldg., Eastgate 37411
(615) 894-1500
C. R. Stanton
FS,AD,COMP,ED,F,LEG,MED,OFF ADM,
 RE,S,TE

KNOXVILLE

KNOXVILLE PERSONNEL SERVICE, INC.
607 Market St. 37902
(615) 524-7325
O. K. Anderson
AD,COMP,F,LEG,MED,OFF ADM,RE,S,TE

MEMPHIS

CROSSTOWN EMPLOYMENT SERVICE
McClure Bldg., 1231 E. Raines Rd., Suite
 207 38116
(901) 396-1780
Ruth M. Farris
AD,COMP,F,LEG,MED,OFF ADM,RE,S,TE

DELTA EMPLOYMENT CORPORATION
805 Memphis Bank Bldg. 38103
(901) 525-0111
Freda Dodd
AD,COMP,ED,F,LEG,MED,OFF ADM,
 RE,S,TE

EXECUTIVE SERVICE, INC.
1212 First National Bank Bldg. 38103
(901) 527-3431
Daniel S. Whipple
AD,COMP,F,LEG,MED,OFF ADM,OS,
 RE,S,TE

EXECUTIVE SERVICE, INC.
4990 Poplar Ave., Suite 205 38117
(901) 682-2451
Daniel S. Whipple
AD,COMP,F,LEG,MED,OFF ADM,OS,
 RE,S,TE

GREAR PERSONNEL SERVICE
766 S. Highland #102 38111
(901) 452-7318
Anne Grear
AD,COMP,ED,F,FS,LEG,MED,OFF ADM,
 RE,S,TE

TENNESSEE—Continued

JAMES PAIR PERSONNEL SERVICE
100 N. Main Bldg., Suite 1029 38103
(901) 527-4301
James Pair, CEC/Opal Robinson
FS

LEAKE-SHAPIRO PERSONNEL SERVICE, INC.
701 Sterick Bldg., 8 N. 3rd St. 38103
(901) 525-1616
Lucille H. Leake
AD,COMP,F,LEG,MED,OFF ADM,
RE,S,TE

LEE WHIPPLE PERSONNEL SERVICE
301 Emmons Bldg., 4745 Poplar Ave. 38117
(901) 684-1411
R. Lee Whipple
AD,COMP,ED,F,FS,LEG,MED, OFF ADM,
OS,RE,S,TE

ROTH YOUNG PERSONNEL SERVICE OF MEMPHIS, INC.
Suite 1409, 1331 Union Ave. 38104
(901) 278-5573
Floyd E. Williams
AD,F,MED,OFF ADM,RE,S,TE

NASHVILLE

DEALY-ROURKE PERSONNEL SERVICE
Suite 121, 1808 W. End Bldg. 37219
(615) 329-1771
Robert C. Rourke
AD,COMP,F,FS,LEG,OFF ADM,S,TE

KEY PERSONNEL SERVICE
1817 Parkway Towers 37219
(615) 255-5722
Dick Dorney/Dottie Dorney
AD,COMP,F,LEG,OFF ADM,RE,S,TE

OCCUPATIONAL PLACEMENT SERVICE, INC.
16th Floor, Third National Bank Bldg. 37219
(615) 255-1156
Jack C. Ramer/Kenneth G. Rogers
AD,COMP,ED,F,LEG,MED,OFF ADM,
RE,S,TE

PROGRESSIVE PERSONNEL SERVICE
1701 West End Ave. 37203
(615) 254-6683
(Mrs.) Irene S. Philbin
AD,COMP,ED,F,FS,LEG,OFF ADM,
RE,S,TE

TEXAS

ABILENE

AAA PERSONNEL SERVICE
1265 S. Danville Dr. 79605
692-4630
Mary Douglas
AD,COMP,ED,F,LEG,MED,OFF ADM,
RE,S,TE

LASSITER EMPLOYMENT SERVICE
1341 N. 2nd St. 79601
(915) 672-1355
Joe E. Lassiter
AD,COMP,ED,F,FS,LEG,OFF ADM,S,TE

AMARILLO

FRASIER EMPLOYMENT SERVICE
2805 Wolflin Ave. 79109
(806) 355-5691
U. L. "Bud" Frasier/Virginia Frasier
AD,COMP,FS,LEG,MED,OFF ADM,RE,S,TE

SHAW & ASSOCIATES
815 Fisk Bldg., P.O. Box 1948 79105
(806) 376-5511
J. Allen/Dorothy Shaw
FS

VANCE EMPLOYMENT SERVICE
Suite 217, Barfield Bldg. 79101
(806) 372-3456
Berlin Vance
AD,COMP,F,LEG,MED,OFF ADM,OS,
RE,S,TE

ARLINGTON

MIDWAY PERSONNEL SERVICE
818 A E. Abram 76010
(817) 277-6644, 261-0783
Jim Stessel
FS

PARKER PLACEMENT SERVICE
123 W. Main, Suite 107 76010
(817) 277-6183
Marjorie Parker
AD,F,LEG,MED,OFF ADM,S,TE

AUSTIN

EVINS PERSONNEL CONSULTANTS, INC.
959 Reinli 78751
(512) 454-9561
Mary E. Evins
AD,COMP,ED,F,FS,LEG,MED,OFF ADM,
OS,RE,S,TE

SNELLING AND SNELLING
1011 Congress Ave. 78701
(512) 477-5761
E. J. Hart
AD,COMP,ED,F,LEG,MED,OFF ADM,
OS,RE,S,TE

TARRANT EMPLOYMENT
122 Perry-Brooks Bldg. 78701
(512) 477-5737
C. Hugh Tarrant
FS

BEAUMONT

DELTA EMPLOYMENT SERVICE
520 San Jacinto Bldg. 77701
(713) 835-1493
(Mrs.) Violet L. Last
AD,COMP,ED,F,LEG,MED,OFF ADM,
OS,RE,S,TE

GARFIELD EMPLOYMENT SERVICE
2462 Calder Ave. 77706
(713) 838-4777
(Mrs.) Anette Hein
OFF ADM,S,TE

SNELLING AND SNELLING
620 Beaumont Savings Bldg. 77701
(713) 835-4971, 838-0421
George A. Rigely/Helen M. Rigely
AD,COMP,ED,F,FS,LEG,MED,OFF ADM,
RE,S,TE

DALLAS

ANCHOR EMPLOYMENT SERVICE
Suite 405, 1512 Commerce St. 75201
(214) 741-6114, 747-8898
(Mrs.) Mae Lindsay
AD,COMP,F,FS,LEG,OFF ADM,S,TE

availABILITY OF METROPOLITAN DALLAS
1607 Main St. 75201
(214) 748-0551
W. Fred Davies
FS

BRAND EMPLOYMENT SERVICE
130 Casa Linda Plaza 75218
(214) 327-4561
(Mrs.) Carrie Lou Brandon
AD,COMP,ED,F,LEG,MED,OFF ADM,
RE,S,TE

CLOUD EMPLOYMENT SERVICE
907 Dallas Athletic Club Bldg., 1805 Elm St. 75201
(214) 747-4821
(Mrs.) Neil Cloud DuVall
AD,COMP,ED,F,LEG,MED,OFF ADM,
OS,RE,S,TE

COCKRELL-HULL EMPLOYMENT SERVICE, INC.
Frito-Lay Tower, Suite #150 75235
(214) 357-3951
C. D. Buckalew
AD,COMP,ED,F,LEG,OFF ADM,RE,S,TE

CONTINENTAL PERSONNEL SPEC., INC.
7701 Stemmons Freeway 75247
(214) 638-5064
Suzette Shushok/F. X. Shushok
FS

FULTON EMPLOYMENT SERVICE, INC.
1309 Main, Suite 421 75202
(214) 748-7271
Evelyn Fulton
AD,COMP,F,LEG,MED,OFF ADM,RE,S,TE

GOULD-MASSEY PERSONNEL SERVICE
211 N. Ervay 75201
(214) 747-7771
Louise Gould/Helen Massey
AD,COMP,ED,F,LEG,OFF ADM,RE,S

TEXAS—Continued

GROVE EMPLOYMENT SERVICE, INC.
2037 S. Buckner 75217
(214) 391-4191
Margie F. Howard
AD,COMP,ED,F,FS,LEG,MED,OFF ADM,
OS,RE,S,TE

METRO PERSONNEL SYSTEM, INC.
911 Exchange Bank Bldg. 75235
(214) 357-1531
Patricia Plackard
AD,COMP,F,FS,LEG,MED,OFF ADM,
RE,S,TE

OAK CLIFF PERSONNEL SERVICE
1210 Oak Cliff Bank Tower 75208
(214) 948-3516
R. Leslie Gleaves
AD,COMP,F,LEG,MED,OFF ADM,RE,S,TE

ROBERT HALF PERSONNEL AGENCIES OF DALLAS, INC.
1170 Hartford Bldg. 75201
(214) 742-9171
Roger Davidson
COMP,F

TEXAS MEDICAL & PROFESSIONAL BUREAU
14 Mezzanine, Medical Arts Bldg. 75201
(214) 747-8575
Tom Blakley
ED,F,MED,OFF ADM,OS

WHATLEY EMPLOYMENT SERVICE
1407 Main, Suite 810 75201
(214) 742-9481
(Mrs.) Lois Whatley
AD,COMP,ED,F,FS,LEG,MED,OFF ADM,
RE,S,TE

EL PASO

B D A EMPLOYMENT AGENCY
Suite 13-E, El Paso National Bank Bldg.
79901
(915) 532-5969
Dorothea J. Osborn/John C. Rucker, Jr.
COMP,F,MED,OFF ADM,RE,S,TE

WILSON EMPLOYMENT SERVICE
1212 El Paso National Bank Bldg. 79901
(915) 544-1414
(Mrs.) Charlie B. Bessinger
AD,COMP,ED,F,LEG,MED,OFF ADM,
RE,S,TE

FORT WORTH

ABC EMPLOYMENT SERVICES
2516 Jacksboro Hwy. 76114
(817) 336-2471
Vard Miller/Margaret Miller
AD,COMP,F,FS,LEG,MED,OFF ADM,
RE,S,TE

AMERICAN EMPLOYMENT SERVICE
1618 Continental National Bank Bldg.
76102
(817) 332-4136
Willis J. Robinson
FS,AD,COMP,F,LEG,OFF ADM,RE,S,TE

AUSTIN EMPLOYMENT SERVICE
1550 W. Rosedale, 402 Medical Tower
Bldg. 76104
(817) 335-2433
Louise Wallace/M. G. Wallace
AD,COMP,F,LEG,MED,OFF ADM,RE,
S,TE

AUTRY EMPLOYMENT SERVICE
503 Sinclair Bldg., 106 W. 5th St. 76102
(817) 332-7801
(Mrs.) Mayme B. Autry
AD,COMP,F,FS,OFF ADM,S,TE

BABICH & ASSOCIATES, INC.
2111 Continental Life Bldg., 714 Main St.
76102
(817) 336-7261
(Miss) Mildred Babich
AD,COMP,F,LEG,MED,OFF ADM,RE,S,TE

COMMERCIAL EMPLOYMENT SERVICE
813 Fort Worth National Bank Bldg.
76102
(817) 335-5856
(Miss) Sidney Richey
AD,COMP,F,LEG,MED,OFF ADM,S,TE

GENERAL EMPLOYMENT BUREAU
607 W. First St. 76102
(817) 332-4311
Ronald Ballard/Dorothy Harris
AD,COMP,F,FS,LEG,MED,OFF ADM,
RE,S,TE

HAYES PERSONNEL SERVICE
603 Continental Life Bldg. 76102
(817) 332-7645
Ray Allen Hayes
AD,COMP,F,FS,LEG,OFF ADM,RE,S,TE

SNELLING AND SNELLING
810 Houston St. 76102
(817) 332-9331
C. L. Slaton
AD,COMP,F,FS,LEG,MED,OFF ADM,
RE,S,TE

HOUSTON

C/M OF HOUSTON, INC., CAREER MANAGEMENT ASSOCIATES
711 Fannin, Suite 914 77002
(713) 225-2212
L. M. Cherbonnier/E. A. Weiss
AD,COMP,F,OFF ADM,RE,S,TE

JOHN L. CLOUD PLACEMENT SERVICE
1329 Americana Bldg. 77002
(713) 227-6354
John L. Cloud
AD,COMP,F,LEG,MED,OFF ADM,OS,
RE,S,TE

KEY PERSONNEL
806 Main, Suite 1210 77002
(713) 224-9251
Janet Milling
AD,COMP,F,LEG,MED,OFF ADM,OS,
S,TE

LYMAN PERSONNEL SERVICES, INC.
3815 Buffalo Speedway 77006
(713) 526-8911
(Mrs.) Peggy Lyman/Harrison G. Lyman
AD,COMP,F,LEG,OFF ADM,RE,S,TE

MacDONALD PLACEMENT SERVICE, INC.
Suite 349, Post Oak Bank Bldg. 77027
(713) 621-4651
Malcolm W. MacDonald
AD,COMP,ED,F,LEG,OFF ADM,OS,
RE,S,TE

M. DAVID LOWE PERSONNEL SERVICES, INC.
400 Houston Natural Gas Bldg., 1200 Travis
St. 77002
(713) 224-5711
M. David Lowe
AD,COMP,F,FS,LEG,OFF ADM,RE,S,TE

METROPOLITAN EMPLOYMENT SERVICE, INC.
1101 First National Life Bldg., 806 Main
77002
(713) 225-1411
Vic Koenig
AD,COMP,F,FS,LEG,MED,OFF ADM,
RE,S,TE

QUINBY EMPLOYMENT SERVICE
406 Bankers Mortgage Bldg. 77002
(713) 223-2391
Rodney B. Quinby
COMP,F,LEG,MED,OFF ADM, S,TE

SHAMROCK EMPLOYMENT SERVICE
2334 Houston Natural Gas Bldg., 1200
Travis 77002
(713) 225-0806
Joseph B. Collerain
AD,COMP,F,LEG,MED,OFF ADM,OS,
S,TE,FS

SKYLINE EMPLOYMENT SERVICE
3100 Richmond, Suite 106 77006
(713) 526-3761
Robert L. & Marguerite A. Hanson
AD,COMP,F,LEG,MED,OFF ADM,S,TE

SNELLING AND SNELLING
1212 Main St. 77002
(713) 228-1541
Henry W. Rosenwald/Marion M.
Rosenwald
AD,COMP,F,LEG,OFF ADM,RE,S,TE

WINN EMPLOYMENT SERVICE
1309 Esperson Bldg. 77002
(713) 224-6045
Sid Gould
COMP,F,FS,LEG,OFF ADM,RE,S,TE

TEXAS—Continued

PASADENA

ABLE EMPLOYMENT AGENCY
808 E. Thomas 77502
(713) 477-3134
(Mrs.) Betty J. Whitley
COMP,F,OFF ADM,S,TE

BRUCE EMPLOYMENT AGENCY
714 E. Southmore 77502
(713) 473-9251
Stella A. Walters
COMP,F,LEG,OFF ADM,S,TE

CHANNEL EMPLOYMENT AGENCY
709 S. Shaver 77502
(713) 477-1491
Vera Maddry
F,LEG,S,TE

**NEWMAN-JOHNSON EMPLOYMENT
SERVICE**
414 First Pasadena State Bank Bldg.,
P.O. Box 1015 77501
(713) 473-1753
Margaret B. Johnson/
Jessie Belle Newman
COMP,F,FS,MED,OFF ADM,S,TE

PASADENA EMPLOYMENT SERVICE
217 Campbell Bldg. 77502
(713) 472-5538
William H. Coyle, Jr.
AD,COMP,ED,F,FS,LEG,MED,OFF ADM,
RE,S,TE

SAN ANTONIO

EMPLOYMENT PERSONNEL NORTH
1154 North Star Mall 78216
(512) 344-9735
Elizabeth K. Farley
AD,COMP,ED,F,LEG,MED,OFF ADM,
RE,S,TE

KING EMPLOYMENT SERVICE
7801 Broadway 78209
(512) 826-9691
Clara L. Koepsel
AD,COMP,ED,F,FS,LEG,MED,OFF ADM,
RE,S,TE

WACO

A-1 EMPLOYMENT AGENCY
1022 Washington Ave. 76703
(817) 754-5654
W. W. Smith
COMP,F,FS,LEG,OFF ADM,S,TE

CURTIS EMPLOYMENT SERVICE
323 North 7th 76701
(817) 756-1884
(Mrs.) M. C. ("Gen") Meredith
AD,COMP,ED,F,LEG,MED,OFF ADM,
RE,S,TE

UTAH

SALT LAKE CITY

BUREAU OF PERSONNEL
363 E. 33rd South 84115
(801) 486-0053
Ed W. Hoopes
COMP,F,OFF ADM,S,TE

**S.D.I. PERSONNEL-PLACEMENT
AGENCY**
333 S. State St. 84111
(801) 328-9631
Wm. A. Boldt
AD,COMP,F,LEG,MED,OFF ADM,S,TE

VERMONT

BURLINGTON

SNELLING AND SNELLING
200 Main St. 05401
(802) 863-3411
Lyman L. Conger
AD,COMP,ED,F,LEG,MED,OFF ADM,
RE,S,TE

VIRGINIA

NORFOLK

LENDMAN ASSOCIATES, LTD.
P.O. Box 14027 23518
(703) 583-5921
Ernest M. Lendman/Stephen M. Campbell/
Stephen J. Lendman/Richard Wintraub
AD,COMP,F,LEG,MED,OFF ADM,OS,
RE,S,TE

REPUBLIC PERSONNEL SERVICE, INC.
Nine Tidewater Executive Center 23502
(703) 499-5411
J. Donald Varela
FS

SNELLING AND SNELLING
143 Little Creek Rd., W. Wards Corner
23505
(703) 489-3210
Erle H. Austin, Jr.
AD,COMP,F,LEG,MED,OFF ADM,
RE,S,TE

RICHMOND

**SCHNEIDER, HILL & SPANGLER—
RICHMOND, INC.**
200 W. Grace St. 23220
(703) 643-1911
Charles J. Hoey
FS

**SNELLING AND SNELLING OF
RICHMOND, INC.**
801 E. Main St. 23219
(703) 644-7631
Joe Wiggins
FS

VIRGINIA BEACH

**COMMONWEALTH PERSONNEL SERVICE,
INC.**
3707 Virginia Beach Blvd. 23452
(703) 486-3924
Martha C. Hoffman
FS

WASHINGTON

SEATTLE

ACTION PLACEMENTS, INC.
10560 A 5th NE 98125
(206) 363-2613
Florence Waggener
AD,COMP,F,LEG,MED,OFF ADM,
RE,S,TE

CENTRAL MEDICAL DENTAL AGENCY
1507 Medical Dental Bldg. 98101
(206) 623-0061
Nancy Bross
MED

DUNHILL OF SEATTLE, INC.
1411 - 4th Ave. Bldg., Room 415 98101
(206) 624-2024
Dan E. Huston
AD,COMP,ED,F,LEG,OFF ADM,
RE,S,TE

KNAPP AGENCY
1011 Securities Bldg. 98101
(206) 623-2323
Jean Knapp
AD,F,LEG,OFF ADM

**MANAGEMENT RECRUITERS OF
SEATTLE**
Denny Bldg., 2200 - 6th, Suite 1100
98121
(206) 623-6790
Russell C. Murphy
FS

PLACEMENTS UNLIMITED, INC.
637 S. Center 98188
(206) 244-3200
Victor Frank
AD,COMP,ED,F,FS,LEG,MED,OFF ADM,
OS,RE,S,TE

SHIRLEY THOMAS AGENCY
1425 - 4th Ave. 98101
(206) 623-3267
Shirley Thomas
AD,F,LEG,OFF ADM

SNELLING AND SNELLING
144 S.W. 153rd St. 98166
(206) CH 4-7450
F. Jane Steele/E. W. Steele
AD,COMP,ED,F,FS,LEG,MED,OFF ADM,
RE,S,TE

WASHINGTON—Continued

SNELLING AND SNELLING—SEATTLE
1505 - 4th Ave. 98101
(206) 622-5082
Paul D. Balbin
F,FS,LEG,MED,OFF ADM,RE,S,TE

SPOKANE

SNELLING AND SNELLING
701 Bon Marche Bldg. 99201
(509) 624-4141
Clark Hager
FS

TACOMA

TACOMA EMPLOYMENT SERVICE
150½ Pacific Ave. 98402
(206) 272-8491
Margaret Mack (Wild)/Georgia Thompson
AD,COMP,F,LEG,MED,OFF ADM,
RE,S,TE

WEST VIRGINIA

CHARLESTON

CENTRAL EMPLOYMENT SERVICE, INC.
Room 105, 1033 Quarrier Bldg. 25301
(304) 343-5113
C. L. Crawford/Betty Crawford
FS

WISCONSIN

MADISON

availABILITY OF MADISON, INC.
202 N. Midvale Blvd. 53705
(608) 231-2421
Quentin R. Verdier
AD,COMP,ED,F,FS,LEG,MED,OFF ADM,
OS,RE,S,TE

PLACEMENT OF MADISON, INC.
30 W. Mifflin, Suite 910 53703
(608) 257-3551
John C. Fritschler/(Miss) Betty Jensen
FS

QUALIFIED PERSONNEL, INC.
115 E. Main St. 53703
(608) 257-1057
H. Silverberg/Mary L.
Kauper
AD,COMP,F,FS,LEG,MED,OFF ADM,
RE,S,TE

MILWAUKEE

BUREAU FOR PROFESSIONAL EMPLOYMENT, LTD.
1420 Marine Plaza, 111 E. Wisconsin Ave.
53202
(414) 272-3622
Dr. George A. Sievers/
(Mrs.) Florence Sievers
AD,COMP,ED,F,LEG,OFF ADM,RE,S,TE

BUTTERFIELD'S INC.
161 W. Wisconsin Ave., Suite 269 53203
(414) 278-7800
Howard W. Jurack
AD,COMP,ED,F,LEG,MED,OFF ADM,
RE,S,TE

DUNHILL OF MILWAUKEE, INC.
211 W. Wisconsin Ave. 53203
(414) 272-4860
Bradley M. Brin
AD,COMP,F,FS,LEG,MED,OFF ADM,
RE,S,TE

EXECUTIVE PLACEMENT SERVICE, INC.
10425 W. North Ave. 53226
(414) 778-2200
Van B. Hooper
AD,COMP,F,LEG,OFF ADM,RE,S,TE

MANAGEMENT RECRUITERS OF MILWAUKEE, INC.
161 W. Wisconsin Ave., Suite 4189 53203
(414) 273-4430
William C. Healy
AD,COMP,F,LEG,OFF ADM,RE,S,TE

SNELLING AND SNELLING, INC.
105 W. Michigan St., 10th Floor 53203
(414) 271-2242
Elizabeth J. Murray
FS

For a more detailed listing of agencies within specific states, we suggest that you write to the State Chapters of the National Employment Association. Their addresses are given below:

ALABAMA EMPLOYMENT ASSOCIATION
Dudley E. Morgan
Dunhill of Birmingham, Inc.
2207 First National
Southern Natural Building
Birmingham, Alabama 35203   (205) 323-4471

ARIZONA PRIVATE EMPLOYMENT AGENCY ASSOCIATION
Robert D. Urguhart
Dunhill of Phoenix, Inc.
3550 North Central Ave.
Phoenix, Arizona 85719   (602) 264-116

ARKANSAS EMPLOYMENT ASSOCIATION
Roy E. Meadows
Continental Employment Agency, Inc.
285 Tower Building
Little Rock, Arkansas 72201   (501) 375-9121

CALIFORNIA EMPLOYMENT ASSOCIATION
Frederic A. Naglestad
Results Employment Agency
1654 The Alameda
San Jose, California 95126   (408) 295-5647

CAPITAL AREA PERSONNEL SERVICES ASSOCIATION
Myra Lenard
Bob Gray, Inc.
839 17th St., N.W., Suite 200
Washington, D.C. 20006   (202) 638-4277

COLORADO PRIVATE EMPLOYMENT ASSOCIATION
Ron Sampson
Management Recruiters, Inc.
1860 Lincoln St., Lincoln Towers
Denver, Colorado 80203   (303) 292-2980

CONNECTICUT CHAPTER, NATIONAL EMPLOYMENT ASSOCIATION
William F. Markey, Jr.
Management Recruiters, Inc.
60 Washington St., Suite 701
Hartford, Connecticut 06106   (203) 547-0010

DELAWARE, PERSONNEL SERVICES ASSOCIATION OF
Norman N. Schutzman
Snelling & Snelling
919 Washington St.
Wilmington, Delaware 19801   (302) 652-3711

FLORIDA EMPLOYMENT ASSOCIATION
Walter P. Friend
Walt Friend Personnel, Inc.
2747 Art Museum Dr.
Jacksonville, Florida 32207   (904) 396-6902

GEORGIA ASSOCIATION OF PRIVATE EMPLOYMENT AGENCIES
Mrs. Hal Drake
Drake Personnel Service
Lenox Towers
3390 Peachtree Rd., N.E.
Atlanta, Georgia 30326   (404) 261-7136

HAWAII, EMPLOYMENT AGENCY ASSOCIATION OF
Richard Kimball
Kimball Employment
2273 Kala Kaua Ave.
Honolulu, Hawaii 96815   (808) 922-4974

IDAHO STATE PRIVATE EMPLOYMENT AGENCIES ASSOCIATION
Bill Davis
Acme Personnel Service
Sonna Building
Boise, Idaho 83702   (208) 343-1896

ILLINOIS EMPLOYMENT ASSOCIATION
Tom Moran
Career South Personnel, Inc.
4740 West 95th St. (Colonial Savings Bldg.)
Oak Lawn, Illinois 60453   (312) 425-9000

INDIANA, ASSOCIATED EMPLOYMENT AGENCIES OF
Margaret J. Higgins
Human Dynamics Associates
111 South 10th St.
Richmond, Indiana 47374   (317) 966-5594

IOWA STATE ASSOCIATION OF PRIVATE PLACEMENT AGENCIES
Robert Luthro
Future Employment Service
470 Fisher Building
Dubuque, Iowa 52001   (319) 583-8900

KENTUCKY ASSOCIATION OF PRIVATE EMPLOYMENT SERVICES
John M. Considine
Dunhill of Lexington, Inc.
361 Waller Ave.
Lexington, Kentucky 40504   (606) 252-7525

LOUISIANA, PRIVATE EMPLOYMENT SERVICES ASSOCIATION OF
Charles West
Automated Personnel International of New Orleans
226 Carondelet St.
Carondelet Building, Suite 700
New Orleans, Louisiana 70130   (504) 529-1681

MARYLAND EMPLOYMENT AGENCIES ASSOCIATION
William Sweetser
Opportunity Search of Baltimore
Investment Building, Suite G2
Towson, Maryland 21204   (301) 821-0140

MASSACHUSETTS EMPLOYMENT ASSOCIATION
Mrs. Jane Menard
Ad Hoc Personnel Service
101 Pleasant St.
Worcester, Massachusetts 01608   (617) 791-3281

MICHIGAN EMPLOYMENT ASSOCIATION
Mrs. Orimal Hudson
Hudson Personnel
820 Commerce Bldg.
Grand Rapids, Michigan 49502   (616) 451-2993

MINNESOTA EMPLOYMENT AGENCIES ASSOCIATION
G. Ray Kammeier
Employment Counsellors, Inc.
720 Dain Tower
527 Marquette Ave.
Minneapolis, Minnesota 55402   (612) 335-8931

MISSISSIPPI EMPLOYMENT ASSOCIATION
John Hulsebosch
Snelling & Snelling
2nd Floor Baptist Book Store
Jackson, Mississippi 39201   (601) 948-4551

**MISSOURI ASSOCIATION OF PRIVATE EMPLOYMENT
   AGENCIES**
M. L. Davis
Service Specialists Ltd.
220 Ozark Life Building
906 Grand
Kansas City, Missouri 64106   (314) 474-8040

NEBRASKA PLACEMENT SERVICES ASSOCIATION
Carl J. Nolte, Jr.
Sales Consultants of Omaha
7000 West Center Rd.
Omaha, Nebraska 68106   (402) 939-4700

NEVADA ASSOCIATION OF PERSONNEL AGENCIES
Fullmer Barlow
Management Recruiters
210 Las Vegas Boulevard, South
Las Vegas, Nevada 89101   (702) 382-8012

**NEW JERSEY ASSOCIATION OF PRIVATE EMPLOYMENT
   AGENCIES**
Alan B. Taplow
Fanning Personnel of Camden, Inc.
1 Cherry Hill (Mall)
Cherry Hill, New Jersey 08034   (609) 667-3885

**NEW MEXICO, ASSOCIATION OF PRIVATE EMPLOYMENT
   AGENCIES OF**
June Allen
Employment Unlimited, Inc.
205 San Pedro, N.E.
Albuquerque, New Mexico 87108   (505) 265-5891

**NEW YORK, ASSOCIATION OF PERSONNEL
   AGENCIES OF**
David Mendel
Snelling & Snelling
250 Fulton Ave.
Hempstead, L.I., New York 11550   (516) 485-6810

**NORTH CAROLINA, ASSOCIATION OF PRIVATE
   EMPLOYMENT AGENCIES OF**
Robert W. Hanna
Allied Personnel of Charlotte, Inc.
Suite 151, One Charlottetown Center
Charlotte, North Carolina 28204   (704) 332-9095

**NORTH DAKOTA ASSOCIATION OF PRIVATE
   EMPLOYMENT AGENCIES**
Mr. Lynn J. Fieman
Service Specialists, Ltd.
Pioneer Mutual Insurance Building
Fargo, North Dakota 58102   (701) 237-0034

OHIO PRIVATE EMPLOYMENT SERVICES ASSOCIATION
John F. Marshall
Snelling & Snelling
5 West Broad St.
Columbus, Ohio 43215   (614) 221-6471

**OKLAHOMA ASSOCIATION OF PRIVATE EMPLOYMENT
   SERVICES**
Bob Funk
Acme Brindley Personnel Service
2115 Liberty Bank Building
Oklahoma City, Oklahoma 73102   (405) 235-2511

OREGON EMPLOYMENT AGENCIES ASSOCIATION
Mrs. Anne Pagenstecher
Pagenstecher's Placement Agency
1410 S.W. Military Road   Salem Office   (503) 585-6156
Portland, Oregon 97219   Portland Home   (503) 636-5484

**PENNSYLVANIA ASSOCIATION OF PERSONNEL
   SERVICES**
Lawrence J. LaBoon
Metropolitan Personnel
1700 Market St., Suite 2730
Philadelphia, Pennsylvania 19103   (215) 561-5522

**SOUTH CAROLINA ASSOCIATION OF PERSONNEL
   SERVICES**
Fred W. Langdon, Jr.
Speer Personnel Consultants
528 Georgia Ave.
North Augusta, South Carolina 29841   (803) 279-4141

TENNESSEE EMPLOYMENT ASSOCIATION
Eugene Rhodes
Dunhill Placement
100 North Main Building
Memphis, Tennessee 38103   (901) 527-0321

TEXAS PRIVATE EMPLOYMENT ASSOCIATION
John L. Cloud
John L. Cloud Placement Service
1329 Americana Building
811 Dallas Avenue
Houston, Texas 77002   (713) 227-6354

UTAH ASSOCIATION OF EMPLOYMENT AGENCIES
Arthur Richardson
Progressive Personnel
455 East 4th St.
Salt Lake City, Utah 84111   (801) 521-3737

VIRGINIA ASSOCIATION OF PERSONNEL SERVICES
Robert B. Williams
SP Personnel Associates of Richmond
4900 Augusta Avenue, Suite 108
Richmond, Virginia 23230   (703) 358-5531

WASHINGTON EMPLOYMENT AGENCIES ASSOCIATION
Dan E. Huston
Dunhill of Seattle, Inc.
1411 - 4th Avenue Building, Room 415
Seattle, Washington 98101   (206) 624-2024

**WEST VIRGINIA PRIVATE EMPLOYMENT SERVICE
   ASSOCIATION**
James Duckworth
Snelling & Snelling
328½ Seventh St.
Parkersburg, West Virginia 25301   (304) 295-6332

**WISCONSIN ASSOCIATION OF EMPLOYMENT
   AGENCIES**
Bradley Brin
Dunhill of Milwaukee, Inc.
211 West Wisconsin Ave.
Milwaukee, Wisconsin 53203   (414) 272-4860

EXECUTIVE SEARCH FIRMS

Executive Search Firms Defined

Executive search firms (frequently called recruiters or head hunters) work for employers. Many are on a retainer and are paid regardless of when they fill a position. Most of them receive a fee which runs from 20-30% of the annual salary for a given position. The elite among the group will rarely handle any position below $20,000 and a select few restrict their efforts to positions at $40,000 or more. The individuals who work at these firms are normally articulate and polished. They include former personnel executives as well as many people who achieved earlier success in other disciplines.

The top search firms are very highly respected companies with well earned reputations for professionalism and ethics. Many of today's business leaders on both the domestic and international scene have been placed through their efforts. There are however, a great many small companies who call themselves executive search firms but which are actually more in the personnel agency category. Since there generally is no requirement that these firms be licensed, and a phone can put you in business, there are now thousands of operations who employ the "Executive Search" label in some manner. Many of the job hunting counselor firms also use this title as well as the professional counselor title, despite the fact that their claim to the first may have little basis. Our discussion in this section refers to those legitimate firms who meet the description in the first paragraph, and who derive their primary income from this type of operation.

Who the Recruiters Seek

The search firms prefer to reach people who are successful in their companies and who are not looking for a job. These are the individuals who are most easily sold to their clients. They get names of possible candidates from directories, professional and business contacts, articles in the press, etc. The simple act of having to make them aware of your availability will frequently make you a less attractive prospect.

Contacting Search Firms

The best way to utilize a search firm would be to have them contact you. The easiest way to facilitate this is to visibly distinguish yourself by having your name in print as much as possible. Of course, if you know individuals in the field, or your associates can supply you with contacts, you should call them on the phone. As far as their contacting you is concerned, if you can write articles, give speeches, make awards, or otherwise get into the limelight, you will obviously improve your chances. If you can't do this, it will be worth your while to make a direct contact. This is much easier said than done because the larger search firms receive 30-100 resumes per day and some are truly deluged. Many of them file resumes directly in waste paper baskets. Nevertheless, there are firms who read all their mail and who categorize resumes and maintain extensive files. In writing search firms, timing is very critical. Obviously, your chances of reaching firms that are working on assignment which call for your type of background are quite small. However, with a broad enough mailing, you should reach a small percentage of firms that will be working on assignments for which you are qualified.

The Resume Approach

If you have a superior resume, you should consider sending a couple of them with a cover letter to at least the leading search firms. When you write search firms keep your cover letter short. You could state something to the effect that if they have assingments which lead them in search of a top flight _____ executive, that your background should prove of interest. You could be more specific and state that you are certain that you could make a great contribution to almost any of their clients in the capacity of _____, and _____. It generally saves time if you give them either your present earnings or salary requirements.

Another interesting technique which has produced results is to send them a resume which is actually part of an 8½ x 11 file folder. The object of this approach is to facilitate permanent filing of your background for easy reference on their future assignments.

The Letter Approach

Another somewhat "softer sell" approach which has proven effective is to send a letter version of your resume to search firms. An opening paragraph might stress the fact that you are not openly seeking a position at this time, but that during the course of the next six months you hope to consider a number of alternatives at _____ salary level. If you do have the time, this generally proves somewhat more effective than the aforementioned. In either case, your letter or resume will do best if it is directed to an individual at the search firm by name. This is somewhat difficult, although we have provided some names and you can also get names of officers by calling the company, or through a Dun & Bradstreet report.

Remember that your initial objective with recruiters is simply to make a memorable contact. During the course of your search, some of them will eventually get assignments which are in your area.

Summary Comments on Executive Search Firms

Since about half of all executive openings are filled from the outside, executive search firms (working for major corporations) handle a fair percentage of all positions above the $30,000 level. If you are in this salary category, they will be prime candidates for your campaign efforts. Visibility in the press would be your best entree although a direct mailing should prove worthwhile. If you make a mailing and do not hear from them, you should follow-up on your initial contact.

The vast majority of these firms either <u>will not</u> answer you or will reply with a form letter rejection. Some will want to see you and a few will invite you to see them even though they do not have a position at that moment. In this case, we advise that you take advantage of their offer and make the contact, as it may help you at a later date.

If you are at a senior level, you probably already have a fairly wide range of contacts among executive recruiters. They may have approached you for a position or sought your help in getting names of candidates for other assignments. If you have not done so already, we strongly suggest that you cooperate with them as much as possible. In general, the higher your position, the greater will be your dependence on them as a source for interviews.

On the following pages, you will find a broad listing of firms that claim to be active in executive search. All of the <u>largest firms</u> are included in this listing and many of them maintain small regional offices throughout the country. In many cases, the clients of these firms are actually located in many areas of the United States. Management consultant and CPA firms that handle executive search as an auxiliary service are also listed. This listing also covers some firms which are closer to the agency business and which are not search firms in the truest sense. We have listed some of them because they do handle many higher salaried and fee paid positions.

We cannot provide you with a rank order listing of the size of these firms. Like many other businesses there are about 20% of the firms who account for 80% of the search placements. Boyden and Company is probably the largest in terms of volume, while Booz, Allen & Hamilton's Executive Search Division is quite close behind. We have distinguished the firms which are management consultants or CPA's with an MC or CPA notation. We have also listed single and double asterisks next to the company names to signify the following:

> * = Member of the Association of Executive Recruiting Consultants
> ** = Member of the Association of Consulting Management Engineers (ACME)

When executives at these firms have cooperated with us, we have listed the names of individuals that you might contact. Wherever possible we have tried to list the name of the company president, or individuals with considerable search responsibilities. Branch offices have been listed because we believe it will be worth your while to contact them as well as the headquarters office. We know of many instances where a letter to the main office resulted in a form letter reply, while the same letter sent to a regional office ended in a placement. The overseas branches are most likely to be affiliate firms, even in many instances where we have provided an address.

Note: Performance Dynamics also maintains a complete worldwide listing of all firms in the executive search field. However, this listing, which includes thousands of companies, constitutes a separate publication. If the enclosed directory is inadequate for your purposes, you may obtain information by writing to the Publishing Division of Performance Dynamics.

STANLEY B. ADAMS
441 Lexington Ave.
New York, N.Y. 10017
(212) 682-7430
Stanley B. Adams
Marketing Fields

ALBERT & NELLISEN, INC. (MC)
510 Madison Ave.
New York, N.Y. 10021
(212) PL9-1720
EDP Field

AMANSCO INCORPORATED
718 Wallace Avenue
Pittsburgh, Pa. 15221
(412) 241-6678

GORDON H. ANDERSON & ASSOCIATES
168 North Michigan Ave.
Chicago, Ill. 60601
(312) 263-7676
Gordon H. Anderson

GEORGE V. ANDERSON & ASSOCIATES
500 Fifth Ave.
New York, N.Y. 10030
(212) LO 4-6540
George V. Anderson

ANDERSON ROETHLE & ASSOCIATES,
   INC. (MC)
811 East Wisconsin Ave.
Milwaukee, Wisc. 53202
(414) 276-0070
John B. Roethle

ANTELL, WRIGHT & NAGEL
230 Park Ave.
New York, N.Y. 10017
(212) 686-4144
David Chambers

APPOINTMENTS SELECTION LTD.
1 Dover St.
London, W1, England

WILLIAM B. ARNOLD ASSOCIATES
The Equitable Bldg.
1776 So. Jackson St.
Denver, Colo. 80202
(303) 759-9941
William B. Arnold

AVERY & ASSOCIATES (MC)
 936 Huntington Dr.
San Marino, Calif. 91108
(213) 284-3203
William Avery

BADGETT & ASSOCIATES, INC.
1410 Herschel Ave.
Cincinnati, Ohio 45208
(513) 321-0361
Steven Badgett

BALDWIN-STILES & ASSOCIATES, INC.
605 Third Avenue
New York, N.Y. 10016
(212) 661-8666
A. Theron Baldwin

DAVID T. BARRY ASSOCIATES, INC.
527 Washington St.
Wellesley, Mass. 02181
(617) 235-1520
David T. Barry

NATHAN BARRY ASSOCIATES, INC.
29 Commonwealth Ave.
Boston, Mass. 02116
(617) 262-2034
Nathan Barry

THEODORE BARRY AND ASSOCIATES
1151 West Sixth St.
Los Angeles, Calif. 90017
(213) 481-7371
231 East Millbrae Ave.
Millbrae, Calif. 94030
(415) 692-2315
525 "B" St., Suite 621
San Diego, Calif. 92101
(714) 232-3071
2725 4th Ave. South
Seattle, Wash. 98134
(206) MA4-0476
821 17th St.
Denver, Colo. 80202
(303) 892-0335
277 Park Ave.
New York, New York 10017
(212) 758-2440

BARTON MANAGEMENT APPOINTMENTS,
   LTD.
80 Chancery Lane
London, WC 2A, IDD
England
Tel. 01-405-1431
George Dodson-Wells
Financial Fields

BATTALIA, LOTZ & ASSOCIATES, INC.*
342 Madison Ave.
New York, N.Y. 10017
(212) 986-4830
William Battalia
James Lotz
Also: 300 West Adams, Chicago, Ill. 60606
(312) 372-3224

BEACH & SILL, INC.*
420 Lexington Ave.
New York, N.Y. 10017
(212) 679-3731
Samuel H. Beach

BERNDSTON INTERNATIONAL, S.A.
360 Avenue Louise
Brussels 5, Belgium
Tel. 49.60.37

BILLINGTON, FOX, & ELLIS INC.
20 No. Wacker Dr.
Chicago, Ill. 60606
(312) 332-5670
William H. Billington, Jr.
Also: 225 Peachtree St., N.E., Atlanta,
Ga. 30303
(404) 522-2420 Gerald J. Bump
3600 Wilshire Blvd., Los Angeles, Cal. 90005
(213) 386-4700 Harry C. Ellis
1415 Investment Plaza, Cleveland, Ohio 44114
(216) 241-6220 Adrian H. Hasse
280 Park Ave., New York, N.Y. 10022
(212) 986-7800 Alex Reddin
Plus — London

CHARLES A. BINSWANGER ASSOCIATES,
   INC.
725 Jackson Towers
Baltimore, Md. 21201
(301) 728-5000
Charles A. Binswanger
Technical/Scientific Fields

BLENDOW & SELLMER, INC.
P.O. Box 408
Alamo, Calif. 94507
Health & Pharmaceutical Industries
(415) 837-8115
Also: 1023 Burlington, Western Springs,
Ill. 60558
(312) 246-4140
120 Leedom Dr., Media, Pa. 19063
(215) 565-2976

BOOZ, ALLEN & HAMILTON** (MC)
Executive Search Division
135 So. La Salle St.
Chicago, Ill. 60603
(312) 346-1900
Robert Martin
Also: 245 Park Ave., New York, N.Y. 10017
(212) 697-1900 Wayne Dressel
1300 Union Commerce Bldg.
925 Euclid Ave.
Cleveland, Ohio 44114
(216) 696-1900 David G. Tilghman
Bank of America Plaza
555 California St.
San Francisco, Calif. 94104
(415) 391-1900 Thorne S. Foster
Plus: Bethesda, Boston, Dallas, Los Angeles,
Washington, D.C., Dusseldorf, London,
Toronto, Mexico City

BOYDEN ASSOCIATES
260 Madison Ave.
New York, N.Y. 10016
(212) 685-3100
Sidney Boyden
Walter Raleigh
Also: Lennox Towers, 3390 Peachtree Rd.,
N.E., Atlanta, Ga. 30326
(404) 261-6532 Frederick Walters

BOYDEN ASSOCIATES (Cont.)
111 W. Monroe, Chicago, Ill. 60603
(312) 782-1581 Carl Von Ammon
5670 Wilshire Blvd., Los Angeles, Calif. 90036
(213) 933-5563 Paul Papanek
Allegheny Tower, 625 Stanwix St.,
Pittsburgh, Pa. 15200
(412) 391-3020 Thomas L. Denney
1 Maritime Plaza, Golden Gateway Center
San Francisco, Calif. 94111
(415) 981-7900 John Bricker
Seattle First Nat. Bank Bldg.,
Seattle, Wash. 98104
(206) MU2-2640 Bruce Baker
811 Madison Ave., Toledo, Ohio 43624
(419) 255-1160 Richard Y. Moss
1621 Euclid Ave., Cleveland, Ohio 44115
(216) 621-9055 Warren Yrfik
Plus: 58 Pitt St., Sydney, N.S.W. 2000,
Australia Graham Pemefather
149 Avenue Louise, 1050 Brussels,
Belgium C. Stewart Baeder
305 A.I.A. Bldg., One Stubbs Rd.
Hong Kong Charles E. Schlee
Suite 200, 10, Rue de la Scie,
1200 Geneva, Switzerland Thomas A. Moore
11-15 Arlington St., London, S.W. 1,
England Reese Hatchitt
Princesa 25-27, Madrid 8, Spain
Paseo de la Reforma 509, Ilo Piso,
Mexico 5, D.F. Mr. A. Robert Taylor
Av. de la Reforma 3-48, Zona 9, Guatemala City,
Guatemala Mr. Henry A. Du Fion
Praca Dom Jose Gaspar, 134, Conjunto 162,
16º andar, Sao Paulo, Brasil Guy H. Pullen

BRENNAN ASSOCIATES, INC.
375 Park Ave.
New York, N.Y. 10002
(212) 758-2200
William Brennan

LEO BRODY
347 Fifth Ave.
New York, N.Y. 10016
(212) MU 5-6877
Leo Brody
Retail Fields

D.A.K. BROWN & ASSOCIATES (MC)
342 Madison Ave.
New York, N.Y. 10017
(212) 867-5530
Donald Brown
Also: London, Paris

FRANK C. BROWN & COMPANY, INC.**
   (MC)
Executive Search Division
30 Rockefeller Plaza
New York, N.Y. 10020
(212) PL 7-5860
Frank C. Brown
Also: Boston, Miami, Ridgewood, N.J.

THOMAS A. BUFFUM ASSOCIATES*
2 Center Plaza
Boston, Mass. 02108
(617) 227-4350
Thomas A. Buffum

BURKE & O'BRIEN ASSOCIATES
233 Broadway
New York, N.Y. 10007
(212) 962-2811
Martin C. Burke

ALLEN P. BURR & ASSOCIATES*
211 E. 53rd St.
New York, N.Y. 10022
(212) 421-3830
Allen Burr
Marketing/Advertising Fields

ROBERT J. BUSHEE & ASSOCIATES, INC.
300 Sixth Ave. Bldg.
Pittsburgh, Pa. 15222
(412) 471-5750
Robert J. Bushee

E. A. BUTLER ASSOCIATES, INC.
680 Fifth Ave.
New York, N.Y. 10019
(212) 245-1940
Also: 33 W. Court St., Doylestown, Pa. 18901
(215) 348-8700 E. J. Mowry
909 — 17th St., Denver, Colo. 80202
(303) 892-6459 Ralph Moore
10889 Wilshire Blvd., Los Angeles, Cal. 90024
(213) 477-6004 Russell J. Allen
351 California St., San Francisco, Cal. 94108
(415) 421-4541 Clifford Westley
2820 W. Maple Ave., Troy, Mich. 48084
(313) 642-9111 John Barnard
6500 Pearl St., Cleveland, Ohio 44130
(316) 886-2121 Otis H. Bowden
2 No. Riverside Plaza, Chicago, Ill. 60606
(312) 641-0650 E. A. Butler
1245 Sherbrooke St., W. Montreal 109, Canada
(514) 844-3358 Joseph Dore
443 University Ave., Toronto 100,
Ontario, Canada

BUTTRICK & MEGARY, INC.
2 Penn Center Plaza
Philadelphia, Pa. 19107
(215) LO 8-2440
John Kurdziel

P. S. CABOT & CO., LTD.
37-41 Bedford Row
London, W.C. 1, England
Tel. (01) 405-6885

CADILLAC ASSOCIATES, INC.
32 West Randolph St.
Chicago, Ill. 60601
(312) FI 6-9400
Lon D. Barton

CANNY, BOWEN, HOWARD, PECK
   & ASSOCIATES
201 East 50th St.
New York, N.Y. 10022
(212) 758-3400
Frank Canny
Also: 83 Pall Mall, London SW 1, England
George Harris

DANIEL J. CANTOR & CO.
928 Suburban Station Bldg.
Philadelphia, Pa. 19103
(215) LO 3-9646
Daniel J. Cantor
Legal Field

CARR ASSOCIATES
760 Summer St.
Stamford, Conn. 06902
(203) 327-0822
L. Reed Clark

CASE & COMPANY, INC.** (MC)
Executive Search Division
30 Rockefeller Plaza
New York, N.Y. 10020
(212) 581-7730
Dr. John Smith
Also: Atlanta, Chicago, Cleveland,
Los Angeles, San Francisco, Washington,
D.C., Brussells, Madrid, Milan, Paris

H. V. CHAPMAN & ASSOCIATES, LTD.
1491 Yonge St.
Toronto 7, Ontario, Canada
927-5270 R. K. Smith
Also: Calgary, Edmonton, Halifax,
Montreal, Ottawa, Vancouver, Winnipeg

CHERNUCHIN ASSOCIATES
400 Madison Ave.
New York, N.Y. 10017
(212) 486-9090
Dr. Paul Chernuchin

RICHARD CLARKE ASSOCIATES
1270 Ave. of the Americas
New York, N.Y. 10000
(212) LT 1-3400
Richard Clark
Minority Group Recruiting

WILLIAM H. CLARK ASSOCIATES, INC.*
292 Madison Ave.
New York, N.Y. 10017
(212) 889-3434
William H. Clark
Also: 20 N. Wacker Dr., Chicago, Ill. 60606
(312) 641-1290 John W. Fox, John W. Setear

HARREL R. COFFER & ASSOCIATES,
   INC. (MC)
2677 Larkin St.
San Francisco, Calif. 94109
Textile & Chemical Fields
(415) 474-3838

COLE & ASSOCIATES, INC. (MC)
10 Post Office Square
Boston, Mass. 02109
(617) 542-7191
Robert Hennes

COLEMAN & ASSOCIATES
10884 Santa Monica Blvd.
Los Angeles, Calif. 90025
(213) 879-0434
Electronic/Aerospace Fields

CONLEY ASSOCIATES
135 So. La Salle St.
Chicago, Ill. 60603
(312) 263-4680
Gordon Houffeld

HERBERT COOKE ASSOCIATES
611 Aster Blvd.
Rockville, Md. 20850
(301) 424-1343
Herbert Cooke
Technical/EDP Fields
Mgmt. Sciences

HALLAM COOLEY ASSOCIATES, INC.
260 California St.
San Francisco, Calif. 94111
(415) 362-2469
Financial/Service Fields

GRANT COOPER & ASSOCIATES (MC)
1015 Locust St.
St. Louis, Mo.
(314) 621-6888
Personnel/Industrial Relations Fields

J. J. COOPER & ASSOCIATES
20 North Wacker Dr.
Chicago, Ill. 60606
(312) 346-8266
J. J. Cooper
Engineering/Technical Fields

BETTY Z. CORWIN
230 Park Ave.
New York, N.Y. 10017
(212) 689-4860
Miss Betty Corwin
Advertising/Marketing Fields

COUSINS & PREBLE (MC)
208 So. La Salle St.
Chicago, Ill. 60604
(312) 346-8877
George Travers
Scientific/Engineering Fields

CRESAP, McCORMICK & PAGET** (MC)
Executive Search Division
245 Park Ave.
New York, N.Y. 10017
(212) 661-4600
A. T. Ashman

CRESAP, McCORMICK & PAGET**
   (MC) (Cont.)
Also: 100 W. Monroe St., Chicago, Ill. 60603
(312) 263-7125 W. Callander
3600 Wilshire Blvd., Los Angeles, Cal. 90005
(213) 387-5363 Phillip Doherty
Plus: Brussels, Mexico City

CRIS ASSOCIATES
274 Madison Ave.
New York, N.Y. 10017
(212) 685-6663
Helen Cris

ELMER R. DAVIS & ASSOCIATES, INC.*
60 East 24nd St.
New York, N.Y. 10017
(212) MU2-7717
Elmer Davis

CHARLES E. DAY & ASSOCIATES, INC.
610 South Forest Ave.
Ann Arbor, Mich. 48104
(313) 769-7407

DEANE & CO.
1445 San Marino Ave.
San Marino, Calif. 91108

THORNDIKE DELAND ASSOCIATES*
1440 Broadway
New York, N.Y. 10018
(212) 564-8100
Thorndike Deland, Jr.

DELIA ASSOCIATES (MC)
193 Maplewood Ave.
Maplewood, N.J. 07040
(201) 763-6497
Michael Delia
Plastics/Engineering
Packaging Fields

DEVINE, BALDWIN & ASSOCIATES, INC.
250 Park Ave.
New York, N.Y. 10017
(212) 867-5235
J. E. Devine

DEVOTO, BASS, BROOKHOUSER &
   ASSOCIATES, INC.*
120 So. Riverside Plaza
Chicago, Ill. 60606
(312) 346-8278
Donald E. DeVoto

DRAKE-BEAM & ASSOCIATES (MC)
Executive Search Div.
280 Park Ave.
New York, N.Y. 10017
(212) 826-8890
James Cabrera

DRUMMOND ASSOCIATES, INC.
265 Monmouth Park Highway
West Long Branch, N.J. 07764
(201) 542-6464
Chester Feinberg
MBA Recruiting

DUFFY, BISHOW & DAVIS
3440 Wilshire Blvd.
Los Angeles, Calif. 90005
(213) 385-2441
John A. Duffy

ANTHONY EASTMAN & ASSOCIATES (MC)
39 So. La Salle St.
Chicago, Ill. 60603
(312) 726-8195
L. M. Snyder
Also: Brussels, Munich

EASTMAN-FULGHUM INTERNATIONAL, S.A.
5 Place du Champs de Mars
Brussels 5, Belgium
Tel. 12-01-90

JOHN G. EDMUNDSON & ASSOCIATES
1545 Wilshire Blvd.
Los Angeles, Calif. 90017
(213) 484-1490
John G. Edmundson

EINSTEIN ASSOCIATES, INC.
405 Lexington Ave.
New York, N.Y. 10017
(212) 867-8700
Kurt Einstein

ENION ASSOCIATES, INC. (MC)
3 Penn Center Plaza
Philadelphia, Pa. 19102
(215) 568-4475
Industrial/Architectural

ERNST & ERNST (CPA)
Executive Search Division
1300 Union Commerce Bldg.
925 Euclid Ave.
Cleveland, Ohio 44115
(216) 861-5000 Victor Towne
Also: Offices in all major cities with
Executive Search in New York @
140 Broadway, New York, N.Y. 10005
(212) 943-7800 Jacques Andre

EUROSEARCH CONSULTANTS, S.A.
Square Eugene Plaskey 92-94
1040 Brussels, Belgium
Tel. (02) 36-38-11
Robert J. Donnay
Also: Amsterdam, Dusseldorf, London,
Milan, Paris

WALTER EVERS AND CO.
Union Commerce Bldg.
Cleveland, Ohio 44115
(216) 861-6353

EXECUTIVE APPOINTMENTS, LTD.
78 Wigmore St.
London, W1, England

EXECUTIVE DEVELOPMENT CORP.
120 Sylvan Ave.
Englewood Cliffs, N.J. 07632
(212) 593-0870 Marc Savage, John Thomas

EXECUTIVE MANNING CORPORATION
444 Madison Ave.
New York, N.Y. 10022
(212) EL 5-6635
William A. Hertan
Also: 1001 Conn. Ave., N.W.,
Washington, D.C. 20036

EXECUTIVE RECRUITMENT
    INTERNATIONAL
50 Rte. Acacias
1227 Geneva, Switzerland
Tel. 44-33-59

EXECUTIVE SEARCH LTD.
45 Brompton Rd.
London, SW3, England

EXECUTIVE SERVICE CORPORATION
6 East 45th St.
New York, N.Y. 10017
(212) MU2-4000
Thomas Harris
Also: Union Commerce Bldg.
Cleveland, Ohio 44115
(216) 621-6540

FAIRBANKS ASSOCIATES INC. (MC)
509 Madison Ave.
New York, N.Y. 10022
(212) 755-5615
Publishing/Trade Association Fields
John Murphy

J. H. FELLER & ASSOCIATES (MC)
Magnolia Ave., Larkspur, Calif.
(415) 924-2135
J. H. Feller
Health Fields

CHARLES S. FERNOW
227 27th St.
Avalon, N.J. 08202

FINLAY HUTCHINS INC.
7033 North Kedzie
Chicago, Ill. 60626
(312) 973-1142

TERENCE N. FLANAGAN ASSOCIATES
89 Summit Rd.
Summit, N.J. 07091
(201) 273-1800
Terence N. Flanagan

FOERTSCH-READY, INC.
595 Madison Ave.
New York, N.Y. 10022
(212) 421-3710
C. Edwin Fitzgerald

FORDYCE & ANDREWS & HASKELL, INC.*
230 Park Ave.
New York, N.Y. 10017
(212) 689-3644
Robert Fordyce

FOX-MORRIS ASSOCIATES
1500 Chestnut St.
Philadelphia, Pa. 19102
(215) 561-6300
Warren Nuessle
Also: 777 Third Ave., New York, N.Y. 10017
(212) 486-9750 Mr. Walter McNichols
2115 Concord Pike, Wilmington, Del. 19803
(302) 654-4465 George Whitwell

BERTRAND FRANK ASSOCIATES INC.**
    (MC)
475 Fifth Ave.
New York, N.Y. 10017
(212) MU5-4460
Bertrand Frank
Also: Zug, Switzerland
Apparel/Textile Fields

FREDERICKS AND MARSHALL
15910 Ventura Blvd.
Encino, Calif. 91316
(213) 981-0100

FRY CONSULTANTS, INC. (MC)
Executive Search Division
10 So. Riverside Plaza
Chicago, Ill. 60606
(312) 236-5040
Jack Cunningham
Also: 6 E. 43rd St., New York, N.Y. 10017
(212) 986-1166 David Moore
3540 Wilshire Blvd., Los Angeles, Calif. 90005
(213) 385-3223 Joseph Pagromich
Plus: Kaiserstasse 1
6 Frankfurt/Main 1
Frankfurt, West Germany
Dr. Bruno Hoke
Kraftstrasse 29
8044 Zurich
Zurich, Switzerland
Al Hofstetter
Plus: Atlanta, Nashville, Washington, D.C.

GARNETT, STIXROD, STRAUB
    & ASSOCIATES, INC.
50 East 46th St.
New York, N.Y. 10017
(212) 689-8731
A. Y. P. Garnett

GEARY ASSOCIATES, INC.
230 Park Ave.
New York, N.Y. 10017
(212) MU 9-3330

N. W. GIBSON ASSOCIATES
5900 Wilshire Blvd.
Los Angeles, Calif. 90036
(213) 939-3126

HADLEY LOCKWOOD, INC.
110 Wall St.
New York, N.Y. 10017
(212) HA 5-4405
Curt Lockwood
Brokerage/Financial Fields

HALBRECHT ASSOCIATES, INC.
2 Greenwich Plaza
Greenwich, Conn. 06830
(203) 661-1660
Herbert Halbrecht
Tech./Scient./EDP Fields
Also: Washington, D.C.

HALEY ASSOCIATES
375 Park Ave.
New York, N.Y. 10022
(212) 421-7860
Robert L. Gette

P. K. HALSTEAD ASSOCIATES, INC. (MC)
2005 Palmer Ave.
Larchmont, N.Y. 10538
(914) TE 4-0472
P. K. Halstead
Retail Fields

HANDY ASSOCIATES, INC. (MC)
405 Park Ave.
New York, N.Y. 10022
(212) 755-1911
Mrs. Pearl Meyer
Also: Buenos Aires, Hong Kong, London,
Paris, Tokyo, Zurich

JACK G. DICKSON ASSOCIATES
420 Lexington Ave.
New York, N.Y. 10017
(212) LE 2-6824
William W. Harvey

HASKINS & SELLS (CPA)
Executive Search Division
1114 Ave. of Americas
New York, N.Y. 10004
(212) 422-9600
Everett Johnson

FRANK W. HASTINGS ASSOCIATES, INC.
420 Lexington Ave.
New York, N.Y. 10017
(212) 532-7451
Frank W. Hastings

ROBERT H. HAYES AND ASSOCIATES, INC.
430 North Michigan Ave.
Chicago, Ill. 60611
(312) 321-1714

F. P. HEALY & COMPANY, INC.
342 Madison Ave.
New York, N.Y. 10017
(212) 661-0366
Frank P. Healy

HEIDRICK & STRUGGLES, INC.*
20 North Wacker Dr.
Chicago, Ill. 60606
(312) 272-8811
Margaret Phelan
Also: 245 Park Ave., New York, N.Y. 10017
(212) 867-9876 Gerald Roche
1809 E. 9th St., Cleveland, Ohio 44114
(216) 241-7410 Donald C. Williams
445 So. Figueroa, Los Angeles, Calif. 90017
(213) 624-8891 John R. Schlosser
555 California St., San Francisco, Cal. 94104
(415) 981-2854 Frank P. Bacci

HERGENRATHER & ASSOCIATES
3435 Wilshire Blvd.
Los Angeles, Calif. 90005
(213) 385-0181
Edward Hergenrather

HODGE-CRONIN & ASSOCIATES, INC.*
9575 West Higgins Rd.
Rosemont, Ill. 60018
(312) 692-2041
William Hodge

HOFF ASSOCIATES
200 Park Ave.
New York, N.Y. 10017
(212) MU 2-4043
Miss Ann Hoff

DANIEL D. HOWARD ASSOCIATES,
    INC.** (MC)
Executive Search Division
307 North Michigan Ave.
Chicago, Ill. 60601
(312) 372-7041
Daniel D. Howard

WARD HOWELL ASSOCIATES, INC.
122 East 42nd St.
New York, N.Y. 10017
(212) 697-3730
Ward Howell
Also: 8 Grafton St.,
London, SW 1, England

HPA INC. (THE LAWYERS REGISTER)
101 Park Ave.
New York, N.Y. 10000
(212) 757-1490
Collier Weeks

HR RESEARCH ASSOCIATES, INC.
260 California St.
San Francisco, Calif. 94111
(415) 362-1454

HUBBARD, PENNIMAN, BUCK & HOY, INC.
110 North Wacker Dr.
Chicago, Ill. 60606
(312) 726-7576
(Marketing, Sales)

THE HUNT COMPANY
501 Fifth Ave.
New York, N.Y. 10017
(212) 972-1122

PAUL HUTCHINS ASSOCIATES
919 Third Ave.
New York, N.Y. 10017
(212) 752-9969
Paul Hutchins
EDP Fields

INTERCONTINENTAL MANAGEMENT
    SERVICES (MC)
Executive Search Division
120 Broadway
New York, N.Y. 10005
(212) 233-9240
Benjamin Schneider

INTERNATIONAL EXECUTIVE
    SELECTION, S.A.
19 Boulevard de Suisse
Monte-Carlo, Monaco
Tel. 30-41-21
Also: London

JESSUP & COMPANY
1026 — 17th St., N.W.
Washington, D.C. 20036
(202) 638-4644
Joseph L. Jessup

JEWELL, FARMER & SHAEFFER,
    INC. (MC)
60 East 42nd St.
New York, N.Y. 10017
(212) MU 7-6060
Keith Jewell

JOHNSON & MILITANTE
5151 No. Harlem Ave.
Chicago, Ill. 60656
(312) 792-2323
Vince Militante
Electrical/Other Industries

J. W. JOLDERS (MC)
6210½ West San Vincente
Los Angeles, Calif. 90048
(213) 935-3111
J. W. Jolders

KAHLERT ASSOCIATES
201 East 42nd St.
New York, N.Y. 10017
(212) 682-3131
James Kahlert
Also: Los Angeles, Chicago

A. T. KEARNEY & COMPANY** (MC)
A. T. KEARNEY PERSONNEL
    SERVICES DIV.
100 So. Wacker Dr.
Chicago, Ill. 60606
(312) 782-2868
James Arnold
Also: 437 Madison Ave., New York, N.Y.
    10022
(212) 751-7040 Robert Kayser
Plus: Cleveland, Los Angeles, San Francisco,
Washington, D.C., Dusseldorf, Milan,
Paris, London

KEATING, DUMONT & GRIMM, INC.
342 Madison Ave.
New York, N.Y. 10017
(212) 661-5590
Pierson Keating

JACK KENNEDY ASSOCIATES
520 No. Michigan Ave.
Chicago, Ill. 60611
(312) 828-9474
Jack Kennedy
Advertising/Publishing/Communications/
Marketing Fields

WILLIAM KEY & PARTNERS, LTD.
4 Half Moon St.
London W 1 Y 7RA, England
W. F. Key
Operations Research/EDP Fields

KIENBAUM BERATUNGEN GmbH
Hindenburgstrasse 4-8
5270 Gummersbach, West Germany

KIERNAN AND COMPANY, INC.
515 Madison Ave.
New York, N.Y. 10022
(212) 755-9800
Paul Kiernan
Also: 73-75 Mortimer St.,
London, W 1, England

WARREN KING & ASSOCIATES (MC)
20 No. Wacker Dr.
Chicago, Ill. 60606
(312) 726-0481
Warren King

KORN/FERRY & ASSOCIATES
1901 Avenue of the Stars
Los Angeles, Calif. 90067
(213) 879-1834

KORN/FERRY & ASSOCIATES (Cont.)
Also: 936 Huntington Dr., San Marino, Calif.
(213) 284-3203
277 Park Ave., New York, N.Y. 10017
(212) 838-3929
260 Peachtree St., Atlanta, Ga. 30303
(404) 577-7542
One Shell Plaza, Suite 3270, Houston,
Texas 77002
(713) 223-0336

MARSHALL S. LACHNER ASSOCIATES
420 Lexington Ave.
New York, N.Y. 10017
(212) MU 3-3568
Marshall S. Lachner

LESTER B. KNIGHT & ASSOCIATES** (MC)
Executive Search Division
549 West Randolph St.
Chicago, Ill. 60606
(312) 346-2100
Lester B. Knight
Also: N.Y.; Zug, Switzerland; London;
Dusseldorf; Karlstead, Sweden

WILLIAM M. KORDSIEMAN
& ASSOCIATES (MC)
100 West Monroe St.
Chicago, Ill. 60603
(312) RA6-7580
Retail/Appliance Fields

KREMPLE & MEADE*
1900 Ave. of the Stars
Los Angeles, Calif. 90067
(213) 553-3156
Robert Kremple

E. THOMAS LALUMIA ASSOCIATES, INC.
420 Lexington Ave.
New York, N.Y. 10017
(212) 889-7720
E. Thomas Lalumia
EDP/Marketing/Acctg./Personnel Fields

LAMALIE ASSOCIATES
100 Erieview Plaza
Cleveland, Ohio 44114
(216) 522-1650
Also: 11 E. Adams St., Chicago, Ill. 60603
(312) 939-2951

WARREN LAMB ASSOCIATES, LTD.
Westmoreland House
127-131 Regent St.
London W 1 R, 7HA, England
Tel. 01-437-0238
Warren Lamb

LAMSON-GRIFFITHS ASSOCIATES, INC.
(MC)
20 No. Wacker Dr.
Chicago, Ill. 60606
(312) 332-4571
John Griffiths

ROBERT E. LARSON & ASSOCIATES
622 North Cass St., Suite 411
Milwaukee, Wisc. 53202
(414) 271-3433

LAUER & HOLBROOK, INC.
208 South LaSalle St.
Chicago, Ill. 60604
(312) 372-7050

LAUGERY, de LABRUSSE & ASSOCIATES
38 Rue de Lisbonne
75 Paris 8e, France
Tel. 387-55-09, 522-83-10
Gustave Laugery
Also: Amsterdam, Brussels, Dusseldorf,
London, Milan

JACK LAWRENCE & COMPANY, INC.
375 Park Ave.
New York, N.Y. 10022
(212) 758-4073
Jack Lawrence

LAWRENCE-LEITER & COMPANY** (MC)
Executive Search Division
114 West 10th St.
Kansas City, Mo. 64105
(816) 474-8340
William Beeson

LAWYER'S PLACEMENT SERVICE
1155 East 60th St.
Chicago, Ill. 60637
(312) 493-0533
Mrs. Frances Utley

ROBERT LEE & PARTNERS
24 Berkeley Square
London, WC1, England

LEWIN & COMPANY (MC)
501 Madison Ave.
New York, N.Y. 10022
(212) 421-0772
A. W. Lewin
Marketing/Advertising/P.R. Fields

ERNEST LOEN & ASSOCIATES
7250 Franklin
Hollywood, Calif. 90057
(213) 874-2113
Ernest T. Leon
Technical/Scientific Fields

ARTHUR J. LOVELEY ASSOCIATES
521 Fifth Ave.
New York, N.Y. 10017
(212) 682-8110

FRED LUSTIG AND ASSOCIATES*
405 Lexington Ave.
New York, N.Y. 10017
(212) MU 7-0427
Fred Lustig

LYBRAND, ROSS BROS.,
& MONTGOMERY (CPA)
Executive Search Division
1251 Ave. of Americas
New York, N.Y. 10004
Bernard Lybrand
(212) 489-1100
Also: Major U.S. Cities and London, Paris

MADDEN ASSOCIATES, INC.
Suite 1357
2 North Riverside Plaza
Chicago, Ill. 60606
(312) 372-2798

ROBERT MADIGAN ASSOCIATES, INC.
60 East 42nd St.
New York, N.Y. 10017
(212) 867-6550

MANAGEMENT ENTERPRISES
4040 No. Lincoln Blvd.
Oklahoma City, Okla. 73105
(405) 424-4685
Thomas J. Harris

MANAGEMENT SELECTION GROUP LTD.
17 Stratton St.
London, W1, England

THOMAS MANGUM COMPANY
315 West Ninth St.
Los Angeles, Calif. 90015
(213) 623-5221
Thomas Mangum

F. L. MANNIX & CO., INC. (MC)
65 William St.
Wellesley, Mass. 02181
(617) 237-1921
F. L. Mannix
Technical/Industrial Relations Fields

MARC ASSOCIATES, INC.
1150 Suburban Station Bldg.
Philadelphia, Pa. 19103
(215) 568-6996
Ronald Stevens

MARSHALL CONSULTANTS, INC.
360 E. 65th St.
New York, N.Y. 10022
(212) 628-8400
Larry Marshall
Communications/P.R./Publishing Fields

JOHN M. MARTIN & ASSOCIATES (MC)
4055 Wilshire Blvd.
Los Angeles, Calif. 90005
(213) 386-5772
John M. Martin

McCANN ASSOCIATES (MC)
2755 Philmont Ave.
Huntington Valley, Pa. 19006
(215) WI 7-5775
Forbes McCann
Government/Public Administration Fields

McCARTNEY & ASSOCIATES
1545 Waukegan Rd.
Glenview, Ill. 60025

McCELLAND, KIERSTEAD & FENN (MC)
200 Park Ave.
New York, N.Y. 10017
(212) YU 6-2515
Peter Fenn
Financial Fields

RICHARD F. McCORMACK & ASSOCIATES
2127 E. Lee Wynn Dr.
Sarasota, Fla.
Richard F. McCormack

McCORMACK SERVICES
Box 204
Verona, N.J. 07044
Robert McCormack

NATION-WIDE RECRUITING
23101 Sherman Way
Canoga Park, Calif. 91304
(213) 387-1840
Bernie Weiner

FRITZ NEAGLE ASSOCIATES (MC)
230 Park Ave.
New York, N.Y. 10017
(212) MU 9-3788
Fritz E. Neagle, Jr.
Consumer Product Fields

FRANK NOETTLING ASSOCIATES
200 Park Ave.
New York, N.Y. 10017
(212) 687-0550
Frank Noettling

DAVID NORTH & ASSOCIATES
120 East 56th St.
New York, N.Y. 10022
(212) 421-9650
David North
Also: Chicago, Boston, San Francisco,
London, Paris, Toronto

OLIVER & ROZNER ASSOCIATES, INC.
1 East 53rd St.
New York, N.Y. 10022
(212) 688-1850
Frank Oliver

PACKARD ASSOCIATES (MC)
3 Water Lane, Plandome Manor
Manhasset, N.Y. 11030
(516) 627-9232
Joseph Packard

JOHN PAISIOS & ASSOCIATES
332 South Michigan Ave.
Chicago, Ill. 60604
(312) 922-8836

PARIS SURVEY
36, Avenue Hoche
Paris 8, France
Tel. 622-47-82

CHARLES PARTHUM & ASSOCIATES (MC)
2040 W. Wisconsin Ave.
Milwaukee, Wisc. 53233
(414) 342-2900
Charles Parthum

BRUCE PAYNE & ASSOCIATES, INC. (MC)
Executive Search Division
Time & Life Bldg.
Rockefeller Center West
New York, N.Y. 10020
(212) 581-5500
Bruce Payne
Also: Boston, Los Angeles, Mexico City,
Buenos Aires, San Paulo, Brazil;
Zug, Switzerland

THE P. E. CONSULTING GROUP
12 Grosvenor Place
London, SW1, England

PEAT, MARWICK, MITCHELL & CO. (CPA)
Executive Search Division
345 Park Ave.
New York, N.Y. 10017
(212) 758-9700
Garth Parker

JAMES PEPPER & ASSOCIATES
Avenida Paulista 2202
Sao Paulo, Brazil
Tel. 287-1604, 287-3982
James Pepper
Financial Fields

PERFORMANCE DYNAMICS INC.
Executive Search Division
17 Grove Ave.
Verona, N.J. 07044
Mitchell Lyman

THE PERSONNEL LABORATORY, INC.
500 Summer St.
Stamford, Conn.
(203) 325-4348
King Whitney, Jr.

J. R. PIERCE ASSOCIATES
3960 Wilshire Blvd.
Los Angeles, Calif. 90005
(213) 386-1276
J. R. Pierce

PLANNING DYNAMICS INC.
Executive Search Division
Three Gateway Center
Pittsburgh, Pa. 15222
(412) 261-6084
Charles D. Reese, Jr.

PLANNING RESEARCH CORP.
1100 Glendon Ave.
Los Angeles, Calif. 90024
(213) 272-9321
Frank Dietz

HENRY PONZIO ASSOCIATES, INC.
415 Lexington Ave.
New York, N.Y. 10017
(212) 661-3119
Henry A. Ponzio
EDP/Engineering/Finance/Personnel Fields

ARTHUR J. PRESCOTT, INC.
400 Madison Ave.
New York, N.Y. 10017
(212) PL 1-4630
Arthur J. Prescott

PRICE WATERHOUSE & CO. (CPA)
Executive Search Division
60 Broad St.
New York, N.Y. 10004
(212) 422-6000
Matthew Beecher

PROMODAG
17, Avenue des Marronniers
94-Nugent-sur-Marne, France

ALBERT RAMOND & ASSOCIATES, INC.**
   (MC)
1615 Tribune Tower
Chicago, Ill. 60611
(312) WH 3-2323

PAUL R. RAY & CO., INC. (MC)
1212 First Nat. Bank Bldg.
Fort Worth, Texas 76100
(817) 336-4476
Paul R. Ray
Also: 200 Park Ave., New York, N.Y.
(212) 687-0046
9841 Airport Blvd.
Los Angeles, Calif.

REEVES/NEWELL & ASSOCIATES
636 Acanto
Los Angeles, Cal. 90049
(213) 476-1988
F. L. Reeves

REGEHR & FULGHUM ASSOCIATES
Sonnenstrasse 33, 8 Munich 15
West Germany
Tel. 59-55-65

RUSSELL REYNOLDS ASSOCIATES, INC.
245 Park Ave.
New York, N.Y. 10017
(212) 682-8622

JOSEPH L. RODGERS & CO.*
155 East 38th St.
New York, N.Y. 10016
(212) MU 2-0755
Joseph L. Rodgers
All fields, but retailing emphasis

ROGERS, SLADE & HILLS, INC.** (MC)
Executive Search Division
30 East 42nd St.
New York, N.Y. 10017
(212) 682-2550
Ralph Rogers

ROMAC & ASSOCIATES
200 Boylston St.
Chestnut Hill, Mass. 02116
(617) 969-4010
Robert J. Bond
Accounting/EDP Fields

P. S. ROSS & PARTNERS (MC)
Place Ville Marie
Montreal 113, Quebec, Canada
Tel. 514-861-7481
David W. Soles
Also: Ottawa, Quebec, Toronto, Hamilton,
Vancouver, Winnipeg, Edmonton, Saint John

C. J. SAMMOND & ASSOCIATES, INC.
437 Fifth Ave.
New York, N.Y. 10016
(212) 685-1350

SAMSON, BELAIR, RIDDELL, STEAD INC.
630 Dorchester Blvd., West
Montreal 101, Quebec, Canada
Tel. (514) 848-9461
James A. McCoubrey
Also: Toronto

GEORGE D. SANDEL & ASSOCIATES (MC)
60 Hickory Dr.
Waltham, Mass. 02154
(617) 893-0713

SANFORD MANAGEMENT SERVICES,
　INC. (MC)
1212 Wilshire Blvd.
Los Angeles, Calif. 90017
(213) 481-7575

JERRY SANS ASSOCIATES
18 East 41st St.
New York, N.Y. 10017
(212) 532-1189
Jerry Sans
EDP/Eng./Archit./& Advertising

J. L. SAROIAN & ASSOCIATES
1858 Indianapolis St.
Whiting, Ind. 46394
(219) 659-1180
J. L. Saroian
Chemical/Electronic Fields

R. M. SCHMITZ & COMPANY, INC.
Prudential Plaza
Chicago, Ill. 60601
(312) 372-9225

F. R. SCHWAB & ASSOCIATES
645 Madison Ave.
New York, N.Y. 10022
(212) PL 8-6800
F. R. Schwab

WILLIAM A. SHARON ASSOCIATES, INC.
515 Madison Ave.
New York, N.Y. 10022
(212) 755-9563

SIBSON AND COMPANY, INC.
444 Madison Ave.
New York, N.Y. 10022
(212) 421-9310
Robert E. Sibson
Also: East Brunswick, N.J.

JOHN W. SILER & ASSOCIATES
5261 North Port Washington Rd.
Milwaukee, Wisc. 53217
(414) 962-9400

SORZANO, ARMSTRONG & REISTAD, INC.
270 Madison Avenue
New York, N.Y. 10016
(212) MU7-0390

NORMAN SPENCER & COMPANY LTD.
14 Brandon St.
Wellington, C1, New Zealand

SPENCER STUART & ASSOCIATES* (MC)
477 Madison Ave.
New York, N.Y. 10022
(212) 758-9222
Also: 500 No. Michigan Ave., Chicago, Ill. 60611
(312) 822-0080　Guy W. Simpler
Plus: London, Paris, Zurich, Frankfurt, Madrid

SPRIGGS & COMPANY
875 No. Michigan Ave.
Chicago, Ill. 60602
(312) 751-1200
Robert D. Spriggs

STACK ASSOCIATES
230 Park Ave.
New York, N.Y. 10017
(212) 889-1135

PAUL STAFFORD ASSOCIATES, LTD.*
45 Rockefeller Plaza
New York, N.Y. 10020
(212) 765-7700
Paul Stafford
Also: 875 No. Michigan Ave.,
Chicago, Ill. 60611
(312) 664-9402

STAUB, WARMBOLD & ASSOCIATES, INC.*
919 Third Ave.
New York, N.Y. 10022
(212) 758-8200
Robert A. Staub
S. A. Kondoleon
Also: 137 Avenue Louise,
Brussels 5, Belgium
Herbert Greenberg
Parque Espana, 49-4
Mexico 11, D.F. Mexico
Enrique Sod

JOHN HOLT STETHEM & COMPANY, LTD.
1155 Dorchester Blvd., West
Montreal 102, Quebec, Canada
Tel. 866-1904
Mrs. B. Garneau Nadeau
Also: Toronto

STEVENSON & KELLOGG, LTD.** (MC)
Executive Search Division
150 Eglinton Avenue East
Toronto 12, Ontario, Canada
(416) 483-4313
M. E. Money
Also: Halifax, Montreal, Vancouver

STEVENSON, JORDAN, & HARRISON (MC)
200 Park Ave.
New York, N.Y. 10017
(212) 867-1280
Andrew Kazarinoff
Also: Chicago, Washington, D.C.,
Montreal, Toronto

STOCKBROKER'S REGISTER, INC.
799 Boylston St.
Boston, Mass. 02116
(617) 261-8200
Also: 150 Broadway, New York, N.Y.
(212) 943-7610

L. F. STOWELL & ASSOCIATES, INC.
135 E. 54th St.
New York, N.Y. 10022
(212) 753-9100
Lonsdale F. Stowell

JOHN S. STUDWELL ASSOCIATES, INC.
310 Madison Ave.
New York, N.Y. 10017
(212) 867-5350
John S. Studwell
Also: Lewis Tower Bldg., Phila., Pa.
(215) PE 5-4017

STURM, BURROWS & CO.
1420 Walnut St.
Philadelphia, Pa.
(215) KI 6-4111
Garfield C. Burrows
Frederick C. Sturm

GEORGE SULLIVAN ASSOCIATES*
Box 338
Rumson, N.J. 07760
(201) 741-4544
George Sullivan

SUMMERMOUR & ASSOCIATES, INC. (MC)
230 Peachtree St., N.W.
Atlanta, Ga. 30303
(404) 577-4632
Textile/Apparel Fields
Also: Charlotte, Nashville, N.Y.

GEORGE M. SUNDAY & ASSOCIATES, INC.
6 East Monroe St.
Chicago, Ill. 60603
(312) AN 3-1970
Lawrence D. Flynn

VICTOR TABAKA & ASSOCIATES
1800 Peachtree Rd., N.W.
Atlanta, Ga. 30309
(404) 351-3305
Victor Tabaka

J. M. TANKERSLEY & ASSOCIATES (MC)
419 Bradford St.
Gainesville, Ga. 30501
(404) 536-2436
J. M. Tankersley
Animal Health Fields

TECMARK ASSOCIATES
101 Park Ave.
New York, N.Y. 10017
(212) 683-8108
Donald Valentine

TEMPLE ASSOCIATES, INC.
19 Temple Place
Boston, Mass. 02111
(617) 482-3443
Financial Fields

ALEXANDRE TIC et CIE
10, Rue Royale
Paris 8, France

JOHN TYZACK & PARTNERS SELECTION
   LTD.
10 Hallam Street
London, W1, England

TOMSETT CONSULTING ASSOCIATES
402 Frick Bldg.
Pittsburgh, Pa. 15219
(412) 471-2050
Max Walker

LEE TODD ASSOCIATES
85 East End Ave.
New York, N.Y. 10028
(212) RH 4-3466
Lee Todd
Health Fields

STEPHEN TODD ASSOCIATES
15 William St.
New York, N.Y. 10005
(212) 422-6130
Stephen Todd
Investment/Financial Fields

TOUCHE, ROSS, BAILEY & SMART (CPA)
Executive Search Division
80 Pine St.
New York, N.Y. 10005
(212) 489-1600
Dr. Gordon Armbruster

URWICK, ORR & PARTNERS, LTD.
14 Hobart Pl.
London, SW 1, England
L. F. Urwick

VAN HORN ASSOCIATES
277 Park Ave.
New York, N.Y. 10017
(212) 826-6056
E. B. Van Horn

WILLIAM VAN NOSTRAND
   & ASSOCIATES (MC)
50 East 42nd St.
New York, N.Y. 10017
(212) 687-4386
William Van Nostrand

VOGEL & ASSOCIATES
759 No. Milwaukee
Milwaukee, Wisc.
(414) 273-7111

GORDON WAHLS & COMPANY
33 Second St.
Media, Pa. 19063
(215) 565-0800
Gordon Wahls
Scientific/Industrial Relations Fields

NELSON WALKER ASSOCIATES, INC.
   (MC)
52 Vanderbilt Ave.
New York, N.Y. 10017
(212) 889-8640
John Smyth

WEBB, OWEN ASSOCIATES
353 Lexington Ave.
New York, N.Y. 10016
(212) 725-5750
William B. Owen

WERMERT & ASSOCIATES, INC.
110 Charlotte Place
Englewood Cliffs, N.J. 07632
(201) 568-1317
Gilbert Wermert

WESTCOTT ASSOCIATES
39 South La Salle St.
Chicago, Ill. 60603
(312) 332-6336

WESTWOOD RESEARCH, INC.
10889 Wilshire Blvd.
Los Angeles, Calif. 90024
(213) 478-2567
Lorenzio I. Dwyer, Jr.
Also: 1660 "L" St., N.W.
Washington, D.C. 20036
(202) 659-3612

WILLIAM H. WILLIS, INC.
445 Park Ave.
New York, N.Y. 10022
(212) PI 2-3456
William H. Willis, Jr.

WILKINSON, SEDWICK & YELVERTON,
   INC. (MC)
255 California St.
San Francisco, Calif. 94111
(415) 981-6060
Dr. Robert Crisera
Also: 200 Park Ave., New York, N.Y. 10017
(212) 986-2244
2200 — 6th Ave., Seattle, Wash. 98121
(206) MA 2-5800
3435 Wilshire Blvd., Los Angeles, Calif. 90005
(213) 381-7075
Emphasizes Industrial Relations/
Personnel Fields

WINTER-KAHN, NIELSEN-ROSS
   & BUCKWALTER, INC. (MC)
222 Wisconsin Bldg.
Lake Forest, Ill. 60045
(312) 234-2400
Also: Chicago

WOODS, GORDON & COMPANY (MC)
Royal Trust Tower
Toronto Dominion Center
Toronto 111, Ontario, Canada
Tel. (416) 368-4761
Jas. W. Mills
Also: Calgary, Edmonton, Ontario,
Montreal, Ottawa, Vancouver, London,
Hamilton, Kitchener, Winnipeg

WORDEN & RISBERG (MC)
The Fiedlity Bldg.
123 So. Broad St.
Philadelphia, Pa. 19109
(215) PE 5-3300
Peter Bowen

WYTMAR & COMPANY, INC.*
10 So. Riverside Plaza
Chicago, Ill. 60606
(312) 236-1350
James W. Jacobs
Also: Paris, Dusseldorf

ARTHUR YOUNG & COMPANY (CPA)
Executive Search Division
277 Park Ave.
New York, N.Y. 10017
(212) 922-2000
Edwin Mruk

JORG ZAUBER ASSOCIATES
Berliner Allee 48
Dusseldorf, West Germany

EGON ZEHNDER INTERNATIONAL S.A.
    (MC)
5, Place du Champs de Mars
B — Brussels 5
Tel. (02) 13-41-40
Alain A. Hauzeur
Also: Bahnhofstrasse 1, 8001 Zurich,
Switzerland
Tel. 27-27-69
W. P. Siegenthaler
Plus: Paris, Mr. Ph. Bouvard
London, Mr. R. A. B. Gowlland
Copenhagen, Mr. J. Friisberg

ZIMMER, HUBBARD, LANGLIE & MOORE INC.
777 Summer St.
Stamford, Conn. 06902
(203) 325-2677
Emile Zimmer

SAMPSON-NEILL ASSOCIATES INC.
543 Valley Road
Montclair, N.J. 07043
(201) 783-9600
Martin C. Sampson, M.D.
Health Fields

8.

PROFESSIONAL ASSOCIATIONS

&

UNUSUAL APPROACHES FOR GENERATING INTERVIEWS

PROFESSIONAL SOCIETIES, ALUMNI AND TRADE ASSOCIATIONS

There are many professional organizations, alumni groups and trade associations that act as intermediaries between job hunters and corporations. You don't have to be an active participant or loyal fund raiser to avail yourself of their potential for job hunting assistance. Their general effectiveness can vary greatly dependent upon the specific organization and the individual in charge. Most of these groups function as resume clearing houses and they rarely charge either the job hunter or the corporation a fee. As a general rule, we suggest that you don't use these sources until your campaign is well under way.

If you are in a delicate position it might be unwise to leave your normal resume with these groups. If this is the case we suggest that you provide them with a resume which is not identified. Your basic resume less your name and address, as well as present and past employment should suffice. This would still give firms all the information they need to evaluate whether or not your background matched their needs. If you know the Director of the organization on a personal basis, you could let him reveal additional information at his discretion. This would include information as to employers and salary.

Directories which list exhibitors at trade shows are often a fine source for names of both firms and key executives in an industry. Copies of these directories are usually available without charge from the trade associations.

The Encyclopedia of Associations lists the names and addresses of thousands of these groups. In general we believe they are most effective for men who are specialists and who seek between $10,000 and $20,000. There is no doubt that many of them can prove very effective for accountants, lawyers, doctors, engineers, and other specialty occupations.

UNUSUAL APPROACHES FOR GENERATING INTERVIEWS

During the course of your campaign, you might consider experimenting with some unusual approaches for generating interviews. Creativity is so rarely displayed by job hunters that almost any aggressive off-beat approach can be quite effective if executed tactfully.

Telephone

For example, you might attempt to arrange interviews through telephoning executives on a direct basis. It is surprisingly easy to reach executives at any level by phone. If you had already sent an executive a letter and were in the area, you will probably find it worthwhile to call. A good time to call is usually just after 5:00 P.M. At that time most secretaries have generally departed and executives will answer their own phones. If you find that the person you want is never available at that time, then adjust your strategy and try reaching him early in the morning, before regular secretarial hours.

Telegram

There is also nothing quite like a telegram because you can be sure your telegram will be read. You could save this expensive approach for an answer to an ad, or to approach an executive in a company that is very important to you. In the telegram you can briefly summarize your key qualifications and say that your resume and/or letter will shortly follow.

Special Delivery or Registered Letters

Another different way to seek a position is to use a special delivery or registered letter. Anything that arrived registered would have a better chance of being read by the executive to whom it was addressed. Any of these approaches that is carefully worded in good taste will go a long way toward convincing a firm that you really want to work for them.

Newsletters

Another medium you might investigate includes the editors and publishers of Newsletters. The growth in popularity of Newsletters has resulted in a considerable number of such publications being available. Some of them are carefully read by executives at all levels including corporate presidents. In general, they are enjoying a growing influence as outside communications sources. Many of them offer to act as an exchange meeting place between executives and employers seeking executive talent. They are informed of openings and will forward your resume if you are the type of executive material the employer is seeking.

Other Rarely Used Approaches

There are many other creative approaches which students and young managers have successfully used to generate interviews. In general, the success of a dramatic approach depends on the creativity being applied in good taste. We have seen men adapt almost all of the sales approaches commonly used in selling both products and services. This includes odd-shaped pop-open brochures as well as printed invitations which facilitate company consideration of an applicant by completing a self-addressed and postage-paid card. Other people have had their resumes delivered by a messenger service in envelopes marked rush and personal. Some have also found it effective to send letters to outsiders who are on a firm's Board of Directors. Being able to suggest a good executive candidate reflects well on any Director, and you may find them very receptive.

9.

COMMERCIAL JOB HUNTING SERVICES

This book is intended to provide job hunters with the strategy advice they need to locate an attractive position. However, for people who are still unsure of certain factors regarding their campaign, or who do not have the time to execute a job search themselves, there are commercial services available. You can consider retaining professional assistance for help in virtually any area of job hunting.

Because of the rapid growth in firms who service job hunters, we have included this section for anyone who may be considering the use of such services.

General Explanation and Definitions

There is an expanding number of firms who go by names such as the following:

> Employment Consultants
> Career Counselors
> Career Advisors
> Executive Placement Consultants
> Executive Marketers
> Career Advancement Specialists
> Executive Job Counselors

Quite frankly, there are so many labels being used that it can be immensely confusing from anyone's viewpoint. While some firms have been in this business for quite some time, the increase in job mobility during the last decade has greatly accelerated the growth of this industry.

Regardless of the particular label a company uses, these are generally firms which offer services for which the individual job hunter must pay a fee. They should not be confused with executive search firms who are retained by corporations. They also differ from a personnel agency in that their fees are generally paid regardless of whether an individual actually locates a position. (Personnel agencies only collect their fees from the individual or the company when a person begins work with the new employer.)

Because of the rapid development of this business, an individual job hunter needs to be extremely careful in shopping for these services. In some cities, a number of these firms have received a notable amount of adverse publicity in recent years. This has generally stemmed from the complaints of unhappy clients who paid large sums of money to these firms, but who felt they received little in return. Most of the criticism has been directed at firms that provide extensive counseling and psychological testing services, which are then supplemented by a resume writing and small mailing.

The Nature of the Services Available

The exact services which various companies offer differ substantially, and probably no two firms offer the same range of services. However, as a general rule, we feel that their functions can be grouped according to the following classifications:

1. CAREER COUNSELORS   —   These firms provide services for individuals who are not sure of their abilities; goals; what occupation they should pursue; or how to go about achieving their goals. They typically seek to help people resolve questions such as:

    Are you in the right field?

    Do you belong in a large or a small company?

    Do you really achieve the satisfaction you need in your job?

    What is it that you really want to seek?

    Is your work as rewarding as you should have achieved at this stage?

    A good counselor can help bring into perspective things which the individual may have in the back of his mind but can't nail down. Sometimes just speaking with a counselor will help make a person feel better about a decision that he is facing.

    Counselors also act to help people review their present situation before they leave a job. The cliche "the grass is always greener" has a lot of meaning when it comes to the way many view management jobs. Many counseling firms work to a large extent with people who are at an emotional low point in their careers. Frequently these people lack any real understanding of failure and success. Failure is something which is rarely dramatic, although many people feel like failures as soon as they have suddenly lost a position. Their actual loss of the position may be due to an employment cut-back, impending merger, a personality clash, or a myriad of other problems. A real failure is normally established in bits and pieces of patterns visible to any objective counselor. For that matter, people rarely achieve rapid success in the corporate environment. Unless you happen to be very lucky, corporate success is something which will be achieved only through a building process.

The fear of a possible change is also something which can sometimes be resolved through working with a good counselor. Many individuals do an injustice to their careers by not searching for a new position. The fear of change that holds them back is primarily a case of fear of the unknown. People who change jobs after working for a single company a long time are usually amazed three months later at just how easily they managed the transition. It is almost invariably smoother than people expect, as most people lose confidence in their adaptability when they are in one firm too long.

When it comes to actually purchasing the services of a counseling firm, you are usually buying services which fit within one or more of the following groups:

A.   Aptitude and psychological testing –Normally to help these firms help their clients in career direction. Some firms stress their ability to help a person to get to know himself. Others may use them only to help individuals prepare for such tests.

B.   Discussions with individuals about themselves and the job market – This is to help the company determine what financial and responsibility goals are possible achievements given someone's background. They also counsel people on how to improve their position without having to leave the present employer.

C.   Personal counseling during the course of a client's job campaign – This service is basically a review of a client's interview experiences in hopes of helping him overcome his shortcomings. It is generally done in connection with a job hunter's execution of his own campaign.

2.   RESUME WRITERS AND DISTRIBUTORS – These firms generally do the following:

A.   Preparation and printing of resumes and the preparation of appropriate cover letters to accompany the resume.

B.   Circulation of your resume – In this case, the firms may send letters with your resume to firms which may have an interest in your background. They may do this under your name or if you wish to remain anonymous, they may use a file reference (E.G. #B459) and send them out under their company letterhead. (NOTE: Career counselors will frequently offer these two services as an extension of their counseling program.)

3. EXECUTIVE MARKETERS — These are the firms who offer specific job hunting services to individuals. They are retained by job hunters who have defined position and financial objectives, and should be distinguished from the firms who do extensive personal counseling. A person may retain one of these companies for the execution of an entire job campaign or simply for review of a resume which the job hunter has written. The specific services which they offer usually include:

A. Resume analysis — Individuals may have their resumes and cover letters analyzed and critiqued.

B. Resume preparation — The companies will create resumes and letters appropriate for the individual's goals.

C. Third party representation — Some of these firms will execute mailings for individuals on their letterheads; essentially representing them in order to protect the individual's secrecy.

D. Reference validation — Individuals who are worried about their references may have these firms check them in advance of their campaign.

E. Market research — These firms will develop a mailing list for a person's direct letter campaign (names and addresses of companies along with the names of executives for the individual job hunter to contact).

F. Interview role-playing — These firms may be retained to help individuals develop finesse in the interviewing situation. Some companies employ video-tape during give and take workshop sessions.

G. Total job campaign assistance — Individual job hunters can purchase complete job campaign assistance from these companies. Companies can be retained to do all of the work incident to the generation of interviews. These companies would create all written materials and would answer advertisements, make mailings to executive search firms, and corporations. They would do this on a basis where they either (1) sign the individual's name to the correspondence, (2) use their own company name, or (3) use the name of one of their individuals acting as a third party representative.

H. Typing and administrative services — If an individual job hunter has retained one of these firms for some area of assistance, they can usually purchase typing, secretarial, and mailing services.

4.   JOB REGISTERS – There are some firms who fall in between the types of firms above and personnel agencies. They will frequently advertise that their services cost nothing if you do not get a new job. As a client you may register with them for a fee which can range from $10 to $600. Some of them follow a procedure which subsequently refunds the fee if the individual accepts a job arranged through their placement efforts. In placing him they act as an agency that gets their fee from the company. They are generally known as Computer, Executive Placement or Register firms and will frequently claim to have listings for all ranges of positions.

If you are not in a hurry, some of these services can work out very well. However, individuals should be sure that they understand two things quite clearly. The first is what will happen to their fee if they get a job through their own efforts. The second is the time period necessary before a person can get a refund if no job offers are forthcoming.

Some Negatives about Many of These Services

We do work with job hunters ourselves, and have conducted a great many job campaigns for individuals in almost every situation. However, commercial job hunting services industry has recently been blighted by the practices of some firms. We agree that certain firms can do a disservice to their clients, and a considerable number have been guilty of one or more of the following:

(1)   The resumes and letters prepared by some firms, while accomplishment oriented and fairly well-written, often tend to look alike. Most firms follow a basic format to help keep costs in line and to expedite the writing process. The result is that their resumes (or letters) bear a resemblance which makes them readily identifiable by most seasoned personnel and search executives. In turn, some of these people frequently place less faith in what they read and react negatively concerning the individual's creativity and ability to express himself. Some also assume that the individual is someone with problems or otherwise he would not be using counseling services.

(2)   Some firms which circulate resumes or letters on behalf of an individual frequently do so in a very haphazard fashion. Instead of addressing letters by personal name, they send letters addressed to "President – XYZ Corporation". Some of them also send form letters rather than individually typed correspondence. A common result (between the form letter and the stereotyped resume) is that far fewer interviews per contact may be produced than the person might have achieved on his own.

(3)   A serious disservice rendered by some firms to their clients sometimes involves the organizations to whom some of them circulate letters and resumes. Executives have had

their resumes (or letters) sent to firms — which they specifically told the counselor not to contact — including their present employer. This type of mistake is surely the occassional result of poor administrative control. However, where a person's career is concerned, the margin for this type of error obviously must be zero.

(4)   One last factor of consequence has to do with the quality of individual counselors. Some of these firms have expanded so rapidly that they have the same personnel problems as any growing firm, namely inexperience and in some cases, rapid turnover.

Their Contracts and Guarantees

Where a large assignment is concerned, the standard method of operation for most firms involves having a client sign a contract. The contract specifies fees and terms of payment as well as the firm's responsibilities. Many of these contracts have a way of absolving the counseling firms of any liability without guaranteeing any specific results.

If you are a prospective client of a job counselor, consider the exact wording in the contract most carefully. At the present time, an individual cannot hold these firms responsible for any oral promises, unless they are written into the contract. If an individual in one of these firms makes certain promises of delivery, be it offers of interviews or job offers, the client should request that it be written into the contract. Some of these firms have been accused of making implications and promises, both in their advertisements and in personal conversations, on which they don't deliver. A counselor may allude to having placed many executives in top positions, or to having a vast network of industry contacts. However, this is no guarantee that such statements are true, or that such previous success or contacts will result in your locating a position equal to or better than what you presently enjoy.

While the job hunting counselors usually have a general brochure available, most do not publish literature or have anything in writing which clearly spells out the exact nature of their service, or precisely what they will do for a client. Their reason for this is they claim every individual is a separate case and that they customize their service to meet the needs of the individual. As a general rule, their exact activities are somewhat shrouded in secrecy and can be only confirmed in personal discussions.

The Fees They Charge

The fees which many firms charge are frequently based on an individual's present earnings (i.e. 10-15% of present annual earnings). However, they can run a wide range from $100 to $8,000 depending on the breadth of service an individual desires as well as his present earnings. The average fee in the New York area is probably somewhere in the neighborhood of $1,400 to $2,000. It is worth noting that while most base their fees on a percentage formula, there are unfortunately others which have a trial and error fee system in that they essentially charge what they believe the traffic will bear. Very few have a fee system which is directly related to the costs which they incur on behalf of a client.

Even where there is a fee system which may be related directly to the cost of working for a client, all job hunting services can be quite expensive. Like many other service firms, these companies must charge substantially more than they pay their individual executives in order to meet their payroll, cover their overhead and earn a profit. The actual setting of hourly rates in this industry is not much different from the consulting industry at large. An established rule of thumb for a firm who has attractive New York City offices would be to bill an individual three times the actual hourly wage which is paid to the consultant working with the client. The established rule being that the first third of the billing rate covers the payroll; the second third — the overhead; and the last third makes a contribution to profits. In practice, the actual range of billing rates varies with a firm's overhead. They do run from one and one half times the salary rate to as high as five times the rate paid the individual consultant.

While this rate structure may seem high, almost all service firms operate on a similar basis. The fact remains that the good consultant firms should be able to produce at a rate many times in excess of what you could accomplish in the same period and some can offer invaluable assistance. You have to carefully weigh the potential advantage in time and dollars; along with the value to you of a potential job change; and view these against the out-of-pocket costs of retaining them.

Be Careful in Your Selection

If you consider using the service of one of these firms, you should be very careful in your selection. The firms in this field are usually not required to be professionally licensed by either the cities or states in which they operate, and like any other business, some firms are much more reliable than others. If you would like to have professional assistance in your campaign, we suggest that you start by retaining a company solely for the purpose of analyzing your resume or creating an entirely new resume and cover letters. It's almost always interesting for an individual job hunter to see what a professional can do with his background, and this service really represents your best investment. If you decide on more complete assistance, the information herein should provide you with a good basis for questions when you have discussions with a given company. If you do use a firm to execute your entire campaign, we strongly suggest that you insist on receiving blind carbon copies of all correspondence initiated on your behalf. You should also be sure to insist upon both a personal and creative approach designed solely to meet the objectives you have stated. While some commercial job hunting services can be an immense help to certain people, this is an area in which the age-old phrase "Caveat Emptor" should certainly be kept in mind.

10.

MAINTAINING SECRECY

&

THE HANDLING OF REFERENCES

AND APPLICATION FORMS

LOOKING FOR A POSITION IN TOTAL SECRECY

There is a very real need to free individuals from the fear of having their employer learn of their job search. Unfortunately for job hunters, there can never be positive assurance of job hunting secrecy. However, we can suggest certain unconventional approaches which will minimize your chances of being discovered. The following alternative methods have all proven effective in allowing individuals to explore opportunities without revealing their identities.

Post Office Box Number Approach (Using a Box # as your Address)

For a period of three months you could get a box number at a post office that is not in your own community. You should be able to get one at a post office convenient enough for you to check a few times a week. You would then be free to send your resume (less your name) and unsigned letters in answer to blind advertisements. You could state that the delicate nature of your present position necessitates absolute anonymity until you know who they are, or can identify or establish a mutual interest in confidence.

This anonymous approach can be surprisingly effective in getting interviews. You don't have to tell too much about yourself and can more easily avoid highlighting any liabilities you may have.

We have felt that its success is directly related to its' mystery appeal. Since it is rarely used, the individual on the receiving end may give you an interview simply because of the curiosity factor.

Third Party Letter Approach

Another way to approach this problem of looking for a job in secret is to make use of the third party letter. Here we refer to your using a friend's name in answering advertisements, mailing direct letters and so forth. Your letters would speak of someone he knows that has such and such qualities, etc. This third party approach can be troublesome and less efficient in terms of time. On the other hand, boastful statements are obviously in much better taste when they come from someone else. The third party letter really acts as an endorsement and can enable you to be presented in a more forceful manner.

Third Party Letter — with You as the Third Party

Another derivation of the same approach is for you to answer all advertisements with a letter, and send letters to companies wherein you state that you know of a party and are acting on behalf of that party. You can state your own qualities and then divulge that you are the actual applicant at an appropriate time when you feel secure.

If you consider using any of these and want to use a resume rather than just a letter, you will obviously require an additional special format resume. To best protect your anonymity, it should be a simple type-written resume which does not contain the names of any of your employers or schools, as well as your name and address. It should essentially be restricted to your objectives, duties, accomplishments, types of degrees, marital and military status.

As previously indicated, there is no technique which can eliminate all risk. However, we have known individuals who circulated up to 500 resumes under the cover of a box number and a third party, and who were effective at achieving their goals.

THE QUESTION OF REFERENCES

Be Discreet in Disclosing References

We believe it is unwise to give the names of references until you feel a job offer will be extended. If you give out your references too frequently, you may find that these people become annoyed. Their eventual reference, which may be necessary to secure the job you want, might not end up as a strong endorsement. If you're filling out a lot of employment applications which request references, you might simply indicate that they will be furnished at a later date if there is a mutual interest.

How to Check Questionable References

If you have any doubt about your references or about your past employer's opinion of you, you should have them checked in advance of your campaign. On many occasions people have received lukewarm or bad references which were contrary to their expectations. If you have some doubts, we recommend that you have a friend at another company make a phone call to the references in question — in the guise of an employer who is considering hiring you. As an alternative, you could consider doing the same thing by letter. In this case your friend would send a letter to the reference (or employer). It would tell him that you had applied for a position with that company and that your application was receiving his serious attention. Your friend could then state that since you had listed his name, that his opinion as to your quality of work, character, dates of employment, and earnings would be appreciated. Your friend could also ask his opinion on your ability to work effectively with all levels of management. If you receive either no reply or what you consider a less than adequate response from a given individual, you should then go to that reference and indicate that he cost you an excellent job opportunity. You will have to do this in good taste but you should be firm and show your disappointment. Chances are that it would never happen again, since giving you an inadequate reference would not be worth the trouble that the individual might cause for himself. If this doesn't work out, be sure to give advance notice to your potential employer that differences existed between you and the reference in question.

The whole area of cross-checking your references can be extremely delicate. Making a check on yourself can completely backfire if you handle it the wrong way.

We know of one instance where a gentleman had quit an organization but was concerned about the reference he would receive. He decided to do his own reference check through a post office box number which was one hundred miles from the former employer. He invented a bogus organization, gave it the box number address and had stationary printed. He subsequently sent a letter to the personnel executive explaining that he was an applicant for a job and requested a reference. He signed the letter with a name which he invented.

Approximately five days later, the job applicant received a letter at the box number. Unfortunately, it was addressed to him, rather than the name of the firm he had invented. The letter read, "Dear John, I am astonished that you would stoop to such a low activity as that which you have tried to perpetrate." The letter was signed by the personnel executive at his former employer.

It was at this stage that the job applicant came to our firm for advice! Needless to say, he was totally shocked at having been discovered and very worried about the danger of losing that reference forever. It turned out to only be the beginning of his problems since he had also sent the same letter to three other executives at the same organization.

When this gentleman's problem was unravelled, it turned out that he grossly underestimated the personnel executive with whom he was dealing. That gentleman had felt the letter was a bogus because of the box number and the absence of a phone number; he then wrote his reply, drove the hundred miles and handed the envelope to a postal employee. At the same time he indicated that he had forgotten the job applicant's box number and name of his firm. In essence, he tricked the post office into revealing that the job applicant was the owner of the box number. The moral of this case is obvious. If you choose to check your references, make sure you do the job well.

Make Use of Outstanding References

Outstanding references can be a tremendous help to almost any person. You should try to cultivate references from men with impressive titles. Listing references which include senators, congressmen, generals, chief executives, editors and publishers, or other men in the public limelight will impress almost anyone. If you have these kinds of references, you should obviously use them whenever they might be of assistance in your job campaign. References frequently make the final impression for or against an individual.

THE HANDLING OF APPLICATION FORMS

Application forms frequently offer job hunters a totally unique source of frustration. Completing them can be immensely time consuming. Furthermore, the forms always manage to highlight liabilities and allow minimum room for expression of achievements. In fact, if you have definite liabilities, these forms may be a major block in your campaign and one which will limit your interview exposure.

As a general rule, you should try to make sure that an interesting position is available before completing them. An even better policy is to try to avoid them entirely. However, if you are answering ads or sending letters to firms, you will almost certainly receive letters back with application forms. In many cases you will have to complete them prior to getting an interview. The only advice we can supply you concerning this source of frustration is listed below:

(1)   When filling out applications, always type or print neatly, and keep erasures to a minimum. Never fill them out in a hurry, and always fill them out at home. If someone requests that you complete one in an office lobby prior to an interview, simply indicate that you would rather fill it out at your own convenience

(2)   If the salary objective is requested on a given form, you should generally leave it blank. It is virtually impossible to guess accurately about how much a position is worth, and stating your objective can only limit your ability to negotiate.

(3)   As previously indicated, you should generally avoid filling in references until you are sure a mutual interest exists.

(4)   When you complete your occupational history, be sure to expand on the accomplishments and duties section by referring them to your resume. (Then attach another copy of your resume.)

(5)   Make sure that you reflect an active personality on questions concerning hobbies. A good mixture of sports, civic affairs, and bridge is usually satisfactory.

(6)   Questions along the line of "Have you been arrested or denied credit within the last five years?" – invite the obvious response!

(7)   If an application requests college grades, and you happened to be near the bottom of your class, be sure to cite an appropriate number of part time jobs while working your way through college!

(8)   When you return your application form, be sure to attach a well-written cover letter which clearly restates your desire to explore the particular opportunity.

11.

THE HANDLING OF PSYCHOLOGICAL TESTS

In the late 1950's and early 1960's both psychological and aptitude testing were really in vogue. In recent years the use of testing in personnel selection has declined. Short aptitude tests are still commonly used but primarily at the very junior levels.

The reasons which have prompted a decline in testing are quite numerous. The principal factor is that many firms have found that some very talented people would rather go elsewhere than submit to testing. In addition, there is a major fallacy related to most written psychological tests. This is the fact that even the most carefully prepared built-in-lie questions can often be finessed by a knowledgeable test-taker. Such a person can project whatever image he believes appropriate. One other factor of considerable significance is simply that the validity of most tests for screening executives has rarely been established in any concrete form.

In the course of your campaign you will still probably encounter firms which insist that you submit to various tests as an employment requirement. Unless you enjoy taking tests or are a real test-taker and can turn this to an advantage, you shouldn't be willing to take them. Almost all tests are simply a screening out device — never screening in — as you will still need all the qualities necessary for any other job.

Today tests are used primarily as a crutch or perhaps at the whim of a particular personnel executive. You can decline taking them by simply indicating that at your level you can certainly stand on your record (past accomplishments and education), and that you would be happy to supply whatever business and personal references they might request. If they are really interested in you, they will accede to your request.

(If the truth be known, the facts are that test taking should be a two-way street. It would certainly be just as important for you to know more about your direct superior as it would be for the company to know more about you.)

If you find yourself in a situation where you simply cannot avoid taking some tests, you should approach them with care. You will normally be at a disadvantage because some of the more widely used tests have fallen into the hands of many job hunters who then are careful to project an excellent but not quite perfect image. We have encountered a great many people who have obtained access to the short aptitude tests through various friends in the personnel field. With reproduction being such an easy thing today, almost anyone who has been on the administering side of such tests is likely to have file copies somewhere at home. Our whole point in this paragraph is that even if you have excellent aptitude, and are psychologically well-balanced, it is likely that you will only perform at a level achieved by many other applicants for the same position. On the other hand, if you have some weak areas, you are almost certain to be rejected because of the performance of others who will have some form of access or experience with the tests.

There are some excellent books written on all phases and types of testing. The best ones are of the textbook variety and are used in teaching psychological testing at the University level. They do explain all of the various well-known tests and include information that would be very useful to test-takers. Although it is quite old, The Organization Man by William Whyte contains some provocative discussion on tests as well as advice to test-takers. This book is widely available in paperback form. Another interesting book (also available in paperback) is The Brain Watchers by Martin Gross. It is a general indictment of the whole testing industry and has some cogent material on how to score well on tests.

If you really wanted to learn more about testing, as well as about yourself, we suggest that you consider the testing services available through most major universities. You can arrange to take almost any type of test through the psychology department of these institutions. While they can be somewhat expensive, the fees are usually far below the other commercial sources which offer testing services. The American Personnel Guidance Association can also supply you with the names of individual counselors who give tests. They are located at 1607 New Hampshire Ave., N.W., Washington, D.C. 20009.

SOME BRIEF PREPARATION FOR PSYCHOLOGICAL TESTS

The object of almost all psychological tests is to enable a firm to obtain a description of your strengths and weaknesses. However, during all interviews and tests, your object is to project an image which will enable you to get job offers. Unfortunately, these two objectives will almost be in a direct conflict.

There is presently a wide range of different types of tests in use. The techniques employed can range from arduous discussions with a psychologist, to tests where you view a series of inkblots and describe what you see. The most common tests, however, are of the written variety. These tests normally ask you questions about what you think of your parents, friends, superiors, and yourself. They will generally ask you about the influence which you perceive these people as having exercised on you. They also probe for your opinion on how these people view your personality.

From your point of view, the most difficult thing about these tests will relate to your ability to project a consistent image. If you are unable to do this, the firm will assume that you either lack intelligence or were not cooperating on their tests. Achieving consistency is difficult because almost all tests will ask similar questions (with changed phrasing) in different parts of the same test.

They are usually referred to as built-in lie detectors, and can be difficult to finesse when you are subjected to a battery of tests over a broken time schedule.

In order to provide you with general guidance as well as specific assistance re this consistency problem, we think you should participate in a short exercise.

The next page contains a list of 187 words. These words comprise almost all of the general personality and ability traits that are likely to be measured by any type of psychological test. The words themselves actually form the basic vocabulary used in the summary analysis of many psychological tests. By summary analysis, we mean the final test profile which describes an individual in terms of his strengths and weaknesses. This list is probably complete enough to permit a profile description of you or any individual you know.

TEST INSTRUCTIONS

Assume that an employer (who had an interesting position) instructed you as follows:

> In three minutes, go through the list of words and check those positive and negative factors which most consistently apply to you.

> You can check any number of positive factors that apply, but you must check a minimum of 10 negative factors.

Now, go to the next page and allow yourself no more than three minutes. Don't just scan them! Get a pencil and complete the test! (You can always erase your checkmarks and try it on your wife, husband, girlfriend, etc. later!)

GENERALLY POSITIVE

active	detailed	honest	poised
adaptable	determined	imaginative	positive
aggressive	dignified	independent	practical
alert	diplomatic	individualist	productive
ambitious	discerning	inspiring	proud
analytical	disciplined	intellectual	purposeful
argumentive	discreet	intuitive	realistic
artistic	discriminating	just	reliable
astute	economical	keen	resourceful
attentive	efficient	kind	respected
broad-minded	eloquent	logical	self-reliant
composed	energetic	loyal	sense-of-humor
congenial	enterprising	methodical	shrewd
conscientious	enthusiastic	modest	sincere
considerate	esteemed	objective	sociable
consistent	exacting	observant	sophisticated
constructive	extroverted	opinionated	sympathetic
contemplative	fair	optimistic	systematic
courageous	forceful	orderly	tactful
courteous	forward-thinker	outspoken	talented
creative	frank	patient	thoughtful
cultured	friendly	perceptive	tolerant
daring	generous	perfectionist	truthful
democratic	genuine	personable	visionary
dependable	good-natured	philosophical	

GENERALLY NEGATIVE

abrupt	domineering	introverted	self-conscious
agitator	easily depressed	jealous	selfish
agnostic	eccentric	lavish	sensitive
anti-social	egotistical	lethargic	sentimental
arrogant	embittered	mean	shallow
avaricious	emotional	mutinous	simple
awkward	excitable	naive	skeptic
belligerent	extravagant	narrow-minded	squeamish
bizarre	fabricator	negligent	stubborn
bogus	fastidious	obstinate	submissive
bungler	forgetful	paltry	superficial
capricious	fragile	pessimistic	suspicious
clumsy	impractical	pompous	tempermental
complacent	impulsive	possessive	trivial
conceited	inconsiderate	pretentious	two-faced
conventional	inconsistent	rash	uncertain
corrupt	incorrigible	repugnant	unobservant
covetous	indifferent	reserved	unreliable
crafty	inhibited	restless	unscrupulous
deceitful	irritable	sarcastic	unsophisticated
despondent	insubordinate	secretive	vacillating
discourteous	intolerable	self-centered	vicious

Now that you have completed checking the positive and negative factors, be totally honest with yourself in admitting how well you'd come out if the interviewer confronted you as follows:

SITUATION A

The interviewer asks you to describe to him verbally, taking as long as you desired, the reasons prompting your selection of each word. In explaining your rationale, you are required to refer to actual examples of accomplishments in specific situations. You must also state the names of other individuals in the situations you describe (e.g. your employer, a business associate, your father, etc.).

SITUATION B

The interviewer takes your completed list, and then invites you back for more interviewing in one week. At that time, he gives you the same list, but with all of the words intermingled together, and asks you to again complete the test.

SITUATION C

The interviewer takes your completed list and informs you that instead of subjecting applicants to lengthy tests, that their policy is to send the same list to your references and former supervisors. These people would be asked to describe you by checking the words under the same ground rules. The interviewer says they seek to obtain comparable statements about you from a number of sources and to effect a simple confirmation of your self-image.

The Lessons to be Learned From This Exercise

The first point is something that you undoubtedly already know. On any given test you are at the mercy of the methodology and the individual doing the interpretation. In the best of situations, there is much to be desired in terms of true objectivity. The forced choice test, which is most common, is particularly difficult because you frequently receive inadequate instructions. When you looked at the test words you probably thought that "this describes me sometimes, in some settings, but not in others, etc.". Or perhaps you thought that a great many of the words applied to you at some time or other, but that there were great variations in degree of application. These types of frustrations however, are exactly what you will be up against when you try to be forthright on written psychological tests.

The second point to be observed is that many tests are evaluated as much by what you fail to check, as by what you do check. Furthermore, they are almost always full of synonyms. You might find it worthwhile to go back and look at the positive qualities which you failed to check. You should consider what they might reveal to someone about positive characteristics which you don't believe you possess. Insofar as synonyms are concerned, there are many words on the tests which have almost identical meaning. Many people who administer tests assume that if you check one word you should also check others with the same meaning (e.g. reliable and dependable). Any failure to do so subsequently reflects on either your honesty or intelligence.

The third point of this exercise is that it presents you with a problem which you will face on all types of tests. Namely, the question about how good an image to project. If you presented too perfect an image, the people conducting the test may not believe you. They may also catch you in your fabrication by presenting you with a situation similar to examples A and C. On the other hand, you obviously don't want to project too many weaknesses. If you did this you might fail to meet the criteria established for the job.

The best approach to both of these questions is to project a normal less-than-perfect image. Everyone has faults and a person without weakness just does not exist. However, you should lean to the positive qualities and project the negatives which would be least likely to affect your ability to do any given job. For example, being "reserved" may not be a negative at all. The same holds true for "skeptic", "sensitive", "sentimental", etc. Some of the words on the negative list can actually be desirable in a specific situation. Likewise, some of the words listed as positive factors could be considered undesirable traits. Some negatives are also much worse than others. For example, being "belligerent" may certainly be unattractive, however it is probably far better than being "corrupt" or "deceitful". What you will need to project will depend upon your occupation, and your perception of what the employer desires.

If you can honestly say that none of the assumed test situations created any feeling of panic, then you are probably a master at test taking who has nothing to worry about. If however, you reacted to this exercise as 95% of other people, there are some wise lessons to be learned.

REFERENCE SITUATION A --- If you really expected to face the first situation, as you might in a session with a psychologist, you could be prepared. The first thing you should do is to go over the words on the list. They can help to refresh your understanding of yourself, as well as to serve as the basis for the image you want to project. If you understand yourself, and know the image you want, you will have a much easier time reading the object of any question in any test situation. Almost any questions you will face, will have as an object, the identification or the presence of one of the traits on the list.

REFERENCE SITUATION B --- If you were faced with the second situation you would probably have a hard time maintaining your consistency. This would be particularly true if you had not done some serious advance thinking about the image you desired to project. You can beat this type of situation by having a keen awareness of synonyms and antonyms, and by sticking firmly to your pattern of answering questions.

REFERENCE SITUATION C --- If an employer presented you with the third situation, either forget about the job, or don't let it worry you at all! While employers do look for consistency in any reference check, the lack of it is no condemnation of any person. In fact, if you really were an adaptable individual, you would probably be wise in projecting different attributes in different social and business situations.

We believe you will find it worthwhile to do some thinking about the words on the test exercise. In order to facilitate this, the list below restates the words in groups that have a certain homogeneity. We suggest that you refer back to these words for ideas when writing your resume.

FAMILY GROUPINGS OF WORDS WITH SOME HOMOGENEITY

GENERALLY POSITIVE

courteous	fair	reliable	realistic	outspoken	observant
sociable	just	dependable	practical	argumentative	attentive
personable	democratic	loyal	economical	opinionated	alert
friendly	broad-minded	honest	efficient	extroverted	
congenial	objective	truthful			logical
good-natured	daring		proud	talented	analytical
thoughtful	courageous		eloquent		intuitive
contemplative	composed	disciplined	dignified	sense-of-humor	perceptive
considerate	poised	determined	esteemed		discerning
kind	sophisticated	purposeful	inspiring	artistic	astute
sympathetic	cultured	constructive			keen
generous	consistent	productive	active	optimistic	shrewd
tolerant	orderly		energetic	positive	intellectual
patient	methodical		enthusiastic	forward-thinker	philosophical
genuine	systematic	creative	aggressive	visionary	tactful
sincere	detailed	imaginative	ambitious	individual	discreet
conscientious	perfectionist	resourceful	forceful	independent	diplomatic
		adaptable	exacting	self-reliant	modest
				enterprising	

GENERALLY NEGATIVE

abrupt	emotional	corrupt	inhibited	despondent	egotistical
awkward	temperamental	two-faced	self-conscious	easily depressed	pretentious
clumsy	excitable	incorrigible	sensitive	pessimistic	arrogant
bungler	impulsive	unscrupulous	introverted		pompous
ineffectual	rash		submissive	conventional	
		jealous		simple	stubborn
capricious	squeamish	possessive		shallow	obstinate
forgetful	fastidious	covetous	vacillating		narrow-minded
negligent	bizarre	avaricious	uncertain	sentimental	impractical
unobservant	eccentric				
unreliable	agitator	trivial		anti-social	naive
complacent	insubordinate	paltry	discourteous	belligerent	unsophisticated
lethargic	mutinous	selfish	inconsiderate	repugnant	
indifferent	secretive	skeptic	sarcastic	intolerable	superficial
restless	fabricator	agnostic	embittered	domineering	bogus
inconsistent	crafty	fragile	vicious	self-centered	extravagant
irritable	deceitful	reserved	mean	conceited	lavish

12.

THE INTERVIEW

&

SALARY NEGOTIATIONS AND CONTRACTS

THE INTERVIEW

Comments about "How to be Interviewed" are rather time worn. However, we do feel it is worthwhile to review even the obvious things for those who have not gone through interviewing recently.

Be Informed . . . . . About the Firms You Visit

You should always try to be informed about a company before you go to an interview. This means knowing a firms's products, markets, number of employees, current stock quotation, growth record, sales, profits, and general reputation. Nothing is more impressive in an interview, or expresses your interest more dramatically than your being knowledgeable about the firm with whom you are speaking. Even if you are in senior management you might do well by doing some extra homework. Frankly, the higher your position the more this can work to your advantage vis-a-vis your competition for a job.

You can get information about firms from brokerage houses, annual reports, Fortune's 500 Listing, Moody's Manuals, and special annual issues of trade magazines. Advertising Age and Forbes are two sources which have special information on large corporations once a year. F&S Indexes give references to recent articles on a given firm, cover over 500 leading businesses, financial and trade magazines, and are available in most libraries. A check of the Wall Street Journal or New York Times Index would also alert you to recent developments concerning a given firm.

Prior to accepting a position, you would be wise to have an associate (or your bank) order a Dun & Bradstreet report if the firm is not large and well known. Besides a credit evaluation the Dun & Bradstreet reports usually provide some information about the company's officers.

The Interview . . . . Things You Should Do

In the interview, some of the obvious things you should make an effort to do include the following:

(1)   Be prompt, friendly, relaxed, and neatly groomed. Maintain good posture. As far as dress is concerned, a blue suit is still the best compromise for all the types of people you will meet. Worn suits, frayed shirts, and shoes with holes in them won't help you. The same holds true for heavy cosmetics, mod watches, bow ties and sunglasses.

(2)   Find out what happened to the last person in the job, and if possible, get his name.

(3)   Be a good listener, but certainly not reticent about asking penetrating questions.

(4)   Sell yourself but use psychology and play to the ego of the interviewer. Compliment him on something in his office that may mean something to him.

(5)   Be enthusiastic, confident, and ambitious, but as controlled as the situation demands. You should project a well-thought-out image of yourself for a given position. In addition to the image criteria that relates to your own occupational field, you would probably be wise to convey sincerity, dedication, professionalism, and a high energy level.

(6)   Gear your comments to stress sales, profits, costs and growth wherever possible.

(7)   Protect the confidence of your present employer.

(8)   Maintain your dignity at all times.

(9)   When there's too much silence, be ready to raise questions for which you have prepared answers.

(10)   Indicate that you admire certain achievements of the organization.

(11)   Underplay your need for a new job.

(12)   Identify some of the new organization's problems and attempt to relate your discussion to them. Highlight your past experience which is relevant to the potential solution of these problems.

(13)   Lastly, if you are asked, you should always state that your health is excellent.

THE INTERVIEW 141

The Interview . . . . . Things You Should Avoid

Some of the things you should avoid doing are the following:

(1) Don't fill out applications in waiting rooms.

(2) Don't be interviewed by junior substitutes or subjected to hasty interviews over the phone.

(3) Don't submit to an inquisition or tripartite interview (unless absolutely necessary).

(4) Try to avoid arriving too early for an interview.

(5) Never apologize for any of your liabilities.

(6) Be careful about posing a threat to your prospective boss's position.

(7) Never read the mail on your interviewer's desk; nervously drum your fingers; look at your watch; or exhibit other signs of nervousness or boredom.

(8) You should generally avoid arguments and discussions on race, religion, or politics.

(9) Also, despite projecting confidence, you should never imply you can do everything or work miracles.

(10) In general, try to avoid naming your references until the very end.

(11) Don't permit yourself to get flustered by the presence of unusual decor, strange lighting, uncomfortable chairs, an interviewer's nervous tapping, or phone interruptions.

(12) Never bring unsolicited samples of your work or give out confidential information about your past employer.

Notes: Certain occupational areas may require exception to this. For example, if you happen to be a copywriter or an art director, you obviously would be wise to maintain an impressive portfolio of your work, and to use it as evidence of your accomplishments.

(13) Avoid being critical of your past organization or specific people (even if your criticism is warrented). Never forget that someday you might want to return or get other assistance from their executives.

(14) Don't permit your time to be arbitrarily wasted by firms that have the time to interview you but who don't have a position available. Try to make sure that they either have a position available or that you are being interviewed by a person with the authority to create a position.

(15) You should always find out to whom your position specifically reports and try to ascertain his skill in your area. A look at the organization chart to identify the importance of the function (from a reporting standpoint) may also be worthwhile.

(16) Never be pressured into accepting a job at a lower level that you seek.

(17) Never accept the offer of a job during the interview. Take some time to think over any offer, even if it seems to be just what you want.

Beware of Bargain Hunters

You should also be aware of companies always looking for inexpensive buys and whose only promise relates to nebulous statements about future possibilities. If you accept a job with one of these firms, you will almost certainly be unhappy in the future. Don't be reticient concerning the firm's policy re salary reviews. Again, you should try to find out the average frequency and percent increase that is given for excellent performance.

After the Interview — Follow-up with a Short Letter

The interview follow-up is one of the most neglected job hunting techniques. If you are at all interested in a position you should always follow-up the interview with a letter. Adherence to this one principle, will positively bring you job hunting results which you otherwise would not achieve. Your letter should not be a standard thank you but rather a short letter which once again spells out your prime assets and accomplishments. You might find it useful to touch on the major subjects discussed, and if possible to use names and language which reflect the company environment. If your follow-up letter does not bring a reply, you should follow-up via phone with continued enthusiasm. In the long run this type of aggressiveness, if handled diplomatically, will surely prove effective. The idea is to keep selling yourself but to do it tactfully.

Developing Polish in an Interviewing Situation

Though every interview (and interviewer) is different, there are steps you can take to ready yourself. Some of the more basic questions for which you should always have answers prepared are listed on the next page. Despite an excellent ability to get interviews, people have lost out by hesitancy and lack of poise in handling these types of questions. Remember that above all, you should learn from your interviewing mistakes. Almost any person can develop great interviewing polish with experience.

Questions Which Can Be Difficult If You Are Not Prepared For Them

These are the types of questions which form the basis of what is frequently labeled as a stress interview. Very competent interviewers can fire these questions at individuals in rapid succession. They are difficult to answer if you are not prepared and will test your knowledge, poise, ability to think quickly, and confidence! When combined with other pressures of an uncomfortable office, and an interviewer's intentionally pressuring personality, they can throw almost any executive way off balance!

While this may seem like a menial task, we strongly recommend that you spend some time developing your answers to these questions and verbalize them out loud in a private room. Even if you are an accomplished speaker, you will be amazed at how much you gain through such an exercise. It is really not altogether different from a politician preparing for an open press conference and practice will enable you to project a knowledgeable and confident image.

What are your short range objectives?

What are your long range objectives?

What do you look for in a job?

Why are you leaving your present position?

What can you do for us that someone else cannot do?

Why should we hire you?

Can you work under pressure, deadlines, etc?

What is your philosophy of management?

Do you prefer staff or line work? Why?

What kind of salary are you worth?

What are your five biggest accomplishments in:
your present or last job?
your career so far?

What is your biggest strength? Weakness?

How long would it take you to make a contribution to our firm?

How long would you stay with us?

How do you feel about people from minority groups?

If you could start again, what would you do different?

What new goals or objectives have you established recently?

How have you changed the nature of your job?

What position do you expect to have in five years?

What do you think of your boss?

Why haven't you obtained a job so far?

What features of your previous jobs have you disliked?

Would you describe a few situations in which your work was criticized?

Would you object to working for a woman?

How would you evaluate your present firm?

Do you generally speak to people before they speak to you?

How would you describe the essence of success?

What was the last book you read? movie you saw? sporting event you attended? etc.

In your present position, what problems have you identified that had previously been overlooked?

What interests you most about the position we have? the least?

Don't you feel you might be better off in a different size company? different type company?

Why aren't you earning more at your age?

Will you be out to take your boss's job?

Are you creative? — give an example.

Are you analytical? — give an example.

Are you a good manager? — give an example.

Are you a leader? — give an example

How would you describe your own personality?

Have you helped increase sales? profits? — how?

Have you helped reduce costs? — how?

What do your subordinates think of you?

Have you fired people before?

Have you hired people before? — what do you look for?

Why do you want to work for us?

If you had your choice of jobs and companies, where would you go?

What other types of jobs are you considering? What companies?

Why do you feel you have top management potential?

Tell us all about yourself.

Obviously, we cannot provide answers for you to the previous questions. Every case is certainly an individual one and the answers which you must be prepared to give will depend on your own goals and situation. The psychology at play in a difficult interviewing situation is really the most important thing.

For example, you must be prepared to articulate some short and long range objectives and what you look for in a job. You've also got to have a good sound reason for wanting to leave your present job, but one which does not sound like sour grapes. Your biggest accomplishments and biggest strengths can be thought out and geared to what you believe the particular interviewer is seeking. When you're asked for your biggest weakness, you've also got to appear mortal! The idea here would be to give a weakness which from the interviewer's viewpoint isn't much of a weakness. Some alternative approaches to answers which use this psychology are listed below:

What is your biggest weakness?

"Well, I really don't feel I have a weakness which significantly effects my working ability. I guess at times I have a tendency to be impatient and occasionally push people too hard to get a job done. Patience isn't my strongest virtue."

What do you think of your boss?

"He's an outstanding man. I have a great deal of respect for him and have enjoyed working with him very much."

How long would it take you to make a contribution to our firm?

"Well, I hope to be able to make a contribution in a very short time. Obviously it will take some time to get my feet wet and to get used to certain operating procedures. There are a number of things which I have accomplished before that I may be able to institute once I gain a better understanding of your organization."

How long would you stay with us?

"As I mentioned to you, I'm looking for a career opportunity. However, I'm a realist. Obviously if I don't do the job you won't want me around; and if there is no opportunity for me it won't be the type of environment I'd enjoy."

What position do you expect to have in five years?

"That really depends on the type of job I accept and the particular company I join. In some companies I might hope to be president in that length of time; while in other firms, a job with a far lesser title may prove equally enjoyable and rewarding. I guess the answer really depends on the responsibility which I am given."

What's wrong with your present firm?

"I really don't feel there is anything wrong with the firm. I have enjoyed working there very much and think that there are some really top people in management. I feel it would be a good company for the long pull but I am ready to handle additional responsibility right now. Unfortunately, my own short term growth prospects are limited because of the lack of promotional opportunities."

Why are you leaving your present position?

"I'm anxious to earn more money and take on added responsibility. In addition to enjoying my work, I'd like to expand my knowledge. Quite frankly, there isn't much opportunity in my present position."

Even if you're undecided about a number of things, or uncertain of your own abilities in certain areas, you want to project a firm and consistent image. Once you have received the job offer you can carefully weigh the positives and negatives, and whether you think you can deliver what would be expected.

Concluding Comments on Interviewing

People who are professional job hunters are invariably masters at the entire interviewing process. A skillful job hunter will recognize tell-tale signs of how well the interview is going and adjust his behavior accordingly. It is generally a good sign if the interviewer does more talking than you do; if he knows your resume background before you begin the interview; or if he really begins speaking in terms of you solving his problems. You must also master the art of complimenting in a genuine and sincere manner. If you are being interviewed by a man in personnel, you should be sure to find some way to express your interest in that field and your recognition of the responsibility which it involves. You should always remember that your primary objective in any preliminary interview is to somehow leave an impression that is more favorable for what that interviewer is seeking than the many other candidates who are competing with you.

There will always be some questions to which you do not have answers, however after a while, you will find that even difficult situations leave you relatively unruffled. When you find yourself in a situation where the job is not for you, then you should seize the opportunity to see if you can have them consider you for other positions. If this is not possible then you should try to gain information concerning leads to positions in other firms.

Despite the level of job hunting skill which you possess, you will be rejected for the vast majority of positions for which you are interviewed. You will be rejected because you spoke too much, too soft, or too loud for a given interviewer; or because you weren't liked, appeared too average or just like another person; or because your salary demands were too high. If, you have done your homework, however, you will not be rejected because your appearance was not as good as it should have been; because your record was weak in spots without your having a suitable explanation; because you lacked interest in their company; because your background was not communicated as being well-rounded enough; because you were not communicative enough during the interview; or because your initiative was not suitably demonstrated by the accomplishments you reviewed. Even in the best of situations you are going to lose quite often. A key factor will be your ability to avoid discouragement over set backs.

As a final comment on interviewing, we suggest that when appropriate you develop a tactful means of applying pressure yourself. Don't let firms keep you on a string while they search for a still-better prospect. There will certainly be occasions where you have been interviewed by everyone concerned -

where they have had time to fully evaluate your qualification — but where they simply delay extending a concrete offer. In such cases, you should indicate that while you want very much to join them, other opportunities which are concrete, require that you have a decision within a week.

SALARIES, NEGOTIATIONS AND CONTRACTS

Where the Higher Salaries Exist

The greatest number of higher salaried positions generally exist in the large corporations and in larger cities, and the higher your salary requirement, the fewer the jobs which will be available. Companies also vary in their salary policies, as some are universally lower paying than others. You should be able to identify low paying firms from personal contacts, or in an early interviewing stage.

Salary Range and Raise Systems

The salary for a given job usually has a range set in advance. At the very least, an employer will have an idea of what he is willing to pay for the position. This is true even if the firm claims that salary for a position is "open". One exception to the situation just cited would be the case where an employer wanted to hire you and was willing to create a new position to bring you aboard. This is the instance where you will have your best opportunity for negotiating attractive compensation.

The most common salary range systems ordinarily have a range established which differs by half the amount of the minimum salary. For example, a company may have a position which can pay from $20,000 to $30,000. While they hope to hire an individual at the lowest figure possible, the usual procedure is to allow the direct superior to offer any amount between the minimum (i.e. $20,000) and the mid-point ($25,000). In general, the lower the amount at which an individual is hired, the higher the annual percentage increase for which he is eligible. As an alternative, some companies follow a policy that states that the lower a person's salary (within the range) the more frequent the salary review. For example, a policy might state that if an individual is between the minimum and the mid-point, he is eligible for an annual review. However, if he is between the mid-point and the maximum, he is only eligible for a salary review on an 18-month basis. You should do your best to find out what an employer hopes to pay (and the range established) and skip it entirely if it is significantly below your personal goals.

When to State Your Present Salary

If your salary is relatively low, you should generally avoid stating it before an interview. Obviously you don't want to negotiate from your present salary base and divulging it in advance would only put you at a disadvantage. We do know of individuals who have conducted campaigns without ever providing their current income. However, in spite of a few success stories, we doubt that there are many potential employers who will tolerate your excuses for not giving them the information. Nevertheless, you should attempt to avoid salary discussion for as long as possible if your earnings are far below that which you hope to attain.

If you earn a high salary for your age or education, then you should state it as early as possible (perhaps even in your letter) as a sign of your accomplishments. If you did not care to mention a figure in your letter you could cite the percentage growth you have made over a certain period of time. While a high salary requirement can rule you out, you will avoid wasting time on positions which would eventually prove disappointing. Obviously, you should always refer to your total earnings if you are eligible for a bonus, commision, stock option, or other fringe incentives.

Do Not be Quick to Compromise

If you're presently employed we think that during the initial stages of your campaign you should stick to your salary objective. Start by shooting for what you are worth and be fairly inflexible. The philosophy is to sell quality rather than lower price. This is what the top executives in growing companies want to buy, and if they think you're the right person, a few thousand dollars will rarely stand in their way.

Negotiating for Maximum Salary

Regardless of your talents, most prospective employers will evaluate your potential worth to them in terms of your present earnings. For example, if you were earning $22,000 you probably would not be considered for a $35,000 position. However, you could have the same set of credentials but be earning $30,000 and a given firm might be glad to consider you an eligible applicant. This is actually one of the most near-sighted practices of American business today. Strict adherence to this policy usually reflects an excessive influence being exerted by either an unenlightened staff or old-line executives in a corporation. Fortunately, there are a growing number of firms and executives who are well aware that accomplishments are a much better measure of talent than previous earnings. In order to gain a large increase in salary you are going to have to seek out this latter type of executive and waste little time with the former.

When it comes to financial matters, there can be no doubt that your competition will include some very imaginative liars. However, before you exaggerate your present level of earnings you should be aware that it is very easy for a firm to check out your real earnings. In actual practice, most firms will not seek a verification of present salary, and if you did exaggerate your earnings, you may simply be lucky. However, if anyone in the firm does have reason to suspect your claim, they have a number of avenues open to them. Some of these are as follows:

(1) They may ask to see a payroll stub from your present employer.

(2) They may ask to see a copy of your last income tax or W-2 form.

(3) They may attempt to make a written or phone verification (after you have been hired) with your former supervisor and/or personnel department.

(4) They may rely on an outside agency for an investigation of your background and earnings. Many of these firms can perform a very accurate check on any earnings claim.

If you have a low salary and feel you must exaggerate to be considered for the position you seek, be sure to hedge in terms of an expected bonus or increase in salary. In other words, state your present salary as it is, but if you have a remote chance of shortly receiving a raise or an annual bonus, be sure to make that level of earnings the basis for your negotiations.

Before negotiating for salary, try to be sure that an offer is going to be extended. We generally advise not to begin negotiating until you're on pretty safe ground. Judging the firmness of an offer can obviously be very difficult. When negotiating it is best to never make overly concrete demands. However, you should clearly state your worth at the maximum figure possible. (You could obviously make it clear that you have already had opportunities offered at $ xxxxx level.) Very few firms will rule you out or withdraw an offer simply because you believe you are worth more. In addition, there is always the chance that they will meet your maximum figure. Even if they do not plan on budging from a lower figure, and you accept the job, firms generally feel better when they believe they are getting a valuable and sought-after individual. If a firm is apparently unwilling to raise their first offer, a compromise you might consider would be to negotiate for a bonus, stock options or an earlier than normal review. In the case of higher executives, negotiation for stock options and fringes is something that should be automatic. In fact in the higher tax brackets, the total financial package would be the basis for any negotiations.

The fine art of salary negotiations is practiced by very few individuals. If you are aggressively seeking employment, you will immediately be placed at a disadvantage when it comes to salary negotiations. In all discussions, your overall object is to have a firm want you as much as possible. Ideally, you hope to have them first make up their mind on hiring you, and secondly, to become anxious to have you accept any offer they will extend. As with any form of negotiations, one of your principal objectives in all salary discussions will be to phrase your demands so that your financial request seems as reasonable as possible.

As a job hunter, your most difficult decision may involve your evaluation of comparative offers. Unfortunately, there is very little in the way of "rule of thumb" advice which we can provide. From our experience, we have found that it does help many individuals if they take the time to write everything about comparative offers down on paper. While it is always convenient if the highest offer is also the position with the most growth potential, things rarely, if ever, seem to work out that way.

CONTRACTS

It is very difficult to generalize about employment contracts. In recent years, many firms have taken a stronger stand against them. Their reasons for doing so revolve around the simple fact that employees are usually guaranteed compensation for a certain length of time, as long as they work to the best of their abilities in normal business hours. The employers are guaranteed very little and the individual can usually break them quite easily. On the other hand, corporations are usually forced into a financial settlement if they choose to dismiss an executive under contract. When arguments over broken contracts cannot be resolved, the courts will almost always rule in favor of the individual.

Despite corporate policies against contracts, it is difficult to conceive of any firm who would be willing to lose a sought-after executive, simply because they want to maintain their policy. A contract is just one more element in the total negotiation package. In any given situation a contract may be just as negotiable as questions relating to salary, bonuses, and stock option participation.

If you can possibly arrange it, a contract will usually be to your advantage. While you can always be dropped, a contract can provide you a measure of financial security and a certain degree of independence from corporate politics. In many cases, the mere possession of a contract may be the most significant status symbol that exists in a firm. For senior executives a contract usually has a higher priority than amount of salary. This is especially true if a corporation may experience turnover in top management, or if a firm is likely to be the subject of a merger of acquisition.

As a general rule, we suggest that you should never be reluctant to ask for a contract. A request, as opposed to a demand, will never result in a revoked job offer, and again there is always the chance that they may accede to your request. Don't be deterred by the fact that you have heard that the firm does not give contracts. There is always a first time for everything, and as previously mentioned, if a firm really wants you, a contract request will not stand in their way. You should be aware, however, that your first request may result in a number of negatively phrased routine questions. The most common ploy of employers is to question your request as a lack of confidence in the firm, their management, or in your own ability. They may also ask you if you are the kind of executive who values security more than opportunity. You should anticipate comments such as

> "Bill, your contract request makes me wonder if you have the self-confidence and entrepreneurial qualities which you've indicated. We're also very concerned about your trust in us. If our relationship is going to be as successful as we all plan, I think it should begin on a note of mutual trust and integrity."

As long as you anticipate them, these types of questions should be easy to finesse. There is usually only one major disadvantage that goes along with most contracts. If you request one, your employer may insist on inserting a protective clause which would limit your ability to take future employment with a competitor. The insertion of such a clause is often requested as a show of good faith, and is quite hard to negate without creating serious doubt in the mind of your new employer.

If you are at an executive level, there are certain firms with whom you must be very firm in your request for a contract. These would include: companies in financial trouble; firms that are merger or acquisition candidates or those which have just been merged or acquired; family controlled and private companies; and companies where one individual operates the firm or is known to personally dominate the environment. In these cases you should seek a three-year contract covering your minimum compensation, and which also has provisions for bonuses, deferred compensation, moving expenses, annual re-negotiation upwards and profit sharing. You also may be able to negotiate life insurance; release without penalty in case of merger; salary benefits to your family in case of death; special reimbursement for foreign service; and consulting fees in the event of termination after the end of the contract period. In any event, don't treat contract terms lightly and be sure to review all the fine print with a competent lawyer.

SALARY CHART

This Annual Salary	=	This Monthly Salary	=	This Bimonthly Salary	=	This Salary Every 2 Weeks	=	This Weekly Salary	This Annual Salary	=	This Monthly Salary	=	This Bimonthly Salary	=	This Salary Every 2 Weeks	=	This Weekly Salary
10000		833		417		385		192	14800		1233		617		569		285
10100		842		421		388		194	14900		1242		621		573		287
10200		850		425		392		196	15000		1250		625		577		288
10300		858		429		396		198	15200		1267		633		585		292
10400		867		433		400		200	15400		1283		642		592		296
10500		875		438		404		202	15600		1300		650		600		300
10600		883		442		408		204	15800		1317		658		608		304
10700		892		446		412		206	16000		1333		667		615		308
10800		900		450		415		208	16200		1350		675		623		312
10900		908		454		419		210	16400		1367		683		631		315
11000		917		458		423		212	16600		1383		692		638		319
11100		925		463		427		213	16800		1400		700		646		323
11200		933		467		431		215	17000		1417		708		654		327
11300		942		471		435		217	17200		1433		717		662		331
11400		950		475		438		219	17400		1450		725		669		335
11500		958		479		442		221	17600		1467		733		677		338
11600		967		483		446		223	17800		1483		742		685		342
11700		975		488		450		225	18000		1500		750		692		346
11800		983		492		454		227	18200		1517		758		700		350
11900		992		496		458		229	18400		1533		767		708		354
12000		1000		500		461		231	18600		1550		775		715		358
12100		1008		504		465		233	18800		1567		783		723		362
12200		1017		508		469		235	19000		1583		792		731		365
12300		1025		513		473		237	19200		1600		800		738		369
12400		1033		517		477		238	19400		1617		808		746		373
12500		1042		521		481		240	19600		1633		817		754		377
12600		1050		525		485		242	19800		1650		825		761		381
12700		1058		529		488		244	20000		1667		833		769		385
12800		1067		533		492		246	20500		1708		854		788		394
12900		1075		538		496		248	21000		1750		875		808		404
13000		1083		542		500		250	21500		1792		896		827		413
13100		1092		546		504		252	22000		1833		917		846		423
13200		1100		550		508		254	22500		1875		938		865		433
13300		1108		554		512		256	23000		1917		958		885		442
13400		1117		558		515		258	23500		1958		979		904		452
13500		1125		563		519		260	24000		2000		1000		923		462
13600		1133		567		523		262	24500		2042		1021		942		471
13700		1142		558		527		263	25000		2083		1042		962		481
13800		1150		575		531		265	25500		2125		1063		981		490
13900		1158		579		535		267	26000		2167		1083		1000		500
14000		1167		583		538		269	26500		2208		1104		1019		510
14100		1175		588		542		271	27000		2245		1125		1038		519
14200		1183		592		546		273	27500		2292		1146		1058		529
14300		1192		596		550		275	28000		2333		1167		1077		538
14400		1200		600		554		277	28500		2375		1188		1096		548
14500		1208		604		558		279	29000		2417		1208		1115		558
14600		1217		608		562		281	29500		2458		1229		1135		567
14700		1225		613		565		283	30000		2500		1250		1154		577

SALARY CHART (Cont.)

This Annual Salary	=	This Monthly Salary	= This Bimonthly Salary	= This Salary Every 2 Weeks	= This Weekly Salary	This Annual Salary	= This Monthly Salary	= This Bimonthly Salary	= This Salary Every 2 Weeks	= This Weekly Salary
30500		2542	1271	1173	587	45500	3792	1896	1750	875
31000		2583	1292	1192	596	46000	3833	1917	1769	885
31500		2625	1313	1211	606	46500	3875	1938	1788	894
32000		2667	1333	1231	615	47000	3917	1958	1808	904
32500		2708	1354	1250	625	47500	3958	1979	1827	913
33000		2750	1375	1269	635	48000	4000	2000	1846	923
33500		2792	1396	1288	644	48500	4042	2021	1865	933
34000		2833	1417	1308	654	49000	4083	2042	1884	942
34500		2875	1438	1327	663	49500	4125	2063	1904	952
35000		2917	1458	1346	673	50000	4167	2084	1923	962
35500		2958	1479	1365	683	50500	4208	2104	1942	971
36000		3000	1500	1385	692	51000	4250	2125	1961	981
36500		3042	1521	1404	702	51500	4291	2146	1981	990
37000		3083	1542	1423	712	52000	4333	2167	2000	1000
37500		3125	1563	1442	721	52500	4375	2188	2019	1010
38000		3167	1583	1461	731	53000	4416	2209	2038	1019
38500		3208	1604	1481	704	53500	4458	2229	2058	1029
39000		3250	1625	1500	750	54000	4500	2250	2077	1038
39500		3292	1646	1519	760	54500	4541	2271	2096	1048
40000		3333	1667	1538	769	55000	4583	2292	2115	1058
40500		3375	1688	1558	779	55500	4625	2313	2135	1067
41000		3417	1708	1577	788	56000	4666	2334	2154	1077
41500		3458	1729	1596	798	56500	4708	2354	2173	1086
42000		3500	1750	1615	808	57000	4750	2375	2192	1096
42500		3542	1771	1635	817	57500	4791	2396	2211	1106
43000		3583	1792	1654	827	58000	4833	2417	2231	1115
43500		3625	1813	1673	837	58500	4875	2438	2250	1125
44000		3667	1833	1692	846	59000	4916	2459	2269	1135
44500		3708	1854	1711	856	59500	4958	2479	2288	1144
45000		3750	1875	1731	865	60000	5000	2500	2308	1154

13.

DEVELOPING AN OUTSTANDING RESUME

As we have previously indicated, the quality of the resumes circulated by most people is very poor. The average resume is plain looking; either too short or too long for the individual's objectives; filled with dull uninteresting words; and typified by errors such as misspelled words, uneven margins, etc. So that you may have some perspective, we have included in the following sections, a variety of resume examples which would be among the best 50 of a typical 1,000 submitted in answer to advertisements. While these resume examples are not completely outstanding, they generally have some important elements in common. They usually begin with a summary and are accomplishment-oriented. In addition they sell ability, and experience rather than simply the latter. Your object should be to develop materials which equal or surpass these examples. When you accomplish this you will have increased your own competence and will have a significant competitive advantage throughout your campaign.

Your Resume must have a Superior Appearance

The type of resume which is most likely to produce exceptional results is one that is clean and distinctive in appearance. It should be an attention-getter which is prepared in good taste, and which as a starter, simply looks more attractive and readable than competitive resumes. To accomplish this we suggest the following:

Paper Appearance — Since almost everyone uses white bond paper, we suggest that you use something different. A grey or beige paper which has a lightly textured, linen, or pebbled finish will stand out among any number of resumes. A paper of about 20 to 50 lb. weight should be effective. Since stationery stores will not carry these papers, you will have to phone a "Paper Supplier" and request samples. If it is convenient, it is best to stop by and visit one of these firms. They usually have a fairly wide selection of quality papers in stock. If you are considering the use of back-to-back printing, be sure to ask them if the paper you select will take printing on both sides without a show-through effect. For an 8½ x 11 size you should be able to find a quality paper for $10 to $15 per 1,000 sheets, and the supplier can usually get you matching envelopes if you desire.

Paper Size and Format — While size is of less significance, we also suggest that you consider preparing a resume in something other than the standard 8½ x 11 form. Obviously, there is no single "best" format. However, a creative approach here may just give you the difference which will set you apart from the crowd and insure readership. For example:

(1)   You could consider a smaller size such as 7 x 10 or 6 x 9, perhaps a 4 x 9 foldout which would fit nicely in a standard business envelope.

You could have your resume printed on both sides of 8½ x 11 paper, but then fold the paper into an 8½ x 5½ booklet. This type of approach makes a resume seem more personal since it is more like a letter. It also vastly improves readership because the effect of overwhelming detail is lessened.

(2)   Another derivation of the above would be to start with legal size paper, have it folded into three equal cuts, and utilize only five of the sides which are available for printing.

Type Style — Nothing looks or reads better than a varityped resume. A resume which is typed on an IBM Selectric Composer will be far more readable than anything done on a standard IBM electric or selectric typewriters. Using "Cold Type" (which is the Yellow Page listing for this typing service) gives you a wide range of distinctive type styles to choose from, and also permits you to get far more words on a page. You can easily select a type which gives 15-18 characters per inch instead of the standard 10 or 12, and improve your readability at the same time. One of the nice things you can do with this type is to actually use more than one type style in your resume. Captions and subheadings could be in a style which are different but complementary to the style selected for your basic copy. You can also vary the darkness of the type as three weights are usually available (light, medium, and heavy). If you decide to have your resume done on the IBM Selectric Composer, we suggest their 11-point Univers Medium, typed with one point leaded, as a very readable and attractive style.

Resume Construction

Here again the thing you wish to avoid is having a standard resume which looks like all the other hundreds of dull pieces of paper. This seems so very simple, yet it is something that is almost always overlooked and its importance cannot be overstated. You want to develop a resume that is alive and interesting and that sells you without the reader being aware of the sale. There are many creative ways you can construct your resume and the examples in the next section will give you some ideas. From our experience a style that almost always proves effective includes the following:

(1)   A short statement of your objectives, which mentions the specific position titles that you are capable of filling. (You may list four or five such titles in your objective.) This accomplishes a few things. A) It immediately gives the reader a feeling that you are a solid individual who knows what he wants, as well as someone who knows where he can be most effective. B) It enables a firm to immediately spot a position goal that

coincides (in title) with the position they have available. C) By listing a number of position titles, you will have a broad resume which can be effective in all sorts of circumstances.

(2)   A short capsule summary of your main selling points. It should be designed to sell your ability and experience, (95% of all resumes only do the latter) and will have to be carefully worded and reasonably brief. If you use a paper with a creative appearance, along with a creative format, the use of the objective and summary will insure that your main selling points will be read. We believe this to be absolutely true even if your resume is submitted in answer to an advertisement to which 1,000 other candidates respond. An example of an objective and summary is listed below:

> **OBJECTIVE** - A position of senior sales and profit responsibility offering career opportunity as well as immediate challenge. Am particularly qualified to make a contribution as a Director, of such functions as Marketing, New Products, Marketing Services, Planning and Market Development.
>
> **SUMMARY** - Am presently Director of Marketing with a division of a major drug corporation. In a $200 million division of the same firm, I had been Senior Product Manager. Previous positions held with firms in the food, drug, and appliance industries include Salesman, Regional Sales Manager, and Assistant Product Manager. My accomplishments in every position are substantiated by rapid salary growth.
>
> Am 42 years old, married and have BA and MS degrees and a distinguished record as a Naval Officer. Personal qualities include analytical and creative ability, managerial skill, great initiative and an ability to get things done. Am well traveled and experienced at working with the highest levels of management.

The Copy in Your Resume

The resume is an introduction which is supposed to create a desire on the part of a firm or individual to want to see you personally. However, an effective resume really plays a greater role. For example, even after you have been interviewed, the chances are that your resume will be read again, perhaps by the individual who saw you as well as by other people in the organization. A good resume will keep selling for you throughout the interview and negotiation process.

The copy in your resume must, of course, be well-written. As previously stated, it should be alive and interesting, with emphasis on accomplishments rather than duties. The more you project your career as a series of progressive accomplishments, the more effective your resume will be. These accomplishments should be sales, profit, cost control-oriented where possible. In listing your accomplishments, remember that this is not the time to be modest. You must use exciting words, which have some sell to them, and yet which can be handled in a manner which minimizes the fact that this is your opinion of yourself. This is the area in which your skill at resume writing will really be tested. We have seen many opportunities lost by people who undersold themselves and their past accomplishments. Your aim is to present yourself in the most favorable light possible. You can be sure that your alert competition will be doing the same.

When you're drafting copy for your resume, you should remember the following:

1) Use full descriptions rather than abbreviations (i.e. American Management Association instead of A.M.A.)

2) When referring to dollar figures, write them out as numbers (i.e. $5,000,000 instead of five million dollars)

3) Use exact chronological dates if your situation permits (this adds to the believability of your copy)

4) If one of your former employers has changed their corporate name, indicate the present name with the former designation (i.e. CITGO, formerly Cities Service Corporation)

5) If it is possible, it is generally wise to include some material of a warm and personal nature.

Despite what you may have heard, resumes can be very effective regardless of length. We have prepared effective resumes which were from one to five pages in length. In general, a two-page resume will suffice, especially if you use "cold type" which permits many more words to the page.

Overcoming Specific Liabilities

Almost any job hunter will have certain liabilities which must be overcome. You will probably have to develop a strategy for dealing with some particular problem situation. This strategy will have to be applied both in your resume and during all interviews. Although it may seem obvious, you should always remember that employers seek to buy a maximum of assets and a minimum of liabilities. Since your initial object is to get interviews, your resume and letters should disclose as few weaknesses as possible. During the interview, you can personally explain your shortcomings if it seems necessary. The most common shortcomings of individual job hunters include the following:

* Being too young

* Being too old

* Having experience which is very narrow

* Having a record of too frequent job changes

* Lack of a college degree

* Being unemployed

Being Too Young

Individuals who perceive their youth as a liability are indicating that others view their lack of suitable experience as a negative, relative to their salary and position objectives. Our experiences indicates that "youth" is the easiest of the frequently cited liabilities to turn into an asset. In your resume or letter you will do best if you find some way to actually mention things like aggressiveness, drive, ability to learn quickly, and natural problem-solving talents. You would be wise to comment on any part-time experience or extra-curricular accomplishments which will evidence these abilities. Comments on hobbies can also be used to very effectively project an interesting type of personality and background. This is true whether the hobbies be car racing, sky diving, being an expert skier, bridge player, etc. You might also consider using a small discreet photograph which projects more maturity than your age alone would indicate.

There are a growing number of companies who have very young management teams and who are willing to pay salaries which are high relative to a person's age. Because they are young executives themselves, they often seek talented young people who might rapidly produce in responsible positions. If you feel youth is a problem relative to the position or the salary level you were seeking, you should probably conduct a broader than usual job campaign. In the course of a large scale campaign, you'll almost be sure to reach many of the types of people just mentioned.

If you happen to be a graduating student, we believe that virtually all of the strategy advice in this book will have application. In working on job campaigns for students, we have become convinced that a broad scale direct letter campaign will produce better job offers than most people could otherwise achieve. Obviously students have the alternative of relying upon interviews which are set up through their college placement centers. While this is certainly a source to be used, an individual effort at a creative campaign will probably turn up job offers which involve more responsibility than the usual beginning positions with large corporations. For students interested in opportunities within a small business, a full scale campaign should be launched a few months before graduation. This sort of time schedule may seem very close, however, small businesses normally do not have training programs or other jobs which would be open for any length of time. Achieving job hunting success in this type of situation involves the necessity of almost perfect timing in terms of a graduate's availability and the opening in a company.

Being Too Old

It's always quite interesting for us to listen to the myths which people readily accept about age barriers and job hunting. In job seeking, older age can certainly prove to be a negative. However, we think it is quite unfortunate that so many unhappily employed people believe they are too old to change jobs. Even though they may not consciously realize it, the truth is that they are probably using age as a convenient excuse. Most of the time individuals either lack the confidence to try, don't know how to go about it, or are not willing to go through the work a job campaign requires. Winning a new job is never an easy task. The same holds true for getting settled in a different environment and becoming a success in a new firm. However, despite difficulties in adjustment, and the stresses associated with proving yourself again, a good job change can bring you a totally new feeling about life. If you change you may find that the mental stimulation, excitement, and new associates, end up making for an atmosphere which makes you feel much younger.

In the late 1960's and early 1970's the job market seemed to place more emphasis on youth than ever before. For a while it seemed as though every business journal was constantly relating stories about young millionaires and young presidents who met with rapid success. However, as a result of the recession and high unemployment levels during 1970, 1971, and 1972, there seems to have been a definite shift toward the favoring of experience over youth. In fact, at the present time more young people are losing opportunities for jobs because of lack of suitable experience than any other reason. If you happen to be one of the people who thinks he is too senior-in-age, you might reflect on this thought for a second. At the same time consider the fact that you must have accumulated experience which could be of value to literally hundreds, if not thousands, of firms. Your major concern should not involve whether or not to seek a job. The key question is how to reach the right people in the right companies.

What does being too old really mean? In the United States half the population is over 26. To some people being too old is surpassing this magic number. In the job market, being too old actually has less to do with age than it does with responsibility and salary progress in business. We simply cannot accept the belief that being over 40, or even over 50, is tantamount to having an insurmountable negative. To be sure, as you get older job hunting will usually become more difficult, and particularly so in certain fields and industries. However, the prime reason for this is usually that as people rise up the organizational pyramid, there is a corresponding decrease in the number of additional positions available.

All age problems in job hunting are relative. Being too young could mean that you're 45 and shooting for a top spot in an industry where 90% of the top executives are 10 years your senior. On the other hand, being too old could be a case of being 32 in the advertising field and only earning $10,000. If we had to generalize about the period when age becomes a barrier, we would have to say that it is only at that point where you mentally accept it as an obstacle. Because of differences in fields, industries, and individual progress records, it is really impossible for anyone to state an age number where things will become more difficult. We would agree that in most cases being 40 is not quite as good as being 39. However, for the majority we'd guess that the truly critical stage is when people reach their mid-fifties. Even then, if you execute a broad campaign, you will eventually pick-off a new position.

In some cases it may take six to twelve months of effort, but since job hunting is a percentage game, you will eventually win out.

The main point we wish to communicate is simply that you should avoid making the common mistake of not trying because you feel your age makes the job hunt impossible. In general, the older you are the higher position you should seek, although we do not think you should rule out positions involving a salary cut. Approximately 80% of all executives over 40 who lose their jobs, end up accepting positions of lesser responsibility. However with the advice in this book, if you happen to be in this situation, you should be able to make sure that you're in the other 20%. Some people in this category accept lower salaries because the differences between insurance and pension plans are of more significance than an increment of annual take home income.

In terms of resume content, many people have to struggle to even begin to condense twenty or thirty years of experience into two or three pages. After a great deal of work, the typical product of most efforts is a resume which is not much more than a chronological history of job descriptions. In most cases, your focus should not become chronological history but should emphasize problems which you have faced and solutions which came about through your efforts. You should have very little problem in finding the way to persuasively state accomplishments which say to readers . . . "I can do the same thing or more for you." There is also no doubt that you will have to rely more on letters than resumes, since information in letters can be more easily slanted to cover your age, length of experience, and dates. You will find it useful to make a point to stress your sound business judgement, your ability to work in any type of environment, with all levels of management, and your drive (which is of course, what many believe senior talent does not possess).

As far as your resume is concerned, you can avoid mentioning your age, emphasize only recent work experience, and disclose your age once you have the interviews. You might also consider, although very carefully, the use of a small and discreet photograph. This can be quite delicate as you may be providing one more piece of information that will keep you from getting interviews. Nevertheless, if you have the right appearance, and a photograph which projects dignity and perhaps more youth than you possess, you might find it effective.

In terms of contacts you should orient your campaign toward executives in your own age bracket or older. These people will obviously represent your best percentage chance. The birth dates of executives are included in many reference guides. For example, Dun and Bradstreet's Reference Book of Corporate Management provides full background information on the Officers of America's largest 2500 corporations. It covers dates of birth, colleges attended, previous employment, directorships held and other potentially useful information. While you will orient your campaign to senior-in-age executives, you will have to forget any prejudices you may have about working for someone who is many years your junior. If you are seeking a top spot there will be a number of younger executives who will seek the complementary relationship which your age and maturity will bring. You may also have another advantage with some of them in that you are less likely to be seen as a competitive threat.

The first impression a job hunter gives is always of critical importance. It is our feeling that the first five minutes of any interview are more significant than all the other minutes put together. As you become older, the need to make a good first impression will become even more vital. If you're out of shape and run-down, start exercising, get some color in your face (either real or artificial sun tan), consider dyeing your hair or getting a hairpiece, and investigate some of the more youthful style eyeglass frames which are available. You may feel uneasy about some of these thoughts, but if you really want to get a new job, they will give you a big advantage. Too often people worry about what friends and long-time associates will say when they see their new appearance. The fact remains that most of your potential employers will have never seen you before and we have seen these efforts make critical differences time and time again.

Many individuals who feel their age represents a problem, will also be considering the special job hunting problems associated with career changing. In recent years there has been a great deal written on this subject. More people than ever are shifting career fields, because their abilities, interests, and life styles have shifted so greatly. In addition, many people have found themselves in specialty areas for which there is no immediate market. Thousands of individuals within the aerospace and defense sector have simply been forced to look for new jobs in entirely new fields.

While we are aware of many career change — success stories, they are usually the result of careful planning. If you haven't planned on a career change, it will be practically impossible for you to achieve something offering the responsibility and the income of your present or prior job. Changing career fields is something that should be planned. In order to move into a responsible job in another field, a person should have some experience, education or both.

It is very possible to train for another occupation through attending night school, graduate school programs and the like. However, this is always a time-consuming process. This time requirement along with the general risk of changing careers is presently discouraging many people who are otherwise anxious to move in this direction.

At the present time there are literally thousands of occupations which experienced individuals could explore. Many individuals successfully expand hobbies into occupations. The fields which have recently been favorites for those who have established themselves in other areas, include the following:

commercial artist	executive recruiter	travel agent
journalist	securities broker	personnel agent
photographer	builder	archeologist
interior designer	social worker	market research analyst
writer	professor	financial analyst
librarian	musician	government positions (city, state, federal)
local accountant	real estate agent	importer
consultant	sports commentator	exporter
life insurance agent	painter	legal and medical related occupations

There are of course many other occupational areas which individuals may wish to consider. If you find yourself in a position where you choose to launch a new career, you may find it worth while to talk to a professional career counselor. At the very least, this may stimulate your mind in terms of the wide range of opportunities there are available. The Federal Government also has numerous publications which provide information on the thousands of occupations pursued in America. The "U.S. Department of Labor's Dictionary of Occupational Titles" lists more than 30,000 classifications. Another publication which will also provide interesting information is the "College Placement Handbook". This gives data on the many fields and careers open to college graduates and is published annually by the College Placement Council in Bethlehem, Pennsylvania. The "Guide to U.S. Civil Service Jobs", published by the U.S. Government Printing Office in Washington, D.C. may also prove worthwhile.

When you are seeking work in an entirely new field, the job hunting process becomes considerably more difficult. You may have to develop a series of letters which highlight the different facets of your experience which would be appropriate for the new field you wish to explore. When you're attempting a career change, letters will prove far more productive than resumes. In fact, the normal avenues for seeking employment such as utilizing agencies, recruiters, answering ads, etc. will not work very well for you. Our experience indicates that people have had the best results by sending out hundreds of letters focusing on small businesses and answering advertisements in the "business opportunities" sections of major newspapers. If you happen to be fortunate enough to have an investment available, you obviously can consider starting your own business or buying a franchise. In this case you will also be using the "business opportunities" sections.

As we mentioned, the key to making a successful career change involves sound career planning. If you anticipate some problems or simply desire to make a change, you will be wise to begin studying, planning, and working while still in your current field. With our changing education systems, high divorce rate, expanding communications, career shifts at almost any age will become more routine. By the end of the decade, the maintenance of dual capabilities and dual careers will have become a common practice.

Having Experience which is Narrow

If you have single industry or company experience you should consider using two resumes. One would be directed at the industry where you have experience while the other should be a functional resume which does not disclose the firm(s) or industry where you have all your working experience. An example of a functional resume is included in the next section. In this functional resume you can stress accomplishments by area of work. Your cover letter, that accompanies the resume, could indicate something to the effect that your position is delicate and that company anonymity is a necessity, but that details on employers will be submitted if there is a mutual interest.

Having a Record of Too Many Job Changes

Job hoppers are people who have not shown much progression within companies, and who usually have a record of many lateral job changes. Almost any potential employer will be wary of you if this is the kind of record you have. However, there is a big difference between job hoppers and men who have achieved great progress both within firms and through changing jobs. There is certainly no stigma attached to the latter. Your job changing will really not be a liability if you can point to a salary progress or state your growth in percentage terms. In fact, there is no better evidence of employer satisfaction than a record of salary growth.

If your employers have been relatively unknown firms, as opposed to "blue chip" companies, you should again consider the use of a functional resume. This type of resume can obviously prove useful if you're afraid of being cited for too many job changes. As previously stated, a functional resume is one which can completely omit names or number of companies with whom you have been associated. If you feel that you should list each job change, your resume should include the general reasons for leaving each firm rather than leaving it to the imagination of the reader. Acceptable reasons for leaving certainly include factors such as mergers or acquisitions; departure of talented superiors; a need for more challenge; changes in corporate growth policy; a desire to locate somewhere else in the country; and the extension of a financial offer which was too attractive to turn down.

Lack of Proper Education

Though you may not have a degree, you should be able to cite various schools which you have attended, as well as courses, management seminars, military schools, and special training. If you combine this with statements that you have the ability to learn quickly, as well as creative, analytical and writing abilities, you will go a long way toward overcoming this liability. With this particular liability the need for stressing accomplishments is more significant than ever. This is particularly true if you are a senior executive. In this case, an effective statement of accomplishments will almost always overcome any lack of formal education.

Being Unemployed

If you've just been fired, encouraged to leave, laid off, or otherwise dehired, the first thing to remember is not to panic. If you do panic, you are going to lose your polish, confidence and ability to think clearly and execute a good campaign.

Being fired today is far from an unknown tragedy. It happens to corporate presidents and vice-presidents all the time, and at a faster percentage rate than at middle management levels. People may not admit it and be quick to claim they quit all their previous positions, but it is likely that many of the executives who interview you will have shared the same experience at some stage of their career. In fact, it is a very rare individual who can succeed in moving up the corporate ladder without being fired at least once during his career. Being fired, or asked to leave, doesn't mean failure in everyone else's eyes, even though you may feel tremendously down just after the ax has fallen.

More often than not people get fired because of a personality conflict, or secondly because someone at the top demands a change due to the political pressures being applied to him. The number three reason for firings relates to those situations where cost reductions are dictated because of internal programs or mergers, and these frequently result in terminations which reflect little concern for individual performance. The first reason we mentioned is the most significant. This concerns those situations where people could not get along with their boss or at least not the way the boss wanted! The fact is that a lot of bosses, at any level, are often uninspiring, difficult to get along with, sometimes neurotic, insecure and not all that competent themselves. If you take a good objective look at yourself, you will probably have to admit to some of the same qualities at various times in your own career. Getting all the way to the top in most corporations requires as much political finesse as natural ability, and if you just lost at this game, all we can advise is that you sharpen your political intuition in the future.

The major point we want to make for those who find themselves unemployed, is simply that it is not synonymous with failure, and won't be unless you let it happen. Being unemployed does mean that you'll be carrying a great handicap. Regardless of the circumstances, you are probably already aware that the great majority of firms prefer to look just at those who are presently employed. Nevertheless, because we have a country with unlimited business opportunities, almost anyone can turn a poor position into a greater success with some hard work. The ability to bounce back after a bad experience is probably the truest indication that you really possess the top fibre that we'd all like to have. If you are in this position just take the applicable advice in this manual and really go to work on a campaign.

The most common technique of executives who are unemployed for a long period of time is to come up with a consulting enterprise which evidences continuity of employment. About all it takes is a phone and some stationery. Remember that a telephone answering service can act as an office for you. They will respond to incoming calls based on the exact instructions you give them. Even if you do not care to go the consulting route, an answering service will sound far more professional than your wife and children.

Another technique is to simply not indicate a termination of employment on your resume. You can always state that the resume was prepared before you mutually decided to terminate your relationship.

If you find yourself in a position of having suddenly lost your job, we suggest the following:

(1)   Get your unemployment compensation forms completed – Unless you have a lot of capital, don't let your pride stand in the way of your accepting a weekly unemployment check. Almost everyone who loses a job ends up being unemployed for much longer than they expected.

(2)   Be prepared for a disappointment – Being an unemployed person means you will encounter more false leads, generate consistently unwarrented optimism over opportunities, and encounter more disappointment than you've ever experienced. You will also find it a tremendous emotional strain and, if you are out a long time, will probably have family problems on a much greater scale.

(3)   Don't take a vacation – Start on your campaign immediately. You will have a great advantage over employed individuals since you will be able to devote your entire effort to job hunting.

(4)   Get access to a business phone – You might be able to use the number of a friend who can have his secretary take messages for you – or list a phone number (separate from your home phone) under your own consulting service.

(5)   Invest in your campaign – Even though you may be very limited financially, the investment will pay fifty times over. We suggest that you begin by completing a financial plan which accepts the fact that you may be unemployed for the next six months. In the course of planning we suggest that you eliminate all unnecessary entertainment, household luxuries, etc., but that you allow sufficient funds to enable you to dress as though you have been promoted and to actively pursue a first class job campaign. In order to do this you will need to be in a position where you can follow-up every lead, even long shots, and you may have to retain a typist to get out the maximum number of letters and resumes. You may very well have to use every possible technique in this book including "position wanted" advertisements.

(6)   Don't be over anxious – or too available. Never beg for a position. Everyone likes to hire talent which is hard to find. Don't show up in advance of your interview time, and don't always be available at the first suggested time for further interviews.

(7)   Accept your first reasonable offer – even if it is not ideal, but continue your campaign in full force for four more weeks. This is pure and simple insurance, and if something vastly superior develops, you can sit down and talk it over with your new employer. Also do not make the mistake of thinking you can always get a job at a salary cut. It can frequently be more difficult to get a lower paying job, for which you are over-qualified, than an equal or better position.

(8)   If you have been out for a long time – then forget everything you've been trying up to now. Obviously the materials you've been using have failed to do the job for you. Your new starting point is to prepare three totally different and outstanding resumes. They should have appearances and orientations which are not similar to one another and which have little noticeable resemblance to your former materials. Slant these three resumes to three different types of jobs which you could fill and mail them to the appropriate officers in as many corporations as possible. At the same time develop one standard letter which incorporates your ability to fill these different types of positions and launch a mailing (without a resume) to every applicable executive search firm and branch office listed in this book. In both the resumes and letter be sure either to fill your employment gap with consultant work or give no indication that you are presently unemployed. Don't worry about your materials reaching firms you've previously contacted. In almost all cases they will have no record of the previous correspondence.

(9)   If you are forty years of age and unemployed, you might consider contacting a Forty Plus Club in a city year you. Forty Plus Clubs are co-operative and non-profit organizations of management executives, each of whom is at least 40 years of age and is currently unemployed. These clubs act as no-fee clearing houses for available executives, and essentially act to desseminate details of their qualifications to employers in need of their services. Anyone who is at least 40 years of age and who has had a successful executive career will receive consideration from these clubs. All Forty Plus Clubs in different cities have different qualifications for membership. Since some time each week must be devoted to club work, any individual must live within commuting distance of the location at which a particular club is located.

The way Forty Plus Clubs usually function is that individuals working on behalf of each club keep contact with prospective employers in each metropolitan area. They work to obtain job orders and particular specifications. Where appropriate, a committee at each club sends the resumes of members of the club to these prospective employers and arranges interviews. The clubs are financed by initial contributions from each person who is admitted. Each member then contributes a minimal fee each week for maintenance, The clubs usually have typewriters available and may be used as a business address and phone answering service. For information on Forty Plus Clubs in the United States and Canada you may write to the addresses following:

40 Plus of New York, Inc.
15 Park Row
New York, N.Y. 10038
Phone 212-BE3-6086

40 Plus of Philadelphia
1715 Chestnut Street
Philadelphia, Pa. 19103

40 Plus of Washington, Inc.
810 18th Street, N.W.
Washington, D.C. 20006
Phone 202-638-2125

40 Plus of Greater Cincinnati, Inc.,
408 American Building
Fourth and Sycamore Streets
Cincinnati, Ohio 45202

40 Plus of Chicago
343 S. Dearborn Street
Chicago, Illinois 60604
Phone 312-341-0040

40 Plus of Denver, Inc.
251 E. 12th Avenue
Denver, Colorado 80203
Phone 303-222-1551

40 Plus of Northern California
1990 Embarcadero
Oakland, California, 94606
Phone 415-534-4154

40 Plus of Southern California, Inc.
672 S. Lafayette Park Place
Los Angeles, California 90057
Phone 213-388-2301

40 Plus of Houston
1919 Travis
Houston, Texas 77002

40 Plus of Tucson
Chamber of Commerce Building
Tucson, Arizona

40 Plus of Hawaii
141 Merchants Street
Honolulu, Hawaii 96813

40 Plus of Canada
Suite 603
57 Bloor Street West
Toronto, Ontario, Canada 189

Some Comment for Feminine Job Hunters

Our firm receives a substantial amount of mail from women, who consider their femininity to be a definite liability in the job market. From our viewpoint we do not completely agree with this statement. Certainly there is little doubt that women face added barriers in the job market. However, despite these barriers, we know of countless examples where the strategy advice in this book has been applied with great success by women at all salary levels.

Being young is still the primary barrier for women when it comes to job hunting. Despite improved birth control methods, people consider a woman too young as long as she is able to have children. No woman should be offended if an employer inquires about her family plans relative to a business career. In fact if you happen to be planning a career in a business world, you would be best advised to volunteer the information.

In the last decade women have made great progress in the business world. Nevertheless, women are still excluded from executive suites in many industries. The obvious exceptions being advertising, publishing, journalism, show business, cosmetics, the arts, science, etc. Women still have their best opportunities in areas where success is not closely related to large scale supervision of male personnel.

Equal opportunity for women in business is not likely to evolve from legislation. When it comes to searching for the good jobs, women will continue to have to earn their stripes in a biased environment. Any female job hunter should consider carefully the reasons why various male employers do reject women candidates. The usual negatives include a belief that a female candidate may be too fragile; not possess a shrewd enough mind; lack the ability to handle junior men effectively; be overly emotional; and a not-too-unusual masculine fear of feminine competition.

The female job hunter will generally do best by taking a fairly conservative approach to job hunting. The things of a personal nature which female job hunters should avoid include the obvious: too much make-up, heavy perfume, tasteless jewelry, mod clothing, short skirts, unappropriate hair coloring, wigs, etc.

A women seeking a job in middle management will need to focus on projecting qualities of genuineness, integrity, intelligence, taste, drive and creativity. The latter two, namely drive and creativity, are particularly important.

Management level opportunities for women will rapidly expand in the next decade. Any woman who combines above average ability with some shrewd knowledge of job hunting may actually have a competitive edge over her fellow competitiors, despite the bias of the market place.

Summary Comments on Resumes and Liabilities

The importance of your resume is something which really cannot be overstated. This is particularly true for anyone who is seeking a position at a large increase in salary. One of your greatest advantages in your job campaign will be the fact that your average competitor will be using a resume which does not do his talent or background justice. This is not to say that those competitors will not be proud of their resumes. Almost to an individual, they will have labored over the preparation of their resume, shown it to their wife or girl friend and received numerous compliments. It's exactly that kind of exercise which has led so many talented people directly down the road to job hunting despair. The fact is that there are very few people whose opinions will be of value in judging the potential effectiveness of your resume. Even the average resume produced by individuals who have had years of experience in the personnel field leave a great deal to be desired. Personnel officers invariably have a preference for resumes which make their life easy. They will say the best resume is one which gives them the immediate facts which can enable them to reach a quick decision on their interest. However, your best interest will not be served by giving the personnel officers a set of statistics. The objective of your resume is to sell interest in you, even if you are not precisely what the employer had in mind.

The most effective resume in helping you meet this objective will normally be one which is accomplishment-oriented and which sells ability as well as experience. It will be a resume designed to overcome your liabilities and will be very well written. A distinctive appearance, based on a good format, high quality paper and vari-typed copy, will greatly improve your readership. Even if your resume met these criteria, there will be people who at times will tell you that your resume isn't what it should be; that it is too professional; that it isn't easy to read or that it does not provide the facts. What you need to do is simply produce the best document possible, given the advice at your disposal. If you are uncertain of its potential effectiveness you can have a professional firm critique it, or you can proceed to test it with a small mailing.

We normally suggest that if your objectives are varied that you consider using a few different resumes and that you plan to selectively distribute each one of them. With a distribution using the techniques covered in other sections you will maximize your chances of success. If you choose to stay with a single resume, we urge you to include an objective which specifically mentions the titles of various positions you could handle.

To conduct a complete campaign, you will probably need 500 to 800 resumes. Printing them in this quantity will cost about $3.00 (per page) for 100 copies. However, if you are uncertain or likely to change your resume, be sure to start with a smaller quantity. If you are in a remote location, adherence to the advice in this section will be even more important. The chances are you may require a greater number of resumes and will also have to place greater reliance on them than a job hunter in a more favorable location.

If you feel you have very serious shortcomings which may limit your ability to generate interviews, you should give consideration to a campaign which relies entirely on letters as your vehicle for opening doors. As mentioned in an earlier chapter, the use of well-written letters provides the ideal means of covering-up shortcomings as you can focus exclusively on accomplishments and personel assets that might interest a given firm.

COLD TYPE EXAMPLE

The use of an IBM "Selectric" composer permits you to vary type styles; the number of characters per inch, the spacing between lines and the boldness of the lettering itself. Examples of the variations are illustrated below.

TYPE STYLES (only a few of the available styles are illustrated)

This is an example of 11 Pt. Univers Medium on the IBM Selectric Composer.
This is an example of 11 Pt. Univers Italic Medium on the IBM Selectric Composer.
This is an example of 11 Pt. Press Roman Medium on the IBM Selectric Composer.
This is an example of 12 Pt. Bodoni Book Medium on the IBM Selectric Composer.
This is an example of 12 Pt. Pyramid Medium on the IBM Selectric Composer.

Number of Characters Per Inch

This is an example of 8 Pt. Univers Medium on the IBM Selectric Composer.
This is an example of 10 Pt. Univers Medium on the IBM Selectric Composer.
This is an example of 11 Pt. Univers Medium on the IBM Selectric Composer.

Spacing Between Lines

This is 11 Pt. Univers Medium typed solid on the IBM Selectric Composer.
This is 11 Pt. Univers Medium typed solid on the IBM Selectric Composer.
This is 11 Pt. Univers Medium typed solid on the IBM Selectric Composer.

This is 11 Pt. Univers Medium typed 1 Pt. leaded on the IBM Selectric Composer.
This is 11 Pt. Univers Medium typed 1 Pt. leaded on the IBM Selectric Composer.
This is 11 Pt. Univers Medium typed 1 Pt. leaded on the IBM Selectric Composer.

This is 11 Pt. Univers Medium typed 2 Pt. leaded on the IBM Selectric Composer.
This is 11 Pt. Univers Medium typed 2 Pt. leaded on the IBM Selectric Composer.
This is 11 Pt. Univers Medium typed 2 Pt. leaded on the IBM Selectric Composer.

This is 11 Pt. Univers Medium typed 3 Pt. leaded on the IBM Selectric Composer.
This is 11 Pt. Univers Medium typed 3 Pt. leaded on the IBM Selectric Composer.
This is 11 Pt. Univers Medium typed 3 Pt. leaded on the IBM Selectric Composer.

Boldness of Lettering

This is an example of 11 Pt. Univers Light on the IBM Selectric Composer.
This is an example of 11 Pt. Univers Medium on the IBM Selectric Composer.
This is an example of 11 Pt. Univers Bold on the IBM Selectric Composer.

14.

EXAMPLES OF RESUMES AND LETTERS

This section consists of examples of letters and resumes. While intentionally fictionalized, they conform in essence to materials which have proven effective, and in some cases are similar to the efforts which professional firms would produce for a considerable fee. They are included so that you can adapt or copy the style or phrases which best suit your personal situation. Examples of the following are covered:

LETTER EXAMPLES

FOR SENDING TO FIRMS:

Direct Letters
Direct Cover Letters
3rd Party Letters
Letters for Following-up Interviews

FOR ANSWERING ADVERTISEMENTS:

Cover Letters
Letter-Only Replies
3rd Party Letter Replies

FOR SENDING TO EXECUTIVE SEARCH FIRMS:

Cover Letters
Letter-Only Examples

RESUME EXAMPLES

Letter-Resume Combination
Single Page Resumes
Foldout Resumes
Blind Resume
Functional Resumes
Regular 2 Page Resumes
3 Page Foldout Resume
3 Page Resumes

EXAMPLE OF DIRECT LETTER

(with resume attached)

(Graduating College Senior)

January, 1867

Dear _____:

My name is Thomas Alva Edison. This coming June I will have the privilege of graduating from college and hope to pursue a career in electronics. My qualifications are . . . . .

These might very well have been the opening statements of Thomas Edison's resume upon his graduation from college. At that point in his career he had virtually no experience to offer. All he probably could speak of was his own opinion of his imagination and devotion to his field. Somewhere along the line, someone decided to take a chance on his abilities and an historic career was launched.

I would never claim to have the genius of Edison, but I do possess imagination, drive and a similar devotion to my field of engineering. Of even more importance is the interest I have always had in your company. I hope that you, too, will give me the opportunity for an interview that someone once gave him.

Thanks for your consideration. My resume is attached.

Sincerely,

EXAMPLE OF DIRECT LETTER

(A Sea Captain — Changing Fields)

Dear _____ :

I am a fairly young (44) SEA CAPTAIN, about to retire.

I'm writing you because I would like to become part of your company in an Administrative capacity which could utilize my extensive experience in all phases of the maritime industry, broad knowledge of most countries of the world, and talent for directing people.

I have achieved notable success as:

CAPTAIN of luxury lines, freighters, and modern container ships, for major American and Foreign Steamship Companies.

PORT CAPTAIN in a large port.

My expertise covers:

Ship operation and scheduling	Safety programs
Cargo handling and storage	Accident investigation
Marine claims	Labor relations
Passenger relations	Personnel management

I'm fluent in all the Romance languages, and have a working knowledge of Russian and Greek.

I have also authored many published articles on maritime subjects, and am a recognized authority on maritime current events.

I would like very much to meet with you to discuss, in depth, the ways in which my varied background could serve your company.

Sincerely,

EXAMPLE OF DIRECT LETTER

(A 24 Year Old Market Researcher)

Dear _____ :

If your company needs someone with well-developed professional talents to participate in market research, then some of the things I have done may interest you.

As an industrial market research assistant, I have done the following:

Analyzed and interpreted statistical data for a basic supplier, studied characteristics of the industry, and defined all major marketing problems.

Prepared and edited management consulting reports involving marketing problems.

Developed all promotional and technical service publications on a chemical company's 150 products.

Screened for important findings, in 15 technical areas, some 350 internal research and development reports.

Released the key findings to, and acted as the liaison with, ten other domestic and overseas affiliates in the reciprocal exchange of R&D information.

Prepared manuals summarizing the marketing activities and economic environments of a company's 15 foreign sales subsidiaries. Consolidated and analyzed their operating and marketing statements for regular monthly management review.

Have been taking EDP and market research courses on my own initiative to supplement my knowledge and usefulness in this particular area. Also have experience in abstracting information for more accurate computerization and retrieval by information specialists.

I hold an MBA degree in management from Stanford.

I would be glad to meet with you at your convenience.

Yours very truly,

EXAMPLE OF DIRECT LETTER

(Young Financial Executive)

Dear Sir:

As Chief Financial Officer of a growing firm, I thought you might be interested in employing a young executive with my following background and goals.

— A total of 11 years of solid growth in accounting and financial management.

— Presently corporate controller of a medium sized international pulp and paper manufacturer with consolidated sales above $100,000,000.

— Previously financial analyst, SEC specialist, (international and domestic) and consolidation consultant with a worldwide conglomerate.

— Earlier line experience as controller with a small heavy equipment manufacturer.

— Four years experience with a "Big-Eight" public accounting firm.

— An outstanding salary growth record.

I consider myself a sophisticated financial professional. I am looking for a position in management which will offer a challenge and a chance to grow, in an organization where everyday financial activities are in the mainstream of current business operations.

If you are intersted please let me know and I'll be glad to furnish more details.

Thank you.

EXAMPLE OF DIRECT LETTER

(A Young Man Seeking His First Job)

Dear _____ :

I've been quite concerned about how a young man can go about getting a point across to a top executive like yourself.

The point being -- I feel I am bright, industrious and personable -- and that I have all the necessary ingredients for successful management development.

Raised in an atmosphere of business (my Father is a prominent retailer), I have always been preparing myself for a business career.

While still in college, I launched two successful business ventures. One, a clothes manufacturing company, grossed $30,000 in its first year. The other, an Italian restaurant, was so popular I franchised it and was netting $900 a month before I sold out prior to graduation. I also managed to work out 15 months of part time work with two leading consultant firms, thereby gaining additional exposure to business problems.

I now have college, the Navy, and, an additional two years of business education behind me. I have a knowledge of general business procedures, cost accounting, computer application, banking, underwriting and marketing.

I'd welcome the opportunity to discuss the posibilities of joining your organization and would be happy to furnish a more detailed background -- hopefully at an interview.

I'll look forward to hearing from you.

Sincerely yours,

EXAMPLE OF DIRECT LETTER

(Staff/Line Manufacturing Manager)

Dear Sir:

I'm contacting you because I'm interested in _____ and I believe you could be interested in my capabilities as a Staff/Line Manufacturing Executive who can provide positive profit-producing results. Since I'm presently employed, please treat this contact in confidence.

My experience, knowledge and skills are in: Manufacturing Management; Plant Management; Production Management; Engineering; Systems & Procedures; Project Management; Industrial Relations; Construction; Quality Control; Production; Inventory Control; EDP Methods; Budgets; Costs; Research & Development; PERT; Capital Expenditures and Planning. From my knowledge of your firm I believe I could make this experience provide strong assistance to the Top Management in your organization. For example,

> . . . as Director of Manufacturing for Benton Products, Inc., I directed, managed and supervised the planning of production, material handling, layout and construction, of a new plant and equipment for a new line of products. The new line justified a 80% expansion of plant space, together with $500,000,00 of equipment. My Company now enjoys a top position among its competitors in this field. Also,

> . . . when assigned as Plant Manager and faced with a strong possibility of a union, I wrote and issued a policy manual designed in the manner of a union contract, which outlined a corrective disciplinary program and provided a grievance procedure. Results: Plant now has ten times more employees and they have rejected five organizing bids by three major unions.

My formal background includes a B.A. in 1951 from the Williams College with major studies in General Science, together with a B.M.E. Degree from Detroit University.

I'm 40, married with three children. We're free to relocate, and I'm free to travel to enhance my present career situation. Since there's so much more to relate, I'd appreciate the opportunity for a personal meeting. I'm confident it could be both interesting and mutually profitable. Naturally, I'll be pleased to put my time at your disposal for the purpose of an interview. May I hear from you?

Yours truly,

EXAMPLE OF DIRECT LETTER

(with resume attached)

(A Technical-Oriented Executive Assistant)

Dear_____ :

Do you have any problems in communicating management aims and policies to your technical and scientific people? And interpreting the problems of many complex and technical projects to management? If so, I would like to discuss my ability to help you.

I have twelve years' experience as a "right hand man", who has been getting jobs done by persistent follow-through on many government defense projects.

I believe that most of my success is due to the fact that I communicate well with technical and creative people, coordinating their efforts with the aims of general management. I am also considered an effective technical writer and speaker.

I have a great deal of experience with prime and subcontractors on sensitive and secret government projects. I have also consistently helped conclude such projects profitably and on time.

May I see you at your earliest convenience?

My resume is attached.

Very truly yours,

EXAMPLE OF DIRECT LETTER

(with resume attached)

(A Technical Executive)

Dear Mr. _____ :

For quite some time I have been an interested follower of _____. I don't know whether you can use a top scientific executive at this time, but I thought I'd bring my qualifications to your attention.

My recent experience has involved working closely with top executives such as yourself in a marketing, R&D, and sometimes an acquisition capacity. I have held a variety of line and staff management positions, and I think that by virtue of this I am quite familiar with the types of problems which you and your executive team face.

As a Consultant I have worked on a wide variety of problems for clients at a billing rate established by my employer of $600 per day.

I consider myself to be a technically oriented professional who can produce immediate results in almost any environment and believe I could do the same thing for you on a career basis, and certainly at a small fraction of the above billing rate.

I'm attaching a resume which summarizes my background on the first page. If you can use someone with my types of skills I'd certainly enjoy having the chance to talk with you.

Sincerely,

EXAMPLE OF DIRECT LETTER

(with resume attached)

(An Experienced R & D Executive)

Dear _____ :

I would like to meet you and discuss the contributions which I believe I can make to your firm in the area of Research.

I have broad experience in the planning and execution of basic and applied research, in making practical applications of this research, and in solving manufacturing process and product problems. I can also offer experience in the administration of research, developing budgets, evaluating research programs, recruiting, and personnel evaluation.

My product knowledge includes quality control, fabrication processes and problems, and product evaluation and improvement in the metals field. I have had direct experience from the research point of view in tinplate cans, electrolytic capacitor foil and instrumentation for research.

These are some examples of what I have done in the environment in which I have been working:

* I recognized the need for greatly improved surface quality for steel products and instituted a research program to attain this on a production basis. The company invested $2 million in new furnace capacity as a result of my basic research.

* Economic justification for a multi-million dollar rolling mill was based to a very large extent on my ability to supervise development of a suitable rolling fluid.

* At my recommendation, we made a $200,000 investment in research equipment and recaptured a market which the company had lost through technical obsolescence.

* A process for making aluminum in a new way became technically feasible through my research, and a patent obtained from it.

Attached is a resume which further outlines some of my qualifications. May we meet to discuss the contributions which I know I can make to your firm.

Sincerely yours,

EXAMPLE OF DIRECT LETTER
(with resume attached)
(An Unemployed Top Executive)

Dear Mr. _____ :

About a year ago I had dropped you a note expressing my interest in the progress you were making with your company. While at the time you didn't have any openings I do remember appreciating the courtesy of a personal reply.

I know without asking that you have little time to devote to screening letters from ambitious job candidates. However, because of my continued interest in the firm, and the fact that I feel strongly that I could make an immediate contribution, I thought I would write again.

Since writing you last, my experience has continued to involve working closely with top executives such as yourself, in a communications, marketing, and sometimes acquisitions capacity. By virtue of this and my prior experience in line and staff positions, I think I am quite familiar with most of the types of problems that you and your executive team must cope with on a daily basis.

I have been reading about the problems which you have with your _____ product line. With the limitations of the marketplace in that sector, I'd guess that you are more concerned than ever with insuring successful new product, acquisition, and venture efforts. As I'm sure you'd agree, success in these areas depends on having dedicated individuals, with a lot of drive, and most of all with a talent for generating growth. Without meaning to sound overly confident, I do consider myself one of the more knowledgeable and action type executives in these areas.

At the present time I have just left my position with a small but successful industrial firm, due to some irreconcilable differences with the owner. I had done an excellent job with them, and in fact had received an attractive raise just two months ago.

On the chance that your requirements have changed since I wrote you last, I'm enclosing a resume which has my background summarized on the first page. If you had a half hour sometime, I'd certainly enjoy having the opportunity of giving you some of my ideas on how I might contribute to your growth. My thanks again.

Sincerely,

EXAMPLE OF 3rd PARTY LETTER

(A 37-Year Old Engineering-Marketing Executive)

Dear _____ :

An associate, an experienced and capable Engineering-Marketing Director, has expressed a desire to put his abilities to work for your company. Because he is currently employed within your industry he asked me to contact you.

Since his overseas military service in 1951 as a platoon leader, he has acquired experience in sales, marketing and a broad business proficiency. He has a solid problem solving foundation in sales engineering, sales promotion, budgeting, forecasting, presentations, displays, new product planning, and market research. This performance background stems from seventeen (17) years demonstrable achievements with three major producers of electrical products.

He holds an M.E. degree and has been schooled in American Management Association courses, in Advertising and in Corporate Long Range Planning.

Here is an example of his resourcefulness: He initiated a project for the development of a comparator by which customers' results are accurately predicted for use by production. He resolved a technical problem and economically placed his company in a position to compete for previously lost business, with potential savings of between $350,000 and $600,000 business annually.

There is much about his conceptual and marketing abilities that cannot be reflected in print. An interview would reveal them and I would be delighted to arrange it.

Sincerely,

EXAMPLE OF 3rd PARTY LETTER

(A 57-Year Old Financial Executive)

Dear _____ :

A business associate of mine with 30 years of financial experience has asked me to contact you in his behalf.

He has a thorough knowledge of finance operations, including methods and procedures, EDP systems and programming, records retention, contracts and negotiable instruments.

Also, he has a long record of success working with correspondent and other firms in updating systems to improve efficiency and reduce costs. He is exceptionally effective in customer relations and is well received by top executives of large corporations.

Highly reliable and a good organizer with administrative skills, he is a perfectionist who takes pride in quality work. Although demanding of himself and others, he is highly regarded by his subordinates.

He has the poise, appearance, and experience to bring prestige, dignity, authority and respect to any financial institution.

There is more detailed information available at your request. To arrange an interview, or to obtain additional information, please call or write me at the address below:

Cordially yours,

EXAMPLE OF 3rd PARTY LETTER

(A 35-Year Old P.R. Executive)

Dear _____:

A friend of mine, an Assistant Marketing Manager/Public Relations has asked me to contact you. He has a BA degree from Oberlin College and did graduate work at both Oregon and California Universities.

He is heavily experienced in the publishing and graphic arts industries, and very skilled in the planning and programming of PR campaigns. He is also excellent at creative writing for media, merchandising, POP materials and in-store promotions. In the last year, he has also personally created materials for sales training, promotional tie-ins, film production and narration, and news releases.

He has over 12 years experience in leading publishing companies, marketing and advertising agencies.

For interview arrangements, or for further information including references, please phone or contact the undersigned.

I look forward to your early reply.

Sincerely yours,

EXAMPLE OF A LETTER WHICH FOLLOWS-UP AN INTERVIEW

Dear Mr. _____:

I think the position we discussed the other day sounds exceptionally challenging. After reviewing your comments about the job requirements I am convinced that I could make a rapid contribution toward your continued growth.

Since you are going to reach a decision quickly I would like to mention several additional things which I feel qualify me for the job we discussed.

1. Proven ability to generate fresh ideas and creative solutions to difficult problems.

2. Experience in the area of program planning and development.

3. Ability to successfully manage many projects at the same time.

4. A facility for working effectively with people at all levels of management.

5. Experience in administration, general management and presentations.

6. An intense desire to do an outstanding job in anything which I undertake.

7. Unquestioned loyalty and integrity.

Please feel free to discuss any of these things with the references which I provided to Mr. Roberts.

I will look forward to hearing from you.

Very truly yours,

EXAMPLE OF A LETTER WHICH FOLLOWS-UP AN INTERVIEW

Dear Mr. _____ :

I just wanted to say how much I enjoyed our conversation on Monday afternoon. The Corporate Planning position which you described sounded both challenging and interesting.

As I had mentioned to you, my previous experience in the corporate planning area included work for both General Motors and the Singer Company. While at Singer, I had been the primary force behind the development of the corporation's first Five Year Plan. If either you or Mr. Jones were interested, I would be glad to sketch out in more detail, the exact accomplishments which I made in this area.

I will be out of town next week, Mr. Smith. However, after that I certainly hope we can explore things further at your convenience. As I had previously stated, I am very confident about the contribution which I could make in your Planning Department.

Thank you again for your time.

Sincerely,

EXAMPLE OF A LETTER WHICH FOLLOWS-UP AN INTERVIEW

Dear Mr. _____ :

This is to clarify my experience and orientation, and their relevance to your requirements for a President with strong marketing management skills.

I am a Generalist, as demonstrated by my experience, responsibility and success in a range of management assignments. I am however a Marketer by inclination and by the nature of my two most recent positions. Evidence of this is my present staff, here in Hong Kong, which consists entirely of Marketing, Sales and Product Managers; whereas the Operations, Manufacturing, and Research Management, which report to me, are located at the plant level. In this division, Management means Marketing.

Nevertheless, the marketing of industrial products differs from the marketing of consumer products in its demand for TOTAL management planning and implementation. Consumer marketing can be a virtuoso performance by the marketing department, while the other corporate departments merely provide support. Industrial marketing demands the full coordination and contribution of all departments; manufacturing, engineering, distribution, sales and service, with marketing acting as the orchestrator rather than the soloist.

The success of my present firm, and I believe yours as well, demands a chief executive who will insure that the marketing goals are everyone's goals, and that everyone's goal is the company's progress and profit.

The purpose of this brief is to confirm these points:

> *General Management is my occupation*
> *Marketing is my skill*
> *Success is my story and remains my goal*

I would not seek nor accept an assignment unless I were confident that it would add luster, not tarnish, to a career that shines rather brightly so far.

I'd certainly like to explore your requirements further. If I'm not for the job, I'll be as apt to tell you as you are to tell me.

> *Sincerely,*

EXAMPLE OF A LETTER WHICH FOLLOWS-UP AN INTERVIEW

Dear Sir:

I certainly enjoyed the chance to meet with you briefly on Tuesday. I feel I could do an excellent job for you because of my proven capabilities as a technically-oriented, <u>Field Sales Management Executive.</u>

I say this because:

1) As Technical Sales Representative for General Electric, I was assigned responsibility for an account that had fallen off badly with my company. The program I developed and carried out to improve this situation increased annual sales to them from $12,000.00 to $380,000.00 within three years.

2) Another account had fallen from $1,900,000.00 to $360,000.00 when I took it over. My execution of my plans to rebuild this account increased the sales volume from this one source to $800,000.00 within three years.

3) When appointed District Sales Manager of Olin, I reorganized their office and programmed their effort. Within two years, the 8 million dollar volume I had inherited had been increased to 11 million dollars.

There is much more I could relate, and I feel a meeting with your Sales Manager could prove mutually profitable. I'm in the process of preparing a complete resume and will forward it to you this week.

Cordially,

EXAMPLE OF A LETTER WHICH FOLLOWS-UP AN INTERVIEW

Dear Mr. _____ :

Since our meeting last week, I have been giving a great deal of thought to the particular problem areas which we discussed. As I am sure you agree, the establishment of a corporate staff is something which requires the leadership of an effective planner and manager.

Mr. Williams, I really think that I could do an excellent job for you and believe that both of the above qualities represent areas where I have particular strength. I think that my ten years consulting experience and my previous seven years as a corporate executive have provided me with a particular sensitivity for the types of problems you face.

After our meeting on Tuesday, I also met with Mr. Burns. Our discussion was quite provocative and I was very impressed with his own expertise in this area. He certainly shares your enthusiasm concerning the future of the corporation and of the corporate function in particular.

One thing which we discussed at length involved the nature of the relationships between the corporate staff and the various division Presidents. The diplomacy and professionalism which you require represent skills which I believe I have greatly refined during the course of my career.

My thanks again for your time. I certainly would be interested in exploring the position further.

Sincerely,

EXAMPLE OF COVER LETTER FOR ANSWER TO ADVERTISEMENT

(with resume attached)

(Industrial President)

Dear Mr. _____:

I am very interested in your recent advertisement as my background and interests match your requirements for a President.

My experience covers every aspect of managing a business, from personal selling to the overall guidance and general management of a nationally distributed multi product — multi factory organization.

My record on the strict return on assets basis has few equals. This ability to produce profits while maximizing sales has produced an unbroken record of success in every challenge I have faced. The factories under my supervision have been considered among the most efficient in North America, and their engineering and design won international acclaim.

New businesses have been created and have flourished under my supervision; namely export, educational electronics, and O.E.M. sales businesses. For my present employer, I have initiated color television marketing and manufacturing in Canada.

My total group responsibility produced sales increases from 33 million to 90 million in the last six years. Market share has improved from as low as fifth to a first position in major product categories, while return on assets have been highest in the corporation.

I believe these qualifications should be of interest to you. I shall look forward to meeting you soon. My resume is attached.

Sincerely yours,

EXAMPLE OF COVER LETTER FOR ANSWER TO ADVERTISEMENT

(with resume attached)

(A Sales Engineer and Training Director)

Dear_____ :

I am seeking a position with your company as Sales Training Director.

Having degrees in Engineering and in Management Sciences, my background covers product research and development, test engineering, application and liaison engineering, patents, cost analysis, market research, and product advertising coordination.

In my present position as Manager of Training, I am responsible for training programs, product development and material engineers, technical sales engineers, engineering supervisors and distributor sales personnel.

I know your markets; have taught the use of sales aids and demonstrators; and have written technical magazine articles and data books for design and application reference. I have also designed, constructed, equipped, and used a communications and education center.

My familiarity with your equipment ranges from pull-tape talking toys to space capsule trainers; from technicolor cartridge-loaded movies to video tape closed circuits; and a variety in between.

As a company producing such devices, you may find my experience in this field useful to your product development operation. I would be glad to discuss additional details of my background with you in a personal interview.

Since I am currently employed, please treat this letter and resume confidentially.

Sincerely,

EXAMPLE OF COVER LETTER FOR ANSWER TO AN ADVERTISEMENT

(with resume attached)

(A Young Regional Sales Manager)

Dear_____ :

I want to convince you that I am the man to fill your new Regional Sales Manager vacancy.

As Regional Sales Manager, I set up a branch office for a consumer products company in the liquor industry that increased sales and profits 24% and 58% respectively, in the first year of operation. . . . .then moved into a larger territory and reversed a $25,000 monthly losing trend into a 7% annual sales gain and $96,000 profit.

I think I could do as well for you and I'd like to try. I'm seeking a regional sales manager's position that offers growth for a young man (28), who can prove his value.

My background includes administrative and supervisory responsibilities in direct and distributor sales to supermarkets, smaller retail dealers and institutions. I am experienced in the areas of hiring, training, and motivating people; in addition to budgets, quotas, sales forecasts, promotions and other sales-oriented functions.

I'm single, a graduate of Princeton, with educational credentials in many areas in addition to my marketing and business administration skills.

May I have the opportunity to further discuss my qualifications at a personal interview.

I will look forward to hearing from you.

Sincerely,

EXAMPLE OF COVER LETTER FOR ANSWER TO AN ADVERTISEMENT

(with resume attached)

(An Industrial Marketing Executive - Changing Industries)

Dear Sir:

Since you are seeking an executive with broad experience to direct your company's total marketing effort, you may be interested in my qualifications.

The attached resume indicates that my major experience has been in chemical, agricultural and pharmaceutical operations. Missing, however, is any general commentary on the nature of this experience.

This, I believe, is most significant because it has enabled me to develop marketing and management skills applicable beyond the specific industries in which I have worked.

This experience includes forming a company within a company, with a totally new operating identity. Organizing, staffing and managing two marketing divisions. Directing a major re-organization to implement a change in corporate objectives and to provide marketing staff support for international operations.

It also includes initiating analysis and planning that have generated profitable, diversified growth in a number of distinctly different markets. And directing successful entries into several of these new markets.

While I have worked as a line Marketing Director with both sales and P&L responsibility, my actual function has been closer to that of a business unit manager. Thus, I have had broad working experience in most areas of general business management.

For example, I initiated -- and my division managed -- alternate production and distribution operations, as well as an independent EDP program, when corporate areas were not able to provide adequate support at acceptable cost or performance levels.

My present compensation is in the $30,000 range. My attitude toward salary in a new position would be influenced by such factors as the attractiveness of the opportunity, the company, location, other forms of compensation.

If my background interests you, I will be glad to furnish any additional information you may require.

Sincerely,

EXAMPLE OF LETTER RESPONSE TO ADVERTISEMENT

(A Divisional General Manager)

Gentlemen:

As General Division Manager of an electronic manufacturing firm, I doubled output in less than a year and converted a previous loss situation into a gross profit of 30% on sales of $9 million.

Judging from your advertisement, you may be interested in a man with my breadth of business experience. Here are some of the other things I have done:

In a staff capacity, prepared a five year Business Plan for a $35 million Division covering market forecast, product line strategies, R&D, and return on investment.

Performed Management Consultation studies of four different Divisions including in-depth analysis and recommendations for future operations.

Headed Systems Task Force which developed and installed a computerized management information system for a $80 million corporation.

Exercised financial planning and control over a $5.4 million centralized Administrative Services operation.

In a line capacity, served as a manufacturing foreman, factory superintendent, assistant plant manager, and Division general manager.

Sold military and commercial products and services as a sales engineer, District sales manager, and Headquarters product line manager.

Set up Baltimore Office for a major computer manufacturer. Directed all sales to the Federal Government plus commercial sales for bank, utility and process control applications.

I am a graduate of the Northwestern Business School, MBA 1952, and of Amherst College, BA in Chemistry 1948. My income requirement is $35,000.

I will be happy to discuss further details of my experience with you in a personal interview.

Very truly yours,

EXAMPLE OF LETTER RESPONSE TO AN ADVERTISEMENT

(A Planning/Acquisitions Executive)

Dear Sir:

I am interested in the acquisitions position which you have advertised.

I am a Chemical Engineer, 38 years old and married with two children. I have 30 hours toward a Master's Degree in Business Administration. Summarized below are some of my more important qualifications which are related to your position.

I am now a Planning Associate for a major Company. In this position I am concerned primarily with new business areas, functioning as an internal financial consultant on matters concerning financial analysis, profit projections, new projects, and acquisitions.

As a member of a three-man business planning team, I appraised the capabilities of a 80 million dollar division of a large chemical company, analyzed the options for future development, and recommended a forward strategy which resulted in the formation of a new Division.

I have utilized discounted cash flow techniques to analyze major expansion projects and to set prices on business assets. Typically, I estimated the purchase price for a 70 million dollar mineral reserve; 2) the economics of a 40 million dollar fertilizer project; 3) the design of a 10 million dollar distribution system; 4) other items totaling about 130 million dollars during a recent three year period.

I evaluated the purchase of a partial interest in a 10 million dollar company and the sale of the partial interest in two other 20 million dollar subsidiaries. I am now involved in work relations with a recently acquired 100 million dollar subsidiary.

I prepared the first meaningfully documented 5 year profit plan for a 10 million dollar specialty chemical operation. Since these specialty chemicals often had a short commercial life, I developed special techniques to facilitate forecasting beyond the visible product horizon.

Earlier, I controlled the deployment of resources in a 5 million dollar research department. I set accomplishment objectives and timetables, and evaluated results recommending actions on the basis of my evaluations.

I have exhibited creativity and personal drive in all my professional activities, and can offer excellent references at an appropriate date. Most of my assignments over the past sixteen years have required good analytical and communication skills, as well as resourcefulness.

Should you find my qualifications of interest, please identify your company to the above box number.

EXAMPLE OF LETTER RESPONSE TO ADVERTISEMENT

(Unemployed General Manager)

Dear Sir:

In the interest of keeping this brief, I will outline a few of my accomplishments during my 21 year work career.

With a Leading Sales Consultant Firm . . . During the past 12 months, I have opened a new office and this operation is both successful and profitable.

With Barco, Inc., a Toledo, Ohio specialty chemical/metallurgical manufacturer for $10\frac{1}{2}$ years . . . . .

1) As Vice President-Division Manager, increased sales from 5 million to 10 million in $4\frac{1}{2}$ years, in a highly competitive industry.

2) Increased profits threefold while supporting a large new product development program. (Had full P&L accountability).

3) Planned, organized, executed, motivated and inspected the activities of over 60 people in sales, service, R&D and engineering.

4) Established short and long range sales forecasts, market planning and research, pricing and product strategies and detailed budgets.

5) As Assistant General Manager ($1\frac{1}{2}$ years) assumed all general management duties while regular General Manager was out sick for one year. In addition, during this period established a direct cost system, a production/inventory control system and developed a methods engineering group.

6) As Sales Manager - Foundry Division ($1\frac{1}{2}$ years) increased sales by 40%.

7) Developed the first comprehensive salesmen's training program. By training the salesmen to utilize an engineered sales approach rather than a commodity approach, sales and account penetration were greatly improved.

8) Established a product manager function which in an industry of fast product change and obsolescence, allowed the company to better innovate and anticipate customer needs.

Page 2

9) Established the most effective advertising department in this industry utilizing direct mail, space, publicity and trade shows to their fullest capabilities.

10) As Regional Sales Manager (3 years) increased sales over 300% through my seven direct salesmen. (four of the seven were sufficiently well trained during this period, that they subsequently advanced to management positions.)

As a Self Employed Manufacturer's Representative in Des Moines, Iowa, increased gross commissions in my territory from $4,000/year to $28,000/year in five years while representing light industrial machinery and mill supply lines.

As a Salesman for Walworth Company in Des Moines . . . . . increased sales many fold during my four plus years while representing this valve and fitting manufacturer.

I can offer the following personal qualifications:
A) A demonstrated record of achievement, leadership and hard work
B) The ability to learn new technology and techniques rapidly
C) A builder, a developer of people
D) Highly motivated, results oriented regardless of the obstacles.

I hold a B.S. in Mathematics from the University of Rochester (three years of Mechanical Engineering) plus have attended numerous A.M.A. and university sponsored seminars. I am 44, married, with two teenage children and am a Veteran.

Present salary is $3,000/month plus percent of the office profit. Compensation requirement would be $40,000 - $45,000/year.

This letter gives a partial picture of my background and experience. I will be happy to fill in the rest of that picture during a personal interview.

Sincerely,

EXAMPLE OF LETTER RESPONSE TO AN ADVERTISEMENT

(International Executive)

Dear Sir:

I have recently returned to the United States after spending 10 years in Europe, the Far East and Latin America, spear-heading and consolidating General Motors Corporation's overseas expansion. Since 1959 sales revenue increased from $70 million to over $2.7 billion last year with corresponding increases in profits.

The international market, particularly Europe, has become very competitive as the speed of mergers and acquisitions has increased. But the international market is still profitable and should continue to remain so, as economic growth is expected to increase more rapidly overseas than in the United States. In this new decade while your company can continue its successful growth pattern I would like to think that your overseas operations will contribute a greater share of profit dollars to your overall profit picture.

I am writing to you because your advertisement indicates you may be interested in someone with my experience in international operations. If so, here are some of the things I have done.

As Manager of Market and Profit Planning and Special Assignments of G.M.'s Latin American Operations and head-quartered in Acapulco: —

Spent 6 months in Lima in 1970 and initiated and implemented sales incentive, sales promotion and cost reduction programs in our Peruvian assembly company which turned an annual $700,000 loss into a profit of $600,000 and disposed of a $6 million excess inventory of passenger cars and trucks.

In 1969 tackled G.M.'s number one Latin American problem - the inadequacy of the dealer body. I revamped Distribution in 9 countries and made substantial progress in another 5 countries.

Developed the $800 million revenue side of G.M.'s 10 Latin American profit centers. In addition, strengthened profit plan controls and initiated monthly profit planning by careful forecasting of sales. This allowed production schedules to be realistically established and hence controlled inventories and improved the cash flow.

Sincerely,

When Planning Executive for General Motors International and head-quartered in Zurich, Switzerland: —

Personally negotiated with the governments of Great Britain, South Africa, Australia, India, Pakistan, Turkey, Greece, Peru, Colombia, Singapore and Malaysia on behalf of G.M. In addition, wrote the main ingredients of the current Automotive Laws for the governments of Malaysia and Turkey and wrote most of the Guarantees G.M. gave to the British government.

During this period 12 General Motors manufacturing/assembly companies were established. These were in Australia, South Africa, the Philippines, Turkey, the Netherlands, Argentina, Colombia, Mexico, Peru and Venezuela for an investment of about $900 million. Distributor-owned companies were also established in India, Pakistan and Singapore.

Managed the distributor-owned company during my eight months' stay in Pakistan.

Formulated Action Programs to establish Distribution Companies in Norway, Denmark, Sweden, Belgium, Holland and Austria for G.M. Group passenger cars and commercial vehicles.

Negotiated with the Agency for International Development (AID) in Washington on behalf of several overseas G.M. companies and borrowed $6 million in local currency for the Turkish company.

Made applications for Investment Funds for overseas expansion, on behalf of G.M. International, to General Motors Corporation's top executive committee - the Administrative Committee.

I was born in London, England; U.S. citizen by Act of Congress; married with two young children and with Degrees from three Universities; Cambridge (Engineering), Michigan (Economics and Business Administration), and Honors M.A. and B.A. Degrees in Economics and Business Administration from Pennsylvania University.

If you desire to discuss my business experience in greater detail I shall be happy to do so in a personal interview.

Very truly yours,

EXAMPLE OF 3RD PARTY ANSWER TO AN ADVERTISEMENT

(An Unemployed General Executive)

Dear _____ :

Your advertisement states that you require a mature, experienced Sales Manager. An associate of mine could be profitable to your company.

This is what he has done. . . . . .

In 1958 he joined a small company manufacturing cameras for industrial and consumer use. Commencing as Sales Manager, he moved into marketing and shortly thereafter, became President and Chief Executive Officer of the company. With full profit responsibility he successfully discharged every duty in the area of Personnel, Production, Engineering, Sales, Marketing and Finance.

Prior to that time, he held the position of Salesman for one of America's major producers of photographic goods. His first position following his graduation from school was with an important American designer and manufacturer of machinery, in engineering, methods and other related disciplines.

This man reflects every conceivable qualification and asset for any growth company.

At 46, he is in perfect health, married, one child and mobile.

He holds a B.S. in Business, majored in Business Management and minored in Engineering.

If you feel, as I do, that this man's capabilities present a strong and potential profit for your organization, I would be delighted to arrange an interview at your convenience.

Sincerely yours,

EXAMPLE OF LETTER TO EXECUTIVE SEARCH FIRMS

(with resume attached)

Dear Mr. _____ :

I don't know how often your search assignments involve
a request for a young junior executive, but I thought I
would write you on the chance that you might be able
to assist me.

This June I will be receiving my M.B.A. degree
from the University of Michigan's graduate school.
While a great many firms will be coming to campus I
feel very reticent about accepting the rather routine
type of training positions which most large corporations
offer, even at an attractive salary.

While I have no full time business experience, I have
held a variety of part time positions while in undergraduate and graduate school. Along with my military experience as a Captain I think they have provided me
with far more than the usual familiarity with business
problems in my specialty areas.

I am enclosing a resume which summarizes my experience,
and if you have any clients who can offer challenging
positions to young men, I'd certainly be interested in exploring them.

Sincerely,

EXAMPLE OF LETTER TO EXECUTIVE SEARCH FIRMS

(with resume attached)

Dear Sir:

If in the course of your search assignments, you have a requirement for a _____ executive, I would be interested in exploring any attractive opportunities.

My own experience has included both line and staff positions and I have substantial experience in working for the Chief Executive level of major corporations.

I have enclosed two resumes and would be glad to meet with you if there is anything which might be of interest.

Sincerely,

EXAMPLE OF LETTER TO EXECUTIVE SEARCH FIRMS

Dear _____ :

I have played a key role in designing, implementing and refining a renowned Financial Planning and Control System, which has been credited with much of my firm's financial progress in the last decade.

Now I am seeking a new association, with a company which can benefit from my several years of financial and administrative management experience. Some accomplishments which may interest your clients include the following:

- Designed and installed mechanized plant operating systems, serving the full gamut of manufacturing plants' operational paperwork, management control and financial report requirements. Now used as a standard at many plants worldwide, savings exceed $20 million per year.

- Planned the centralized Communications and Data Processing Operation, which consolidated the headquarters' computer capacity into one of the world's most powerful business data processing and message switching centers. Savings exceed $2.8 million per year.

- Published the corporate Accounting Control Manual, and re-structured it for standardized application at plants, sales organizations and subsidiary companies worldwide.

- Established annual companywide forms purchase specifications, and administered the U.S. forms control and quantity-buy programs. Savings exceed $3.8 million per year.

- Directed the first company wide systems review task-force team to structure a corporate Management Information System. Two major systems now fully developed and operational are:

  a) The U.S. Hourly Labor Planning and Control System, which serves plants' personnel administration and cost control requirements, and provides by-product computer input to the central Payroll and Labor Relations Personnel Profile systems. Savings exceed $3 million per year.

b) The U.S.-Mexico Traffic Information and Control System -- Our first on-line, real-time system – which reduced personnel, excess transportation, demurrage and in-transit inventory costs. Savings exceed $2 million per year, plus the intangible benefit of improved ability to protect critical production schedules at North American Plants.

• As Systems Control Director for one large world wide manufacturing and sales division, serving the information and control requirements of such diverse staff and line functions as engineering, purchasing, manufacturing scheduling, production, sales, cost and general accounting etc.:

a) Built mathematical simulation models of the higher profit areas of the business to improve management decision tools in optimizing profit plans.

b) Converted to third-generation computers at the three U.S. and European computer sites. Savings, including capacity gains, exceed $800,000 per year.

c) Completely resystematized the Parts and Accessories Distribution, Inventory Control and Accounting systems at one European "master" and ten U.S. regional depots. Savings exceed $900,000 per year, plus the intangible benefits of improved customer order service, higher percent order fill performance, quicker inventory turnover, and reduced investment in inventories.

d) Effected major modifications to the Warranty Policy/Product Quality Analysis System which helped reduce warranty costs $2 million per year by tightening administrative controls, and providing earlier warning on product quality problems

• Developed recommendations to improve the clerical and computer processing at the centralized U.S. salary and hourly payroll operation. Savings exceed $3 million per year.

• Negotiated positive bank reconciliation from major banks, using check register magnetic tape outputs as automatic input to the banks' computers. Savings exceed $2 million per year.

If your clients could use a financial and administrative executive who is thoroughly familiar with modern management and control methods, I would like to discuss my qualifications with you in a personal interview. I am confident I can convince you that I can produce the same beneficial results for your clients that I have attained for my present employer.

In an interview I'd be glad to give you a full resume in substantiation of my experience, plus personal and business references of the highest caliber.

Yours very truly,

THE LETTER - RESUME

The letter-resume on the next two pages deserves some explanation. Though shown on separate sheets, it was printed on both sides of 8½ x 11 paper, folded in the center, and used as a four-sided brochure. In our illustration the fourth and first sides appear together. This is the manner in which this kind of format must be typed on 8½ x 11 paper.

This particular format is intended to eliminate the need for having a separate cover letter and resume. While it cannot be personally addressed, it does maintain a personal note and offers immense convenience for a volume campaign. It is a format that is particularly suited for men in remote areas or others who may conduct a letter campaign making many hundreds of contacts.

It is also a format which might be used by men who wanted to explore opportunities in different fields. For example, in this case the words in [brackets] can easily be changed (after printing) to reflect a different objective. The letter can then be re-printed and mailed to a different list of firms.

The resume which follows on the third page is an example of a general resume which would be necessary in support of the letter-resume. It contains the same information but has no specific objective and could be used with Personnel Agencies and other placement organizations.

RESUME EXAMPLE: MILITARY OFFICER SEEKING CIVILIAN JOB

Lt. Alan Williams . . . .

SUMMARY OF DETAILS

EDUCATION
BA degree @ University of Minnesota '64 (English major)
USN Flight Training School - 15 months
USN Nuclear Weapons School - 2 weeks
USN Flight Instructor School - 6 weeks

MILITARY ASSIGNMENTS
9/64 to 10/65 Flight training @ Pensacola/NAS Corpus Christi
6/66 to 12/68 Division Officer @ NAS Patuxent River
1/68 to 4/69 A/C Commander @ NAS Patuxent River
4/68 to 4/69 Material Officer @ NAS Patuxent River
5/69 to Pres. Instructor Pilot @ NAS Pensacola

PERSONAL DATA
Date of Birth   May 13, 1942
Height   6'3"
Weight   200 pounds
Married, one child
Original Home   Denver, Colorado

OTHER INTERESTS
Golf---bowling---stereo systems---photography--- also have Commercial Pilot's license.

REFERENCES
Would be glad to supply military, academic, or personal references upon request.

Lt. Alan Williams
5900 East Shore Drive
Pensacola, Florida 32505

Phone (904) 432-6802

Dear Sir:

I am writing your firm because I would like to have the opportunity to be considered for employment as an [Investment Account Executive].

In June of 1970 I will be released from military service as a Naval Officer. I feel I have the aggressiveness, intelligence, and personality to make a contribution to any growing [brokerage firm] in a very minimum of time.

My qualifications for such a position include:

* An ability to sell and work well with all types of people.

* A great amount of drive and the interest and desire to work long hours.

* Some knowledge of the market and the brokerage business, which while supported only by personal interest, is accelerating rapidly.

I believe that my achievements in the past, while primarily in the military environment, are indicative of both my aptitude and versatility. These include:

Lt. Alan Williams . . . .

I will have been in the Navy for 6 years since graduating from college. Because of the Viet Nam conflict and a shortage of experienced pilots, my tour of duty was extended for one year.

I am leaving the Navy despite having an excellent record because my greatest interest is in working for a [brokerage firm]. I feel I have the maturity and ability to be even more successful in this capacity.

As for personal data, I will be 28 years old in May, am 6'3'' and 200 pounds, and married with one child.

I have traveled extensively throughout all of Europe, as well as Iceland, Canada, Puerto Rico, Bermuda, and all of the United States, and would be willing to relocate wherever there is a challenging opportunity, a competitive atmosphere, and a chance for me to prove my worth.

If you expect to have any openings in June where a man with my aptitudes and background could begin his career, I would certainly welcome the opportunity to talk to you.

Sincerely,

Lt. Alan Williams . . . .

* Winning a $10,000 scholarship to the University of Minnesota, from whom I received a BA degree in 1964, with a major in English.

* Earning a considerable amount of money while in college by working during every available vacation.

* After 15 months training became a Navy Pilot. Subsequently designated Aircraft Commander above several more senior officers. This position included responsibility for a combat ready crew of 5 Officers and 8 Enlisted men along with an aircraft valued at $5 million.

* Was cited for administrative abilities in addition to my skill as a pilot. As Material Officer, I was responsible for material and procurement in a squadron with assets over $70 million and an annual operating budget of almost $1 million.

* Four years of continuous experience as a supervisor, instructor, and leader. Each required the ability to communicate well with others, to make prompt decisions, and to gain the confidence of superiors as well as subordinates.

SUPPORT RESUME FOR MILITARY OFFICER SEEKING CIVILIAN JOB

Lt. Alan Williams   5900 East Shore Drive, Pensacola, Florida 32505   (904)432-6802

In June I will be released from extended military service as a Navy Pilot. I will have been in the Navy for 6 years since graduating from college. My objective is to find a challenging position where I can use my best abilities.

* An ability to sell and work well with all types of people.

* A great amount of drive and the interest and desire to work long hours.

* Strong analytical and writing abilities.

I believe that my accomplishments are indicative of both my aptitude and versatility. Some of them are as follows:

* Won a $10,000 scholarship to the University of Rochester and received a BA degree with a major in English. Participated in many extra-curricular and athletic activities, and earned a considerable amount of money by working every available vacation.

* After 15 months training became a Navy Pilot. Subsequently designated Aircraft Commander above several more senior officers. This position included responsibility for a combat-ready crew of 5 Officers and 8 Enlisted men along with an aircraft valued at $5 million.

* Was cited for administrative abilities in addition to my skill as a pilot. As Material Officer, I was responsible for material and procurement in a squadron with assets over $70 million and an annual operating budget of almost $1 million.

* Four years of continuous achievements as a supervisor, instructor, and leader. Each required the ability to communicate well, to make prompt decisions, and to gain the confidence of superiors and subordinates.

MILITARY ASSIGNMENTS
9/64 to 10/65 Flt. Trng. @ NAS Pensacola & Corpus Christi
6/66 to 12/68 Division Officer @ NAS Patuxent River
1/68 to 4/69 A/C Commander @ NAS Patuxent River
4/68 to 4/69 Material Officer @ NAS Patuxent River
5/69 to Pres. Instructor Pilot @ NAS Pensacola

PERSONAL DATA
Age - 28
Height - 6'3"
Weight - 200 lbs.
Married, one child
Orig. Home - Denver, Colo.

EDUCATION
BA degree @ Univ. of Minnesota '64 (English)
USN Flight Training School - 15 months
USN Nuclear Weapons School - 2 weeks
USN Flight Instructor School - 6 weeks

OTHER INTERESTS
Golf---bowling---
stereo systems ---
photography --- also
have Commercial Pilot's
license.

I have traveled extensively throughout all of the United States, Europe, Iceland, Canada, Puerto Rico and Bermuda and would be willing to relocate wherever there is a challenging opportunity, a competitive atmosphere, and a chance to prove my worth.

SINGLE PAGE RESUME EXAMPLE: SALES EXECUTIVE

J. MARCUS BERNSTEIN
41 Elm Road
Bronxville, New York 10552
(212) 682-4731

EMPLOYMENT HISTORY

1967 July to Present . . . .
LTV, Inc. - N.Y.C. Sales $20,000,000
Manufacturer of tape cartridge playback equipment and pre-recorded tape cartridges.
Position: Assistant to the Executive Vice-President

1964 April to 1967 July . . . .
Jarvis Radio - Div. of Magnox Corp., Bethpage, N.Y. Sales $6,400,000
Manufacturer of hi-fidelity components and communications equipment.
Position: National Sales Manager promoted to General Manager.

1962 June to 1964 Mar. . . . .
B.P.I. Technical Communications Inc. — White Plains, N.Y. Sales $2,000,000
Manufacturers of Citizens Band two-way radio equipment.
Position: National Sales Manager.

1960 Feb. to 1962 May . . . .
Arco Inc. —Blakey, Ohio
Retail photographic suppliers cooperative.
Position: Group Sales Coordinator

EXPERIENCE

A. SALES . . . .
Successfully marketed products through most levels of distribution.
Considerable volume with premium users as well as catalog and stamp plan firms.
Import/export experience.
Determined new uses for products and developed the appropriate industrial accounts resulting in unusual and large volume sales.
Direct mail know-how.
Cognizant of distribution patterns in several industries; Electronics, Photographic, Record.

B. SALES PROMOTION . . . .
Formulated advertising budgets and campaigns.
Designed p.o.p. materials, displays, racks and exhibits.
Prepared literature, catalogs and service manuals.
Working knowledge of the graphic arts.
Participated and supervised at numerous trade shows.
Heavy experience with Advertising Agencies and Public Relations organizations.

C. PRODUCT DEVELOPMENT . . .
Determined product desirability in the market place.
Involvement at most levels of product design.
Liaison with engineers, designers and production personnel.
Experience includes design of cartons, labels and packaging.
Knowledge of patent and trade-mark regulations.

D. MANAGEMENT . . . .
Formulated corporate policy and programs in sales, merchandising and marketing.
Hired, trained and supervised field sales personnel and sales rep organizations.
Managed manufacturing facility employing several hundred people.
Prepared stockholder reports.

E. MISCELLANEOUS . . . .
Controlled the progress of millions of dollars in merchandise from order placement with overseas facilities, until its arrival at the warehouse.
Established repair and service facilities.
Capable of handling voluminous correspondence.
Seasoned traveler. . . 500,000 air miles.

PERSONAL DATA

34 years of age, single, 6'3", 195 lbs. Excellent health.
College: New York University, three years, evenings.
 Industrial Distribution Major. "A" student.
Veteran: U.S. Air Force, 3 years
 Air Traffic Control — Tower Operator

Determined, innovative, practical, versatile, objective, personable, decisive, a driver . . .

Effective at attorneys' offices, union negotiations, jobbers warehouse, board meetings, shirt-sleeve confabs, Tokyo factories, convention panels, or on either side of a desk . . .

RESUME EXAMPLE: ASSISTANT TO CHIEF EXECUTIVE

This is also an example of a resume in the format of an 8½ x 5½ folder. The first and fourth sides are typed together, as are the second and third pages. Printing is then done back-to-back.

JOSEPH STEVENS

• 41 Central Road, Montclair, N.J. • (201) 226-2988 •

Objective: Qualified for Assistant to Chief Executive or as a Director of such functions as Marketing Research, Marketing Services, Planning, Market Development, and New Products.

General Background: Employed with a billion dollar consumer corporation in the drug industry. During the last 12 months I have been Assistant to the President.

This involves traveling with him, briefing him on marketing developments, participating in profit planning and budget reviews of divisions, handling marketing questions from the financial community, and working on corporate-wide marketing problems.

Previous corporate responsibility under V.P.-Development as Director of New Business included extensive work in the areas of new products, market development, and acquisitions.

In a large division of the same firm, I had been Director of Marketing Research and before that Assistant Director. The former was in a department handling 60-70 projects per month, with a staff of 30 and a budget in excess of a million dollars.

Before joining this firm I held a number of consumer-oriented positions in the leisure time industry. In most recent sequence these include Market Research Manager/Market Analyst/Assistant to a Regional Sales Manager/and Salesman.

My accomplishments in all positions are substantiated by rapid salary growth. Am 33 years old, have BA and MBA degrees, both with academic honors. Also had a distinguished record as a Naval Officer. Personal qualities include great initiative and ability to get things done. . .administrative skills. . .strong creative, writing and analytical abilities. Am well traveled, experienced at making presentations and at working with highest level of large corporate management.

Page 4

Education/Personal/& Other Experience

From 8/60 to 8/61 I attended the University of Pittsburgh's Graduate Business School on a full time basis. Studied under a University Fellowship (a grant of $2,000) and consulted to British Petroleum, Gulf Oil Corporation, and Firth Sterling Steel Corporation.

From 9/59 to 8/61 I was a Lieutenant in the U.S. Navy. Reporting to Base Commanders, I managed all budgeting, procurement, and distribution activities of several installations, and had a large staff under my supervision. Received recognition as an "Outstanding Supply Officer" (an award limited to 10% of eligible Lieutenants), and was awarded a Regular Commission and full scholarship to Graduate Business School (both of which I declined).

Degrees include BA from Villanova University '57 (economics and psychology) and an MBA from the University of Virginia '61. Was on the Dean's List at both schools and was 1 of 5 class officers of my MBA class. As an undergraduate, I had numerous activities, held jobs all summers and formed a successful sales business on campus.

Have also attended numerous professional schools in the military and in business (the most recent of which was a two-week executive course at Harvard.)

Other part time work experience not previously cited included work as a copywriter, photographer, and owner of a small mail order firm. Am 33 years old. . .married with two children. . .6'2''. . .180 lbs.

I have always been known as someone whose ethics and character are of the highest caliber; who enjoys giving a 100% effort; and who inspires subordinates to the same level of performance. I feel equally effective in both sophisticated environments and in situations requiring basic approaches to building sales and profits.

Page 2

Present Employer — Since March 1964 - with a leading drug corporation. Currently assisting the President. Previously reported to V.P.-Marketing as Director of Market Analysis. Other positions included Director of Marketing Research and Assistant Director. Major contributions have led to more than a 50% increase in earnings. Some accomplishments are as follows:

* In present position major accomplishments have related to my ability to keep the top Officer informed, and in helping him exercise effective control of decentralized operations.

* When I reported to the V.P. Development, I created, analyzed, and wrote large amounts myself. Also handled the entire effort relating to two new drug products; from idea creation and concept testing, through name and package design (and testing), and development of the marketing plan, advertising strategy, and copy with our agencies.

* Developed a system for alerting management to acquisition opportunities and provided the complete analysis/recommendations of entire industries as well as specific companies.

In a divisional Marketing Research department, where I had a large staff and budget, prime duties were as operations manager. Traveled widely giving presentations.

* Over a two year period, significantly upgraded the entire staff through internal reorganization, intensive training, and recruiting.

* Instituted a complete market intelligence system and developed the corporation's first Five Year Plan.

* Created a large scale continuous P.O.P. advertising/merchandising research program, and a program for measuring market shares in local areas.

* Reshaped and integrated the communication of Nielsen and other market data into a form that greatly aided decision making.

* Guided the corporation's market information and sales analysis activities through EDP conversion, and incorporation into M.I.S. system.

Page 3

Previous Employer — from February 1963 to March 1964 as Marketing Research Manager Photronics Inc. Received a salary increase of 20% after 10 months with this firm, but resigned because acquisition of the firm limited further growth.

* This position consisted of responsibility for a small market research function. It involved participation in the establishment of marketing strategies. Principal efforts were directed at appraising management's research needs, and subsequently designing and executing programs to meet those needs.

* Specific responsibilities included the management of a budget, supervision of a small staff, and the direction of consumer/dealer studies, media research, as well as the development of a marketing information system. Also developed programs for measuring advertising effectiveness, market evaluations, etc.

* Experience included initiating, supervising and writing various phases of marketing research, negotiating contracts with outside suppliers, and the handling of presentations. Most notable achievements related to contributions on new consumer products.

From August 1961 to February 1963 I was with the Consumer Photographic Division of Eastman Kodak. Started as a Salesman, moved to Assistant to a Regional Sales Manager, and then to a Market Analyst. Resigned from this firm, turning down an attractive promotion to Product Manager, because personal considerations necessitated relocation in the New York City area.

* Reported to the National Sales Manager in last position. Provided information and analysis as a basis for sales management decision making. Advanced rapidly and was responsible for sales forecasting, market analysis, and distribution analysis. Worked closely with product managers, sales and agency personnel. Other projects related to new products planning, analysis of new markets, promotion strategy, and competitive activity.

HEDGE ROBERTS
221 East 74th Street
New York, New York

Phone: (212) 535-6678

Objectives: — Account Executive, or other position requiring **creative, analytical and sales** abilities.

General
Background:
— 26 years old
— 6' 180 lbs.
— Excellent health
— Military Service completed
— BBA & MS degrees
— 2 years marketing experience with consumer package goods firm.

Previous
Part-Time
Experience:
— Interviewer for a radio station
— Real estate salesman
— Manager of a college cafeteria
— Army Instructor
— Advertising manager for retail outlets.

Other
Interests
— Photography
— Writing (have published)
— Motorcycling
— Sky diving (27x)
— Pilot
— Automotive racing
— Skiing

Accomplishments with present employer are evidenced by a 48% salary increase in first year. Available at $12,000 - $14,000, depending on location and growth opportunity.

RESUME EXAMPLE:
ACCOUNT EXECUTIVE

NOTE: This is an example of a 4 panel resume. Printing is done back to back and resume is then folded into a 3-2/3" x 8-1/2" Brochure. The panel on the right represents the front of the resume.

MISCELLANEOUS DATA

— received my BBA & M.S. degrees from Ohio State University. Major — Marketing.

— served two years in the U.S. Air Force as Personnel Specialist

— prior to graduation, I had been employed by WCOL radio in Columbus, Ohio.

In addition to the skills already cited, I can offer an employer personal qualities which include:

— integrity

— a great deal of drive

— **a desire to generate new ideas and achieve more efficient operations in anything in which I am involved.**

Presently a Market Analyst with a Leading Consumer Package Goods Firm. Started June, 1968

Initial assignment with present firm was as an analyst involved in **analyzing, writing** and **presenting** to management market information concerned with: Sales (units and dollars), Shares (package-brand-company), Distribution (store-count and all commodity), Advertising (dollar expenditures and share of Industry) and out-of-stock situations as indicated to the firm by the A. C. Nielsen Services, etc.

After four months was assigned as Market Analyst in a newly formed and unique research group. As member of a seven-man team, responsibilities include complete project direction. In this capacity, am fully responsible for all activities involved in the execution of market studies on a local basis throughout the United States. This job has required over 60 hours of work per week and has resulted in a great refinement of my report writing, analytical and presentation skills.

The job includes direct project responsibility for:

—insuring successful execution of field survey work
—editing survey data prior to data processing
—coordination with EDP suppliers
—analysis of data
—final writing of reports
—presentation of reports to sales and marketing management.

The material covered in the market studies relates to:

—brand distribution and market shares
—product and package trends
—point-of-purchase advertising
—comparative sales patterns in various outlet types

In addition to the above, I have had a major role in the development and subsequent refinement of this research effort. This program is unique in its ability to provide accurate actionable information to management in a minimum of time. The corporation has invested $250,000 in the development of this program and my own authority has extended over projects involving expenditures of more than $50,000.

Additional creative contributions to this program have included the writing of instruction books; the designing of questionnaires; establishment of the **unique** and **creative** report format which represented a break-through in communications); the development of presentations and the presentations themselves.

I have also been actively involved in selling this program to local sales managers; the establishment of TAB specifications, and the scheduling of projects through all of their various phases. All work has required close contact with a variety of people (and levels of management) as well as extensive traveling.

BLIND RESUME EXAMPLE: EXPERIENCED P.R. DIRECTOR

AVAILABLE

CREATIVE COMMUNICATOR

Able to initiate, write, supervise, and produce audio-visual and printed materials for sales training and promotion programs. Thirteen years' broad experience with three major industires; 17 awards for writing and photography. $18,000. References on request.

Box 191
San Diego, California

*Public Relations - Promotion Specialist
Expert in Industrial Communications
Thirteen years' broad range experience with three major industries.

* Present position: Senior Writer/Editor - Major Defense Company

* Graduated Northwestern University School of Journalism, BSJ degree, February 1953. Voted "Outstanding Journalism Graduate" - awarded Sigma Delta Chi Special Award.

* Earned 17 subsequent awards including four consecutive Freedoms Foundation awards, two Newspaper National Snapshot awards, citations from International Council of Industrial Editors, Treasury Department, Manufacturing Chemists Association, United Appeal and Community Fund; plaques from the Detroit Advertising Club and California Public Relations Association, an "Oscar" from Financial World magazine, and "Outstanding Community Leader" award from the Greater San Diego Civic Center.

* More than 350 articles published in industrial magazines, trade journals and magazine supplements.

* Designed, wrote and taught courses in Creative Thinking at major defense company. Lectured on Communications and Creativity to many organizations, civic, and church groups. Among them, Central California Industrial Editors, Toastmasters International (at District Meeting), Industrial Management Club, Ethical Hypnotists, Unitarian Church, Florida Scholastic Association (keynote speaker at state convention), Winter Park Camera Club.

* Started community newspaper for Civic Center, continuing as Editor. Have free lance public relations - promotion business called Creative Communications. Accounts include: Mid-California Technical Institute, City of San Diego, San Diego Chamber of Commerce, Loch Haven Art Center, Johnny Bremer's Pizza (Putt-Putt Pizza, Chug-Chug Chicken), Swanky Franky, and Creativeering Associates among others.

* Was member of Public Relations Society of America, National Management Association, Toastmasters International, Sigma Delta Chi, International Council of Industrial Editors, Northern Michigan Industrial Editors Association, Industrial Editors Association of New York; Vice-President of Central California Industrial Editors Association, Program Chairman and Editor of monthly newsletter; Associate Editor of WESTERN ACCENT, regional publication of Western Council of Industrial Editors.

* Completed 18 courses in writing, publicity, public relations and advertising since 1953. Attended numerous conferences to enhance management skills. Recent conferences include: Editors Conference at University of California, November 1961; Industrial Communications Conference, Yale, October 1962; Miami Conference on Communications Arts, University of Miami, April 1964; Editors Conference at University of Florida, November 1967; Quest for Creativity, Oneida State University, August 1967.

* Married, two boys, ages 10 and 8. Formerly Captain - U.S.A.F.

Box 191
San Diego, California

FUNCTIONAL RESUME EXAMPLE: MARKET RESEARCH EXECUTIVE

BURNS GOFFREY,   423-B Steelton Street
Denver, Colorado
(303) 771-4454

RESEARCH EXECUTIVE with responsibilities including conception, preparation, execution and presentation of research surveys and sales analytical projects.

SUMMARY: Fourteen years diverse experience in performing sound and creative market research and communicating it to management. Skilled in consumer media research, sales analysis and product testing. Experienced at working with salesmen, sales promotion and advertising executives. Have engaged in every phase of the survey operation from field interviewing to presentation.

PRESENTATIONS: WRITTEN & VERBAL	Have written many major types of research reports: effectiveness of point-of-purchase advertising (media); food, beverage and tobacco usage (consumer); rail express shipments (transportation); magazine and newspaper editorial (readership); sales audits in retail outlets (distribution and merchandising). Have addressed sales and committee meetings on findings.
PLANNING ORGANIZING COORDINATING	Devised survey samples. Developed and pretested questionnaires. Performed and directed field interviews. Supervised editing, coding, and tabulation of survey results.
TRAINING SUPERVISION	Trained and supervised interviewing crews for specialized field studies in 21 metropolitan areas in 18 states. Validated and edited their work. Instructed and supervised office personnel in techniques of report tabulation.
SALESMANSHIP LIAISON	Successfully sold membership in trade association through personal sales calls and mail solicitation. Worked closely with magazine advertising salesmen in creating research presentations to clients. Furnished association members with helpful research and promotion data. Experienced in working with outside research organizations.
TECHNICAL KNOWLEDGE	Thorough knowledge of statistical techniques and linear programming. Familiar with the operation of office calculating machines and I.B.M. equipment. Skilled in constructing graphs, charts, and maps.

-2-

BURNS GOFFREY

PROMOTION SERVICE	Wrote several membership promotional booklets containing complete description of association services and activities. Composed copy for sales promotional literature and answered mail and telephone inquiries while employed by trade associations and trade publications.
FOLLOW—THROUGH DETAILS	Developed system to expedite processing of magazine reader service cards used to order literature from advertisements, catalogs, and new product announcements. Issued monthly reports on advertising pages' breakdown for numerous competitive trade journals. Computed liquor per capita consumption figures for all U.S. markets.
PERSONAL	Age: 37; 6'5''; 210 lbs; single; excellent health.
EDUCATION	B.S. Degree in Economics, Miami University.
EMPLOYMENT HISTORY	Assistant Marketing Director Roberts Advertising Agency, 1964-67 Associate Research Director Hartman Publishing Corp., 1962-64 Project Director J.E.L. Steel Company, 1960-62 Field Manager Western Foods Inc., 1954-59 Market Analyst Audits & Surveys Inc., 1952-54 United States Air Force, 1949-51
ORGANIZATIONS	American Statistical Society Lions International

FUNCTIONAL RESUME EXAMPLE: GENERAL MANAGER - WITHOUT COLLEGE DEGREE

WILLIAM CROSS   168 EAST 60th STREET, NEW YORK, NEW YORK 212-RA-6-3463

General
Background

Experienced general management executive -- with a record of over 20 years of proven accomplishments in the areas of sales and marketing/personnel/production and purchasing.

Have held a wide variety of jobs and progressed from Foreman through Vice-President with responsibility for the complete management and sales/profits of a major division.

Am widely traveled and willing to relocate. Presently 46 years old. Education includes 2 years at the University of California. Military service consisted of 4 years in the U.S. Army Infantry (discharged as Captain).

Personal attributes include an ability for complete dedication to a job . . . the ability to affect strong loyalty from subordinates . . . able to work independently or as part of a team . . . a facility for rapid analysis of problem situations and an ability to get things done . . . and a managerial skill for meeting stringent production, sales, or cost objectives.

Areas of Major Experience

personnel . . . .

Have been responsible for large scale work forces, both union and non-union, technical and administrative. Have had full authority for all hiring and termination, the executing of union negotiations and responsibility for salary administration.

Numerous accomplishments in managing a staff skillfully. Proven ability for inspiring loyalty and minimizing absenteeism, turnover, and serious labor problems.

sales/marketing . . . .

Have been responsible for a sales organization which generated a volume at the $7,000,000 level. During a 5-year period, sales and profits were tripled.

Opened new markets for products through contacts on a direct basis with chains as well as through wholesalers, jobbers, etc.

Successfully introduced many new products and built sales on existing line products through expanding distribution.

Page Two . . . . William Cross

Conducted continuous market research which was oriented toward expanding distribution on food products normally sold along ethnic lines.

Fully responsible for development of sales promotions and associated point-of-purchase materials. Directed various promotions under widely varying circumstances.

Have strong personal contacts with officers and owners of various chains including firms such as A&P, Bohack, Hills-Korvette, Jewel Tea, Finast, Safeway, Penn Fruit, Food Fair, etc.

production . . . . Widely experienced in managing production output and problems. Previous positions held include Foreman -- Production Supervisor -- Assistant Plant Manager -- and Plant Manager.

Have a record of accomplishments in all of the above positions. Some examples are the following:

(1) Frequently overhauled production schedules and coordinated work between shifts to effect significant savings in time, direct labor, and overhead costs.

(2) Initiated sweeping quality and product controls which led to superior performance.

(3) Introduced systems of cost and price controls and insured their useful implementation.

(4) Planned and implemented production smoothly on new product additions.

purchasing . . . . Have been completely responsible for the entire purchasing function.

Assisted in the design of new plants in major cities. These included facilities for production/warehousing/and shipping.

Introduced quality control reports for raw products which permitted guides to be established prior to bulk purchasing.

Provided guidance to Plant Managers on problems involving pricing and inventory control.

Instituted procedures and controls which guaranteed the availability of diverse materials to meet critically timed production schedules.

RESUME EXAMPLE: MILITARY OFFICER – ABOUT TO ENTER BUSINESS

Roger Talligson
41 Hanover Street
Glasgow Air Force Base
Montana
(406) 113-4110

. . . . 30 years old; BA in Economics; seven years full and responsible experience in the supervision of personnel and in financial and related business procedures.

. . . . Excellent military record which culminated in the rank of Major and encompassed a wide range of executive functions.

. . . . Qualified in the application of the most advanced management techniques, work measurement activities, cost reduction programs, related accounting and budgeting offices.

. . . . Extensive background in production, inventory, quality controls, and the coordination and expedition of diverse policies, systems and methods.

. . . . Summary - talented junior executive with the ability to direct and motivate employees in the achievement of productive and vital goals;

. . . . Broad management experience, involving responsibility for production, inventory, accounting and related controls and functions:

1967-present   U.S.A.F. EQUIPMENT MANAGEMENT OFFICE
GLASGOW AIR FORCE BASE.

As OFFICER IN CHARGE of all equipment and related budgeting, inventory, etc., on base - supervised military and civilian personnel in practical administrative procedures:

- Responsible for equipment valued at $420,000,000.
- Conducted employee training on inventory and accounting procedures.
- Handled budget of approximately $516,000 for the fiscal year.
- Solved problems regarding shortage of storage space through effective disposition of equipment not-in-use.
- Insured the provision of 3,400 technicians with requisite supplies; succeeded in reserving funds for these supplies and increasing supply percentage.

. . . . Record of achievement in the initiation of effective work program and dynamic cost reduction system, resulting in dramatic savings:

. . . . As OFFICER IN CHARGE OF MATERIEL MANAGEMENT, Glasgow AFB (1966-1967), developed an effective financial program based on personnel participation, resulting in savings of $4,000,000. In addition, initiated and established a "Zero Defects" Program, setting goals and awarding individuals and work centers for their achievements; this base was one of the few with an outstanding rating in this Program.

. . . . Demonstrated ability to establish and direct major operational procedures:

. . . . As CHIEF, EQUIPMENT MANAGEMENT AND PROCEDURES SECTION at another air base (1964-1966), was responsible for equipment research involving the continual study of the latest publications to provide customers with the most current equipment additions, alterations, changes. Conducted extensive studies on time, motion, personnel and resources, resulting in the elimination of overtime for employees and a more efficient filing system. Reviewed and determined authorization of all base equipment, establishing rigid justification requirements for its provision.

. . . . Additional military and civilian experience:

. . . . Served as WAR READINESS SUPPLY CHIEF with a SUPPLY OFFICE, BAFRI Air Base, Iran (1963-1964) obtaining, storing and insuring the serviceability and readiness of all supplies and equipment. Worked as LABORER on farm owned by father during summers (1954-1962) to help defray high school and college expenses.

. . . . Education and Training: personal data:

Graduated from Midwestern College (1959-1962) with a BA degree in Economics; was a member of the College Business Club.

SPECIALIZED MILITARY TRAINING includes completion of USAF OFFICERS TRAINING SCHOOL (1962-1963) with Commission as 2nd Lieutenant and USAF SUPPLY SCHOOLS (1965 and 1967), graduating first in my class.

30 years old; married, 3 children; enjoy golf and bowling, hunting and fishing; member of Air Force Officers Club, Glasgow Air Force Base Non-Appropriated Fund Activity and Housing Council; belong to Lutheran Church; am President for Decoration Committee to Improve Airmen's Dormitories. Own car; willing to travel; free to relocate; available for employment as of September 1, 1970.

Further details and references on request.

The Courtesy of an Interview would be Appreciated.

RESUME EXAMPLE: EXECUTIVE DESIGNER

ANTHONY MACMILLAN

17 MAPLE ROAD, NEWTON, NEW JERSEY   TELEPHONE 201-728-8153

PERSONAL

Born 8/21/25, Married, Two Children, Excellent Health, U.S. Citizen

EDUCATION

Brown University - School of Design

Rhode Island University - Bachelor Industrial Design, 1955
    Magna Cum Laude

California University - Graduate MS. degree in Human Factors

PROFESSIONAL
EXPERIENCE

Creative Design   9/65 - Present
Newton, New Jersey

As Executive Designer and Product Development Head reported to the President.
Created science and art oriented children's discovery kits for a nationally advertised
subscription series. Designed puzzles, games, manipulatives and storage units in support of elementary school teaching system. Conceived and detailed new toys as
well as redesigned old to meet the stringent cost and consumer appeal requirements
of wholesale merchandising program. Designed major displays, exhibits and interiors
including New York Fifth Avenue showroom. These personal achievements have
been in addition to my successful direction of over 40 designers.

Concord Electronics   4/62 - 9/65
Garden City, New York

Section Head in the Creative Development Department. Directed a team of engineers,
industrial designers and draftsmen. Designed electronic equipment under Federal, industrial, military and Space Agency contracts. Specialized in designing for volume
production where cost control, sophisticated engineering and contemporary image
were all important. Projects varied from complex control centers to space vehicle
micro-miniature readouts.

U. S. Design   1960 - 1964
Wesley, Ohio

Designed, subcontracted and sold an extensive line of contemporary residential accessories under the name of U. S. Design. Developed all logo, catalogs and gift show displays. For this purpose maintained a development shop, office, warehouse and shipping facility in Wesley, Ohio. Distributed throughout Eastern Seaboard to top quality
retailers such as Upper Story, Cambridge, and Tiffany's in New York. Established this
business with financing obtained primarily from other simultaneous full-time employment.

Page Two . . . . . Anthony Mac Millan

Daytron Mfg. Co.   5/54 - 4/61
Wayland, Massachusetts

Senior Engineer and Group Head, responsible for the mechanical engineering and industrial design of electronic consoles, equipment cabinets, computer modules and
data display devices. Assignments covered all aspects of R&D from mock-up stage to
manufacturing follow through and environmental test.

McClennen & Jones   1952-1954
Architects
Albany, Georgia

Specified all interior and exterior colors and finishes for schools and office buildings.
Designed lobby murals, mosaic tile walls, custom auditorium seating and stage cur-
tains. Selected furnishings and customized kitchen equipment.

Westinghouse Electric Co.   1944 - 1947
Home Appliance Division
Pittsburgh, Pennsylvania   (interrupted by military service as naval officer)

Performed time and motion studies, established piece-rate standards for production of
home electric appliances. Underwent management training and became labor relations
assistant investigating grievances and negotiating wage rate disputes.

GENERAL   Creative, resourceful, sensitive, purposeful, adaptable.
ABILITIES

EARNINGS   My motivation in seeking a new position is purely financial. While I have enjoyed ex-
               cellent progress in my present position, I believe my achievements have far exceeded
               my financial growth. I would be interested in exploring positions which offered sub-
               stantial responsibility at financial level in excess of $40,000.

REFERENCES   Supplied upon request. Please do not contact former employers until a mutual in-
               terest has been established.

RESUME EXAMPLE: COMPUTER/ACCOUNTING EXECUTIVE

JOHN A. HANDY
River Road, Dallas, Texas
(218) 871-4001

qualifications

Manager of Computer Services and Manager of Accounting Services for a large corporation, with heavy administrative responsibility in both accounting and data processing, and with a manufacturing cost control background; also experienced in the design, installation, and operation of high volume accounting and statistical systems - primarily serving the controllership function. Experienced in organizing, training, and supervising accounting and data processing personnel; the preparation and analysis of financial and operating reports; and the scheduling of personnel and equipment. Accustomed to dealing with all levels of management.

employment

UNIROYAL INC. (1959 - present)

> **MANAGER, COMPUTER SERVICES. .** Responsible for directing the data processing activities of a corporate computer center employing 50 people. The center provides accounting and statistical services for the operating divisions and is characterized by fluctuating high volumes, tight deadlines, and a great number of complicated accounting and statistical systems. Functions include maintenance programming, systems improvement, keypunch, computer operations, and input and output control. While the main systems are currently operated on an NCR 415 Rod Memory Computer, the installation of a tele-communication system utilizing a Honeywell 800 is in process.

> **MANAGER, ACCOUNTING SERVICES. .** Responsible for directing the activities of this corporate accounting service center employing 90 people. Functions included the maintenance of the divisions' ledgers, the preparation of financial and operating reports, preparation of salaried payrolls and the filing of corporate payroll tax returns, and accounting for receivables, payables and property. Disbursement volume reached $400,000,000 and payrolls were world wide.

AMERICAN SEATING CO. (1956 - 1959)

> **PLANT CONTROLLER. . .** Responsible for the accounting activities of the company, including financial statement preparation, cash administration, installation of cost systems and development of inventory control procedures. Primary emphasis was on the installation of a standard cost system for factory cost control purposes and the development of product costs and selling prices.

JOHN A. HANDY . . . . . page 2

FIRTH STERLING STEEL COMPANY (1953 - 1956)

ASSISTANT TO CONTROLLER . . . Responsible for all accounting activities including statement preparation and product profitability reporting. Directed the initial installation of IBM equipment and developed and installed a budget system.

SUPERVISOR, COST DEPARTMENT. . . Responsible for the activities connected with costs and cost control. Devised and installed a shop time keeping system, defined operating departments, developed overhead rates, and computed product breakeven points by applying direct costing techniques.

OKONITE INC. (1950 - 1953)

ASSISTANT CHIEF COST ACCOUNTANT. . . Supervised the activities of the cost department and prepared analysis of government contract profitability. Developed and installed standard material prices, and installed a standard cost system in the process department.

JONES STEEL COMPANY (1947 - 1950)

SENIOR COST ANALYST . . . Primary duty was the analysis and interpretation of standard cost variances. Other duties included the development of standard product costs, forecasting of operating variances, and general maintenance of the system.

education

BBA in Economics, University of Texas

personal

Married, four children. Excellent health. Born 1922. Height 6'5". Wt. 210.

RESUME EXAMPLE: SENIOR INDUSTRIAL EXECUTIVE

JAMES ROBERTS   554 FIFTH AVENUE, PITTSBURGH, PENNA.   (412) 811-4100

PERSONAL STATISTICS

Memberships: American Iron and Steel Institute
Association of Iron and Steel Engineers
American Institute of Mining, Metallurgical and Petroleum Engineers
Registered Professional Engineer, Province of Ontario
Past Director, Cleveland Chapter, AIME

Patents: Hold numerous patents covering platemaking and low temperature devices . . . also copyrights on over 50 articles I have written and published.

Education   Bachelor of Science Mechanical Engineering
Master of Science Mechanical Engineering
University of California 1958

Both degrees were earned in four calendar years; 100% college expenses were provided by self-employment at full and part-time work. Master's thesis resulted in a city adopting all of the proposals contained within the thesis, including a system of one-way streets, off-street parking, etc., all of which are now implemented.

Age: 36   Present compensation $75,000+

DATES OF EMPLOYMENT

September 1969 - Present: U. S. Steel Corporation
August 1966 - August 1969:   Firth Sterling Steel Company
June 1961 - July 1966:   U. S. Steel Corporation
June 1958 - May 1961:   Bethlehem Steel Corporation Ltd.

WORK EXPERIENCE

UNITED STATES STEEL CORPORATION

Assistant to the President. On the President's staff, my duties are quite varied, covering "trouble-shooting" of operating problems in any of the Company's divisions, financial and capital spending, planning, development of personnel objectives, evaluating acquisition proposals, etc.

President of a division. A $60,000,000 manufacturer of pre-engineered buildings with two manufacturing plants and 2,000 employees. I was assigned to take over this division when it became apparent that its president could no longer function due to health reasons. For two years prior to this time, this division had been a money-loser, and my instructions were to return it to a profitable operation and recruit a man to run the division so I could return to the corporate staff in Pittsburgh. This was accomplished in less than six months, and the new president will be able to show a respectable profit in his first year.

FIRTH STERLING STEEL COMPANY

Vice President, Operations. A completely integrated steel producing company, selling carbon steel plates, hot and cold rolled sheet and strip, with $200,000,000 sales and 5,000 employees. I was responsible for the operations of 110 coke ovens and by-products, two blast furnaces, two 180-ton oxygen furnaces, one 60'' blooming mill and 18 soaking pits, a 120'' plate mill, a 40'' continuous hot strip mill, a 40'' cold mill and temper mills, engineering and construction departments, Industrial Engineering Department, 3,000 hourly employees and 400 supervisors.

Assistant Vice President - Operations. Duties as above, with second place responsibility.

Manager of Planning. Reporting to the President, my duties involved total plant maintenance in addition to the engineering and construction of all new facilities, and the long range planning of new products and plants. The major effort, however, was directed to the construction of a $40,000,000 basic oxygen steelmaking facility to replace nine 160-ton open hearth furnaces. This included negotiating all contracts, fundamental design of the facility, intended mode of operation, selection of supervisors and their training. This project was completed in the time allotted, within the budget, and attained the savings in operating costs over the old method as forecasted within three months after start-up.

UNITED STATES STEEL CORPORATION

Superintendent, Oxygen Furnaces Division. Responsible for quality, production and costs from two 400-ton basic oxygen furnaces and related facilities. Part-time responsibility for production from eleven 650-ton open hearth furnaces in absence of immediate supervisor. Member of Planning Task Force for implementations of electric furnaces, continuous casting of billets, vacuum degassing, and installation of second basic oxygen steelmaking shop. Production from the oxygen furnaces increased steadily month after month for a three-year period until it reached 300% of its initial rated capacity and cost savings had tripled their original estimates. This facility, during its first years of operation, was the largest of its kind in the world.

Assistant Superintendent, Oxygen Furnaces Division. Duties were the same as above with the exception of the part-time open hearth and Task Force responsibilities.

Practice Engineer (same division). Duties were to act as coordinator between operating, engineering, and construction departments and outside contractors during the planning, design and erection of the 400-ton oxygen furnaces. Also heavily involved in the selection and training of hourly and salary personnel and overseeing their on-the-job training in other steel mills prior to start-up of the facility.

BETHLEHEM STEEL CORPORATION LTD.

Melter Foreman. A completely integrated steel producing company with $300,000,000 sales and 8,000 employees. Responsible for the production of steel from two 120-ton oxygen furnaces, on a per-shift basis with authority over teeming and mould yard personnel, some 30 hourly people and three supervisors.

Engineering Trainee. Duties included the on-turn performance of every first level supervisory position in connection with steel producing. A training ground which provided maximum exposure and experience in a minimum time.

RESUME EXAMPLE: DATA PROCESSING/SYSTEMS MANAGER

Robert Simmons	30, Married
560 Main St., Apt. #35	(201) 228-6411
Verona, N.J. 07044	Health: Excellent

Summary of Qualifications:

Over seven (7) years diversified business experience with emphasis on the development of business systems. Have functioned as a management consultant, project manager and systems analyst. Responsibilities entailed: problem definition, fact finding, systems design, implementation, supervision of systems and programming personnel, training of clerical personnel and presentations to executive personnel.

ARTHUR ANDERSON & CO., N.Y., N.Y. - Jan. 1967 - Current
Management Consultant

Member of Management Advisory Services; Position involved doing feasibility studies, designing and implementing business systems, supervising systems and programming personnel, training clerical personnel and making presentations to executive personnel.

Manpower Planning System	Designed and directed the implementation of a Manpower Planning System. The main objectives of the system are: 1) Simulation of manpower needs over the coming year 2) Improvement of mens' training and professional development 3) Improvement of manpower utilization 4) Improvement of manpower controls. Computer hardware employed: IBM / 360 Model 30 - DOS
Production Control System	Designed and directed the implementation of a Production Control System for an electrochemical processing company. Objectives of the system were to: 1) Improve order control 2) Improve manpower and production planning 3) Lay the groundwork for a cost system. Computer hardware employed: NCR 395
Inventory Control System	Designed and directed the implementation of an Inventory Control System to better control a foreign car manufacturer's spare parts inventory. Purpose of the system was to reduce warehousing, obsolescence and carrying costs associated with excessive inventories. Computer hardware employed: IBM 1401
Financial Control System	Directed the implementation of a Circulation Accounting System. Objectives of the system were to improve operating and financial controls, reduce operating costs and improve profits. Computer hardware employed: Honeywell 200

Robert Simmons   Page 2

GULF & WESTERN, N.Y., N.Y. - May 1965 - January 1967
Management Engineer

Position encompassed acting as an internal consultant to Gulf & Western's divisions. Directed implementation of special projects and studies designed to improve division operations and profits.

Agricultural Chemicals Division	Directed the implementation of an inventory production distribution linear programming model designed to obtain optimal product mix by terminal for maximum profits. Model covered a three month period and encompassed thirteen (13) terminals, twenty-two (22) products and three (3) producing units. Computer hardware employed: IBM 1401 - IBM 7040
Chemicals Division	Coordinated the development of an activities network inter-relating the Packaging, Purchasing, Quality Control, Marketing and Production activities required as prerequisite to the introduction of new products. Purpose of the network was to control the activities of each functional area to assure timely introduction of new products.
Consumer Division	Assisted in the evaluation of IBM's System 360 and Honeywell's System 200 EDP series. Findings and recommendations were submitted to Consumer Division Management.

INTERNATIONAL BUSINESS MACHINES, N.Y., N.Y. - 1961 - 1965
Systems Engineer

Stock Transfer System	Assisted in the design and installation of a stock transfer system for two Fortune "500" companies. System also produced quarterly dividend checks and proxies.
Credit Report System	Designed a report originating and editing system for credit reports. Purpose of the system was to eliminate costly retyping caused by changes affecting credit ratings of firms.

Instructor of Linear Programming	Sept. 1966 - Jan. 1967 NYU Management Institute (Evenings)
NEW YORK UNIVERSITY GRAD. SCHOOL	1963 - 1965 - Masters in Industrial Engineering. Evening program; Concentration: Management Science.
UNIVERSITY OF CALIFORNIA 1959 - 1961	Bachelor of Industrial Engineering. Alpha Pi Mu - Industrial Engineering Honorary Society

References will be furnished upon request.

RICHARD F. McCORMACK

PERSONAL DATA

Date of Birth: March 8, 1923
Residence: 16 Marshall Terrace, Essex Fells, New Jersey
Telephone: (201) 744-2860   Married -- 4 Children

GENERAL EXPERIENCE

Very broad, embracing responsible positions in General Management, Profit Planning, Regional Sales Management, Plant Management, Research and Development. General Management has covered both consumer products and industrial products. All relevant experience has been obtained in major corporations which employ sophisticated controls and demanding standards.

POSITIONS HELD

1966 - Present

General Manager - Protection Products Division ($34,000,000), Riegel Paper, Inc.

Responsibility - Full profit responsibility for completely decentralized division distributing packaged consumer products. This is a separate entrepreneurship, embracing complete manufacturing, marketing, sales and distribution, research and development, accounting, and personnel departments but operating within corporate guidelines governing capital and legal matters.

Profitability - Increased profit each year. Net profit before taxes increased from less than 2% to 19.5%. Gross profit was increased by cost reductions, price increases of marginal lines, elimination of low profit items, and the introduction of high margin lines. Net profit was aided also by the revision of advertising and promotional budgets, and by a consolidation of staff through reorganization. Sales increased in spite of product line eliminations. R.O.I. over 35%.

Orientation and Growth - The division was changed from a subordinate department, furnishing the corporation with companion items, to a self reliant entrepreneurship. The division was reoriented by restating its charter and its direction. Products were added on the basis of their compatibility with distribution; distribution was broadened to reflect changing consumer buying habits. Market needs and product benefits replaced familiar technology as the motivation for product development and marketing objectives.

Marketing Services, Sales Department and Technical Department were restructured and restaffed to conform to new objectives.

Organization and Motivation - Profit planning, embracing concrete financial objectives, was introduced for the entire division. Monthly review, by each department head, compared performance with plans. Appropriate corrective action or opportunistic action became automatic in a results oriented atmosphere.

Salesmen performances were budgeted and reviewed on individual territory P & L's. Systems of review by objectives were instituted to upgrade salesmen and Sales Managers. Sales compensation was changed to a responsive incentive system.

New Product development procedures were instituted to select and control projects. The Technical Department was reorganized and staffed to emphasize innovation and to reduce the expenditures on service and support activities.

Managerial personnel were encouraged to develop increased capacity by enlarging their assignments, and increasing their responsibility without forsaking adequate control at the top.

POSITIONS HELD (Continued)

1959 - 1966 -- Rexall Inc.

General Manager of the Chemical Division of Rexall Inc., manufacturing reinforced plastic materials, and specialty packaging materials. Full responsibility for P & L. Responsible for Marketing, Manufacturing, Research and Development, financial control.

Led Chemical Division to highest sales and profit in its history. Increased profit from 3% of sales in the last fiscal year before my management, to rate of 9% of sales in two years. Profit (pretax) level represents 19% return on investment compared to 7% under previous management. Plant and facilities were expanded to meet volume needs.

Manager of Manufacturing for a Coated Abrasive Division of Rexall, directing all functions other than sales and finance i.e. Manufacturing, Research and Development, Q.C. Chairman of committee making annual and long-range Marketing-Operational Plan.

As Manager of Manufacturing, moved this division, which had a reputation for poor quality and service, to a position of industry quality and the best service. In my first full year as Manager of Manufacturing, the division reversed from a 7% loss to a 5% profit with no change in net sales, an improvement of $500,000 in pretax results. Increased ACTUAL gross margins in four years from 20% to 35% with no price increase.

SYSTEMS

At Rexall I formed a Management Engineering Department which was given authority to investigate the practices of any department, and to recommend improvements. Starting with my own department, we consistently reduced personnel and improved efficiency of most departments. In this I had to obtain the cooperation and support of department heads who would naturally resist any such study. In virtually every case this cooperation was gained. This Management Engineering group was formed without adding anyone to the payroll. I used Industrial Engineers and Accountants for a few hours a week.

This program led to the development of a system of sales reporting and sales review. In order to sell this as a pilot demonstration, I accepted a part-time assignment as Regional Sales Manager for the region in which the plant was located. The sales review systems are still in general use.

Established manufacturing cost control at supervisory level, gave faster, better control and eliminated clerks. Eliminated dependence of manufacturing department on accounting department and "after the fact" reports.

RELATIONSHIPS

I have always extended and received cooperation at all levels. I work effectively with others and have derived effective cooperation from groups which previously were in conflict.

I have represented my employers at Association meetings; in negotiations with the highest personnel of customers and competitors; in labor negotiations; in foreign ventures; and in numerous community activities.

I have been an officer and board member of various charitable organizations.

EDUCATION

B.S. Chemistry - Colgate University - 1944

M.S. Chemistry - University of Colorado - 1950

RESUME EXAMPLE: NEW PRODUCT - MARKETING EXECUTIVE

MARCUS GOLDMAN

74 21st Street
Columbus, Ohio
(614) 781-4200

NEW PRODUCT MANAGEMENT

9 years experience involving sales for outstanding corporations, and market development and new product management for a multi-million-dollar importer/distributor.

Record of success in market survey and analysis, product evaluation and customer and market liaison.

Thoroughly experienced in sales and marketing strategies, credits, etc.

30 years old, veteran, Bachelor of Arts and Master of Science (Business Administration) from Harvard University. Excellent scholarship and substantial participation in extra-curricular activities.

✓ **Experience in new product management and market development for substantial distributor of industrial products:**

1966 - present (COMPANY NAME ON REQUEST)

This company has sales in excess of $4,000,000. It is an importer of industrial chemicals for resale to Graphic Arts firms.

AS MARKET DEVELOPMENT MANAGER:

- Introduced new products now accounting for 30% of company volume.

- Handled market research through literature and field investigations, customer liaisons, competition analysis, etc.

- Developed effective inventory controls; determined validity of demand for each item, forecast needs and by redistributing inventory improved service -- and built customer satisfaction.

- Successfully dealt with customer resistance to buying imports and fear of delivery risks.

- Had some part in directing sales efforts.

- Maintained customer liaison by sales calls, letter and phone.

MARCUS GOLDMAN
Page Two

√ **Substantial experience in the sale of intangibles & services:**

1961-1965 (MAJOR FIRM - NAME ON REQUEST)

As SALES REPRESENTATIVE, sold 250 accounts consisting of manufacturers, distributors and wholesalers.

Successfully handled credit analysis, customer liaison, interpretive work, and customer service.

Worked with customer sales forces; helped them utilize credit as an effective sales tool.

√ **Demonstrated success in the sales of services for major company:**

1960-1961 (LARGE SERVICE COMPANY)

As a SERVICE SALESMAN, developed clientele through mail advertising, direct contact, referrals and cold-canvassing. Sold $800,000 of services.

** **Military Experience:**

1956-1957 UNITED STATES NAVY, FINANCE CORPS

Responsible for payrolls of 1,000 men: audited contracts with Japanese Government.

** **Education:**

1960	Harvard University, Graduate School of Business	Master of Science in Business Administration
1959	Yale University	Bachelor of Arts degree
1955	Exeter Academy	Graduate

Received honors in Sociology and Economic Theory in college and maintained a high B or low A average.

Played basketball in high school, participated in dramatic activities and was on the crew at college. Worked with Harvard University Players on set design.

** **Personal Data:**

30 years old, married, one daughter, excellent health, own automobile.
References on request.

RESUME EXAMPLE: YOUNG SALES ENGINEER

This is an example of a resume which would be typed on 8½ x 11" sheets but printed on 17" x 22" paper, and then folded in the middle. The type below would appear on the cover. The next 2 pages would represent the inside of the folder and the last page would be blank.

THOMAS SMATHERS

12 OAK HILL ROAD

SPRINGFIELD, ILLINOIS

(217) 888-6543

Brand Manager

Marketing

Marketing Engineer

Market Development

Primary Metals

Young (29) Sales Engineer, 6 years experience in Primary Metals Industry. B.S. in Metallurgical Engineering, California University especially skilled in area of special metals.

Am competent well-organized personal salesman, knowledgeable in all facets technical marketing.

Thomas Smathers
Page Two

THIS ACCOMPLISHMENT SAVED A CUSTOMER $250,000

A large account was faced with increased internal demands for crude alcohols. It was possible to build a new tower costing $100,000 or to convert to bubble tray designs. There were special corrosion problems which led him to recommend quick installment of sieve trays costing $50,000. Additional towers were trayed and savings topped $250,000.

Increased production efficiency in trayed towers without increase in maintenance or down time costs, has been an added bonus. This company now uses zirconium in all their alcohol units.

WHAT OTHERS HAVE SAID ABOUT ME (references available upon request)

A SUPERIOR

"His work justified adding Sales Engineers in other areas whose activities were patterned after his . . . . ."

A COMPETITOR

". . . . . he has outstanding drive, energy, and ambition . . . . . displays a great deal of tenacity when following a project."

AN ASSOCIATE

"He has an unusual ability to meet and impress customers on a 'first time' basis."

A LEADING SUPPLIER

"He has a very good reputation in the industry for his technical and business acumen."

A FORMER EMPLOYER

". . . . . he's a top-notch salesman and a fine engineer . . . . . "

Thomas Smathers
Page Three

CAREER DEVELOPMENT

U.S. Metals, Inc.	Special Primary Metal Products	1967-Present

Field Sales Manager
Manager Market Development
Engineer Assistant
Technical Salesman

Magnesium Industries	Precious Metal Products	1965-1967

Product Metallurgist

Alcoa Aluminum	Aluminum Products	1962-1964

Technical Advisor
Assistant Product Manager

EDUCATION

California University - B.S. Metallurgical Engineering
Michigan University - graduate studies toward M.B.A.

PERSONAL

Age: 29   Married, two children   Will Relocate/Travel

121 East 85th Street
New York, New York

781-1397 (Res.)
241-1700 (Bus.)

Steven X. Powers

Qualified for Position As

INTERNATIONAL EXECUTIVE - GENERAL MANAGER

(Pharmaceutical/Chemical, Operations, Manufacturing, Corporate Development)

... Over 22 years experience with multimillion dollar chemical and pharmaceutical manufacturers in U.S. and Latin America in the full range of general management, plant management, corporate reorganization and development, product diversification and marketing.

... Thoroughly experienced in all phases of international operations, related planning and liaison.

... Completely up-to-date on modern management techniques including PERT, management by objectives, computer applications, etc.

... Adept at market development, financial management and negotiations, management-labor relations, executive and personnel development and training.

... Degrees and other broad education in chemical engineering, pharmaceutical manufacture and engineering, management and business administration. Fluent in Spanish, some Portuguese and Japanese.

... In short, a thoroughly sophisticated executive, completely at home with a proven record of success in international operations.

(Please see following two pages for further details)

* Completely reorganized and revitalized complex chemical and industrial products manufacturing; improved multi-plant efficiencies and profitability:

1968 - PRESENT   Major Conglomerate, Latin American Group

As GENERAL MANAGER of its Chilean subsidiary, have been completely responsible for the manufacture of sugar, margarine, shortenings, edible oils, industrial hydrogenated fats and oils, synthetic resins, formaldehyde, industrial adhesives, organic chemical specialties and paints, resulting in a $15,000,000 volume produced in five plants.

- Supervised a staff of 9 departmental managers, a group of business administration specialists, a lawyer, accountants and 16 chemists and engineers.
- Assured the efficient and profitable operation of various reactors, distillation columns and a wide range of sophisticated chemical equipment.
- Was specifically required to reorganize the company and develop executive personnel.
- Installed a system of training of all personnel in management, administrative and technical areas.
- Reorganized sales and marketing activities.
- Successfully re-established cordial relations with labor unions and achieved their cooperation.
- Initiated a functional organization with clear lines of responsibility, definitive job descriptions and well-selected executives.
- Generally improved technical services for Industrial Products Division; improved marketing and distribution.
- Handled a wide range of financial, business, sales, governmental liaison.

In short, increased profitability in over-all operations, notwithstanding the reduction in personnel from 650 to 325.

* Developed chemical plants in South America, achieved diversification of products, and improved sales by 600%:

1963 - 1968   Union Carbide, Liquid Carbonic Division, Melrose, Illinois

As GENERAL MANAGER in a Colombian subsidiary, was completely responsible for the organizational development and direction of a substantial chemical plant in South America. Was responsible for multimillion dollar sales, involving production from seven plants.

- Supervised a staff of Executives, with the Operations Manager, Controller and Sales Manager reporting directly to me.
- Assigned the task of production development and diversification.
- Reorganized company along function lines; effectuated more efficient operations.
- Supervised the erection of two CO_2 plants and facilities for liquifying gases.
- Put company into chemicals by building a benzoic acid plant.

In summary, instituted systems procedures and processes and diversification, which increased sales by 800%.

OVER. . . .please

* Experience in the manufacture of industrial specialties:

1963   **Bell Manufacturing Company, Miami, Florida**

As PRODUCTION MANAGER, was responsible for manufacture of chemical specialties for the construction industry, including paints and specialties.

*Other Management, Chemical and Pharmaceutical experience in U.S. and Latin America

1961 - 1963	Medico Laboratories - Production Manager	
	Miami, Florida	(Pharmaceuticals)
1956 - 1961	Carry Products Co. - President	
	Havana, Cuba	(Manufacture of industrial adhesives, resins, specialties)
1947 - 1956	Merck Corporation -	General Manager (Chile-Latin America-U.S.A. Plant design and construction, production reorganization)

* Education in U.S. and Latin America:

1934 - 1938	The Citadel
1938 - 1942	Boston College of Pharmacy and Science - Bachelor of Science
1942 - 1943	University of Havana - Degree in Pharmacy
1953 - 1955	International Correspondence Schools - Chemical Engineering
1952	Merck Corporation - Pharmaceutical Manufacturing
1945 - 1947	U. S. Navy - Counter-Intelligence Training

* Affiliations:

American Chemical Society
American Management Association, International Division
American Society of Columbia
Colombo-American Chamber of Commerce

* Personal Data and U.S. Army Service:

50 years old, married, 3 children.
Veteran, U.S. Navy Counter-Intelligence Corps.
Trained in Chinese language and Chinese psychology, all phases of Intelligence activities.

FURTHER DETAILS AND REFERENCES ON REQUEST

3 PAGE RESUME EXAMPLE: FEMALE EDP EXECUTIVE

Lorna Hamilton

Director, Business & Accounting Application Development
NCR Company, Information Service Department.

7 Elm Rd.
Los Angeles, Calif.
(213) 741-1460

Feb. 24, 1925

Married, no children

FUNCTIONAL EXPERIENCE

- **MANAGER - STATISTICS DEPARTMENT**
  Developed and maintained order entry and
  sales analysis reporting system.

- **COORDINATOR - ACCOUNTING DEPT.**
  Developed and coordinated effort on
  E.A.M. cost accounting applications.

- **OFFICE DIRECTOR**
  Established, controlled and maintained
  accounting records, prepared financial
  reports and administered office of
  corporation.

- **ASST. MANAGER - A.R. DEPARTMENT**
  Administered and controlled billing
  activities.

- **MANAGER - E.A.M. DEPARTMENT**
  Established procedures for department
  operations, supervised personnel and
  activities.

- **PRIVATE ASSISTANCE-SERVICES**
  Provided accounting, tax, and management services for corporation, partner-
  ships, and sole proprietors.

INFORMATION SYSTEMS EXPERIENCE

- **CONSULTATION & APPRAISALS**
  Designed automated information system
  for manufacturing concerns. Specifically
  responsible for systems design of all financial areas of business

- **TIME-SHARING APPLICATIONS**
  Implemented manpower skills inventory,
  general ledger accounting, and shop order
  accounting applications utilizing time-
  sharing system with medium scale computer.
  Managed unit engaged in developing
  generalized business and accounting
  applications for Time-Sharing.
  Responsible for and monitored acquisition
  of time-sharing business and finance
  programs and contract documentation from
  a major university.

- **AUTOMATED SYSTEMS**
  Developed, designed and implemented
  applications in Cost, Accounts Receivable,
  Sales Statistics and Payroll areas on medium
  scale computer.

- **PURCHASING, PERSONNEL, & FACILITIES
  ENGINEERING AUTOMATED SYSTEMS**
  Conducted feasibility studies, developed,
  designed and implemented computer systems
  in Purchasing, Personnel, & Facilities
  Engineering, on large scale computers.

Lorna Hamilton . . . Page 2

DATA PROCESSING EXPERIENCE

- **EXPERIENCE PROFILE**

Computer	Systems	Programming
Card	2 yrs.	2 yrs.
Tape	6 yrs.	5 yrs.
Disc	8 yrs.	6 yrs.

EAM		
Card	4 yrs.	

- Hardware

Hardware	Systems	Programming
IBM 1401	2 yrs.	2 yrs.
IBM 1410/ 7010	5 yrs.	5 yrs.
NCR 235/635 Time-Sharing	4 yrs.	3 yrs.
EAM	4 yrs.	

- Computer Languages
  SPS
  AUTOCODER
  COBOL
  FORTRAN
  BASIC

- Communication Systems Programming
  Equipment

Teletype Terminals	X	X

- Special Applications
  NCR 41 Time-Sharing System
  NCR 64 Time-Sharing System

- Professional Instruction
  NCR Time-Sharing System
  BASIC Language
  FORTRAN Language
  Accounting Applications

PROFESSIONAL BACKGROUND

- **EDUCATION PROGRAMS**
  . .FORTRAN Programming
  . .SC-4020 Plotter
  . .Work Planning Workshop for Managers

- **OTHER PROFESSIONAL BACKGROUND**
  . .Columbia University
  . .L.A. College of Commerce -
  C.P.A. Review Course
  . .Carey's Business College -
  Secretarial
  . .American Management Association -
  Manpower Planning & Control
  . .Member, Data Processing Management
  Association
  . .Member, ACM

- **CERTIFICATES**
  . .Statement of Completion in Economics
  Columbia University
  . .Certificate in Data Processing -
  Data Processing Management Assoc.

- **PROFESSIONAL SEMINAR PARTICIPATION**
  . .Speaker at National CPA Annual
  Computer Users Conference, 1965
  . .Seminar speaker to faculty and students
  of Western University.

- **CONTINUITY OF SERVICE**
  . .NCR Company   8 years
  . .IBM Corp.   17 years

- **IBM EDUCATIONAL PROGRAMS**
  . .PROGRAMMING: 1401, 1410, 1301 Disc,
  SC4020, 1410/7010 Operating System,
  Fortran, Cobol, SPS, Autocoder

Lorna Hamilton . . . Page 3

<u>Other Information</u>:

- Performed as management consultant on a four person study team in designing an integrated information system for British Petroleum. My responsibility included all financial areas of the corporation. Made oral presentation to Chairman of the Board and Directors.

- Designed and developed a flexible and generalized time-sharing application.

  This package is slanted to the Certified Public Accountant and Taxation market (potential time-sharing annual revenue of $8,000,000.00). It is the first unique generalized time-sharing package in a new market.

  Seventeen thousand (17,000) copies of the user's manual have been published to date.

- Designed and implemented time-sharing programs that are presently used on a nationwide basis.

- Managed and administered a unit engaged in developing and implementing generalized time-sharing accounting applications slanted to the small business market.

15.

QUESTIONNAIRE FOR RESUME CONTENT

Questionnaire for Resume Content

On the following pages we have included a questionnaire which we have used for writing resumes. It was designed to collect a <u>maximum</u> of pertinent information which we could then <u>selectively</u> consider for inclusion in a resume.

If you are in the process of preparing or rewriting your resume, you should find it useful to scan the questions. They may serve to provoke thought about items which you might otherwise forget to include.

Even if you are a top executive, you may find it useful to actually go through and complete the questionnaire. Though it takes a couple of hours, it offers a convenient and organized means of initially putting on paper everything that a future employer might consider. In addition it can serve as an excellent diary type record for your personal files.

It has been our experience that people who go through this process, invariably find it much easier to actually prepare materials which are an outstanding expression of their own talents.

GENERAL DATA:

Name: _____

Address: _____

_____

Phone #: Home: _____ Bus: _____

Date of Birth: _____

Height: _____ Weight: _____

Marital Status: _____ # Children: _____

LANGUAGE FACILITY & EXTENT OF FLUENCY

(indicate excellent, good, fair, etc.)

(Language)	(Speak)	(Read)	(Write)
_____	_____	_____	_____
_____	_____	_____	_____
_____	_____	_____	_____
_____	_____	_____	_____

TRAVEL & RELOCATION:

Extent of Previous Travel: _____
(countries, area of U.S.)

Willing to travel? (%) _____

Willing to relocate U.S.? _____ Preference: _____

Willing to relocate overseas? _____ Preference: _____

EDUCATION:

(Degree or % Completed & Year)	(School)	(Concentration)	(Class Rank)	(Grade Point Average)*
BA, BS, etc.	_____ _____	_____	_____	_____
MA, MBA, MS, etc.	_____ _____	_____	_____	_____
PhD, LLB, etc.	_____ _____	_____	_____	_____

*If better than average achievement in concentration, please indicate _____.

Courses taken in school relevant to your occupational objectives:
_____
_____
_____

Scholastic honors, scholarships, assistantships, etc.
_____
_____
_____

Extra curricular
activities, achieve-
ments, etc.

_____

_____

_____

Extent of work while
in school (name of
company, summer work,
and % of educational
expenses earned)

_____

_____

_____

Additional professional
training (seminar, conferences, training programs,
correspondence courses,
etc.)

Title of Course	Conducted By	Dates Attended
_____	_____	_____
_____	_____	_____
_____	_____	_____
_____	_____	_____

PRESENT INTERESTS/ACTIVITIES

Professional society, or
business association mem-
berships, offices held,
committees served on:
(also articles, publica-
tions, copyrights, patents,
inventions, etc.)

_____

_____

_____

_____

_____

_____

Civic/political organiza-
tion, memberships, offices
held: - certificates,
professional licenses
held, etc.

_____

_____

_____

_____

Principal recreational
activities (athletic,
hobbies, etc.)

_____

_____

_____

MILITARY SERVICE

Branch of Service: _____

Date Entered: _____   Rank: _____

Date Discharged: _____   Rank: _____

Highest Rank Held: _____

Reserve Status and Rank: _____

Specialized training
schools, etc. type/
length of time

Military Assignments:

(Place)	(Titles/ Specialty)	(Reported to - Title and Rank)	Responsibilities		
			Men	Budget	Materiel

List nature of duties/accomplishments/achievements in each assignment on the pages where we request information on each employment position held.

EMPLOYMENT STATISTICS:

Immediate Salary Objective: $ _____

Immediate Position Objectives:

Carefully list <u>in order of</u>   1. _____
<u>preference</u> the titles of
<u>five</u> positions you believe   2. _____
you could fill at this stage
of your career. Then, <u>check</u> 3. _____
which two, regardless of your
order of preference, you   4. _____
believe you are best quali-
fied for.   5. _____

Long range position objectives: _____

PAST EMPLOYMENT: (start with first job)

	Company	Company	Company	Company	Company
Name of Co.					
Type of Business/ Products					
Division/ Dept.					
Approx Sales Volume					
Location					
Titles Held					
Reported to (Titles)					
Dates					
First/Last Salary					
Reason for leaving Co.					

Which of the words below best describe functions you performed in your last 3 positions? Double check (√√) those which describe functions you continuously performed, and single check (√) those which had application on an occasional basis. Please give careful thought to each word and do not exaggerate. Later on in this questionnaire, we request that if possible, you elaborate on accomplishments related to the words you have double checked.

	Present or Most Recent Position	Next Most Recent Position	Second Most Recent Position
planned			
directed			
controlled			
established			
disapproved			
scheduled			
systematized			
managed			
guided			
conducted			
harmonized			
grouped			
wrote			
conceived			
cataloged			
created·			
trained			
reshaped			
supervised			
improved			
strengthened			
enlarged			
examined			
contracted			
straightened			
organized			
coordinated			
implemented			
approved			
designed			
invented			
arranged			
governed			
presided			
sorted			
analyzed			
distributed			
administered			
indexed			
developed			
presented			
recruited			
moderated			
expanded			
negotiated			
investigated			
rectified			
revised			

COMPLETE THIS AND THE ADJACENT SHEET FOR YOUR PRESENT POSITION

Company: _____ Position: _____ Dates: From: ____ To: ____

General job responsibilities/ description. Be sure to include # of employees supervised directly and indirectly, titles of individuals reporting to you; also budget, equipment and materiel responsibilities, with an indication of whether your influence was direct or indirect.

Significant accomplishments relate to sales/profits/cost savings where possible (i.e. elaborate on items such as installed standard cost system, guided development of 3 new products, developed employee benefits program, generated $50,000 in new business, etc.) - expand on the words you have double checked (✓✓) on the previous page if possible. (This section is particularly vital to preparation of your resume.)

Describe any original reports, papers, documents you prepared or which were prepared under your direction:

_____

List any direct or indirect technical contribution which you made or participated in:

_____

List any administrative or procedural recommendations which you made which were implemented:

_____

List major management decisions (not covered so far) or organizational changes in which you actively participated:

_____

Describe any promotion or transfer to this position with approximate date and amount of salary increase:

_____

**COMPLETE THIS AND THE ADJACENT SHEET FOR YOUR
MOST RECENT PREVIOUS POSITION HELD**

Company: _____ Position: _____ Dates: From: ____ To: ____

General job responsibilities/
description. Be sure to include # of employees supervised directly and indirectly, titles of individuals
reporting to you; also budget, equipment and materiel
responsibilities, with an
indication of whether your
influence was direct or
indirect.

Significant accomplishments
relate to sales/profits/cost
savings where possible (i.e.
elaborate on items such as
installed standard cost system, guided development of
3 new products, developed
employee benefits program,
generated $50,000 in new
business, etc.) - expand
on the words you have
double checked ($\checkmark\checkmark$) on the
previous page if possible.
(This section is particu-
larly vital to preparation
of your resume.)

Describe any original reports, papers, documents you prepared or which were prepared under your direction:

List any direct or indirect technical contribution which you made or participated in:

List any administrative or procedural recommendations which you made which were implemented:

List major management decisions (not covered so far) or organizational changes in which you actively participated:

Describe any promotion or transfer to this position with approximate date and amount of salary increase:

COMPLETE THIS AND THE ADJACENT SHEET FOR YOUR
2ND MOST RECENT PREVIOUS POSITION HELD

Company: _____ Position: _____ Dates: From: ____ To: ____

General job responsibilities/
description. Be sure to include # of employees supervised directly and indirectly, titles of individuals
reporting to you; also budget, equipment and materiel
responsibilities, with an
indication of whether your
influence was direct or
indirect.

Significant accomplishments
relate to sales/profits/cost
savings where possible (i.e.
elaborate on items such as
installed standard cost system, guided development of
3 new products, developed
employee benefits program,
generated $50,000 in new
business, etc.) - expand
on the words you have
double checked (√√) on the
previous page if possible.
(This section is particu-
larly vital to preparation
of your resume.)

Describe any original reports, papers, documents you prepared or which were prepared under your direction:

_____

_____

_____

_____

_____

List any direct or indirect technical contribution which you made or participated in:

_____

_____

_____

_____

_____

List any administrative or procedural recommendations which you made which were implemented:

_____

_____

_____

_____

_____

List major management decisions (not covered so far) or organizational changes in which you actively participated:

_____

_____

_____

_____

_____

Describe any promotion or transfer to this position with approximate date and amount of salary increase:

_____

_____

_____

_____

_____

COMPLETE THIS AND THE ADJACENT SHEET FOR YOUR
3RD MOST RECENT PREVIOUS POSITION HELD

Company: _____ Position: _____ Dates: From: ____ To: ____

General job responsibilities/
description. Be sure to include # of employees supervised directly and indirectly, titles of individuals
reporting to you; also budget, equipment and materiel
responsibilities, with an
indication of whether your
influence was direct or
indirect.

Significant accomplishments
relate to sales/profits/cost
savings where possible (i.e.
elaborate on items such as
installed standard cost system, guided development of
3 new products, developed
employee benefits program,
generated $50,000 in new
business, etc.) - expand
on the words you have
double checked (✓✓) on the
previous page if possible.
(This section is particu-
larly vital to preparation
of your resume.)

Describe any original reports, papers, documents you prepared or which were prepared under your direction:

List any direct or indirect technical contribution which you made or participated in:

List any administrative or procedural recommendations which you made which were implemented:

List major management decisions (not covered so far) or organizational changes in which you actively participated:

Describe any promotion or transfer to this position with approximate date and amount of salary increase:

16.

PLAN OF ACTION & CONCLUDING SUMMARY

SCHEDULING A PLAN-OF-ACTION

It is impossible to prepare an exact layout of campaign steps which will meet the needs of every executive. Each and every person has an individual situation both in terms of his objectives and the alternatives available to him. The schedule below is a plan of action which has been successfully executed by a wide range of junior and senior executives.

Check (✓) if item applies to you	Check (✓) when completed	
		PRELIMINARY ITEMS - recommended for completion before campaign starts
		* Establish a time schedule - set a definite goal for being in a new position (i.e. 10 weeks) and plan on allocating as much time as possible to its accomplishment.
		* Scan or complete the questionnaire for resume content and resume examples.
		* Prepare draft of copy for one or more resumes (depending on how many different position objectives you have).
		* Arrange your copy in a creative format.
		* If possible, have it typed in "cold type" (i.e. on an IBM Selectric Composer).
		* Select and order quality grade of paper and have resume printed.
		* Develop key resume copy in letter form - prepare as many standard letters as you need for different positions you are pursuing.
		* Also determine if you will need an anonymous resume or special format for agencies, etc. If so, prepare them using the same information that is in your basic resume.
		* If you conduct a campaign in secrecy, get a Post Office box number and prepare a format for use as a third party letter.
		* In addition, different standard letters may be required for:
		(1) Sending direct to firms (with or without resume attached)
		(2) Sending to Executive search firms (ditto above)
		(3) Sending to firms with serious problems (ditto above)
		(4) Answering advertisements (to be used in lieu of your resume when the position available differs from your resume orientation).

* Develop short standard cover letter to accompany resumes as an alternative to the above.

* Prepare list of the company addresses and individuals you will contact.

  (1) Prime company prospects (your industry, allied industries, growth firms, etc.)
  (2) Secondary prospects (requiring relocation, etc.)
  (3) Executive search firms
  (4) Firms with serious problems
  (5) Recently promoted executives and their former employers
  (6) Prominent alumni from your college

* Begin cultivating or renewing personal and business contacts which may be useful and keep a record of them.

* Check your references (if necessary).

* Purchase envelopes, personal stationery, stamps, notebook, etc.

* Subscribe for three months to media which list employment opportunities.

* Make arrangements with a local typist for assistance throughout your campaign. Have all your initial mailing materials typed (use advance dating if necessary), sealed, and ready for distribution.

* Check in libraries for position advertisements appearing in last 10 weeks (include advertisements for positions senior to your qualifications and also those which you may have previously answered with a different resume).

* Scan books on psychological testing (if appropriate).

* Prepare answers to difficult interviewing questions.

INITIATION OF CAMPAIGN

* Mail all materials which have been prepared. (Be sure letters are marked private and confidential if directed to corporate presidents.) We believe it is better to concentrate effort in a short period of time. Executives who do this have more offers materialize at about the same time and reduce the chance of having to evaluate offers on a singular basis.

* Check current display and classified advertisements (under various headings) but delay short period before answering.

* Attempt to identify blind advertisements and approach companies on a direct basis.

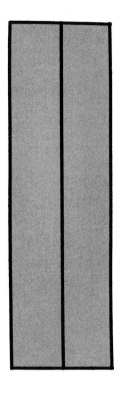

* Check with editors of both general and trade newsletters.

* Contact personnel agencies in reference to specific listings.

* Contact professional societies, trade associations and alumni placement offices.

* Write for details on job hunting services if appropriate.

* Follow-up all initial correspondence which went unanswered or resulted in a form reject.

* Approach personal and business contacts.

* Consider dramatic approaches to firms (use of messenger, phone, telegram, etc.).

* Consider advertisements concerning your own availability carefully. Check success of someone else in your field who advertised in the media you are considering.

We have seen many very successful job hunters execute complete campaigns according to the schedule listed on the preceding pages. While the expense in terms of time and money is not inconsequential, it is invariably very small in relation to the annual increase in income gained.

Remember that timing will be very important throughout your campaign. The executive part of the job market is usually at its peak in the early part of the year and again in the early fall months.

Executing a complete plan does work. However, if you have been a typical job hunter you may have some difficulty getting organized and moving rapidly. Once you do get moving you probably will find that you quickly develop the feeling of confidence that accompanies professionalism in any endeavor. In fact, if you are like most people, your confidence in your job hunting ability is likely to vastly increase your business confidence in general.

For an executive who is presently employed, the preliminary items should take a maximum of four weeks to accomplish. With conscientious application, the total effort should be successfully executed in less than 10 weeks.

CONCLUDING SUMMARY

Remember that the initial objective of your job campaign is to generate interviews. To do this you need a superior resume and well-written persuasive letters. The material cited as examples will provide you with some excellent guidance. You will also need to take approaches which are different from those of your competitors. You want to create an image of yourself as one person among hundreds.

As previously stated, a key to any successful job campaign is organization and confidence. Even with a resume which puts you above your competition, you should not simply rush to firms and agencies. The first thing to do is to read and reread this manual and then lay out your whole campaign. Just having a planned campaign which you can follow will give you a tremendous advantage and save you great amounts of time usually lost through trial and error.

On your campaign, you should do all your spade work first, and then make all of your contacts in a relatively concentrated period. This is a very key point because in this way you will be more likely to have a number of offers come through at the same time.

During the course of your campaign, you should keep copies of all incoming and outgoing correspondence. You should also record the names and telephone numbers of all the contacts you made. Even if you get a very attractive job, the names of many of the contacts you made will be of great service to you should you have to look for a position again.

Remember that you will be much better off if everything you do is individualized. Except in very unusual circumstances we advise job hunters to resist the temptation to run off form letters. The personal nature of individualized materials will have an effect which more than compensates for the extra time required. Also never underestimate the importance of your appearance in the course of your job campaign. Despite everything else, there is nothing that can be more singularly decisive. Don't go into any interview when you are tired, unshaven, or wearing an old suit. Also remember that beards, mustaches, and long side burns are still not in favor in the majority of executive suites.

By all means try to stay employed during your campaign. No matter how attractive your background or what level of executive success you have achieved, you will be under greater pressure and find it is much harder to locate a position when you are unemployed.

If you follow the advice in this book, we strongly believe that you will get a number of offers. As a general rule, we do not think that employed individuals who execute a campaign should accept their first offer. However, if you do receive an offer which is very attractive and accept it you should continue to keep your resume circulating for the first couple of months on the job. This is nothing but pure and simple insurance.

If you are in a remote location or attempting to locate in a distant country or state you will have to work exceptionally hard. We also suggest that you attempt to use every channel for getting interviews and that you execute a very large scale and broad campaign. This will compensate for the smaller percentage response which you will generally experience. You should also give particular emphasis to executing everything in a very concentrated period. All of your materials should be prepared and literally put in the mail at the same time. This will maximize the number of interviews you can explore on any given trip.

The information in this book has summarized proven methods which will give you an immense competitive advantage and which should be invaluable to you throughout your career. To take advantage of them, however, they must be applied. With your knowledge of your own situation, you should be able to directly use, adapt or refine these approaches to exactly meet your own needs. They should also serve to provide the seeds for your development of new and imaginative techniques. Job hunting is never an easy task and requires hard work, calculated risks, patience, and a real ability to avoid discouragement. If you have these abilities, and invest some time, money and energy, your goals will definitely be achievable.

17.

FINANCIAL PLANNING GUIDE

On the next few pages we have put together a general financial planning guide for anyone who may ever find themselves suddenly unemployed. The original source for this guide came to us through the courtesy of the Dow Chemical Corporation and the T.R.W. Corporation.

The starting point for any financial plan involves a close, hard look at anticipated expenses. If you are married, it would be wise to sit down with your wife and approach financial planning with the assumption that you will be out of work for three to six months. Any unfounded optimism at this stage would only leave you in a more difficult position at a later date.

We have divided this guide into three basic sections:

I. The first section involves your projecting anticipated expenses during the period of unemployment.

II. The second section deals with your listing your present cash position and making realistic estimates of possible cash inflows.

III. The third section deals with your potential need to identify sources of additional cash through sale of assets.

I. ANTICIPATED CASH OUTFLOW

We have listed below categories of expenses which are routinely incurred by most individuals. They are only intended as a very general guide. However, from our experience, we find that the people who work through this budgeting exercise will bring into focus areas for potential savings.

One non-routine expense which we have listed will involve the costs of your job campaign. You will have to make an allowance for expenses related to such things as typewriter rental, typing fees, stationery expense, stamps, extra weekly periodicals, phone charges, added transportation, dry cleaning expenses, etc. There can be little doubt that it will cost money for you to find a good job. We advise that you do your best to provide the funds in this area that will enable you to proceed with maximum speed.

	MONTHS					
	1	2	3	4	5	6
Bills and other debts presently outstanding	___	___	___	___	___	___
Interest on debts	___	___	___	___	___	___
Mortgage (or rent)	___	___	___	___	___	___
Life insurance premiums	___	___	___	___	___	___
Medical insurance premiums	___	___	___	___	___	___
Automotive insurance premiums	___	___	___	___	___	___
Other installment payments for which you are obligated	___	___	___	___	___	___
Property taxes	___	___	___	___	___	___
Tuition payments	___	___	___	___	___	___
Club dues	___	___	___	___	___	___
Contributions	___	___	___	___	___	___
Gifts	___	___	___	___	___	___
Lessons: music, tennis, etc.	___	___	___	___	___	___
Food	___	___	___	___	___	___
Clothing	___	___	___	___	___	___
Housewares	___	___	___	___	___	___
Personal items (cosmetics, toiletries, cigarettes, liquor, etc.)	___	___	___	___	___	___
Drugs and medical supplies	___	___	___	___	___	___
Household operations:						
Heating	___	___	___	___	___	___
Electricity	___	___	___	___	___	___
Water	___	___	___	___	___	___
Phone	___	___	___	___	___	___
Subscriptions and daily newspapers, magazines, etc.	___	___	___	___	___	___
Automotive expenses:						
Gas	___	___	___	___	___	___
Maintenance	___	___	___	___	___	___
Local Transportation (taxi, bus)	___	___	___	___	___	___
Other travel	___	___	___	___	___	___
Laundry and dry cleaning	___	___	___	___	___	___
Entertainment	___	___	___	___	___	___
Barber/Beauty shop expenses	___	___	___	___	___	___
TOTAL — All of the above	═══	═══	═══	═══	═══	═══
Estimated job campaign costs	___	___	___	___	___	___
GRAND TOTAL — (Anticipated Cash Outflow)	═══	═══	═══	═══	═══	═══

II. PRESENT CASH POSITION AND ANTICIPATED CASH INFLOW

Listed below are general categories which should be sufficient for you to identify your present cash position and anticipated cash inflow. Those items which exist as totals, rather than monthly income, should be evenly divided among the six months. Once you complete these estimates, you would proceed to compare your availability of cash with the forecasted expenses from Section I.

PRESENT CASH POSITION (INCLUDING ASSETS WHICH CAN BE READILY CONVERTED TO CASH AS REQUIRED)

	MONTHS					
	1	2	3	4	5	6
Cash — Checking account	___	___	___	___	___	___
Savings account	___	___	___	___	___	___
Credit union, etc.	___	___	___	___	___	___
Savings bonds	___	___	___	___	___	___
Stocks	___	___	___	___	___	___
Bonds	___	___	___	___	___	___
Cash value of life insurance policy	___	___	___	___	___	___
Leases (sale value)	___	___	___	___	___	___
Land contracts	___	___	___	___	___	___
TOTAL	___	___	___	___	___	___

ANTICIPATED CASH INFLOW

	MONTHS					
	1	2	3	4	5	6
Severance pay	___	___	___	___	___	___
Unused vacation pay	___	___	___	___	___	___
Retirement funds	___	___	___	___	___	___
Pay in lieu of pension for stock savings plan	___	___	___	___	___	___
Unemployment compensation	___	___	___	___	___	___
Interest from savings account	___	___	___	___	___	___
Interest from bonds	___	___	___	___	___	___
Dividends from stocks	___	___	___	___	___	___
Tax refund	___	___	___	___	___	___
Collectable debts owed to you	___	___	___	___	___	___
Income generated by spouse	___	___	___	___	___	___
Income generated by children	___	___	___	___	___	___
Income generated by your part-time job	___	___	___	___	___	___
TOTAL (Anticipated Cash Position)	___	___	___	___	___	___

III. SUPPLEMENTAL INCOME FROM SALES OF ASSETS, ETC.

We mentioned before that you should approach financial planning with the point of view that you may be unemployed for some time. In completing Sections I and II you may very well find that you are not going to have the cash required for surviving this difficult period. If your situation is very tight, you should obviously attempt to hold down many expenses which would otherwise be normal. Here we refer to things such as entertainment expenses, gifts, contributions, lessons for the children, extra telephones, etc. You could also consider a garage or rummage sale of assets which otherwise might be unused.

If the situation looks very negative, you will have to face up to the possibility of selling certain assets. This is a step which should only be taken after you have exhausted all other avenues for cash generation or expense reduction.

Listed below are some of the categories you might examine as sources for extra cash:

			MONTH			
	1	2	3	4	5	6
Automobiles (second car)						
Automobiles (first car)						
Sporting equipment (boats, planes, motor cycles, snow mobiles, campers)						
Expensive cameras (or other hobby equipment)						
Jewelry						
Musical equipment						
Stamp-coin collection						
Works of art						
Unused furniture						
Old clothing						
Other equipment (unused lawn and farm equipment, appliances, etc.)						
Secondary properties						
Your home						
TOTAL (Supplemental Income)						

SUMMARY

The purpose of this very short guide is to help you identify categories of potential expenses which might be reduced or eliminated. When you are unemployed, it is sometimes difficult to channel funds to the places where they are most needed without actually going through a budgeting exercise. If you may be unemployed for some time, it would be wise for you to consider early communication with any creditors you may have. If you speak to them before you get behind in any payments, you will probably receive better consideration from them as you go along.

Some other things you may wish to consider would include:

1) Borrowing against your life insurance policy rather than cashing it in. Most policies offer a lower interest rate than is currently available, and in the future, a varying payment schedule.

2) A single source loan to consolidate smaller debts. It will be difficult to get a loan from a financial institution while you are unemployed. However, if you have collateral, it is possible. You may be able to secure a loan at a lower interest rate than the interest you will be charged by retail stores and credit card firms.

3) If you are really feeling pressed, sooner or later you may have to consider selling your home. A respected realtor with whom you can frankly review your problem will prove invaluable.

At the time you find yourself unemployed, you should also check into the prevailing government programs. For example, the Federal Food Stamp Program, government programs for paying the travel and interviewing expenses of technical personnel, state funding programs, etc.

18.

REFERENCE MATERIALS

&

FORMS FOR RECORDING CONTACTS

REFERENCE MATERIALS

Sources for Names

If you plan to execute a direct mail campaign you will need to obtain sources for the names of individuals and companies to contact. These sources exist for virtually every field and geographical location, including many unusual occupations and places. We suggest that you first learn what publications are available that may be useful to your campaign, and secondly, determine how to obtain access to them quickly and at minimum cost.

The key reference works listed below should enable you to identify the title and publisher of several sources you could use. Obtaining access to these reference works and the sources you uncover in them may require persistence. Your alternatives include the use of public and private libraries, internal sources within your company or through a business associate, and direct purchase from the publisher.

REFERENCE SOURCES FOR DIRECTORY DESCRIPTIONS

1. Guide to American Directories
   B. Klein & Company, 13 Third Street, Rye, New York (914) 967-4340
   (Describes 3300 directories in approximately 400 subject categories)

2. The Standard Periodical Directory
   Oxbridge Publishing Company, Inc., 150 East 52nd St., N.Y., N.Y. 10022 (212) 751-7590
   (Describes 50,000 periodicals and directories in 230 subject categories)

3. Ulrich's International Periodicals Directory
   R. R. Bowker, Inc., 1180 Ave. of the Americas, N.Y., N.Y. (212) LT1-8800
   (Describes 40,000 periodicals and directories published throughout the world)

4. Trade Directories of the World
   Croner Publications Inc., Queens Village, N.Y. 11428 (212) 464-0866 (also London, U.K.)
   (Trade directories listed by continent, country, and trade or profession. Also lists import/export directories. Price $20)

5. Overseas Newspaper & Periodicals Guide Book
   Communications, Inc., 6535 Wilshire Blvd., Los Angeles, Calif. 90048
   (3,000 trade and technical publications in 130 countries)

Libraries

In most major city library systems there are one or more branch libraries that specialize in business. These libraries, as well as the libraries of any undergraduate or graduate school of business would be likely to have one or more of the directory reference works. Quite frequently, they will also possess a collection of the most widely used directories.

You should not be reticent about asking a librarian to order the directory reference volumes if they are not available. Libraries are a refuge for job hunters. Providing the materials that help people find jobs is one of the most useful social functions any library can perform. Most libraries will purchase any volume that is requested a number of times.

Many libraries will also have the Directory of Special Libraries and Information Centers. This reference work provides information about more than 13,000 special libraries operated by businesses, government agencies, educational institutions, trade associations and professional societies. Many of these are open to you. Your local library may be able to arrange permission for you to visit some that are normally closed to the public.

Stock brokerage offices frequently maintain a small reference library for their clients and prospective customers. Moody's and/or Standard & Poors and other investment directories useful to job hunters are usually available.

Sources At Your Present Place of Employment

In large corporations, both the Purchasing and Market Research departments are likely to possess industry directories. Mail room personnel often know which individuals within an organization subscribe to various trade publications. Trade association and trade show directories would probably be available from the persons in charge of those functions. You should be able to borrow publications you need without disclosing your purpose. If you are unemployed we suggest that you ask a business associate to borrow directories for you.

Buying Your Own Directories

For your convenience we have provided a listing of several hundred of the leading directories which have been useful to job hunters. The first part of this listing consists of the 50 State industrial directories. Virtually all of these provide names and addresses of companies classified by product and geographic location and include names of key personnel. Hundreds of additional city, county, and regional directories are described in the directory reference sources.

Chambers of Commerce and industrial development organizations frequently compile and publish lists of local companies. They will also know of firms that have new or expanded local facilities that need staffing. You should be certain to contact the Chamber of Commerce of any community where you would like to find a job. You can obtain the address by checking the telephone directory or referring to Thomas Register which contains a listing of all U.S. Chambers of Commerce.

Following the listing of State directories is a listing of the major industry directories. Thousands of additional useful publications are listed in the Directory Reference Sources. Purchasing your own copy of a directory is often a practical alternative particularly if you are in a remote location. Sometimes it is possible to split the cost with another job hunter you know or arrange to have your company obtain a copy. Buying a directory enables you to be certain you have the latest edition. Old directories usually have an unacceptable proportion of name listings that have become incorrect.

THE 50 STATE DIRECTORIES

Sources of State Information & State Industrial Directories: State Chamber of Commerce Department, Chamber of Commerce of the U.S.A., 1615 H. St., N.W., Washington, D.C. 20006. $.25

Industrial Alabama: Alabama State Chamber of Commerce, 468 S. Perry St., Montgomery, Ala. 36101. $5.00

Arizona Directory of Manufacturers: Phoenix Chamber of Commerce, 805 N. 2nd St., Phoenix, Ariz. 85004. $2.00

Directory of Arkansas Industries: Arkansas Industrial Development Commission, State Capitol, Little Rock, Ark. 72203. $7.50

California Manufacturers Register: Times-Mirror Press, 115 S. Boyle, Los Angeles, Calif. 90023. $35.00

California Employment Directory: (4,000 major employers with names of personnel directors), California Employment Directory Inc., 580 Market St., San Francisco, Calif. $10.00

Directory of Colorado Manufacturers: Business Research Division, Graduate School of Business Administration, University of Colorado, Boulder, Colo. 80302. $10.00

Directory of Connecticut Manufacturing: Connecticut Labor Department, 200 Folly Brook Blvd., Wethersfield, Conn. 06115. $1.00

Delaware Directory of Manufacturers: Delaware State Chamber of Commerce, 1102 West St., Wilmington, Del. 19801. $7.00

Washington, D.C. Manufacturers & Distributors: Economic Development Committee, Washington Board of Trade, 1616 K St., N.W., Washington, D.C. 20006. $3.50

Directory of Florida Industries: Florida State Chamber of Commerce, Jacksonville, Fla. 32211. $8.00 plus supplement $3.00

Georgia Manufacturing Directory: Georgia Department of Industry & Trade, 100 State Capitol, Atlanta, Ga. $7.50

Directory of Idaho Manufacturers: Idaho Department of Commerce & Development, State Capitol Building, Boise, Idaho 83701. $3.50

Illinois Manufacturers Directory: Manufacturers News Inc., 3 E. Huron St., Chicago, Ill. 60611. 1 year rental $35.00

Indiana Industrial Directory: Indiana State Chamber of Commerce, Board of Trade Building, Indianapolis, Ind. 46204. $12.00

Iowa Manufacturers: Iowa Development Commission, 250 Jewett Building, Des Moines, Iowa 50309. $10.00

Directory of Kansas Manufacturers: Kansas Department of Economic Development, State Office Building, Topeka, Kan. 66612. $5.00

Kentucky Directory of Manufacturers: Kentucky Department of Commerce, Washington & Wapping Sts., Frankfort, Ky. 40601. $5.00

Louisiana Directory of Manufacturers: Department of Commerce and Industry, P.O. Box 44185 Capitol Station, Baton Rouge, La. 70804. $5.00

Buyers Directory of Maine Industries: Department of Economic Development, State Office Building, Agusta, Ma. Free

Directory of Maryland Manufacturers: Maryland Department of Economic Development, Research Division, State Office Building, Anapolis, Md. 21401. $12.50

Industrial Directory of Massachusetts: Massachusetts Department of Commerce Public Document Division, 116 State House, Boston, Mass. 02133. $2.50

Directory of Michigan Manufacturers: Manufacturers Publishing Company, 8543 Puritan Ave., Detroit, Mich. 48238. $40.00

Directory of Minnesota Manufacturers: Minnesota State Department of Business Development, State Office Building, St. Paul, Minn. 55101. $7.50

Mississippi Manufacturers Directory: Mississippi Research and Development Center, Jackson, Miss.

Missouri Directory of Manufacturers: Division of Commerce & Industrial Development, Jefferson Building, Jefferson City, Mo. 65101. $12.50

Montana Directory of Manufacturers: Montana State Planning Board, Sam Mitchell Building, Helena, Mont. 59601. $2.00

Directory of Nebraska Manufacturers: Division of Nebraska Resources, State Capitol, Lincoln, Neb. 68509. $5.00

Nevada Industrial Directory: Nevada Department of Economic Development, State Office Building, Carson City, Nev. 89701. Free

Made In New Hampshire: New Hampshire Department of Resources & Economic Development, State House Annex, Concord, N.H. $1.00

New Jersey State Industrial Directory: New Jersey State Industrial Directory Inc., Port Authority, World Trade Center, New York, N.Y. $40.00

New York State Industrial Directory: New York State Industrial Directory, Inc., Port Authority, World Trade Center, New York, N.Y. $60.00

North Carolina Directory of Manufacturing Firms: North Carolina Department of Labor, Raleigh, N.C. 27602. $5.00

Directory of North Dakota Manufacturers: North Dakota Economic Development Commission, State Capitol, Bismark, N.D. 58501. $2.00

Directory of Ohio Manufacturers: Ohio Department of Industrial Relations, 220 Parsons Ave., Columbus, Ohio 43215. $10.00

Oklahoma Manufacturers Directory: Oklahoma Industrial Development Department, Oklahoma City, Okla. $10.00

Directory of Oregon Manufacturers: State of Oregon Department of Commerce, Planning and Development Division, 560 State Office Building, Portland, Ore. 97201. $5.00

Pennsylvania Industrial Directory: Pennsylvania Department of Internal Affairs, Harrisburg, Pa. 17120. $7.50

Directory of Plants Established Under the Industrialization Program: Economic Development Administration, Office of Econonic Research, Box 2350 6 PO, San Juan, Puerto Rico 00936. Free

Providence Journal Bulletin Almanac: Rhode Island Development Council, Rodger Williams Building, Providence, R.I. 02908. $2.00

Industrial Directory of South Carolina: South Carolina State Development Board, P.O. Box 927, Columbia, S.C. 29202. $7.50

South Dakota Manufacturers Directory: South Carolina Industrial Development Agency, State Office Building, Pierre, S.D. 57501. $3.00

Directory of Tennessee Industries: Tennessee Staff Division For Industrial Development, 240 Cordell Hull Building, Nashville, Tenn. 37219. $7.50

Directory of Texas Manufacturers: Bureau of Business Research, University of Texas, Austin, Tex. 78712. $15.00

Directory of Utah Manufacturers: Utah Committee on Industrial & Employment Planning, 158 Social Hall Ave., Salt Lake City, Utah 84111. Free

Directory of Vermont Manufactured Products: Vermont Development Commission, State Office Building, Montpelier, Vermont

Directory of Virginia Manufacturing & Mining: Virginia State Chamber of Commerce, 611 E. Franklin St., Richmond, Virginia

Washington State Manufacturers Directory: Washington State Department of Commerce, General Administration Building, Olympia, Wash. $10.00

West Virginia Manufacturing Directory: West Virginia Department of Commerce, Planning and Research Division, 1703 Washington St. E., Charleston, W. Va. 25311

Directory of Wisconsin Manufacturers: Wisconsin Manufacturers Association, 324 E. Wisconsin Ave., Milwaukee, Wisc. 53202. $17.00

GENERAL DIRECTORIES

American Men of Science: R. R. Bowher Company, 1180 Ave. of the Americas, New York, N.Y. 10036. $25.00

Central Atlantic States Manufacturers Directory (manufacturers by state & product with executive names): T. K. Sander son Organization, 200 E. 25th St., Baltimore, Md. 21218. $40.00

Directory of New England Manufacturers (13,000 companies classified by state and industry with executive names): George D. Hall Company, 20 Kilby St., Boston, Mass. 02109. $50.00

Dun & Bradstreet Million Dollar Directory (25,000 businesses with net worth over $1 million, classified by product and location, contains executive names): Dun & Bradstreet, 99 Church St., New York, N.Y. 10007. $108.50

Dun & Bradstreet Middle Market Directory (18,000 companies with net worth of $500,000 to 1 million. Classified by industry & location with names of owners): Dun & Bradstreet, 99 Church St., New York, N.Y. 10007. $75.00

Guide to Locating New Products (125 firms that specialize in locating, developing and/or disposing of new products): TTA Information Services Company, 4 West 4th Ave., San Mateo, Calif. 94402. $25.00

Guide to Venture Capital Sources (450 firms with key individual to contact): B. Klein Publications, 11 Third St., Rye, N.Y. 10580. $20.00

Poors Register of Corporations Directors & Executives (260,500 key executives in 32,000 leading companies cross referenced by product and company location. Includes home addresses of executive plus title and duties): Standard & Poors Subsidiary of McGraw Hill, 345 Hudson St., New York, N.Y. 10014

Standard Directory of Advertisers: National Register Publishing Co., 5201 Old Orchard Rd., Skokie, III. $40.00.

The Standard Newsletter Directory (6000 listings of Newletters organized within 224 subject and industry categories): Newsletters Unlimited Subsidiary of Hudson Associates, 370 Lexington Ave., New York, N.Y. $20.00

Thomas' Register (100,000 manufacturers by product and location), (all U.S. Chambers of Commerce): Thomas Publishing Co., 461 Eighth Ave., New York, N.Y. 10001. $30.00

Venture Capital Source Directory (information about 400 organizations supplying venture capital to new businesses. Names individuals who might have knowledge of job openings in new growth businesses): Technimetrics, Inc., 527 Madison Ave., New York, N.Y. 10022. $25.00

Who's Who In Commerce & Industry: Marquis Who's Who, 210 E. Ohio St., Chicago, III. 60611. $27.50

SPECIALIZED DIRECTORIES

ADVERTISING

Standard Directory of Advertising Agencies (4,000 leading advertising agencies in U.S. with key executives, major accounts, geographic index): National Register Publishing Company, Inc., 5201 Old Orchard Rd., Skokie, III. 60076

Who's Who In Advertising (10,000 alphabetically arranged biographical sketches): Who's Who In Advertising, P.O. Box 556, Rye, N.Y. 10580. $42.50

AEROSPACE

American Aircraft Missiles and Satellites Directory (lists manufacturers and executives): Western Aviation Magazine, 2550 Beverly Blvd., Los Angeles, Calif. 90057. $5.00

APPAREL

American Apparel Manufacturers Association Directory (lists member firms and executives): American Apparel Manufacturers Association, 200 K St., N.W., Washington, D.C. 20006. $25.00

AUTOMOBILE INDUSTRY

Wards Automotive Yearbook (auto industry executives): Powers and Company, 550 W. Fort St., Detroit, Mich. 48206. $10.00

BANKING

American Bank Directory (18,000 banks with officers and directors): McFadden Business Publications, 777 W. Peachtree St., Atlanta, Ga. 30308. National Edition $25.00. Individual State Editions $4.00

Bankers Almanac & Yearbook (International commercial banks with executives and directors): Iliffe - NTP Inc., 300 E. 42nd St., New York, N.Y. 10017. $40.00

Who's Who In Banking (biographical reference on bank executives, covering 50 states): Business Press Inc., 32 Broadway, New York, N.Y. 10004. $25.00

CANADA

Canadian Trade Index (13,000 companies classified by product & location. Contains executive names): Canadian Manufacturers Association, 67 Yorge St., Toronto, Ontario, Canada. $24.00

CHEMICALS

Chemical Guide to the United States (major companies and executives): Noyes Development Company, Park Ridge, N.J. 07656. $15.00

COAL

Mac Quown's Directory of Coal Operating Companies (lists American coal mining companies by location, with executives): National Coal Publications, 2401 Mount Royal Blvd., Glenshaw, Pa.

CONSTRUCTION

A.G.C. Directory Issue (major contracting firms by state with key executives): Associated General Contractors of America, 1957 E St., N.W., Washington, D.C. 20006

DRUGS

Executive Directory of the U.S. Pharmaceutical Industry (500 companies, 3,000 executives): Chemical Economic Service, 92 C Nassau St., Princeton, N.J. 08540. $21.00

American Druggist Blue Book (all drug manufacturers): American Druggist, 1790 Broadway, New York, N.Y. $9.00

EDP

The International Directory of Computer and Information System Services (Computer service industry by country and type of service. ·Contains names of principal officers of each firm or institution): Gale Research Company, Book Tower, Detroit, Mich. 48226. $15.00

Who's Who In Data Processing: American Data Processing Inc., Book Building, Detroit, Mich. 48226. $20.00

EDUCATION

Accredited Institutions of Higher Education (lists colleges and universities with names of Presidents): The American Council on Education, 1785 Massachusetts Ave., N.W., Washington, D.C. 20036. $2.00

ELECTRONICS

Who's Who in Electronics (10,000 manufacturers classified by location): B. Klein Publications Inc., 11 Third St., Rye, N.Y. 10580. $20.50

Electrical News Financial Fact Book & Directory (700 publically owned electronics companies with names of board members and officers): Fairchild Publications, Inc., Book Division, 7 East 12th St., New York, N.Y. 10003. $45.00

ENGINEERING – SCIENCE

Directory of Advanced Technology Companies (4,000 firms with product lines and key executives): Computer + Technology Information Inc., 500 Newport Center Drive, Newport Beach, Calif. 92660. $18.00

ENGINEERING – TEACHING/RESEARCH

Directory of Engineering College Research & Graduate Study (lists 190 engineering colleges with names of department chairmen and research directors): B. Klein Publications, Inc., 11 Third St., Rye, N.Y. 10580. $7.00

FOOD

Progressive Grocer's Marketing Guidebook (lists supermarket chain stores and major food wholesalers in 79 major U.S. markets. Contains names of key executives): Progressive Grocer, 420 Lexington Ave., New York, N.Y. 10017. $75.00

National Food Brokers Association Directory (member firms with executive names): National Food Brokers Association, 1916 M St., N.W., Washington, D.C. 20036.

Thomas' Grocery Register (manufacturers and wholesalers of food by product type and state): Thomas Publishing Co., 461 Eighth Ave., New York, N.Y. 10001. $15.00

Quick Frozen Foods Directory (manufacturers with executive names): Cahners Publishing Co., 1776 Broadway, New York, N.Y. $8.00

GAS UTILITY

Browns Directory of North American Gas Companies (executives of American & Canadian Gas utilities): Moore Publishing Company, Ojibway Building, Duluth, Minn. $60.00

Directory of Gas Utility Companies (U.S. utility companies with key executives): Midwest Oil Register, Inc., P.O. Box 7248, Tulsa, Okla. $18.00

GLASS

Glass Factory Directory: National Glass Budget, 912 Empire Bldg., Pittsburg, Pa. 15222. $3.00

IMPORTS

Directory of United States Importers (25,000 companies classified by location and type of product imported. Contains names of owners and key executives): The Journal of Commerce, 445 Marshall St., Phillipsburg, N.J. 08865. $59.00

IMPORT EXPORT

American Register of Importers and Exporters (30,000 importers and exporters classified by product. Contains names of executives): American Register of Importers & Exporters Inc., 90 W. Broadway, New York, N.Y. 10007. $15.00

INSURANCE

The Insurance Almanac (insurance industry executives): Underwriter Printing & Publishing Company, 116 John St., New York, N.Y. 10038. $15.00

INTERNATIONAL – INTERNATIONAL COMPANIES

Directory of American Firms Operating in Foreign Countries (4,200 American companies with overseas subsidiaries. Classified by product and country. Contains name of U.S. executive in charge): World Trade Academy Press Inc., 50 E. 42nd St., New York, N.Y. 10017. $25.00

The International Yellow Pages (300,000 companies in 150 countries): Reuben H. Donnelley Corp., 235 E. 45th St., New York, N.Y. $20.00

International Businessmen's Who's Who (lists executives in international commerce worldwide): International Publications Service, 303 Park Ave. S., New York, N.Y. 10010. $23.00

INVESTMENTS

Investment Banker Broker Almanac (400 top banker/brokers with key executives): Finance Publishing Corporation, 25 E. 73rd St., New York, N.Y.

LABOR UNIONS

Directory of National & International Labor Unions in the U.S. (lists unions with officers names): United States Government Printing Office, Division of Public Documents, Washington, D.C. 20402. $.55

MANAGEMENT CONSULTANTS

Management Consulting (2600 consulting firms with principals and officers names. Arranged by type of consulting and location): Cornell University Graduate School of Business, Publications Section, Ithaca, N.Y. 14850. $15.00

MARKETING

Handbook of Independent Marketing/Advertising Services (200 creative type consulting firms in marketing advertising, packaging, media, and new products fields): Executive Communications, Inc., 54 Park Ave., N.Y., N.Y. 10016. $65.00

METALS

Standard Metal Directory (metal plants with executive names): American Metal Market Co., 525 W. 42nd St., New York, N.Y. $24.00

Who's Who In Steel & Metals: Atlas Publishing Co., 130 W. 42nd St., New York, N.Y. 10036.

MINORITY GROUP

American Negro Reference Guide (Negro newspapers and publications with editor's names): World Mutual Exchange, 79 Wall St., New York, N.Y. 10005. $4.00

OCEANOGRAPHY

GMT World Register of Oceanographic Products and Services: Untel, Inc., 1053 National Press Building, Washington, D.C. 20004 $10.00

OIL

Burmass Oil Directories (Key executives of Midwest & Gulf Area oil companies.): Burmass Oil Directories, P.O. Box 295, Springtown, Texas. $18.00

Oil and Gas Guide (Oilfield suppliers and service companies by type, with executives): Oil and Gas Guide, Claiborne Towers, New Orleans, La.

Oil Well Supply Companies (world-wide listing): Midwest Oil Register, Inc., P.O. Drawer 7248, Tulsa, Okla. 74105. $22.00

Pipeline News Annual Directory (Pipeline products and firms with executives): Oildom Publishing Company, 1217 Hudson Blvd., Bayonne, N.J. 07002. $5.00

Worldwide Personnel Directory of Refining & Gas Processing, The Oil & Gas Journal, Box 1260, Tulsa, Okla. 74101. $30.00

OVERSEAS
List of U.S. Foreign Service Posts (Explains eligibility and examination requirements & opportunities by city): U.S. Department of State, Washington, D.C.

PAPER
Paper Industry Directory of Members & Affiliates (Pulp and paper mill executives): Paper Industry Management Association, 2570 Devon Ave., Des Plaines, Ill. 60018.

PLASTICS
Source Book of New Plastics (Lists leading plastics manufacturers with executives). Reinhold Publishing Company, 430 Park Ave., New York, N.Y. 10022. $9.00

PUBLIC RELATIONS
PR Blue Book (Lists all known PR consultant firms with owners names plus 5,000 PR Directors of major organizations): PR Publishing Co. Inc., Meriden, N.H. $30.00

RAILROADS
Who's Who in Railroading: Simmons-Boardman Publishing Corp., 30 Church St., New York, N.Y. 10007 $20.00

RESEARCH
Research Centers Directory (4,500 Research centers in all fields. Includes names of research directors): Gale Research, Book Tower, Detroit, Mich. 48226. $39.50

RETAILING
Directory of Variety and Junior Department Store Chains (U.S. chains with key executive names): Business Guides, Inc., 2 Park Ave., New York, N.Y. 10016

TEXTILES
Davison's Textile Directory (Textile Mills & Dyers with executives' names): Davison's Publishing Company, Ridgewood, N.J. 07450. $8.50

FORMS FOR RECORDING CONTACTS

On the following pages we have included some examples of forms which you might consider for use during your campaign. As previously mentioned, it is very important that your entire job effort be well-organized.

During the course of your campaign you should record the names and telephone numbers of all the contacts which you make. Having a record in one place will greatly facilitate your follow-up if initial correspondence does not bring the results you desire. As we also mentioned earlier, a record of the contacts you make may be of great service if you seek another position within the next few years.

FIRMS & INDIVIDUALS TO CONTACT

Name and Address of Firm	Individual & Title	Source for Name (i.e. Directory, Personal, etc.)	Contact (Date)	(✓) If Reply Rec'd	Follow-Up (✓) & Date	Interviewed by Date & Phone #

ADVERTISEMENTS ANSWERED

Name & Address of Firm or Box # of Blind Ad	Where Ad Appeared Publication & Date	Date Answered	Check (✓) If Reply Rec'd	Follow-Up (✓) & Date	Interviewed by & Date

EXECUTIVE SEARCH FIRMS TO CONTACT

Name & Address of Firm	Individual & Title	Contact (Date)	(✓) If Reply Rec'd	Follow-Up (✓) & Date	Interviewed by Date & Phone #	Position & Name of Co. Referred to:

PERSONNEL AGENCIES TO CONTACT

279

Name & Address of Firm	Individual & Title	Contact (Date)	(✓) If Reply Rec'd	Interviewed by: Date & Phone #	Referred to: Position & Name of Co.

As authors, personal consultants and search consultants we are very interested in the experiences of individual job hunters at all levels, and welcome comments on your experiences which might be of value to others through incorporation in future publications which we plan to release.

When you reach a point where you are definitely considering new employment, a letter or resume to our Executive Search Division, will be dealt with in confidence and receive a prompt answer indicating if our present search assignments permit us to be of assistance to you.

Performance Dynamics also maintains a separate Consulting Division which offers a wide range of tailored services ranging simply from comments on letters or resumes, through resume writing, and the execution of complete job hunting campaigns. Some of these services can be handled by mail while others obviously require personal visits to our offices. Explanatory literature on most services is available from the Consulting Division.

Performance Dynamics Inc.